The American Vision
Modern Times

California Reading Essentials and Study Guide

Student Workbook

Mc Graw Hill **Glencoe**

New York, New York   Columbus, Ohio   Chicago, Illinois   Peoria, Illinois   Woodland Hills, California

To the Student

The American Vision: Modern Times **California Reading Essentials and Study Guide** is designed to help you use recognized reading strategies to improve your reading-for-information skills. For each section of the student textbook, you are alerted to key content and academic terms. Then, you are asked to draw from prior knowledge, organize your thoughts with a graphic organizer, and follow a process to read and understand the text. The **California Reading Essentials and Study Guide** was prepared to help you get more from your textbook by reading with a purpose.

Using this study tool will also help you learn the California History–Social Science Standards for United States History and Geography: Continuity and Change in the Twentieth Century. The standards that apply to a given section are listed on the first page of that section.

Glencoe

The McGraw·Hill Companies

Send all inquiries to:
Glencoe/McGraw-Hill
8787 Orion Place
Columbus, OH 43240-4027

ISBN: 0-07-872806-1

Printed in the United States of America

6 7 8 9 10 047 10 09 08 07 06

Table of Contents

Chapter 1: Creating a Nation

Section 1: Converging Cultures 1
Section 2: Dissent and Independence 6
Section 3: The Constitution 12

Chapter 2: Growth and Conflict

Section 1: The New Republic 16
Section 2: Growing Division 22
Section 3: Manifest Destiny 28
Section 4: The Civil War 35
Section 5: Reconstruction 43

Chapter 3: The Birth of Modern America

Section 1: Settling the West 49
Section 2: Industrialization 54
Section 3: Immigration and Urbanization 60
Section 4: Early Reforms in a Gilded Age 64
Section 5: Politics and Reform 68

Chapter 4: Becoming a World Power

Section 1: The Imperialist Vision 76
Section 2: The Spanish-American War 80
Section 3: New American Diplomacy 85

Chapter 5: The Progressive Movement

Section 1: The Roots of Progressivism 89
Section 2: Roosevelt in Office 96
Section 3: The Taft Administration 99
Section 4: The Wilson Years 102

Chapter 6: World War I and Its Aftermath 1

Section 1: The United States Enters World War I 106
Section 2: The Home Front 112
Section 3: A Bloody Conflict 116
Section 4: The War's Impact 120

Chapter 7: The Jazz Age

Section 1: A Clash of Values 124
Section 2: Cultural Innovations 129
Section 3: African American Culture 132

Chapter 8: Normalcy and Good Times

Section 1: Presidential Politics 135
Section 2: A Growing Economy 138
Section 3: The Policies of Prosperity 142

Chapter 9: The Great Depression Begins

Section 1: Causes of the Depression..146
Section 2: Life During the Depression 150
Section 3: Hoover Responds..153

Chapter 10: Roosevelt and the New Deal

Section 1: The First New Deal 157
Section 2: The Second New Deal 163
Section 3: The New Deal Coalition 168

Chapter 11: A World in Flames

Section 1: America and the World 172
Section 2: World War II Begins..176
Section 3: The Holocaust..180
Section 4: America Enters the War..183

Chapter 12: America and World War II

Section 1: Mobilizing for War 187
Section 2: The Early Battles 191
Section 3: Life on the Home Front..195
Section 4: Pushing the Axis Back 199
Section 5: The War Ends 203

Chapter 13: The Cold War Begins

Section 1: Origins of the Cold War..208
Section 2: The Early Cold War Years 212
Section 3: The Cold War and American Society 217
Section 4: Eisenhower's Policies 221

Chapter 14: Postwar America

Section 1: Truman and Eisenhower 226
Section 2: The Affluent Society 230
Section 3: Popular Culture of the 1950s 234
Section 4: The Other Side of American Life 237

Chapter 15: The New Frontier and the Great Society

Section 1: The New Frontier 240
Section 2: JFK and the Cold War 244
Section 3: The Great Society 248

Chapter 16: The Civil Rights Movement

Section 1: The Movement Begins 252
Section 2: Challenging Segregation 257
Section 3: New Issues 263

Chapter 17: The Vietnam War

Section 1: The United States Focuses on Vietnam 268
Section 2: Going to War in Vietnam 271
Section 3: Vietnam Divides the Nation 275
Section 4: The War Winds Down 279

Chapter 18: The Politics of Protest

Section 1: The Student Movement and the Counterculture 283
Section 2: The Feminist Movement 287
Section 3: New Approaches to Civil Rights 291
Section 4: Saving the Earth 295

Chapter 19: Politics and Economics

Section 1: The Nixon Administration 299
Section 2: The Watergate Scandal 302
Section 3: Ford and Carter 306
Section 4: The "Me" Decade: Life in the 1970s 311

Chapter 20: Resurgence of Conservatism

Section 1: The New Conservatism 314
Section 2: The Reagan Years 318
Section 3: Life in the 1980s 323
Section 4: The End of the Cold War 328

Chapter 21: Into a New Century

Section 1: The Technological Revolution 332
Section 2: The Clinton Years 336
Section 3: An Interdependent World 342
Section 4: America Enters a New Century 345
Section 5: The War on Terrorism 348

Answer Key 354

California History–Social Science Standards

GRADE ELEVEN

United States History and Geography:
Continuity and Change in the Twentieth Century

11.1 Students analyze the significant events in the founding of the nation and its attempts to realize the philosophy of government described in the Declaration of Independence.

11.1.1 Describe the Enlightenment and the rise of democratic ideas as the context in which the nation was founded.

11.1.2 Analyze the ideological origins of the American Revolution, the Founding Fathers' philosophy of divinely bestowed unalienable natural rights, the debates on the drafting and ratification of the Constitution, and the addition of the Bill of Rights.

11.1.3 Understand the history of the Constitution after 1787 with emphasis on federal versus state authority and growing democratization.

11.1.4 Examine the effects of the Civil War and Reconstruction and of the industrial revolution, including demographic shifts and the emergence in the late nineteenth century of the United States as a world power.

11.2 Students analyze the relationship among the rise of industrialization, large-scale rural-to-urban migration, and massive immigration from Southern and Eastern Europe.

11.2.1 Know the effects of industrialization on living and working conditions, including the portrayal of working conditions and food safety in Upton Sinclair's The Jungle.

11.2.2 Describe the changing landscape, including the growth of cities linked by industry and trade, and the development of cities divided according to race, ethnicity, and class.

11.2.3 Trace the effect of the Americanization movement.

11.2.4 Analyze the effect of urban political machines and responses to them by immigrants and middle-class reformers.

11.2.5 Discuss corporate mergers that produced trusts and cartels and the economic and political policies of industrial leaders.

11.2.6 Trace the economic development of the United States and its emergence as a major industrial power, including its gains from trade and the advantages of its physical geography.

11.2.7 Analyze the similarities and differences between the ideologies of Social Darwinism and Social Gospel (e.g., using biographies of William Graham Sumner, Billy Sunday, Dwight L. Moody).

11.2.8 Examine the effects of political programs and activities of Populists.

11.2.9 Understand the effect of political programs and activities of the Progressives (e.g., federal regulation of railroad transport, Children's Bureau, the Sixteenth Amendment, Theodore Roosevelt, Hiram Johnson).

11.3 Students analyze the role religion played in the founding of America, its lasting moral, social, and political impacts, and issues regarding religious liberty.

11.3.1 Describe the contributions of various religious groups to American civic principles and social reform movements (e.g., civil and human rights, individual responsibility and the work ethic, antimonarchy and self-rule, worker protection, family-centered communities).

11.3.2 Analyze the great religious revivals and the leaders involved in them, including the First Great Awakening, the Second Great Awakening, the Civil War revivals, the Social Gospel Movement, the rise of Christian liberal theology in the nineteenth century, the impact of the Second Vatican Council, and the rise of Christian fundamentalism in current times.

11.3.3 Cite incidences of religious intolerance in the United States (e.g., persecution of Mormons, anti-Catholic sentiment, anti-Semitism).

11.3.4 Discuss the expanding religious pluralism in the United States and California that resulted from large-scale immigration in the twentieth century.

11.3.5 Describe the principles of religious liberty found in the Establishment and Free Exercise clauses of the First Amendment, including the debate on the issue of separation of church and state.

11.4 Students trace the rise of the United States to its role as a world power in the twentieth century.

11.4.1 List the purpose and the effects of the Open Door policy.

11.4.2 Describe the Spanish-American War and U.S. expansion in the South Pacific.

11.4.3 Discuss America's role in the Panama Revolution and the building of the Panama Canal.

11.4.4 Explain Theodore Roosevelt's Big Stick diplomacy, William Taft's Dollar Diplomacy, and Woodrow Wilson's Moral Diplomacy, drawing on relevant speeches.

11.4.5 Analyze the political, economic, and social ramifications of World War I on the home front.

11.4.6 Trace the declining role of Great Britain and the expanding role of the United States in world affairs after World War II.

11.5 Students analyze the major political, social, economic, technological, and cultural developments of the 1920s.

11.5.1 Discuss the policies of Presidents Warren Harding, Calvin Coolidge, and Herbert Hoover.

11.5.2 Analyze the international and domestic events, interests, and philosophies that prompted attacks on civil liberties, including the Palmer Raids, Marcus Garvey's "back-to-Africa" movement, the Ku Klux Klan, immigration quotas and the responses of organizations such as the American Civil Liberties Union, the National Association for the Advancement of Colored People, and the Anti-Defamation League to those attacks.

11.5.3 Examine the passage of the Eighteenth Amendment to the Constitution and the Volstead Act (Prohibition).

11.5.4 Analyze the passage of the Nineteenth Amendment and the changing role of women in society.

11.5.5 Describe the Harlem Renaissance and new trends in literature, music, and art, with special attention to the work of writers (e.g., Zora Neale Hurston, Langston Hughes).

11.5.6 Trace the growth and effects of radio and movies and their role in the worldwide diffusion of popular culture.

11.5.7 Discuss the rise of mass production techniques, the growth of cities, the impact of new technologies (e.g., the automobile, electricity), and the resulting prosperity and effect on the American landscape.

11.6 Students analyze the different explanations for the Great Depression and how the New Deal fundamentally changed the role of the federal government.

11.6.1 Describe the monetary issues of the late nineteenth and early twentieth centuries that gave rise to the establishment of the Federal Reserve and the weaknesses in key sectors of the economy in the late 1920s.

11.6.2 Understand the explanations of the principal causes of the Great Depression and the steps taken by the Federal Reserve, Congress, and Presidents Herbert Hoover and Franklin Delano Roosevelt to combat the economic crisis.

11.6.3 Discuss the human toll of the Depression, natural disasters, and unwise agricultural practices and their effects on the depopulation of rural regions and on political movements of the left and right, with particular attention to the Dust Bowl refugees and their social and economic impacts in California.

11.6.4 Analyze the effects of and the controversies arising from New Deal economic policies and the expanded role of the federal government in society and the economy since the 1930s (e.g., Works Progress Administration, Social Security, National Labor Relations Board, farm programs, regional development policies, and energy development projects such as the Tennessee Valley Authority, California Central Valley Project, and Bonneville Dam).

11.6.5 Trace the advances and retreats of organized labor, from the creation of the American Federation of Labor and the Congress of Industrial Organizations to current issues of a post-industrial, multinational economy, including the United Farm Workers in California.

11.7 Students analyze America's participation in World War II.

11.7.1 Examine the origins of American involvement in the war, with an emphasis on the events that precipitated the attack on Pearl Harbor.

11.7.2 Explain U.S. and Allied wartime strategy, including the major battles of Midway, Normandy, Iwo Jima, Okinawa, and the Battle of the Bulge.

11.7.3 Identify the role and sacrifices of individual American soldiers, as well as the unique contributions of the special fighting forces (e.g., the Tuskegee Airmen, the 442nd Regimental Combat team, the Navajo Code Talkers).

11.7.4 Analyze Roosevelt's foreign policies during World War II (e.g., Four Freedoms speech).

11.7.5 Discuss the constitutional issues and impact of events on the U.S. home front, including the internment of Japanese Americans (e.g., *Fred Korematsu* v. *United States of America*) and the restrictions on German and Italian resident aliens; the response of the administration to Hitler's atrocities against Jews and other groups; the roles of women in military production; the roles and growing political demands of African Americans.

11.7.6 Describe major developments in aviation, weaponry, communication, and medicine and the war's impact on the location of American industry and use of resources.

11.7.7 Discuss the decision to drop atomic bombs and the consequences of the decision (Hiroshima and Nagasaki).

11.7.8 Analyze the effect of massive aid given to Western Europe under the Marshall Plan to rebuild itself after the war and the importance of a rebuilt Europe to the U.S. economy.

11.8 Students analyze the economic boom and social transformation of post–World War II America.

11.8.1 Trace the growth of service sector, white collar, and professional sector jobs in business and government.

11.8.2 Describe the significance of Mexican immigration and its relationship to the agricultural economy, especially in California.

11.8.3 Examine Truman's labor policy and congressional reaction to it.

11.8.4 Analyze new federal government spending on defense, welfare, interest on the national debt, and federal and state spending on education, including the California Master Plan.

11.8.5 Describe the increased powers of the presidency in response to the Great Depression, World War II, and the Cold War.

11.8.6 Discuss the diverse environmental regions of North America, their relationship to local economies, and the origins and prospects of environmental problems in those regions.

11.8.7 Describe the effects on society and the economy of technological developments since 1945, including the computer revolution, changes in communication, advances in medicine, and improvements in agricultural technology.

11.8.8 Discuss forms of popular culture, with emphasis on their origins and geographic diffusion (e.g., jazz and other forms of popular music, professional sports, architectural and artistic styles).

11.9 Students analyze the U.S. foreign policy since World War II.

11.9.1 Discuss the establishment of the United Nations and International Declaration of Human Rights, International Monetary Fund, World Bank, and General Agreement on Tariffs and Trade (GATT) and their importance in shaping modern Europe and maintaining peace and international order.

11.9.2 Understand the role of military alliances, including NATO and SEATO, in deterring communist aggression and maintaining security during the Cold War.

11.9.3 Trace the origins and geopolitical consequences (foreign and domestic) of the Cold War and containment policy, including the following: the era of McCarthyism, instances of domestic Communism (e.g., Alger Hiss) and blacklisting; the Truman Doctrine; the Berlin Blockade; the Korean War; the Bay of Pigs invasion and the Cuban Missile Crisis; atomic testing in the American West, the "mutual assured destruction" doctrine, and disarmament policies; the Vietnam War; Latin American policy.

11.9.4 List the effects of foreign policy on domestic policies and vice versa (e.g., protests during the war in Vietnam, the "nuclear freeze" movement).

11.9.5 Analyze the role of the Reagan administration and other factors in the victory of the West in the Cold War.

11.9.6 Describe U.S. Middle East policy and its strategic, political, and economic interests, including those related to the Gulf War.

11.9.7 Examine relations between the United States and Mexico in the twentieth century, including key economic, political, immigration, and environmental issues.

11.10 Students analyze the development of federal civil rights and voting rights.

11.10.1 Explain how demands of African Americans helped produce a stimulus for civil rights, including President Roosevelt's ban on racial discrimination in defense industries in 1941, and how African Americans' service in World War II produced a stimulus for President Truman's decision to end segregation in the armed forces in 1948.

11.10.2 Examine and analyze the key events, policies, and court cases in the evolution of civil rights, including *Dred Scott* v. *Sanford*, *Plessy* v. *Ferguson*, *Brown* v. *Board of Education*, *Regents of the University of California* v. *Bakke*, and California Proposition 209.

11.10.3 Describe the collaboration on legal strategy between African American and white civil rights lawyers to end racial segregation in higher education.

11.10.4 Examine the roles of civil rights advocates (e.g., A. Philip Randolph, Martin Luther King, Jr., Malcolm X, Thurgood Marshall, James Farmer, Rosa Parks), including the significance of Martin Luther King, Jr.'s "Letter from Birmingham Jail" and "I Have a Dream" speech.

11.10.5 Discuss the diffusion of the civil rights movement of African Americans from the churches of the rural South and the urban North, including the resistance to racial desegregation in Little Rock and Birmingham, and how the advances influenced the agendas, strategies, and effectiveness of the quests of American Indians, Asian Americans, and Hispanic Americans for civil rights and equal opportunities.

11.10.6 Analyze the passage and effects of civil rights and voting rights legislation (e.g., 1964 Civil Rights Act, Voting Rights Act of 1965) and the Twenty-Fourth Amendment, with an emphasis on equality of access to education and to the political process.

11.10.7 Analyze the women's rights movement from the era of Elizabeth Stanton and Susan Anthony and the passage of the Nineteenth Amendment to the movement launched in the 1960s, including differing perspectives on the roles of women.

11.11 Students analyze the major social problems and domestic policy issues in contemporary American society.

11.11.1 Discuss the reasons for the nation's changing immigration policy, with emphasis on how the Immigration Act of 1965 and successor acts have transformed American society.

11.11.2 Discuss the significant domestic policy speeches of Truman, Eisenhower, Kennedy, Johnson, Nixon, Carter, Reagan, Bush, and Clinton (e.g., with regard to education, civil rights, economic policy, environmental policy).

11.11.3 Describe the changing roles of women in society as reflected in the entry of more women into the labor force and the changing family structure.

11.11.4 Explain the constitutional crisis originating from the Watergate scandal.

11.11.5 Trace the impact of, need for, and controversies associated with environmental conservation, expansion of the national park system, and the development of environmental protection laws, with particular attention to the interaction between environmental protection advocates and property right advocates.

11.11.6 Analyze the persistence of poverty and how different analyses of this issue influence welfare reform, health insurance reform, and other social policies.

11.11.7 Explain how the federal, state, and local governments have responded to demographic and social changes such as population shifts to the suburbs, racial concentrations in the cities, Frostbelt-to-Sunbelt migration, international migration, decline of family farms, increases in out-of-wedlock births, and drug abuse.

Study Guide

Chapter 1, Section 1

For use with textbook pages 98–108

CONVERGING CULTURES

CONTENT VOCABULARY

civilization   a highly organized society marked by knowledge of trade, government, the arts, science, and, often, written language *(page 99)*

joint-stock company   form of business organization in which many investors pool funds to raise large amounts of money for large projects *(page 102)*

Pilgrim   a Separatist who journeyed to the American colonies in the 1600s for religious freedom *(page 103)*

subsistence farming   farming only enough food to feed one's family *(page 104)*

proprietary colony   a colony owned by an individual *(page 105)*

indentured servant   an individual who contracts to work for a colonist for a specified number of years in exchange for transportation to the colonies, food, clothing, and shelter *(page 106)*

triangular trade   a three-way trade route that exchanged goods between the American colonies and two other trading partners *(page 107)*

slave codes   a set of laws that formally regulated slavery and defined the relationship between enslaved Africans and free people *(page 107)*

DRAWING FROM EXPERIENCE

Do you know people who have moved to your community from other parts of the country or world? What reasons did they have for moving? What do you think are some positive aspects of moving? What are some negative aspects?

In this section, you will learn about the settlement of the Americas. You will also learn about the kind of society each nation established.

ORGANIZING YOUR THOUGHTS

Use the time line below to help you take notes. List the major events in European exploration of the Americas.

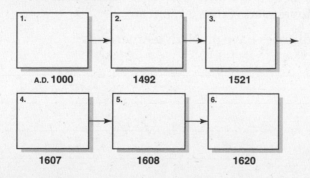

| 1. | 2. | 3. |
| A.D. 1000 | 1492 | 1521 |

| 4. | 5. | 6. |
| 1607 | 1608 | 1620 |

California History-Social Science Standards

11.1 Students analyze the significant events in the founding of the nation and its attempts to realize the philosophy of government described in the Declaration of Independence.

11.3 Students analyze the role religion played in the founding of America, its lasting moral, social and political impacts, and issues regarding religious liberty.

Focuses on: 11.3.1

Study Guide

Chapter 1, Section 1 *(continued)*

READ TO LEARN

• The Earliest Americans *(page 99)*

The first Americans may have arrived here between 15,000 and 30,000 years ago. Nomadic at first, Native Americans learned how to plant and raise crops. The shift to agriculture gradually led to civilization. A **civilization** is a highly organized society marked by advanced knowledge.

The earliest Native American civilizations arose in Central America, or Mesoamerica. The Olmecs were the first, followed by the Maya and the Aztec. Meanwhile, the Hopewell and Mississippian <u>cultures</u> were developing in eastern North America.

Academic Vocabulary
culture: customs, religion, and social practices, generally shared by distinct groups of people (p. 99)

6. What were the first Native American civilizations, and where were they located?

_____

_____

_____

_____

• European Explorations *(page 101)*

For trading purposes, the Europeans wanted to find a direct sailing route to Asia. In 1492, Christopher Columbus landed in the Americas. Although the Vikings had been to northeastern Canada in A.D. 1000, Columbus's later voyage launched a wave of European exploration and settlement.

Europeans soon realized that Columbus had reached a new continent, which they named America in honor of explorer Amerigo Vespucci. The 1494 Treaty of Tordesillas confirmed Spain's right to most of the newly discovered lands in America. A wave of Spanish explorers—with their superior weapons—conquered Native Americans, built settlements, and soon controlled a huge territory in North and South America.

The arrival of Europeans in the Americas changed life for everyone. Native Americans and Europeans exchanged farming methods and crops, inventions, and technologies. Europeans also brought diseases to the Americas that Native Americans had no immunity to, and millions died in widespread epidemics. Military conquests also devastated Native Americans.

7. What effect did European diseases have on Native Americans?

_____

_____

_____

_____

Study Guide

Chapter 1, Section 1 *(continued)*

• Early French and English Settlement *(page 102)*

Soon after Columbus made his historic voyage, France and England began exploring the eastern part of North America. At first, the backers of New France sought profits from fur instead of establishing permanent settlements. In the late 1600s France focused on increasing the size and population of New France. The colony spread from Quebec, down the Mississippi River, to the Gulf of Mexico. The French began growing crops using imported enslaved Africans to do the work.

In 1607, a year before the French founded Quebec, the English founded Jamestown—the first English settlement in the Americas. Jamestown was founded by a **joint-stock company,** a group of private investors who pooled their money to support big projects. The English saw colonies as a vital source of raw materials and as markets for English goods. By 1622 more than 4,500 settlers had <u>immigrated</u> to Virginia. This expansion alarmed the once friendly Native Americans, who attacked in 1622.

In 1620 a small band of Separatists, who came to be known as **Pilgrims,** headed for Virginia on the *Mayflower.* The Separatists, who were persecuted in England for breaking with the Anglican Church, wanted to be able to worship freely. A storm blew them off course and they landed in Cape Cod, Massachusetts. They drew up a plan for self-government called the Mayflower Compact. Government and religion were closely linked in the rapidly growing Massachusetts colony.

> **Academic Vocabulary**
>
> **Immigrate:** entering and establishing oneself in a country other than that of their original nationality (p. 103)

8. Why did the Pilgrims immigrate to America?

_____

_____

_____

_____

• The Thirteen Colonies *(page 103)*

Over the next century the English began establishing colonies all along the eastern shore of the Atlantic Ocean. In New England, Puritan religious intolerance led to dissent. Two dissenters, Roger Williams and Anne Hutchinson, were exiled. They founded towns that became the colony of Rhode Island. Rhode Island featured a total separation of church and state.

Other groups left Massachusetts and founded new colonies. In Connecticut, settlers adopted America's first written constitution, The Fundamental Orders of Connecticut.

New England Puritans valued religious devotion, hard work, obedience, and town life. Local government evolved from town meetings where residents gathered to discuss local problems and issues. Colonists thus came to believe strongly in their right to self-government.

Study Guide

Chapter 1, Section 1 *(continued)*

New England's soil was suitable only for **subsistence farming,** raising only enough food to feed their families. Fishing, lumber, and shipbuilding brought prosperity to New England.

Relations with Native Americans were peaceful until colonial governments demanded that Native Americans follow English laws and customs. Tensions led to King Philip's War. After colonists won in 1678, very few Native Americans were left in New England.

The Dutch claimed much of the land between New England and Virginia, naming it New Netherland. By 1664 New Netherland had become England's main rival in North America. King Charles II of England seized the land, which became the colonies of New England and New Jersey.

South of New York, William Penn founded Pennsylvania, where people of all faiths and, in particular, the Quakers, found a safe haven of religious freedom. Delaware became a colony southeast of Pennsylvania.

The Middle colonies were blessed with good growing conditions. Wheat, which became the main cash crop, brought wealth and new immigrants.

In the South, the proprietary colony of Maryland was established as a refuge for Catholics. A **proprietary colony** was one owned by an individual who could govern it anyway he wanted. Maryland passed the Toleration Act in 1649, granting religious toleration to all Christians.

Virginia continued to thrive, mostly thanks to tobacco. North and South Carolina were established. James Oglethorpe founded Georgia as a place where debtors could start over. Georgia also served to keep Spain from expanding north of Florida.

In the Southern colonies, agriculture was the focus. Plenty of land and a shortage of labor led to the import of enslaved Africans and the indentured servant system. **Indentured servants** signed contracts with American colonists, agreeing to work for a set number of years in exchange for passage to America and free food, clothing, and shelter.

Large landowners dominated Southern society, but were outnumbered by subsistence farmers, tenant farmers (who rented land to farm), and laborers.

By the 1660s, Sir William Berkeley controlled the House of Burgesses—Virginia's legislative assembly. He arranged for the House to limit the vote to people who owned property. The act cut the number of voters in Virginia by half. This angered the backcountry and tenant farmers.

Backcountry farmers also wanted to expand their landholdings. By the 1670s, the only land left was that claimed by Native Americans. Most wealthy planters did not want to risk war with the Native Americans, so they opposed expanding the colony. This angered the backcountry farmers.

In 1675 war broke out between backcountry farmers and the Native Americans of the region. Governor Berkeley did not authorize military action. His lack of response angered the backcountry farmers. In April 1675, a group of backcountry farmers led by a wealthy planter named Nathanial Bacon took action. Bacon

Study Guide

Chapter 1, Section 1 (continued)

organized a militia and attacked the Native Americans. He ran for office and won a seat in the House of Burgesses. The assembly authorized another attack on the Native Americans. The House also restored the vote to all free men.

Bacon was not satisfied with the changes, and a civil war erupted between Bacon and Berkeley. Bacon's Rebellion ended when Bacon became sick and died.

Bacon's Rebellion showed many wealthy planters that they needed to have land available for backcountry farmers in order to keep Virginia society stable. It also resulted in the planters using enslaved Africans more than indentured servants. They used enslaved Africans because enslaved workers would never need their own land. Planters also could use them as collateral to borrow money and expand their plantations. The policies of the English government also encouraged slavery. In 1672 King Charles II granted a charter to the Royal African Company to start a slave trade. The English colonists no longer had to purchase enslaved Africans from the Dutch or the Portuguese.

9. How did the policies of the English government help increase slave labor in Virginia?

_____

_____

_____

- **A Diverse Society** (page 107)

A rise in trade and the population of enslaved Africans changed colonial society. Colonial merchants had developed systems of **triangular trade** involving the colonies, England, Caribbean sugar planters, and Africa. This trade brought great wealth to merchants, who began to build factories which, in turn, fostered the growth of Northern cities.

In the cities, a new society with a distinct social <u>hierarchy</u> developed. Wealthy merchants were at the top, followed by artisans, small business owners, and unskilled laborers. At the bottom were indentured servants and enslaved Africans.

Academic Vocabulary
hierarchy: classification based upon social standing within a group of people (p. 107)

By 1775 there were 540,000 enslaved Africans in the colonies, roughly 20 percent of the population. **Slave codes** denied African captives of their basic human rights. Most enslaved Africans lived on Southern plantations.

Between 1700 and 1775, hundreds of thousands of free white immigrants streamed to the United States. Among them were Germans, Irish, and Jews. Like Jews, women did not receive equal rights in colonial America.

10. What reasons did immigrants have for coming to the American colonies?

_____

_____

_____

Study Guide

Chapter 1, Section 2

For use with textbook pages 109–119

DISSENT AND INDEPENDENCE

CONTENT VOCABULARY

mercantilism   a set of ideas about the world economy and how it works *(page 110)*

Enlightenment   a movement that promoted the idea that people should use reason and natural law to shape society *(page 112)*

Great Awakening   a religious movement that stressed emotionally uniting with God and gained appeal among farmers, workers, and slaves *(page 112)*

customs duty   a tax on imports and exports *(page 113)*

committee of correspondence   committee designed to communicate with other colonies about British activities *(page 115)*

minutemen   a special unit of the militia trained to fight at a minute's notice (page 115)

DRAWING FROM EXPERIENCE

The United States Constitution guarantees freedom of religion. What does that freedom mean? Why is having this freedom important to a democracy?

The last section discussed the settlement of the Americas. This section discusses colonial independence and the establishment of a new government.

ORGANIZING YOUR THOUGHTS

Use the diagram below to help you take notes. Mercantilism was a popular idea in the 1600s and 1700s. List some of the major ideas of mercantilism.

> **California History-Social Science Standards**
>
> **11.1** Students analyze the significant events in the founding of the nation and its attempts to realize the philosophy of government described in the Declaration of Independence.
>
> **11.3** Students analyze the role religion played in the founding of America, its lasting moral, social and political impacts, and issues regarding religious liberty.
>
> **Focuses on:** 11.1.1, 11.1.2, 11.3.2

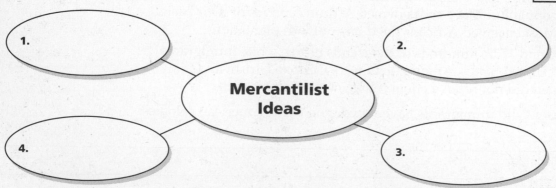

1.

2.

Mercantilist Ideas

4.

3.

Study Guide

Chapter 1, Section 2 *(continued)*

• **Mercantilism and the Glorious Revolution** *(page 110)*

Mercantilism, a set of ideas about the world economy and how it works, was very popular in the 1600s and 1700s. Mercantilists believed that a country could become wealthy by accumulating gold and silver. It could do this by selling more goods to other countries than it bought from them. By doing so, more gold and silver would flow into the country than would flow out. Mercantilists also believed that a country should establish colonies in order to buy raw materials from the colonies and, in turn, sell them manufactured goods. Mercantilism benefited colonies by giving them a ready market for their raw materials. The drawback, however, was that it prevented colonies from selling their goods to other nations. Also, if a colony did not make goods that the home country needed, then that colony could not accumulate the gold and silver it needed to buy manufactured goods.

When King Charles II came to the throne, he decided to regulate trade with the colonies in order to bring wealth to England. In 1660 he asked Parliament to pass the Navigation Act. The act said that all goods coming in and out of the colonies had to be carried on English ships. The act also listed specific raw materials that could be sold only to England or to other English colonies. The list included the major goods that earned money for the colonies. Another navigation act said that all merchants bringing European goods to the colonies had to stop in England, pay taxes, and then ship the goods on English ships.

Colonial merchants were angry, and many broke the new laws. Massachusetts in particular defied the Navigation Acts. King Charles responded by taking away the colony's charter and making it a royal colony.

James II, who succeeded Charles as king, went even further in punishing the colonies. Under his authority, England merged the colonies of Massachusetts, Plymouth, and Rhode Island to create a new royal province called the Dominion of New England. Later, England added Connecticut, New York, and New Jersey to the Dominion.

The king appointed Sir Edmond Andros the first governor-general. His harsh rule made nearly everyone in New England angry.

The English people were growing suspicious of King James II. He rejected the advice of Parliament and offended many of them by openly practicing Catholicism.

The birth of James's son triggered protests against a Catholic heir. Not willing to risk a Catholic dynasty, Parliament asked James's Protestant daughter Mary and her husband William to take the throne. When they arrived, James fled the country. This bloodless change of power became known as the Glorious Revolution.

Study Guide

Chapter 1, Section 2 (continued)

In 1689 Parliament enacted the English Bill of Rights. The document limited the powers of monarchs and listed the rights that Parliament and citizens had, such as the right to a fair jury in legal cases.

As soon as the Massachusetts colonists learned about the English Bill of Rights, an uprising occurred in Boston, and the colonists ousted Andros. The new monarchs permitted Rhode Island and Connecticut to resume their previous form of government, but they issued a new charter for Massachusetts. This charter combined Massachusetts Bay Colony, Plymouth Colony, and Maine into the royal colony of Massachusetts. The new charter allowed the people in the colony to elect an assembly, but the governor was to be appointed by the king. Voters did not have to be members of a Puritan congregation.

During the Glorious Revolution, a political philosopher named **John Locke** wrote a book entitled *Two Treatises of Government*. In the book, Locke argued that a monarch's right to rule had to come from the people. He said that all people were born with certain natural rights. These included the right to life, liberty, and property. He said that people came together to create a government to protect their rights. In return, the people agreed to obey the government's laws. He also said that if a government violated the people's rights, the people were justified in changing their system of government. Locke's ideas influenced American colonists, who would use these ideas to start a revolution against Great Britain.

5. According to John Locke, why did people create a government?

_____

_____

_____

• The Enlightenment and the Great Awakening (page 111)

Two European cultural movements influenced American colonies. The **Enlightenment** championed human reason. The Enlightenment thinkers believed that people could apply natural laws to social, political, and economic relationships, and that people could figure out these laws if they used reason and logic. John Locke was an influential Enlightenment writer. He argued that people were not born sinful, as the Church claimed. Instead, he believed that experience and education could make people better. This thinking influenced beliefs in American society.

Many Americans followed a religious movement that stressed an individual's devoutness and union with God. Ministers spread pietism through revivals, which were large public meetings for preaching and prayer. This rebirth of religious feelings became known as the **Great Awakening.** Two preachers of the Great Awakening were Jonathan Edwards and George Whitefield. Both preachers led religious revivals throughout the colonies.

Academic Vocabulary
logic: a system of thinking based upon likely or reasonable outcomes (p. 112)

Study Guide

Chapter 1, Section 2 *(continued)*

A central idea of the Great Awakening was that people had to be "born again," or have an emotional experience that brings a person to God. Churches that accepted the new ideas, such as the Baptists and Methodists, saw an increase in their membership.

The Great Awakening had a great impact on the South, particularly among backcountry and tenant farmers. Baptist preachers condemned slavery and welcomed Africans at their revivals. As a result, thousands of enslaved Africans joined Baptist congregations. This angered the white planters, who feared that they would lose control of their workforce.

6. Why did many enslaved Africans join Baptist congregations?

_____

_____

_____

_____

_____

• **Growing Rebelliousness** *(page 113)*

In the 1740s, Great Britain and France began fighting for control of the Ohio River Valley. One war, which began in 1754, was called the French and Indian War in North America and the Seven Years' War in Europe. The British won, and the 1763 Treaty of Paris made Great Britain the dominant power in North America.

Great Britain felt that the colonists should share the costs of the war. In the Proclamation Act of 1763, the British restricted colonial expansion into Native American lands west of the Appalachian Mountains in order to avoid costly conflict. Colonists were enraged.

The British discovered that eastern merchants had been smuggling goods without paying **customs duties**—taxes on imports and <u>exports</u>. Britain tightened customs controls and passed unpopular measures, including the Sugar Act of 1764. The Stamp Act of 1765 was the first direct tax on the colonists and opposition was swift. The Declaration of Rights and Grievances was issued, arguing that only the colonists' political representatives, and not Parliament, had the right to tax them. The colonists' boycott of British goods led to the repeal of the Stamp Act in 1766.

In 1767, Britain passed the Townshend Acts, which imposed new customs duties and cracked down on smugglers. When Massachusetts and Virginia resisted, Parliament dissolved their assemblies. On March 5, 1770, violence erupted in Boston and five colonists were killed in a scuffle between colonists and British soldiers. The Boston Massacre could have led to more violence,

Academic Vocabulary
exports: goods produced by one country which are sold and shipped to another (p. 113)

Study Guide

Chapter 1, Section 2 (continued)

but Britain repealed the Townshend Acts—except for the tax on tea—and peace and stability returned temporarily.

7. How did Britain respond to the Boston Massacre?

_____

_____

_____

_____

_____

• **The Road to War** *(page 114)*

The colonists continued to believe that Britain was denying them their rights as English citizens. The colonists created **committees of correspondence** to <u>communicate</u> with the other colonies about the British. The committees helped unify the colonies.

The Tea Act of 1773, which created favorable conditions for the British East India Company, infuriated colonists who feared the British were trying to force them out of business. Colonists blocked British tea ships from American harbors, but Bostonians boarded a British ship and dumped 342 chests of tea overboard—an event known as the Boston Tea Party.

In 1774, Britain passed the Coercive Acts to punish Massachusetts. Shortly after, the Quebec Act denied an elected assembly to colonists who settled in the western territory. Colonists protested these measures, calling them the Intolerable Acts. In 1774, the First Continental Congress, consisting of representatives from 12 colonies, met. They decided to boycott British goods and hold a second Continental Congress in 1775 if the crisis remained unresolved.

The Massachusetts militia began to drill. Concord, Massachusetts, created a special unit of **minutemen** who were to be ready to fight "at a minute's warning."

Americans were divided over the issue of resistance. Loyalists, or Tories, were loyal to Great Britain. Patriots, or Whigs, believed the British had become tyrants.

In April 1775, fighting broke out in Lexington and Concord, Massachusetts, when the British, led by General Gage, tried to seize Patriot arms and munitions. By May 1775, militia troops from all over New England had surrounded Boston, trapping the British. The Second Continental Congress was held in May, and George Washington became the general and commander of the newly organized Colonial Army.

In July 1775, the Continental Congress sent King George III the Olive Branch Petition. The petition asserted the colonists' loyalty to the king and

Academic Vocabulary
communicate: to share information with people or groups (p. 115)

Study Guide

Chapter 1, Section 2 (continued)

asked for a peaceful solution to the problems. King George rejected the petition and declared the colonies "open and avowed enemies." The fighting spread. Thomas Paine's pamphlet *Common Sense* persuasively argued that King George III was a tyrant and that it was time to declare independence. On July 4, 1776, the Continental Congress issued the Declaration of Independence, and the colonies now proclaimed themselves the United States of America.

8. What effect did the pamphlet *Common Sense* have on the colonies?

_____

_____

_____

_____

_____

• Fighting for Independence *(page 117)*

The Continental Army could not match the British Army in size, funding, discipline, or experience, but they did have some advantages. They were fighting on home ground, had help from local militias, and were fighting an enemy that only half-heartedly supported the war.

After early losses, the Americans defeated the British at Saratoga, New York, in 1777. This victory convinced the French to openly support the Americans, and the French became the first country to recognize the United States as an independent nation.

Despite holding the upper hand in the South throughout most of the war, the British were finally forced to surrender at Yorktown, Virginia, in 1781. Parliament then voted to end the war, and the Treaty of Paris was signed in 1783. In this treaty, Britain recognized the United States of America as an independent nation with the Mississippi River as its western border.

9. What advantages did the Continental Army have over the British Army?

_____

_____

_____

_____

_____

Study Guide

Chapter 1, Section 3

For use with textbook pages 124–131

THE CONSTITUTION

CONTENT VOCABULARY

republic   a form of government in which the power resides with a body of citizens who could vote *(page 125)*

recession   an economic slowdown *(page 126)*

popular sovereignty   rule by the people *(page 128)*

federalism   a system of government in which government power is divided between the federal government and the state governments *(page 128)*

separation of powers   a government in which powers of government are divided among three branches *(page 128)*

checks and balances   a system designed to prevent any one of the three branches from becoming too powerful *(page 128)*

veto   to reject *(page 128)*

amendment   change to the Constitution *(page 128)*

ratification   approval *(page 129)*

DRAWING FROM EXPERIENCE

The United States Constitution has lasted for more than 200 years. Why do you think the Constitution has lasted this long?

The last section discussed the War for Independence. This section describes the effects of the war and the writing of the Constitution.

ORGANIZING YOUR THOUGHTS

Use the diagram below to help you take notes. Use the diagram to describe the American political system after the Revolutionary War.

California History-Social Science Standards
11.1 Students analyze the significant events in the founding of the nation and its attempts to realize the philosophy of government described in the Declaration of Independence.
Focuses on: 11.1.1, 11.1.2

1.

2.

3.

4.

5.

Features of New Political System

Study Guide

Chapter 1, Section 3 *(continued)*

READ TO LEARN

- **The Young Nation** *(page 125)*

In the United States of America, royal rule was replaced with a republic. In a **republic** power resides with voting citizens. Virginia's and Massachusetts's state constitutions served as models for other states. These constitutions called for a separation of government power and a list of rights guaranteeing essential freedoms.

The concern for individual liberty in the Revolutionary era led to greater separation of church and state and expanded voting rights. Women and African Americans, however, continued to be denied political rights.

On March 2, 1781, the <u>framework</u> for a central government, called the Articles of Confederation, took effect. The Articles loosely unified the states under a single governing body, the Confederation Congress. The Confederation Congress could negotiate with other nations, raise armies, and declare war, but it could not regulate trade or impose taxes. One of Congress's achievements was the Northwest Ordinance of 1787, which spelled out how states could be established and governed in the Northwest Territory.

Without the power to tax, Congress could not raise enough money to pay its war debts or its expenses, and the country sank into a severe **recession,** or economic slowdown. Shays's Rebellion occurred when Daniel Shays, one of many poor farmers hit hard by the recession, led a protest of new taxes. The incident made clear the weaknesses of the Articles of Confederation. People began to call for a stronger central government.

Academic Vocabulary
framework: a set of guidelines to be followed (p. 126)

6. Why did the Articles of Confederation set up a weak central government?

_____

_____

_____

_____

- **A New Constitution** *(page 126)*

In May 1787, every state except Rhode Island sent delegates to Philadelphia to revise the Articles of Confederation. The delegates quickly decided to abandon the Articles and create a new constitution. The meeting became known as the Constitutional Convention.

All delegates wanted a stronger national government, but other issues split them. Small states wanted an equal number of votes in Congress, but the large states insisted that representation should be based on population. The Great Compromise, suggested by Connecticut's Roger Sherman, solved the issue.

Study Guide

Chapter 1, Section 3 (continued)

Congress would have two houses. In the House of Representatives, representation would be based on population. In the Senate, each state would have equal representation.

The Three-Fifths Compromise stated that every five enslaved people in a state would count as three free persons for determining representation and taxation.

The new Constitution was based on the principle of **popular sovereignty,** or rule by the people. It created a representative democracy in which elected officials speak for the people. The Constitution also set up a **federalist** government that divided power between the national and state governments.

The Constitution established the **separation of powers** among the three branches of government. The legislative branch, or Congress, made the laws. The executive branch, headed by the president, would implement and enforce the laws. The judicial branch—a system of federal courts—would <u>interpret</u> federal laws and render judgment in cases involving these laws. Furthermore, a system of **checks and balances** was created so each branch could monitor and limit the power of the other two.

The delegates understood that the Constitution might need to be <u>revised</u> over time. To allow this to happen, they created a system for making **amendments,** or changes, to the Constitution.

Academic Vocabulary
interpret: to explain the meaning of complex material
revise: to make changes to an original document (p. 128)

7. Why did the Constitution provide for a system of checks and balances?

_____

_____

_____

_____

_____

• The Fight for Ratification (page 129)

On September 28, the Confederation Congress voted to submit the Constitution to the states for **ratification.** To go into effect, 9 of the 13 states had to approve it. Delaware was the first state to do so, on December 7, 1787.

Ratification was not easy as the population was split over the Constitution. Those who supported it were called Federalists; those against it were Antifederalists. Antifederalists were not opposed to federalism, but they were concerned about whether the federal or state governments would be supreme.

Federalists summarized their arguments in a collection of 85 influential essays called *The Federalist.* In Massachusetts, Antifederalists had a majority until Federalists promised to attach a bill of rights to the Constitution. In 1791 the promise led to the adoption of the first ten amendments, or the Bill of Rights.

Study Guide

Chapter 1, Section 3 *(continued)*

The amendments guaranteed the freedom of speech, press, and religion, among others.

On June 21, 1788, New Hampshire became the ninth state to ratify. New York and Virginia, however, had not ratified and without their support many feared the new government would not succeed.

The promise of a bill of rights persuaded the Virginians to ratify, but the vote was close. New York ratified so that it would not have to operate independently of all the surrounding states which had ratified. In 1790, Rhode Island became the thirteenth state to ratify. George Washington was chosen as the first president under the new Constitution.

8. What is the Bill of Rights, and what role did it play in the ratification of the Constitution?

_____

_____

_____

_____

_____

Study Guide

Chapter 2, Section 1

For use with textbook pages 172–181

THE NEW REPUBLIC

CONTENT VOCABULARY

cabinet   a group of advisors to the president *(page 173)*

enumerated powers   powers specifically mentioned in the Constitution *(page 174)*

implied powers   powers not explicitly listed in the Constitution but necessary for the government to do its job *(page 174)*

judicial review   the power of the Supreme Court to decide whether laws passed by Congress were constitutional and to strike down those that were not *(page 175)*

nativism   prejudice or hostility toward foreigners *(page 179)*

labor union   organization of workers who press for better wages and working conditions *(page 179)*

DRAWING FROM EXPERIENCE

How does the government of your community raise the money it needs to pay for community services? How does the government of the United States raise the money? *taxes*

In this section, you will learn how the new government of the United States addressed the challenges it faced.

ORGANIZING YOUR THOUGHTS

Use the outline below to help you take notes. Many actions that strengthened the federal government occurred as a result of American nationalism after the War of 1812. Outline the main actions.

I.   Economic Nationalism

   A.

   B.

   C.

II.   Judicial Nationalism

   A.

   B.

III.   Diplomatic Nationalism

   A.

   B.

California History-Social Science Standards

11.1 Students analyze the significant events in the founding of the nation and its attempts to realize the philosophy of government described in the Declaration of Independence.

11.2 Students analyze the relationship among the rise of industrialization, large-scale rural-to-urban migration, and massive immigration from Southern and Eastern Europe.

Focuses on: 11.1.2, 11.1.3

Study Guide

Chapter 2, Section 1 (continued)

READ TO LEARN

• The Early Years of the Republic (page 173)

One of the first tasks of the new United States was to organize the government. In 1789 Congress created the Department of State, the Department of the Treasury, the Department of War, and the Office of the Attorney General. Then Washington chose his **cabinet**—the individuals who would head these departments and advise him.

In 1791 the Bill of Rights—the first 10 amendments to the Constitution— were ratified. The first 8 amendments protect individual rights against the government.

The new government inherited a huge debt. Alexander Hamilton, the Secretary of the Treasury, wanted to pay off all national and state debts. He also proposed the creation of a national bank to collect taxes, regulate trade, and provide for the common defense. Opponents argued that establishing a bank was not an **enumerated power**—a power specifically mentioned in the Constitution. Hamilton cited Article I, Section 8, which gave the federal government the power to "make all laws which shall be necessary and proper" to fulfill its responsibilities. This <u>clause</u> created **implied powers**—powers not explicitly listed in the Constitution but necessary for the government to do its job. The Bank of the United States was established in 1791 for a 20-year period.

Academic Vocabulary
clause: a distinct section in a written formal document (p. 174)

Hamilton's financial program and the handling of the Whiskey Rebellion, an uprising among Western farmers opposed to a tax on whiskey, split Congress into rival political parties. Federalists like Hamilton favored a strong national government led by the "rich, well born, and able." The Democratic-Republicans, referred to as Republicans, favored strict limits on federal power and protection of states' rights. Madison and Jefferson were prominent Republicans.

Washington's successor was John Adams, a Federalist. Even though Washington had warned Americans of the dangers of party politics and sectionalism, the division between the two parties was deepening. The Federalists passed the Alien and Sedition Acts in 1798. These laws made it a crime to say anything bad about the federal government or federal officials. Aliens, or foreigners living in the country, were often anti-British and tended to vote Republican. The new laws made it harder for them to gain citizenship.

In the election of 1800, there was an unexpected tie between Thomas Jefferson and his running mate Aaron Burr. The Constitution specified that citizens would vote for electors who would vote for president and vice president. This Electoral College voted for two people. The candidate receiving the most votes became president; the runner-up became vice president. Ties were decided in the House of Representatives. The House made Jefferson the president and the Federalists stepped down. The election of 1800 showed that power could be peacefully transferred.

Study Guide

Chapter 2, Section 1 (continued)

2. What did the election of 1800 show?

showed that power could peacefully be stped ~~from~~ transferred.

- ### The Republicans Take Power *(page 175)*

Thomas Jefferson was committed to limiting the scope of government and weakening the Federalists' control of the judiciary. On his last day in office, Adams had appointed dozens of new Federalist judges. Jefferson asked Congress to not allow these last-minute appointments. William Marbury, one of the last minute appointees, took his case to the Supreme Court. Chief Justice John Marshall ruled against Marbury, saying that the law that authorized the Court to issue enforcement orders was unconstitutional. In *Marbury* v. *Madison* (1803), the Court established its right of **judicial review,** the power to decide whether laws are constitutional and to strike down those that are not.

Also in 1803, Jefferson was busy expanding the size of the country. When Napoleon offered to sell the Louisiana Territory and New Orleans, the United States accepted the offer. In the **Louisiana Purchase** the United States doubled in size for a total cost of $15 million, or less than three cents an acre.

When James Madison took office in 1809, he inherited a foreign relations crisis with Britain. The British regularly seized American ships at sea and kidnapped American sailors, a practice called impressment. Americans in the West accused the British of inciting Native Americans to attack settlers. Economic sanctions finally began to have the desired effect, but word of British cooperation came too late—Congress had already declared war.

Conquering Canada was the primary goal in the War of 1812. The Treaty of Ghent, signed in 1814, restored prewar boundaries but did not address the core issues of neutral rights or impressment. But the war did increase U.S. prestige and generated a spirit of patriotism and national unity. It also destroyed the Federalist Party, which had strongly opposed the war.

3. What was the significance of the *Marbury* v. *Madison* case?

The court established the right of judicial review.

Study Guide

Chapter 2, Section 1 (continued)

• The Growth of American Nationalism (page 176)

After the War of 1812, Americans developed national pride. Americans had a greater feeling of loyalty toward the United States than toward their state or region. The Monroe presidency is described as a time of political harmony in the country. One reason for this was because the Republican Party was the only political party that had any power. Also, the war had taught Americans that a stronger national government was advantageous. Republican leaders focused on national growth.

During Monroe's presidency, Congress created a new national bank to replace the First Bank of the United States. They also passed the Tariff of 1816, which protected American manufacturers by taxing imports.

Between 1816 and 1824, chief justice of the United States John Marshall helped unify the nation. He ruled in two cases that established the power of the federal government over the states.

In 1819 the Court decided in *McCulloch v. Maryland* that the Second Bank of the United States was constitutional. The decision said that the "necessary and proper" clause meant that the federal government could use any method to carry out its powers, as long as the method was not expressly forbidden in the Constitution. Marshall also ruled that state governments could not interfere with an agency of the federal government exercising its specific constitutional powers within a state.

In 1824 the Court decided in *Gibbons* v. *Ogden* that the Constitution granted the federal government control over interstate commerce. States could regulate commerce only within their borders. This ruling made it clear that federal law had priority over state law in interstate transportation.

Nationalism also influenced the nation's foreign affairs. Under President Monroe, the United States expanded its borders and became involved in world affairs.

In the early 1800s, many Southerners were angry with Spanish-held Florida. Runaway slaves hid there, aided by the Seminoles. When Spain could not control its border, Andrew Jackson captured Spanish settlements in Florida. Secretary of State John Quincy Adams pressured Spain to agree to a border treaty. In the Adams-Onís Treaty of 1819, Spain ceded all of Florida to the United States.

Spain's Latin American colonies began to rebel in 1809. Several European monarchies discussed the possibility of helping Spain regain control of these colonies. Russia also showed a growing interest in America. In response to this threat, President Monroe issued the Monroe Doctrine. This foreign policy said that the United States would prevent other countries from becoming involved in the political affairs of Latin American countries. The Monroe Doctrine became a long-term foreign policy of the United States.

Study Guide

Chapter 2, Section 1 (continued)

4. What were the outcomes of the Adams-Onís Treaty and the Monroe Doctrine?

_____

_____

_____

_____

_____

• A Growing Nation *(page 178)*

In the early 1800s a transportation revolution occurred. In 1806 Congress funded the building of the National Road—a major east-west highway. Steamboats opened the nation's rivers and waterways to freight and travel. Railroads, which appeared in the early 1800s, helped settle the West and expand trade among regions.

The Industrial Revolution began in Britain in the 1700s. During this time, manufacturers began using large-scale production in factories. Manufactured goods were sold nationwide and overseas.

The United States industrialized quickly because of the American system of free enterprise. There were few government controls, low taxes, and laws favoring businesses.

Industrialization began in the Northeast. The swift-flowing streams provided waterpower for the factories. The Northeast had entrepreneurs and merchants who had money to invest in industry.

Inventions and technological advances helped industry grow in the United States. Eli Whitney made the idea of interchangeable parts popular. In 1832 Samuel F.B. Morse perfected the telegraph. He developed the Morse code for sending messages. Newspapers used the telegraph to quickly collect and share news stories over wires.

Industrialization caused the rise of large cities. Many people moved to urban areas in search of factory jobs and better pay. By 1860 eight cities in the country had populations of over 100,000. Immigrants also contributed to city growth. Many Americans had feelings of **nativism,** a preference for native-born people and a desire to limit immigration. A political party known as the Know-Nothings arose to keep foreigners and Catholics out of politics.

By 1860 there were 1.3 million factory workers in the United States. During the late 1820s and early 1830s, many factory workers joined **labor unions** to improve working conditions. The unions, however, had little power or money. Courts often ruled against early unions.

Despite the trend toward urbanization and industrialization, agriculture was still the nation's leading economic activity. "Cotton was King" in the

Study Guide

Chapter 2, Section 1 *(continued)*

South and provided nearly two-thirds of the total export trade of the United States. The cotton industry was fueled by Eli Whitney's cotton gin and by enslaved labor. The foreign slave trade had been outlawed in 1808, but a high birthrate among enslaved women kept the population growing. By 1850 there were nearly 3.2 million slaves in the South, accounting for nearly 37 percent of the Southern population.

No matter how well treated, all enslaved persons suffered indignities and the complete lack of citizenship rights. Resistance ranged from work slowdowns to violence. Free African Americans had an <u>ambiguous</u> position in Southern society. There was no slavery in the North, but African Americans did not experience real equality.

Academic Vocabulary
ambiguous: to lack a definitive purpose (p. 181)

5. How did industrialization affect cities in the United States?

_____

_____

_____

_____

Study Guide

Chapter 2, Section 2

For use with textbook pages 182–189

GROWING DIVISION AND REFORM

CONTENT VOCABULARY

spoils system   the practice of appointing people to government jobs on the basis of party loyalty and support *(page 184)*

caucus   a system of selecting presidential candidates in which members of a political party choose the nominee for president *(page 184)*

secede   to withdraw *(page 185)*

nullification   to declare invalid *(page 185)*

temperance   abstinence from alcohol *(page 187)*

abolition   an immediate end to slavery *(page 188)*

emancipation   freeing enslaved persons *(page 188)*

DRAWING FROM EXPERIENCE

Have you ever had a disagreement with someone and just could not seem to resolve your differences? Did you try to compromise, or give up something in order to get something else in return? Compromise has been an important problem-solving tool in our country's history.

This section discusses the growing differences between the North and the South.

ORGANIZING YOUR THOUGHTS

Use the chart below to help you take notes. In the early 1800s, many people worked to reform different aspects of society. List the reform that each person or group listed below worked for.

Reformer	Type of Reform
American Colonization Society	1.
William Lloyd Garrison	2.
Prudence Crandall	3.
Frederick Douglass	4
Lucretia Mott	5.
Elizabeth Cady Stanton	6.

California History-Social Science Standards

11.1 Students analyze the significant events in the founding of the nation and its attempts to realize the philosophy of government described in the Declaration of Independence.

11.3 Students analyze the role religion played in the founding of America, its lasting moral, social and political impacts, and issues regarding religious liberty.

11.10 Students analyze the development of federal civil rights and voting rights.

Focuses on: 11.1.3, 11.3.1, 11.3.2, 11.3.3, 11.10.7

Study Guide

Chapter 2, Section 2 (continued)

READ TO LEARN

• The Resurgence of Sectionalism (page 183)

In 1819 the Union had 11 free states and 11 slave states. Missouri applied for statehood as a slave state. This set off the divisive issue as to whether slavery should expand westward. Admitting any new state, either slave or free, would upset the balance of political power in the Senate and start a struggle for political power.

While trying to settle the question of slavery in Missouri, Maine applied for statehood. The Senate decided to combine Maine's request with Missouri's. The result was the Missouri Compromise. It called for admitting Maine as a free state and Missouri as a slave state. An amendment was added to the compromise that prohibited slavery in the Louisiana Purchase territory north of Missouri's southern border. Henry Clay of Kentucky steered the vote through the House of Representatives, which accepted the compromise.

Sectional differences over beliefs and policies were part of the election of 1824. All four candidates in the presidential election of 1824 were from the Republican Party.

Jackson won the popular vote and led in the Electoral College. No candidate, however, won a majority in the Electoral College. The House of Representatives had to vote to select the president out of the three candidates with the highest number of electoral votes. Clay had the least electoral votes, so he was eliminated. Clay, who was Speaker of the House, had great influence there. He threw his support to John Quincy Adams, and Adams won the House vote.

Jackson's supporters accused Clay of winning votes for Adams in return for a cabinet post. Adams and Clay were accused of making a "corrupt bargain." Adams and Clay said they had done nothing wrong. Jackson's supporters took the name Democratic Republicans to point out their differences with Adams's party, the National Republicans. The Democratic Republicans later shortened their name to Democrats.

Starting in the early 1800s, the United States saw a growth of democracy. Hundreds of thousands of males gained voting rights. This was because many states eliminated property ownership as a voting qualification.

John Quincy Adams and Andrew Jackson were the presidential candidates in the election of 1828. The campaign resorted to mudslinging. The candidates criticized each other's personalities and principles.

Jackson won the popular vote and the electoral vote in the election of 1828. Many voters who supported him were from the West and South. They were rural and small-town men who thought Jackson would represent their interests.

President Jackson believed in the capability and intelligence of average Americans. He believed that ordinary citizens should play an active role in government. As a result, Jackson supported the **spoils system,** the practice of appointing people to government jobs on the basis of party loyalty and

Study Guide

Chapter 2, Section 2 *(continued)*

support. Jackson replaced large numbers of government employees with his own supporters. He believed that opening government offices to ordinary citizens increased democracy.

Jackson and his supporters also wanted to make the way presidential candidates were chosen more democratic. At that time, political parties chose presidential candidates through the **caucus** system, in which party members who served in Congress would meet to choose the nominee for president. Jackson believed that this method gave only the well connected the opportunity to hold office. He and his supporters replaced the caucus with the national nominating convention. Delegates from the states met to decide on the party's presidential nominee.

The economy of South Carolina was weakening throughout the early 1800s. Many people blamed the nation's tariffs. South Carolina had to purchase many manufactured goods from Europe. Tariffs placed on these <u>items</u> made them very expensive. In 1828 Congress added a new tariff, which people called the Tariff of Abominations. Many South Carolinians threatened to **secede,** or withdraw, from the union.

Academic Vocabulary

item: a distinct unit in a collection or series (p. 185)

John C. Calhoun, the vice president, was torn between following the country's policies and helping his fellow South Carolinians. Calhoun proposed the idea of **nullification,** which said that states had the right to declare a federal law null, or not valid. He said that states had this right because they had created the union. The issue came up again in 1830 when two senators—Robert Hayne of South Carolina and Daniel Webster of Massachusetts—debated each other on the Senate floor. Hayne supported the right of states to do what they wanted. Webster defended the Union.

President Jackson also defended the Union. When Congress passed another tariff law in 1832, South Carolina was upset and called for secession, while a special state convention voted to nullify the tariffs. Jackson considered this an act of treason. He sent a warship to Charleston, South Carolina, and tensions increased. Senator Henry Clay pushed through a bill that would lower the tariffs gradually until 1842. South Carolina repealed its nullification decision.

Like many other people, President Jackson believed that conflicts with Native Americans would end if they were moved to the uninhabited regions west of the Mississippi River. In 1830 Jackson pushed through Congress the Indian Removal Act, which provided money to relocate Native Americans.

Most Native Americans gave in and resettled in the West. However, the Cherokee of Georgia refused. Two cases reached the Supreme Court. Chief Justice John Marshall sided with the Cherokee and ordered the state of Georgia to honor their property rights. President Jackson, however, did not support the Court's decision.

Eventually, the army was sent to resolve the conflict with the Cherokee. The army forced them out of their homes and marched them west. Thousands of Cherokee died on the journey, which became known as the Trail of Tears. By

Study Guide

Chapter 2, Section 2 *(continued)*

1838 the government had moved the majority of Native Americans east of the Mississippi to reservations. Although most Americans supported the removal policy, some, such as a few National Republicans and some religious denominations, denounced it.

President Jackson opposed the Second Bank of the United States. He believed that it benefited only the wealthy. He removed the government's deposits, which forced the Bank to end. Many people later claimed that Jackson's action contributed to the nation's future financial problems.

In the mid-1830s, the Whig Party formed to oppose President Jackson. The Whigs wanted to expand the federal government and to develop industry and trade. The Whig's ideas were very different from those of Jackson's Democrats, who wanted a limited government.

In the presidential election of 1836, Democrat Martin Van Buren easily defeated the Whigs, who had three candidates. Shortly after he became president, an economic crisis hit the United States. The crisis had been set off by Jackson, who had issued the Specie Circular before leaving office. It ordered that payments for public land must be made in gold or silver, not paper currency. This set off the Panic of 1837. Land sales plummeted and economic growth slowed. Banks and businesses failed, and thousands of farmers lost their land.

The Whigs hoped that the economic crisis would lead to an easy victory over the Democrats in the 1840 presidential election. The Whigs nominated William Henry Harrison for president and John Tyler for vice president. Harrison won, but he died one month after his inauguration, and John Tyler became president.

Tyler actually opposed many Whig policies. As a result, he sided with the Democrats and refused to support a third Bank and a higher tariff. President Tyler also had to deal with foreign relations, particularly with Great Britain. The Webster-Ashburton Treaty established a firm boundary between the United States and Canada.

7. What helped the Whigs defeat President Van Buren in the 1840 election?

_____

_____

_____

Study Guide

Chapter 2, Section 2 (continued)

- ### The Reform Spirit (page 186)

In the 1800s, religious leaders organized a movement to revive Americans' commitment to religion. This movement came to be known as the Second Great Awakening. Ministers attracted thousands of followers in revival meetings, where people sang and prayed. Charles G. Finney, a Presbyterian minister, was an important promoter of the Second Great Awakening. His revivals attracted many followers.

A number of new religions flourished during the mid-1800s. Among these were Unitarianism and Universalism. New Englander Joseph Smith founded the Church of Jesus Christ of Latter-day Saints, whose followers are commonly known as the Mormons. After being harassed in New England for their beliefs, the Mormons moved west. Brigham Young became the leader of the Mormon Church after Joseph Smith's murder.

Lyman Beecher, a revivalist minister, preached the idea of individuals rather than government working to build a better society. He and other religious leaders helped start organizations known as benevolent societies. These organizations focused on spreading God's word and on solving social problems.

Many women participated in the reform movements in the United States. They focused on aspects of American society that they believed needed change.

The optimism of the time and the new stress on individuals led to the creation of new communities. The people who started these communities believed that society corrupted human nature, and the best way to prevent this from happening was to separate people from society.

Many believed that excessive use of alcohol caused many social problems, such as crime and poverty. Reformers stepped up their campaign for **temperance,** or abstinence from alcohol. Temperance groups formed all across the country. Several groups joined together to form the American Temperance Union. Temperance groups also worked for laws to prohibit the sale of liquor.

Some reformers worked to improve prison conditions. Some people also worked for programs to help prisoners rehabilitate themselves rather than simply locking them up. States also began funding schools in which students would become better-educated workers and voters.

In the 1800s, many people believed that the home was the proper place for women. Many women believed that as wives, they were partners with their husbands. Still, some used the reform movement to create schools for girls that taught <u>academic</u> subjects.

In 1848 Lucretia Mott and Elizabeth Cady Stanton organized the Seneca Falls Convention. This was a gathering of women and the start of an organized woman's movement. The convention declared that all men and women are created equal. Stanton also proposed that women focus on gaining the right to vote, and the proposal narrowly passed.

Academic Vocabulary
academic: associated with higher learning at a scholarly institution (p. 188)

Study Guide

Chapter 2, Section 2 *(continued)*

Throughout American history, many Americans had opposed slavery. The first organizations formed to end slavery started in the early 1800s. In 1816 the American Colonization Society (ACS) was formed. The society bought land in West Africa and began shipping free African Americans to a colony they established there. The colony eventually became the country of Liberia. However, most African Americans regarded the United States as their home and did not want to move to another continent.

In the 1830s, the idea of **abolition,** or the immediate end to slavery, gained renewed strength. William Lloyd Garrison was most influential in the development of a national abolitionist movement in the 1830s. He founded Boston's antislavery newspaper, the *Liberator.* In his newspaper, Garrison called for complete **emancipation,** or freeing, of enslaved persons. Garrison founded the American Antislavery Society in 1833. Many women in both the North and South carried on Garrison's abolitionist work.

Free African Americans also took on significant roles in the abolitionist movement. Frederick Douglass, who escaped from slavery in Maryland, was the most famous. He published his own antislavery newspaper, the *North Star.* Another important abolitionist was Sojourner Truth. Her antislavery speeches drew huge crowds.

Many Northerners disapproved of slavery. However, many thought the abolitionist movement was a threat to the existing social system. Some believed that it would create conflict between the North and the South. Others were afraid that it would lead to the influx of freed African Americans to the North, causing housing and job shortages.

Southerners viewed slavery as a necessity to the Southern way of life and to its economy. They defended it by claiming that most slaves did not want freedom because they benefited from their relationship with the slaveholders.

In 1831, a slave rebellion left more than 50 white Virginians dead. Southerners were furious and demanded that abolitionist material not be circulated in the South. Southern postal workers refused to deliver abolitionist newspapers. The House of Representatives refused to debate all abolitionist petitions.

8. How did Southerners respond to the abolitionist movement?

_____

_____

_____

_____

Name _____ Date _____ Class _____

Study Guide

Chapter 2, Section 3

For use with textbook pages 192–201

MANIFEST DESTINY AND CRISIS

CONTENT VOCABULARY

Manifest Destiny   idea that the nation was meant to spread to the Pacific *(page 193)*

annexation   act of adding a new state to the United States *(page 194)*

popular sovereignty   the idea that people living in a territory had the right to decide by voting whether to allow slavery in the territory *(page 196)*

secession   the process of leaving the Union that Southern states threatened *(page 196)*

Underground Railroad   an organized system for helping enslaved persons escape *(page 197)*

transcontinental railroad   railroad that connected the West Coast to the rest of the country *(page 197)*

insurrection   a rebellion *(page 199)*

Confederacy   the new nation declared by the seceding Southern states *(page 201)*

California History-Social Science Standards

11.1 Students analyze the significant events in the founding of the nation and its attempts to realize the philosophy of government described in the Declaration of Independence.

11.2 Students analyze the relationship among the rise of industrialization, large-scale rural-to-urban migration, and massive immigration from Southern and Eastern Europe.

11.10 Students analyze the development of federal civil rights and voting rights.

Focuses on: 11.1.3, 11.2.6, 11.10.2

DRAWING FROM EXPERIENCE

Why did Southern states support slavery? Why did Northerners oppose it? What steps do you think the government could have taken to solve the issue?

In this section, you will learn how the government dealt with slavery in the new territories that were organized after the Mexican War.

ORGANIZING YOUR THOUGHTS

Use the chart below to help you take notes. Several events helped sectional divisions in the 1850s to grow. Explain how each of the events listed in the chart contributed to the growth of sectionalism.

Event	How It Contributed to the Growth of Sectionalism
Dred Scott decision	1.
The Lecompton constitution	2.
John Brown's raid	3.

Study Guide

Chapter 2, Section 3 *(continued)*

READ TO LEARN

• **Manifest Destiny** *(page 193)*

Americans moved west for many reasons, including fertile soil, the fur trade, and trade with Pacific nations. Many Americans believed in **Manifest Destiny,** the idea that the nation was meant to expand to the Pacific.

People who came later to the Midwest pushed on toward California and Oregon. Other nations had already claimed parts of these lands. The United States and Great Britain agreed to settle Oregon together. In the late 1830s, American missionaries came to the Oregon Territory and wrote enthusiastic reports that attracted settlers.

Mexico controlled California. Its distance from Mexico made it difficult to govern. The local California government could not attract enough emigrants from Mexico, so it welcomed foreign settlers, but it remained suspicious about their national loyalties.

Much of the land that pioneers crossed to reach the Pacific was difficult terrain. By the 1840s, they had made several east-west passages, such as the Oregon Trail, the California Trail, and the Santa Fe Trail.

As overland traffic increased, Native Americans on the Great Plains disliked immigration. They were afraid it would change their way of life. The Native Americans in this region relied on buffalo to meet their needs for food, shelter, and clothing. They feared that the increasing number of settlers moving across their hunting grounds would disrupt the wanderings of the buffalo herds.

The federal government wanted peace, so in 1851 the U.S. government and eight Native American groups negotiated the Treaty of Fort Laramie. The Native American groups agreed to live in certain territories. In return, the U.S. government promised that these territories would always belong to the Native Americans.

At first, Mexico had encouraged Americans to settle in the Mexican region of Texas. Tensions developed when Americans refused to accept the conditions of Mexico's offer, and Mexico closed its borders in 1830. American settlers decided to separate from Mexico and finally defeated the Mexicans at the Battle of San Jacinto in 1836. Also in 1836, they voted in favor of **annexation**—absorption—by the United States as a slave state. Because of the slavery issue and the fact that Mexico continued to claim Texas, President Jackson made no move toward annexation.

James K. Polk of Tennessee was the Democratic candidate in the 1844 election. Polk promised to annex Texas and the Oregon Territory. He also promised to buy California from Mexico. His platform appealed to both Northerners and Southerners because it expanded the country and kept a balance between free and slave states. Polk won the election against the Whig candidate Henry Clay.

The American Vision: Modern Times

Study Guide

Chapter 2, Section 3 (continued)

In 1845 Congress passed a joint resolution to annex Texas. In June 1846, Great Britain and the United States divided Oregon along 49° north latitude.

The entry of Texas into the Union angered Mexico, which then broke diplomatic relations with the United States. Matters between the two countries got worse when Mexico and the United States could not agree on the location of Texas's southwestern border. In November 1845, Polk sent John Slidell to Mexico City to purchase California. Mexico's president refused to meet with Slidell.

After Mexico's president refused to discuss the U.S. purchase of California, President Polk ordered General Zachary Taylor and his troops to cross the Nueces River into territory claimed by both the United States and Mexico. Polk wanted Mexico to attack the U.S. troops so he could win popular support for a war. Finally a force of Mexicans attacked Taylor's men. Polk declared war with Mexico, and Congress voted for the war.

Before Polk had signed the declaration of war, settlers in northern California, led by American general John C. Frémont, began an uprising. They easily defeated the Mexican presence there. On June 14, 1846, the settlers declared California independent from Mexico. They called the region the Bear Flag Republic. A few weeks later, American naval forces took possession of California for the United States.

Mexico refused to surrender. Polk sent General Winfield Scott to capture Mexico City. The city was captured in September 1847. On February 2, 1848, Mexico and the United States signed the Treaty of Guadalupe Hidalgo. In this agreement, Mexico gave the United States territory that included what are now the states of California, Utah, and Nevada, as well as most of New Mexico and Arizona and parts of Colorado and Wyoming. Mexico agreed to the Rio Grande as the southern border of Texas. The United States agreed to pay Mexico $15 million and to take over $3.25 million in debt that the Mexican government owed American citizens.

4. What did the United States gain from the Treaty of Guadalupe Hidalgo?

_____

_____

_____

- **Slavery and Western Expansion** (page 195)

The lands acquired after the Mexican War raised the issue of extending slavery westward. In August 1846, Representative David Wilmot proposed an amendment to a bill, which became known as the Wilmot Proviso. It proposed that slavery not be allowed in any territory gained from Mexico. This proposal angered Southerners, who believed Americans had the right to bring

Study Guide

Chapter 2, Section 3 (continued)

along their property, including enslaved laborers, and that Congress had no right to ban slavery in the territories.

Senator Lewis Cass of Michigan proposed an idea that became known as **popular sovereignty.** The idea stated that the citizens of each new territory should decide for themselves if they wanted to permit slavery or not. This idea appealed to many politicians because it removed the issue of expanding slavery from the national government.

In the 1848 presidential election, the major parties decided to avoid the issue of slavery. Many northern opponents of slavery decided to join with members of the abolitionist Liberty Party to form the Free-Soil Party. This party opposed the spread of slavery into western territories.

On election day in 1848, many supporters of the Free-Soiler candidate Martin Van Buren pulled votes from Democrat Lewis Cass. The Whig candidate, Zachary Taylor, won the election.

In 1849 the discovery of gold in California brought thousands of "Forty-Niners," or people who hoped to get wealthy, to California. Soon Californians applied for statehood. California asked to be admitted as a free state.

If California came in as a free state, then the slaveholding states would be in the minority in Congress. Southerners feared losing power in Congress. Many began talking of **secession,** or taking their states out of the Union. In 1850 Senator Henry Clay of Kentucky proposed a compromise to solve the crisis. His resolutions offered concessions to both sides. They included admitting California as a free state, but not placing restrictions on slavery in the rest of the territory from Mexico. Another proposal would add a stronger law about African Americans who had fled north.

Under the Fugitive Slave Act, an individual needed to only point out a person as a runaway for that person to be taken into custody. The law required that any Northerner had to help catch African Americans. If they refused, they could be jailed. Northerners reacted angrily to the law, and antislavery activists disobeyed it. The Northern opposition to slavery increased.

Whites and free African Americans continued helping African Americans escape North through the **Underground Railroad.** This was an organized system in which runaways were transported north and given shelter and food along the way. They were moved to freedom in the Northern states or Canada. Many people, particularly Harriet Tubman, acted as conductors. They made dangerous journeys into the South to guide enslaved persons along the Underground Railroad.

By the early 1850s, Oregon was opened for settlement and California was admitted to the Union. Many Americans believed that they needed a **transcontinental railroad** for further growth in the new territories.

Study Guide

Chapter 2, Section 3 (continued)

Southerners wanted the railroad to start from New Orleans. However, this would require the railroad to pass through northern Mexico. As a result, the United States bought a strip of land for $10 million.

Senator Stephen A. Douglas wanted the railroad to start in Chicago. However, this northern route would require Congress to organize the territory west of Missouri and Iowa. He suggested organizing the region into a new territory to be called Nebraska. Southern Senators responded that to form the new territory, he needed to repeal the Missouri Compromise and allow slavery in the new territory.

Douglas responded by saying that any states organized in the Nebraska territory would be allowed to use popular sovereignty on slavery. He then proposed undoing the Missouri Compromise and dividing the territory into two territories: Nebraska, <u>adjacent</u> to the North, would become a free state; Kansas would become a slave state. Despite opposition, Congress passed the Kansas-Nebraska Act in May 1854.

> **Academic Vocabulary**
>
> **adjacent:** sharing a common border (p. 198)

The conflict over slavery intensified in Kansas. Northern settlers headed for the new territory. In the spring of 1855, thousands of Missourians voted illegally in Kansas and created a pro-slavery legislature. Antislavery settlers held a convention in Kansas and created their own constitution that prohibited slavery. Kansas now had two governments. "Bleeding Kansas," as one newspaper called it, became involved in a civil war between pro-slavery and antislavery settlers.

5. Why did violence break out in the territory of Kansas?

_____

_____

_____

_____

• The Crisis Deepens (page 198)

The Kansas-Nebraska Act brought an end to the Whig Party. Many Northern Whigs joined antislavery Democrats and Free-Soilers to form a new party called the Republican Party. The Republicans wanted to prevent the Southern planters from controlling the federal government. Although Republicans did not agree on whether slavery should be abolished, they did agree that it should be kept out of the territories.

At about the same time, the American Party, known as the Know-Nothings, gained popularity in the Northeast. The American Party was against Catholics and immigrants. Nativist fears helped the party gain seats in Congress and in state legislatures. However, like the Whigs, the Know-Nothings Party split over the issue of the Kansas-Nebraska Act. Eventually it dissolved.

Study Guide

Chapter 2, Section 3 *(continued)*

In the 1856 presidential election, the Republicans nominated John C. Frémont. The Democrats nominated James Buchanan. Buchanan had not spoken out loud about the Kansas-Nebraska Act and easily won the election.

The Supreme Court decided the issue of slavery in the territories by ruling in the case of *Dred Scott* v. *Sandford.* The case centered on Dred Scott, an enslaved man whose Missouri slaveholder had taken him to live in free territory before returning to Missouri. Scott sued to end his slavery, saying that the time spent in free territory meant he was free. The Court decided against Scott. The Court also ruled that the federal government could not prohibit slavery in the territories.

Conflicts continued between pro-slavery and antislavery forces in Kansas. The pro-slavery legislature drafted a constitution in the town of Lecompton in 1857 that would legalize slavery. Antislavery forces voted down the constitution in a territory-wide referendum, or vote on the issue. The Senate voted to accept the Lecompton constitution, but the House of Representatives blocked it. Buchanan and Southern congressional leaders agreed to allow another vote in Kansas on the constitution. In another referendum, settlers in Kansas again voted over-whelmingly against the Lecompton constitution and against allowing slavery in their state. As a result, Kansas did not become a state until 1861.

John Brown was an abolitionist. In 1859 he developed a plan to take over the federal arsenal at Harpers Ferry, Virginia. He wanted to bring about an **insurrection,** or rebellion, against slaveholders. Brown and his followers seized the arsenal, but soon a force of U.S. Marines, under the command of Robert E. Lee, stopped the attack. Brown was sentenced to death by a Virginia Court. Many Northerners viewed Brown as a hero. Most Southerners, however, believed that his plan was proof that Northerners were plotting the murder of slaveholders.

6. Why did John Brown seize the arsenal at Harpers Ferry?

_____

_____

_____

_____

• The Union Dissolves *(page 199)*

The issue of slavery dominated the presidential election of 1860. The Southern Democrats wanted the party to uphold the *Dred Scott* decision and support slaveholders' rights in the territories. Northern Democrats wanted the party to support popular sovereignty. The two groups could not agree on a candidate. As a result, they met again in Baltimore in June 1860 to select their candidate. Northern Democrats endorsed Stephen Douglas as their candidate. The Southern Democrats then walked out and organized their own convention. They

Study Guide

Chapter 2, Section 3 *(continued)*

nominated John C. Breckinridge, the current vice president. Other people who feared the <u>prospect</u> of Southern secession, including many former Whigs, formed the Constitutional Union Party. They nominated John Bell, who supported the Union.

Academic Vocabulary

prospect: someone or something that has the potential of creating positive or negative consequences (p. 200)

The Republicans, who knew they would not be able to get any electoral votes in the South, needed to nominate a candidate who would be able to get the electoral votes in the North. The Republicans turned to Lincoln. During the campaign, the Republicans continued to run on the idea of banning slavery in new territories. They also supported the right of the Southern states to keep slavery in their borders. They supported higher tariffs and a transcontinental railroad.

With the Democrat votes split, the Republicans won the election without Southern support. For many Southerners, having a Republican president meant the end of Southern society and culture. They believed there was no choice but to secede.

South Carolina was the first state to secede. By February 1, 1861, six more states in the Lower South—Mississippi, Florida, Alabama, Georgia, Louisiana, and Texas—had voted to secede.

As the Southern states seceded, Congress tried to find a compromise to save the Union. Senator John J. Crittenden suggested several amendments to the Constitution. Crittenden's Compromise would guarantee slavery where it existed. It would also bring back the Missouri Compromise line. Slavery would be prohibited north of the Missouri Compromise line and allowed south of it. The compromise did not pass Congress. A peace conference also produced no results.

At the same time that some people were working toward compromise, the seceded states called a convention in Alabama and declared themselves to be a new nation—the Confederate States of America, or the **Confederacy.** They drafted their own constitution, which guaranteed slavery in Confederate territory. The convention chose former Mississippi senator Jefferson Davis to be president, who called on the rest of the South to join the Confederacy.

7. What were the results of the convention that the seceded states called?

_____

_____

_____

Study Guide

Chapter 2, Section 4

For use with textbook pages 206–215

THE CIVIL WAR

CONTENT VOCABULARY

martial law   the situation in which the military takes control of an area, replacing civilian authorities and suspending certain civil rights *(page 208)*

greenback   green-colored paper money that was created as a national currency in 1862 *(page 209)*

conscription   the drafting of people for military service *(page 209)*

habeas corpus   a person's right not to be imprisoned unless charged with a crime and given a trial *(page 209)*

attrition   the wearing down of one side by the other through exhaustion of soldiers and resources *(page 209)*

siege   to cut food and supplies and bombard a city until its defenders give up *(page 212)*

mandate   a clear sign from voters that they support a certain policy *(page 214)*

DRAWING FROM EXPERIENCE

Do you know anyone who has served in the military during a war, such as the Vietnam War, the Persian Gulf War, or the current war on terrorism? How do they describe their experiences?

The last section discussed the sectional division leading to the Civil War. This section discusses the progress of the war and the effects on the lives of both soldiers and civilians.

ORGANIZING YOUR THOUGHTS

Use the table below to help you take notes. Both the North and South had several advantages and disadvantages from the policies each side implemented. List them in the table.

> **California History-Social Science Standards**
>
> **11.1** Students analyze the significant events in the founding of the nation and its attempts to realize the philosophy of government described in the Declaration of Independence.
>
> **11.10** Students analyze the development of federal civil rights and voting rights.
>
> **Focuses on:** 11.1.3, 11.1.4, 11.10.2

The Opposing Sides

North		South	
Advantages	**Disadvantages**	**Advantages**	**Disadvantages**
_____	_____	_____	_____
_____	_____	_____	_____
_____	_____	_____	_____

Study Guide

Chapter 2, Section 4 *(continued)*

- **The Civil War Begins** *(page 207)*

   In his inaugural address, President Lincoln again repeated his promise not to interfere with slavery where it existed. He insisted that the Union could not be dissolved, and he announced his intentions to take back the federal property seized by the seceded states.

   In April 1861, Lincoln announced that the federal government intended to send supplies to Fort Sumter. The Confederacy faced a dilemma. To let federal troops in to the South's harbor would be unacceptable for an independent nation, as the South now saw itself. However, to fire on the supply ship would most likely lead to war. Davis decided to take Fort Sumter before the supply ship arrived there. The Confederates demanded that Major Robert Anderson surrender Fort Sumter. Anderson refused, and Confederate forces bombarded the fort until Anderson and his men surrendered. The Civil War had started.

   After Fort Sumter fell, President Lincoln called for volunteers to serve in the military. Many people in the Upper South did not want to secede. However, with a civil war at hand, they believed they had no choice but to secede. Virginia seceded first, and the capital of the Confederacy moved to Richmond, Virginia. By the beginning of June 1861, Arkansas, North Carolina, and Tennessee had also seceded.

   Lincoln tried to keep the slaveholding border states—Delaware, Maryland, Kentucky, and Missouri—from seceding. Delaware seemed safe. However, if Maryland seceded, Washington, D.C., would be surrounded by Confederate territory. To prevent secession, Lincoln placed Baltimore under **martial law.** Under martial law, the military takes control of an area and replaces civilian authorities, and it suspends certain civil rights. At first, Kentucky declared itself neutral. However, in September 1861, Confederate troops occupied the southwest corner of the state. The state convention voted to remain part of the Union. After a struggle between anti-secession and pro-secession forces, Missouri decided against secession.

   2. Why did President Lincoln want to prevent Maryland from seceding?

   _____

   _____

   _____

   _____

   _____

Study Guide

Chapter 2, Section 4 *(continued)*

- **The Opposing Sides** *(page 208)*

On the day that Virginia seceded from the Union, General Winfield Scott asked Robert E. Lee, one of the best senior officers in the United States Army, to command the Union's troops. However, Lee was from Virginia, and so he chose to serve the Confederacy.

Lee was one of hundreds of military officers who chose to support the Confederacy. These officers helped the Confederacy to quickly organize a fighting force. In 1860 the South had seven out of the eight military colleges in the United States, which provided the South with a large number of trained officers. The North had a strong navy. More than three-quarters of the nation's naval officers came from the North. The crews of merchant ships were almost all from the north. They provided the navy with experienced sailors for the Union navy.

The North had several advantages over the South. The North had more people, which made it easier to raise an army and support the war effort.

The North had an economic advantage over the South. It had almost 90 percent of the nation's factories. Thus, the North could provide its troops with ammunition and other supplies.

The South had only one railroad line from the eastern to the western part of the Confederacy. As a result, the Union troops could easily disrupt the South's railroad system and stop the South from moving supplies and troops by rail.

The Union controlled the national treasury. It also continued to get money from tariffs. Congress passed the Legal Tender Act. It created a national currency and allowed the government to print paper money. The paper money became known as **greenbacks** because of its color.

The finances of the Confederacy, which were never very good, grew worse over time. Southern planters were in debt and could not buy bonds. Southern banks were small and did not have enough cash reserves to buy bonds. The Union's blockade of Southern ports reduced trade in the South and, therefore, reduced the amount of money the South could raise by taxing trade. As a result, the South tried to raise money by taxing the people. Many refused to pay taxes. The South also printed paper money, which caused a huge rise in inflation.

President Lincoln faced conflict from members of the Republican Party. Many were abolitionists. However, Lincoln's goal in the Civil War was to preserve the Union. The President also had to deal with the Democrats who challenged his policies.

Some disagreements between Republicans and Democrats had to do with civil rights. In 1862 Congress introduced a militia law that required states to use **conscription,** which is the drafting of people for military service. To enforce the militia law, Lincoln suspended writs of **habeas corpus.** This refers

Study Guide

Chapter 2, Section 4 (continued)

to a person's right not to be imprisoned unless charged with a crime and given a trial. Lincoln suspended writs for those who supported the Confederacy or encouraged others to resist the draft.

The Confederate constitution stressed states' rights. As a result, the power of the central government was limited. Many Southern leaders opposed Jefferson Davis's policies. They opposed forcing people to join the Confederate army and Davis's suspending of writs of habeas corpus.

The United States did not want European nations to interfere in the war. The Confederates wanted Britain to recognize the South and provide it with military assistance against the Union. The Confederates knew that Britain and France depended on Southern cotton for their textile factories. To pressure these countries, many planters stopped selling cotton to them. Both Britain and France chose not to go to war against the United States.

The Civil War was the first modern war. It involved large armies made up mostly of civilian volunteers. It required large amounts of supplies and equipment. By the 1850s, armies began using a new kind of cone-shaped bullet for rifles that was accurate at greater distances. **Attrition**—the wearing down of one side by the other through the using up of soldiers and resources—played an important role as the war dragged on.

The South ran a defensive war of attrition. Davis wanted to force the Union to use its resources until it became tired of the war and agreed to negotiate. Many Southerners disliked this strategy. Instead, Southern troops often went on the offensive. They charged enemy lines and suffered huge casualties.

Union generals proposed their own strategy for defeating the South. It included blockading Confederate ports and sending gunboats down the Mississippi to divide the Confederacy. They believed that this would force the South to run out of resources and surrender. Many Northerners rejected this Anaconda Plan. Lincoln and other Union leaders realized that a long war, focused on destroying the South's armies, had a chance to succeed.

3. What strategy did Union generals develop to defeat the South?

_____

_____

_____

_____

_____

_____

Study Guide

Chapter 2, Section 4 *(continued)*

- **The Early Stages** *(page 210)*

The Union hoped for a quick victory against the South by striking Confederate forces at Bull Run. At first, the attack went well for the Union. Then Confederate reinforcements, led by Thomas J. "Stonewall" Jackson, arrived. The Union defeat made it clear that the North would need a large, well-trained army to defeat the South. The North tried to enlist men by offering a bounty, or a sum of money given as a bonus, to people who agreed to military service for three years. Eventually, however, both the Union and the Confederacy instituted the draft.

President Lincoln wanted to blockade all Confederate ports. Union ships, however, found it difficult to stop all of the blockade runners, or small, fast ships, that the South used to smuggle goods past the blockade. By doing so, the South could at least get some of its cotton to Europe in exchange for goods that it needed.

At the same time that Union ships were blockading Atlantic ports, the Union navy began to prepare to take over New Orleans and gain control of the lower Mississippi River. In April 1862, David G. Farragut led Union forces and within 6 days captured New Orleans.

General Ulysses S. Grant began a campaign to seize control of the Cumberland River and the Tennessee River. Control of these two rivers would cut Tennessee in two and give the Union a river route deep into Confederate territory.

Grant then continued down the Tennessee River. On April 6, 1862, Confederate troops attacked Grant's forces at Shiloh. The Battle of Shiloh resulted in twenty thousand casualties, more than in any other battle up to that point.

In the South, General Robert E. Lee began a series of attacks on the Union army. These attacks became known as the Seven Days' Battle. Lee inflicted heavy casualties and forced the Union army to retreat.

Lee's forces then attacked the Union forces defending Washington. This led to another battle at Bull Run, with the North retreating. Lee then decided to invade Maryland. Both he and Jefferson Davis believed that invading the North would force the North to accept the South's independence. They also thought that the invasion would help gain recognition from Britain. In addition, they hoped the invasion would help Peace Democrats gain control of Congress in the next election.

When Lee invaded Maryland, General George B. McClellan and his troops took positions along Antietam Creek, east of Lee's location. The Battle of Antietam was the bloodiest one-day battle in the war. McClellan inflicted so many casualties on Lee's troops that Lee was forced to retreat to Virginia. Lee's defeat kept Britain from giving the Confederacy recognition and support. The defeat also convinced Lincoln that it was time to end slavery.

Study Guide

Chapter 2, Section 4 (continued)

Democrats opposed ending slavery. Republicans were split on the issue. As Northern casualties increased, however, many began to agree that slavery had to end.

On September 22, 1862, Lincoln announced that he would issue the Emancipation Proclamation—a decree freeing all enslaved persons in states still in rebellion after January 1, 1863. The Proclamation changed the purpose of the war from preserving the Union to ending slavery.

By the end of 1862, the South's transportation system was destroyed. Union troops were located in several agricultural regions. As a result, the South experienced severe food shortages. Many Confederate soldiers deserted and returned home to help their families. The food shortages led to riots in several places in the South.

At the same time, the North was experiencing an economic boom. Northern factories supplied troops with ammunition, clothes, and other necessities. Northern farmers, many of whom were women, used mechanized reapers and mowers. This made farming possible with fewer workers. Women also worked in industries to fill the labor shortages there.

Both Union and Confederate soldiers suffered hardships during the war.

The Emancipation Proclamation officially allowed African Americans to enlist in the Union army and navy. Thousands of African Americans enlisted in the military.

Women helped in the war effort at home by managing family farms and businesses. Many women also served as nurses and doctors to soldiers on the battlefields. Clara Barton and many other women nursed soldiers on the battlefield. This was a turning point for the American nursing profession.

4. Why did thousands of African Americans enlist in the Union army and navy after the Emancipation Proclamation?

_____

_____

_____

_____

_____

• The Turning Point (page 212)

The Union wanted to capture Vicksburg, Mississippi, the last major Confederate stronghold on the river. Doing so would cut the South in two.

Grant began two attacks on Vicksburg, but both times the Confederates stopped the attacks and caused high casualties for the Union troops. Grant then decided to put Vicksburg under **siege**—cut off its food and supplies and

Study Guide

Chapter 2, Section 4 *(continued)*

bombard the city until the Confederates gave up. The Confederates surrendered on July 4, 1863. The Union victory cut the Confederacy in two.

In 1863 Lee decided to invade the North. Some of Lee's troops headed into the town of Gettysburg. There they met the Union cavalry. On July 1, 1863, the Confederates pushed the Union troops out of the town and into the hills to the south. The main troops of both armies moved to the scene of the fighting.

Lee attacked on July 2, but the Union forces held their ground. On July 3, Lee ordered General George E. Pickett and General A. P. Hill to lead 15,000 men in an attack on the Union forces. The attack became known as Pickett's Charge. The Union forces opened fire on the Confederates, causing more than 7,000 casualties. Pickett's Charge did not break the Union lines. Lee withdrew his troops from Gettysburg and retreated to Virginia. At Gettysburg, the Union had 23,000 casualties. The Confederacy had 28,000 casualties, more than a third of Lee's forces.

The Battle of Gettysburg was a turning point of the war in the East. For the rest of the war, the Confederate forces would stay on the defensive and the Union army would continue to advance.

In November 1863, President Lincoln came to Gettysburg to dedicate a part of the battlefield as a military cemetery. The speech, known as the Gettysburg Address, became one of the best-known speeches in American history. In it, Lincoln reminded his listeners that the nation was "Conceived in liberty, and dedicated to the proposition that all men are created equal."

> **Academic Vocabulary**
>
> **conceive:** to create from nothing (p. 213)

The Union wanted to take Chattanooga to control a major railroad running south to Atlanta. This would allow the Union to advance into Georgia. General Grant's forces were able to scatter the Confederate soldiers who blocked the way to the city. Lincoln rewarded Grant's victories in Chattanooga and in Vicksburg by appointing him general in chief of the Union forces.

General Grant placed Union forces in the West under the command of his most trusted subordinate, General William Sherman. Then in the spring of 1864, Grant headed to Washington, D.C., to lead the Union troops against General Lee. He was determined to continue fighting the Confederates until they surrendered. He fought the Confederates near Fredericksburg, Virginia, and then near Spotsylvania Courthouse. Grant could not break Confederate lines there, so he headed toward Cold Harbor. This was an important crossroads northeast of Richmond. Grant launched an all-out attack on Lee's forces, but failed. The Union suffered heavy casualties.

> **Academic Vocabulary**
>
> **subordinate:** to be under the authority of a superior (p. 213)

General Grant ordered General Philip Sheridan to lead the cavalry in a raid outside Richmond. Grant wanted the raid to distract Lee's troops while he headed south past Richmond. When Grant reached Petersburg, he ordered his troops to put the city under siege.

Study Guide

Chapter 2, Section 4 *(continued)*

While Grant fought Lee, the Union navy led by David Farragut closed the port of Mobile, Alabama. Mobile was the last major Confederate port on the Gulf of Mexico.

General Sherman's forces worked to encircle Atlanta. Confederate troops evacuated Atlanta, and Sherman and his troops occupied it.

On November 15, 1864, Sherman began the March to the Sea, cutting a path of destruction through Georgia that was in places 60 miles wide. His troops looted houses, burned crops, and killed cattle. By December 21, 1864, the troops reached the coast and seized the city of Savannah. Sherman then headed north into South Carolina. The troops burned and pillaged, or looted, everything in front of them.

The capture of Atlanta had come just in time to revitalize Northern support for the war and for Lincoln, who won another term in the election of 1864. Lincoln believed that his re-election was a **mandate,** a clear sign from the voters, to end slavery permanently by amending the Constitution. On January 31, 1865, the Thirteenth Amendment, which banned slavery in the United States, passed the House of Representatives and was sent to the states for ratification.

At the same time, General Lee withdrew from Petersburg and tried to escape Grant's forces. However, General Sheridan's cavalry got ahead of Lee's troops and blocked the road at Appomattox Courthouse. With his troops surrounded and outnumbered, Lee surrendered to Grant on April 9, 1865. As part of the terms for surrender, Grant guaranteed that the United States would not prosecute Confederate soldiers for treason.

After the end of the war, Lincoln's advisers warned him not to appear unescorted in public. However, Lincoln went to Ford's Theater with his wife on April 14, 1865. During the play, John Wilkes Booth slipped behind him and shot the president. Lincoln's assassination shocked the nation.

The North's victory saved the Union. It strengthened the power of the federal government over the states. It changed American society by ending the enslavement of millions of African Americans. The war devastated the society and the economy of the South.

5. How did President Lincoln view his reelection in 1865?

_____

_____

_____

_____

_____

Study Guide

Chapter 2, Section 5

For use with textbook pages 218–225

RECONSTRUCTION

CONTENT VOCABULARY

Reconstruction   the rebuilding of the nation after the Civil War *(page 219)*

amnesty   pardon *(page 219)*

pocket veto   the rejection of a bill by the president by leaving the bill unsigned until after Congress adjourns *(page 220)*

freedmen   freed African Americans *(page 220)*

black codes   a series of laws passed by Southern legislatures, which severely limited African Americans' rights in the South *(page 221)*

impeach   to bring charges of a crime against a government official *(page 222)*

tenant farmers   farmers who paid rent for the land they farmed *(page 225)*

sharecroppers   farmers who paid a share of their crops to cover their rent and the equipment they needed *(page 225)*

DRAWING FROM EXPERIENCE

What do you think life was like for Southern planters after the Civil War? For African Americans?

In this section, you will learn about Lincoln's plan to reunite the nation. You will also learn what life was like in the South after the Civil War.

ORGANIZING YOUR THOUGHTS

Use the diagram below to help you take notes. President Lincoln and the Republicans in Congress differed on how the Confederate states were to be readmitted to the Union. List the goals of the Republicans in the diagram.

California History-Social Science Standards

11.1 Students analyze the significant events in the founding of the nation and its attempts to realize the philosophy of government described in the Declaration of Independence.

11.10 Students analyze the development of federal civil rights and voting rights.

Focuses on: 11.1.3, 11.1.4, 11.10.2

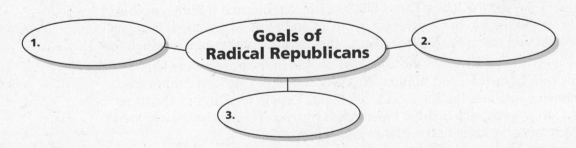

Study Guide

Chapter 2, Section 5 *(continued)*

• Reconstruction Begins *(page 219)*

The South was destroyed after the Civil War. Its economy was in shambles. The president and Congress had to deal with **Reconstruction,** or rebuilding the nation after the war. They had to decide how the former Confederate states would come back into the Union.

President Lincoln wanted a plan that would bring the South into the Union without punishing it for treason. His plan offered a general **amnesty,** or pardon, to all Southerners who took an oath of loyalty to the United Sates and accepted the Union's stand on slavery. When 10 percent of a state's voters took the oath, the state could set up a new government.

A group of Republicans, led by Thaddeus Stevens, opposed Lincoln's plan. They did not want to reconcile with the South. This group became known as the Radical Republicans. They had three goals. They wanted to prevent Confederate leaders from returning to power after the war. They wanted the Republican Party to become powerful in the South. They wanted the federal government to help African Americans gain political equality by guaranteeing their right to vote in the South.

The Republicans knew that after the South came back to the Union, they would gain more seats in Congress. They feared that they would lose control of Congress unless they found a way to guarantee voting rights to African Americans. Because African Americans generally supported the Republicans, giving African Americans voting rights would benefit the Republicans.

Moderate Republicans thought Lincoln's plan was too easy on the South, but they thought the Radical Republicans were going too far. As a result, the moderates and radicals came up with a plan that they both could support as an alternative to Lincoln's plan. They introduced the Wade-Davis Bill to Congress. The bill called for a majority of the adult white men in a former Confederate state to take an oath of loyalty to the Union. The state could then hold a convention to create a new state government. The state would have to abolish slavery, reject all debts the state had taken on as part of the Confederacy, and not allow former government and military officials the right to vote or to hold public office.

Congress passed the Wade-Davis Bill, but Lincoln blocked it with a **pocket veto.** He let the session of Congress come to an end without signing it into law. Lincoln believed that a harsh treatment of the South would not be productive.

After the war, hundreds of thousands of people in the South were left unemployed, homeless, and hungry. Thousands of freed African Americans, or **freedmen,** were looking for food and shelter. To help feed and clothe these people, Congress established the Freedmen's Bureau. The bureau also helped freed African Americans find work on plantations.

Some Northerners believed that the federal government should take lands of Confederates and give it to freed African Americans. Others, however, believed

Study Guide

Chapter 2, Section 5 (continued)

that taking land from plantation owners was against the idea of individual property rights. Congress refused to support the idea of taking land away.

Andrew Johnson became president after Lincoln was assassinated. His plan for Reconstruction was similar to that of Lincoln's. In the summer of 1865 he began to put his plan in place. The plan offered to pardon all former citizens of the Confederacy who took an oath of loyalty to the Union and to return their property. Confederate officers and officials were not eligible for the pardon. To return to the Union, each state had to call a convention to ratify the Thirteenth Amendment. For the most part, the Confederate states met these conditions.

When Congress met in December 1865, many members became angry when they realized that Southern voters had elected many former Confederate officers and political leaders. Many Republicans voted to reject the new Southern members of Congress.

Republicans were also angry about a series of laws that Southern legislatures had passed. Known as **black codes,** these laws limited African Americans' rights in the South. The codes were intended to keep African Americans in a condition similar to slavery.

4. Why did some Southern legislatures pass the black codes?

_____

_____

_____

_____

- **Congressional Reconstruction** (page 221)

Many moderate Republicans were upset that many former Confederates were members of Congress. They were also upset about the black codes. As a result, they joined the radicals. In late 1865, House and Senate Republicans created a Joint Committee on Reconstruction to set up their own plan for Reconstruction.

In March 1866, Congress passed the Civil Rights Act of 1866. It gave citizenship to all persons born in the United States except Native Americans. It allowed African Americans to own property and to be treated equally in court. The Republicans also introduced the Fourteenth Amendment to the Constitution. It granted citizenship to all persons born or naturalized in the United States. It also said that no state could deny any person equal protection of the laws.

President Johnson hoped the Northern voters would turn against the Radical Republicans in the 1866 election and support his Reconstruction plan. However, the Republicans won, and they had a three-to-one majority in Congress. They now could override any presidential veto. They also believed they had a mandate from the people to pass their own Reconstruction program.

Study Guide

Chapter 2, Section 5 (continued)

In March 1867, Congress passed the Military Reconstruction Act. It divided the Confederacy into five military districts. A Union general was placed in charge of each district. Each former Confederate state had to hold a convention to set up a constitution that Congress accepted. These constitutions had to give the right to vote to all male citizens, regardless of race. Each state also had to ratify the Fourteenth Amendment before it could send representatives to Congress.

The Republicans knew that President Johnson could interfere with their plans. To limit Johnson, Congress passed the Command of the Army Act, which required all orders from the president to go through the general of the army's office. Congress also passed the Tenure of Office Act. It required the Senate to approve the removal of any government official whose appointment had required the Senate's consent.

Johnson challenged the law by firing Secretary of War Stanton. A few days later, the House of Representatives voted to **impeach** Johnson, charging him with "high crimes and misdemeanors" in office. The main charge was that Johnson had broken the law by not upholding the Tenure of Office Act. The Senate then put the president on trial. The Senate voted in May 1868. It was just one vote short of convicting Johnson.

Although Johnson remained in office, he had very little power left. He did not run for reelection in the 1868 presidential election. The Republicans nominated General Ulysses S. Grant. He won, and the Republicans kept their majorities in both houses of Congress.

Congress continued with its Reconstruction program. It passed the Fifteenth Amendment to the Constitution. The amendment guaranteed African Americans the right to vote.

5. Why was the victory of the Republicans in the 1866 congressional elections significant?

_____

_____

_____

• Reconstruction and Republican Rule (page 223)

By late 1870, all the Southern states had rejoined the Union. Many Northerners moved to the South as Reconstruction began. Some were elected to the South's new state governments. Some Southerners referred to the Northerners as carpetbaggers. Many looked at the carpetbaggers as intruders who were trying to take advantage of the South's condition. Southerners also disliked the white Southerners who worked with the Republicans and supported Reconstruction. These people were referred to as scalawags.

Thousands of African Americans took part in governing the South. Hundreds of African Americans served as delegates to the state constitutional conventions. They won election to many local offices and to the state legislatures.

The American Vision: Modern Times

Study Guide

Chapter 2, Section 5 (continued)

African Americans also wanted to get an education. The Freedmen's Bureau established schools for African Americans across the South. By 1876 about 40 percent of all African American children attended school.

African Americans in the South also worked to establish their own churches. Churches housed schools and hosted social events and political meetings.

Although African Americans participated in the government, they did not control it. The Republican Party took power in the South because poor white Southerners supported it. They resented the planters and the Democratic Party that had ruled the South before the Civil War.

Republican governments in the South repealed the black codes. They set up state hospitals and institutions for orphans and the mentally ill. To improve the infrastructure, they rebuilt roads, railroads, and bridges. They paid for these improvements by borrowing money and setting high property taxes. Those property owners who could not afford the taxes lost their property.

Many Southern whites resented African Americans. Some organized secret societies such as the Ku Klux Klan. Ku Klux Klan members terrorized African Americans, Republican supporters, teachers in African American schools, and others.

As violence between the Klan and Republicans and African American militias increased, Grant and Congress took action. Congress passed three Enforcement Acts in 1870 and 1871. One outlawed the activities of the Ku Klux Klan. Under this law, thousands of Ku Klux Klan members were arrested. However, only a few hundred were actually convicted or served any time in prison.

Grant's political inexperience helped divide the Republican Party. Scandals hurt Grant's second administration.

Grant's administration also experienced an economic crisis. The crisis started in 1873 when a powerful bank declared bankruptcy. A wave of fear known as the Panic of 1873 spread through the nation.

The scandals and the economic troubles hurt the Republicans in the congressional elections of 1874. The Democrats won control of the House and gained seats in the Senate.

6. How did African Americans fair under Republican rule?

_____

_____

_____

Academic Vocabulary
infrastructure: the basic facilities or services of a system or organization (p. 223)

Study Guide

Chapter 2, Section 5 (continued)

- **Reconstruction Ends** (*page 224*)

With more Democrats in Congress, Republicans had difficulty enforcing Reconstruction. Many Northerners were also focusing more on government scandals and their own economic problems than with the situation in the South.

Southern Democrats had worked to regain control of their state and local governments. They often intimidated African American and white Republican voters and used election fraud to make political gains. Democrats saw the elections as a struggle between African Americans and whites. They received the support of white owners of small farms by promising to lower high taxes passed during Republican rule. By 1876 the Democrats had taken control of most of the state legislatures in the South.

For the election of 1876, the Republicans nominated Rutherford B. Hayes, who wanted to end Reconstruction. The Democrats nominated Samuel Tilden. On election day, neither candidate won the majority of the electoral votes. Twenty votes were in dispute. Congressional leaders worked out an agreement, which became known as the Compromise of 1877. Although no one is sure if a deal was actually made, the terms of the compromise most likely included a promise by the Republicans to pull federal troops out of the South if Hayes was elected. In April 1877, Hayes did pull the troops out, and Reconstruction came to an end.

President Hayes called for an end to the nation's regional conflicts. Many Southern leaders realized that the South could not return to the kind of agricultural economy it had before the Civil War. These Southerners called for a "New South."

Powerful white Southerners joined forces with Northern financiers to bring about economic changes to some parts of the South. Money from the North helped build railroads and industries across the South. However, the South remained mostly agricultural. By 1900 Southern manufacturing establishments equaled only 4 percent of its number of farms.

The end of Reconstruction brought an end to African Americans' hopes for gaining land in the South. Many African Americans returned to plantations, where they became **tenant farmers,** paying rent for the land they farmed. Most of these farmers eventually became **sharecroppers.** Sharecroppers paid their rent with a share of their crops rather than with cash. In addition to rent, their payment included the cost of seeds, tools, and the animals they needed. Although sharecropping allowed African American farmers to control their own work schedule and working conditions, it also trapped sharecroppers on the land because they could not make enough money to pay off their debts and leave the land. The Civil War ended slavery, but Reconstruction's failure left many Southerners trapped in economic <u>circumstances</u> beyond their control.

Academic Vocabulary
circumstances: factors in a problem that determine its solution (p. 225)

7. After Reconstruction, why were many African Americans trapped on the land they farmed?

_____

_____

The American Vision: Modern Times

Study Guide

Chapter 3, Section 1

For use with textbook pages 236–242

SETTLING THE WEST

CONTENT VOCABULARY

placer mining   the process of removing mineral ore by hand *(page 237)*

quartz mining   the process of removing ore by digging deep beneath the surface *(page 237)*

vigilance committee   self-appointed volunteers who tracked down and punished wrongdoers *(page 238)*

open range   vast areas of grassland owned by the federal government *(page 238)*

long drive   cattle run in which herds were moved great distances to a rail line, where they were shipped to market *(page 239)*

homestead   a tract of public land available for settlement *(page 240)*

assimilate   to be absorbed into *(page 242)*

DRAWING FROM EXPERIENCE

What images come to mind when you hear the word *cowhands?* What kind of life do you think they had? What kind of work did they do? Where do most of your ideas about cowboys come from?

In this section, you will learn about the start of the mining industry in the West. You will also learn how ranchers helped to settle large areas of the West.

ORGANIZING YOUR THOUGHTS

Use the diagram below to help you take notes. The Great Plains was at first thought of as a desert. List the reasons that helped to change that image of the Great Plains and encourage settlement there.

California History-Social Science Standards

11.1 Students analyze the significant events in the founding of the nation and its attempts to realize the philosophy of government described in the Declaration of Independence.

11.2 Students analyze the relationship among the rise of industrialization, large-scale rural-to-urban migration, and massive immigration from Southern and Eastern Europe.

Focuses on: 11.1.4, 11.2.6

1.

2.

3.

4.

Things That Encouraged Settlement of the West

Study Guide

Chapter 3, Section 1 (continued)

READ TO LEARN

- ## Growth of the Mining Industry (page 237)

The discovery of minerals in the West led to a flood of people hoping to strike it rich. At first, the prospectors would try to <u>extract</u> the mineral ore by hand. This process was called **placer mining.** After these deposits diminished, corporations would move in to dig beneath the surface. This process was called **quartz mining.**

Academic Vocabulary
extract: to remove by force (p. 237)

In 1859 a prospector named Henry Comstock staked a claim in Six-Mile Canyon, Nevada. There he found nearly pure silver ore. News of the strike brought huge numbers of miners to Virginia City, Nevada. The town soon became a boomtown with thousands of people, shops, newspapers, and a hotel. When the silver deposits ran out and the mines closed, the once booming town became a ghost town, like many other towns in the West.

During boom times, crime was a problem in the mining towns. Prospectors fought over claims, and thieves roamed the streets. There was little law enforcement. As a result, volunteers sometimes formed **vigilance committees** to find and punish wrongdoers.

Men were usually the first settlers in mining towns. However, the towns soon attracted women. Some owned property and were leaders of the community. Others worked as cooks. Some women worked at places called "hurdy-gurdy" houses, where they danced with men for the price of a drink.

Mining also led to the development of towns in Colorado, the Dakota Territory, and Montana. Although there was plenty of gold and silver in the mountains in Colorado, much of it was below the surface and difficult to get out. A big strike happened in the late 1870s in Leadville, where deep deposits of lead contained large amounts of silver. By 1879 thousands of people were pouring into Leadville, which became a well-known boomtown.

The gold and silver found in Colorado were worth more than one billion dollars. This led to the building of railroads through the Rocky Mountains. The railroad helped change Denver into the second largest city in the West.

Gold was discovered in the Black Hills of the Dakota Territory, and copper was discovered in Montana. The discoveries led to a rush of settlers and the development of boomtowns in the 1870s and 1880s. In 1889, Congress divided the Dakota Territory. North Dakota, South Dakota, and Montana became new states.

5. Who made the greatest profits from mining in the West?

_____

_____

_____

Study Guide

Chapter 3, Section 1 (continued)

- ## Ranching and Farming the Plains (page 238)

After the Civil War, many Americans headed west to build cattle ranches on the Great Plains. In the early 1800s, Americans believed that the Great Plains had too little water and tough prairie grasses for cattle from the East. However, Texas had a breed of cattle, the longhorn, that was <u>adapted</u> to living on the Great Plains. This breed had descended from a breed of Spanish cattle that had been brought to Mexico two hundred years earlier.

Mexicans had begun cattle ranching in New Mexico, California, and Texas before these places were part of the United States. Cattle ranching grew in part because of the **open range**—a vast area of grassland owned by the federal government. The open range made up a large part of the Great Plains. This provided land for ranchers to graze their herds free of charge. Mexican cowhands developed the tools and equipment used for rounding up and driving cattle.

<u>Prior</u> the Civil War, there was little reason for ranchers to round up the cattle. Beef prices were low, and it was not practical to move the cattle to eastern markets. However, the Civil War and the building of railroads changed this situation. During the Civil War, eastern cattle were slaughtered to provide food for the armies. After the war, beef prices rose sharply. This made it worthwhile to round up the longhorns and move them east.

By the end of the Civil War, railroad lines reached to the Great Plains. They ended at Abilene and Dodge City in Kansas and in Sedalia, Missouri. Cattle ranchers realized that they could make a profit if they rounded up and drove their cattle north to the railroad. There they could be sold for profit and shipped east. In 1866 ranchers rounded up thousands of longhorns and drove them to Sedalia, Missouri. This first **long drive** was a success. The cattle sold for 10 times the price they could have gotten in Texas. Several long drive trails soon opened.

In the late 1800s, several things changed the image of the Great Plains as being a desert. Railroad companies sold land along the rail lines that they built through the Plains. They sold the land at low prices, attracting settlers there. Railroads opened offices throughout the United States and Europe. They advertised the Plains as being a ticket to prosperity. A Nebraskan encouraged settlement by claiming that farming the Plains would increase rainfall there. In the 1870s, the weather seemed to support that claim. Starting then, rainfall on the Plains was well above average. This helped to change the popular belief that the region was a desert.

The government supported settlement of the Great Plains by passing the Homestead Act in 1862. An individual could file for a **homestead,** or a tract of public land available for settlement, for a $10 registration fee. People could claim up to 160 acres of public land. They could receive title to that land after living there for five years.

Academic Vocabulary
adapt: to change in order to meet the demands of a certain environment or circumstance (p. 238)

Academic Vocabulary
prior: happening before an event (p. 238)

Study Guide

Chapter 3, Section 1 (continued)

The environment was harsh for the settlers on the Plains. Summer temperatures soared above 100°F, and winters brought blizzards. Prairie fires were a danger, and sometimes grasshoppers destroyed crops.

New farming methods and inventions helped to make farming on the Great Plains profitable. Wheat could stand drought better than some other crops. As a result, wheat became an important crop to the Great Plains. The Wheat Belt eventually included much of the Dakotas and the western parts of Nebraska and Kansas.

By the 1880s, the Wheat Belt helped to make the United States the world's leading exporter of wheat. However, the nation faced competition from other wheat-producing countries. In the 1890s, an oversupply of wheat on the market caused prices to drop.

6. What was the Homestead Act?

_____

_____

_____

- **Native Americans** (page 241)

Most of the Native Americans who lived on the Great Plains were nomads who roamed great distances. They followed the buffalo—their main source of food.

The groups of Native Americans on the Great Plains had differences, but they were similar in many ways. They lived in extended family networks. Plains Indian nations were divided into bands of up to 500 people each. A governing council headed each band. Most members of the band participated in making decisions for the group. Gender determined the tasks an individual had to do. Most Plains Indians practiced a religion that was based on a belief in the spiritual power of the natural world.

Native Americans resisted the advance of settlers on their lands. They resented the broken treaties of the government and the forced movement from their lands. They resisted by attacking wagon trains and ranches. Eventually the resistance turned into a war.

In 1867 Congress formed an Indian Peace Commission. It proposed to create two large reservations—one for the Sioux and another for southern Plains Indians. Agents from the Bureau of Indian Affairs would run the reservations. However, many Native Americans refused to move to the reservations. Those who did move faced miserable conditions.

By the 1870s, many Native Americans had left the reservations. They hated their life there and joined those who did not move there to hunt buffalo on the open Plains. However, the buffalo were being killed off by the thousands by

Study Guide

Chapter 3, Section 1 *(continued)*

migrants, professional buffalo hunters, and sharpshooters clearing rail lines for railroad companies.

Some Native Americans tried to resist government efforts to force them back on reservations. The Lakota Sioux, led by Sitting Bull, fled to Canada. Other Lakota were forced back on the reservation. Chief Joseph and the Nez Perce also had to surrender.

The Lakota continued to perform the Ghost Dance, a ritual that was important to them, on the Lakota Sioux Reservation. They did so against the orders of the government agent at the reservation. The government agent blamed the refusal to stop the Ghost Dance on Sitting Bull. When forces came to arrest him, Sitting Bull resisted. He died in an exchange of gunfire. The Native Americans who participated in the Ghost Dance then fled the reservation. The troops went after them. On December 29, 1890, a battle broke out at Wounded Knee Creek. About 25 soldiers and 200 Lakota were killed.

Some Americans had opposed the government's treatment of Native Americans. Helen Hunt Jackson's book, *A Century of Dishonor*, described the government's broken promises and attacks on Native Americans. Her descriptions led to discussions, even in Congress, of better treatment of Native Americans. Some people believed that the Native Americans' situation would improve if they could **assimilate,** or be absorbed, into American culture as citizens and landowners. This meant breaking up the reservations into individual allotments, or pieces of land, where families could support themselves.

In 1887 Congress passed the Dawes Act. It gave each head of a household 160 acres of reservation land for farming. Although some Native Americans succeeded as farmers, many did not want to be farmers. Many found that the size of the land they received was too small to be profitable.

In the end, the idea of assimilation failed. There was no satisfactory solution to the problem of the Native Americans. The Plains Indians were doomed because they depended on the buffalo for food, shelter, and clothing. Once the herds were wiped out, the Native Americans could not keep up their way of life. Few were willing to adopt the settlers' way of life.

7. What did some people in the late 1800s believe was necessary to improve the situation of Native Americans?

_____

_____

_____

_____

_____

Study Guide

Chapter 3, Section 2

For use with textbook pages 243–251

INDUSTRIALIZATION

CONTENT VOCABULARY

gross national product   the total value of all goods and services produced by a country *(page 244)*

entrepreneurs   people who risk their capital in organizing and running a business *(page 245)*

laissez-faire   belief that government should not interfere in a nation's economy *(page 245)*

corporation   an organization owned by many people but treated by law as though it were a single person *(page 248)*

vertical integration   the joining of different types of businesses that are involved in the operation of a particular company *(page 249)*

horizontal integration   the joining of many firms involved in the same type of business into one large corporation *(page 249)*

monopoly   total control of a type of industry by one person or one company *(page 249)*

marxism   theory of socialism in which workers would struggle to create a society without classes *(page 250)*

industrial union   unions that represented all craft workers and common laborers in a particular industry *(page 250)*

closed shop   a system in which companies could only hire union members *(page 251)*

DRAWING FROM EXPERIENCE

What are unions? Why do people join unions? Do you think unions are important for workers? Why or why not?

This section discusses the reaction of workers to big businesses—the rise of unions.

California History-Social Science Standards

11.1 Students analyze the significant events in the founding of the nation and its attempts to realize the philosophy of government described in the Declaration of Independence.

11.2 Students analyze the relationship among the rise of industrialization, large-scale rural-to-urban migration, and massive immigration from Southern and Eastern Europe.

11.6 Students analyze the different explanations for the Great Depression and how the New Deal fundamentally changed the role of the federal government.

Focuses on: 11.1.4, 11.2.1, 11.2.5, 11.2.6, 11.6.5

Study Guide

Chapter 3, Section 2 (continued)

Use the diagram below to help you take notes. Employers in the late 1800s tried to stop unions from forming. Describe four of these actions in the chart.

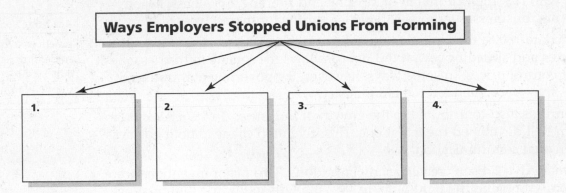

Ways Employers Stopped Unions From Forming

1.

2.

3.

4.

READ TO LEARN

- **The United States Industrializes** *(page 244)*

    After the Civil War, industry grew rapidly. Many people left their farms to find work in factories. By the early 1900s, the United States had become one of the world's leading industrial nations. By 1914 the **gross national product** (GNP), or the total value of all goods and services produced by a country— was eight times greater than it had been at the end of the Civil War.

    One reason that industries expanded was that the United States had many natural resources that industries needed. Factories could get these resources cheaply without having to import them. Many resources were located in the West. The transcontinental railroad brought settlers to the region and moved the resources to the factories in the East.

    At the same time, a new resource—petroleum—was being developed. This resource was in demand even before the automobile was invented. Petroleum could be turned into kerosene, which was used in lanterns and stoves. The American oil industry was built on the demand for kerosene. Oil production helped to expand the nation's economy.

    In addition to natural resources, a population increase provided factories with a larger workforce. It also provided a demand for the goods that these factories produced. The population increase was the result of large families and an increase in immigrants. Between 1870 and 1910, about 20 million immigrants came to the United States.

    The United States's industries also expanded because of the free enterprise system. In the late 1800s, Americans took on a **laissez-faire** policy toward the economy. Those who supported it believed that the government should not interfere in the economy. Laissez-faire relies on supply and demand, not the

Study Guide

Chapter 3, Section 2 *(continued)*

government, to set prices and wages. The theory states that a free market, in which companies compete, leads to more wealth for everyone. It also proposes that taxes should be low and the government's debt should be kept limited. The idea of gaining wealth attracted people into businesses. **Entrepreneurs,** or people who risk their capital in organizing and running a business, began developing businesses in hopes of making profits for themselves.

In the late 1800s, the United States government <u>practiced</u> laissez-faire. It kept taxes and spending low. It did not pass laws to regulate industries, and it did not control prices. In some ways, however, the government introduced policies that were intended to help industry.

Inventions also contributed to the growth of industries. In 1876 Alexander Graham Bell developed the telephone. This invention changed both business and personal communication.

Thomas Alva Edison created many inventions. Two major inventions were the phonograph and the light bulb. In 1882 the Edison Electric Illuminating Company began to supply electric power to customers in New York City. Electric power changed American society.

New methods and inventions increased production in many industries. These changes resulted in lower prices for American consumers.

Academic Vocabulary
practice: to do something repeatedly so it becomes the standard (p. 245)

5. How did the invention of the telephone change American society?

_____

_____

_____

_____

• The Railroads: Linking the Nation *(page 246)*

In 1862 President Lincoln signed the Pacific Railway Act. This law called for the building of a transcontinental railroad by the Union Pacific and the Central Pacific railroad companies. To encourage the companies, the government gave each company land along the route of the tracks. On May 10, 1869, the first transcontinental railroad was completed.

By 1865 the United States had hundreds of unconnected railroad lines. Railroads began to combine them into fewer connected rail lines. To make rail service more reliable, in 1883 the American Railway Association divided the country into four time zones where the same time was kept.

The large railroad systems benefited the nation in many ways. They could shift rail cars from one section of the country to another. Long-distance transportation was faster. New technology allowed railroads to put longer and heavier trains on their lines. More powerful locomotives helped make railroad operations more efficient and less expensive. Railroads also united people from different regions of the country.

Study Guide

Chapter 3, Section 2 *(continued)*

The government helped encourage railroad building by giving many railroad companies land grants. Railroads would then sell the land to settlers and businesses to raise the money they needed to build the railroad. By the 1860s, the railroads owned an area of land larger than New England, New York, and Pennsylvania combined. Some railroad companies earned enough money from the land grants to pay for the entire cost of building their lines.

Some railroad entrepreneurs in the late 1800s got their wealth by cheating investors and taxpayers, bribing government officials, and cheating on their contracts. Bribery occurred often with federal and state governments.

Not all railroad entrepreneurs were robber barons, or people who loot an industry and give nothing back. James J. Hill, an entrepreneur, built the Great Northern Railroad without federal land grants. The Great Northern became the most successful transcontinental railroad and the only one that did not eventually go bankrupt.

6. What was a robber baron?

_____

_____

_____

_____

• The Rise of Big Business *(page 248)*

By 1900 big businesses dominated the nation's economy. Big businesses became possible because of the **corporation.** This is an organization owned by many people but treated by law as though it were a single person. The people who own a corporation are called stockholders. They own shares of ownership called stock. By issuing stock, a corporation can raise large amounts of money while spreading out the financial risk. Corporations used the money they received from selling stock to invest in new technologies, to hire many workers, and to buy many machines.

Small businesses had high operating costs, so they could not compete with big businesses and many went out of business. Many people criticized the corporations for cutting prices. They believed that these corporations used their wealth to drive small companies out of business.

To make his business even bigger, Andrew Carnegie, the owner of a steel company, began the **vertical integration** of the steel industry. A vertically integrated company owns all the different businesses that it depends on to run. Carnegie's company bought coal mines and iron ore fields. Owning these companies saved Carnegie money and made his company bigger.

Business leaders also looked to **horizontal integration,** which involved combining many companies involved in the same business into one large corporation. When a single company gains control of an entire market—from

Study Guide

Chapter 3, Section 2 (continued)

raw materials to <u>distribution</u>—it becomes a **monopoly.** Many people opposed monopolies because they believed that a monopoly could charge whatever price it wanted for its products. Some people, however, believed that monopolies helped to keep prices low because raising prices would cause the competition to reappear.

Many states made it illegal for a company to own stock in another company without getting permission from the state legislature. As a result, in 1882 the Standard Oil Company formed the first trust. This was a new way of combining companies that did not go against the laws that made owning other companies illegal. A trust is a legal <u>concept</u> that allows a person to manage another person's property. The person who manages another person's property is called a trustee.

Many companies also created a new organization called a holding company. A holding company owns the stock of companies that produce goods. The holding company controls all the companies, combining them into one large corporation.

> | Academic Vocabulary |
> | --- |
> | **distribution:** the act of shipping products from a central location to a vast amount of customers (p. 248) |

> | Academic Vocabulary |
> | --- |
> | **concept:** an abstract idea which can be put into practice (p. 249) |

7. In what two ways did Andrew Carnegie and other business leaders try to make their businesses larger?

_____

_____

_____

- **Unions** (page 249)

Conditions for workers in industries were difficult. Work was monotonous and repetitive. Workers often worked in unhealthy and unsafe environments. However, industrialization brought people a higher standard of living.

The difference in the standard of living between the wealthy owners and the working class was great. Many workers decided that the best way to improve their conditions was to organize into unions.

Workers who wanted to organize unions faced several problems. No laws gave them the right to organize. Some people thought that unions threatened American institutions. Others believed that unions were influenced by **Marxism**—the ideas of Karl Marx. Marx believed the basic force that shaped society was the conflict between workers and owners. He believed that eventually workers would revolt, take control of the factories, and overthrow the government. He believed that then the government would take all private property and distribute wealth evenly among everyone. Marxism greatly influenced European unions.

As Marxist ideas spread in Europe, thousands of European immigrants began arriving in the United States. Some Americans began associating

Study Guide

Chapter 3, Section 2 (continued)

European immigrants with anarchism. Because many workers were European immigrants, these Americans also became suspicious of unions.

Employers had to deal with trade unions because they needed the skills the workers in the unions had. However, they thought unions interfered with property rights. Employers of large corporations particularly opposed **industrial unions.** These unions represented all craft workers and common laborers in a particular industry.

Employers tried to stop unions from forming in their companies in several ways. They required workers to sign contracts promising not to join unions. They hired detectives to point out union organizers. Those who tried to start a union or strike were fired and placed on a blacklist—a list of "troublemakers." Once a worker was blacklisted, a person found it almost impossible to get hired. If workers did form a union, companies often used a lockout to break it. The employers locked workers out of the factory and refused to pay them. If the union called a strike, employers would hire replacement workers.

Although industrial unions were not very successful in the late 1800s, trade unions were. Over twenty of the nation's trade unions organized the American Federation of Labor (AFL). Samuel Gompers was the union's first leader. He believed that unions should stay out of politics. He believed that they should fight for things such as higher wages and better working conditions. He preferred negotiation over strikes. The AFL had three goals. It tried to convince companies to recognize unions and to agree to negotiations. It pushed for **closed shops,** in which companies hired only union members. It pushed for an eight-hour workday.

By 1900 the AFL was the largest union in the country. However, by 1900 most workers in the nation were still not union members.

After the Civil War, the number of women who earned wages increased. About one-third of these women worked as servants. Another third worked as teachers, nurses, or secretaries. The final third were industrial workers. Many of these women worked in clothing and food processing factories. Women were paid less than men, and most unions did not include women. As a result, in 1903 two women founded the Women's Trade Union League (WTUL). This was the first union organized to address women's labor issues.

8. What were three goals of the American Federation of Labor?

_____

_____

_____

_____

Study Guide

Chapter 3, Section 3

For use with textbook pages 254–261

IMMIGRATION AND URBANIZATION

CONTENT VOCABULARY

nativism an extreme dislike for foreigners by native-born people and a desire to limit immigration *(page 257)*

tenement dark and crowded multi-family apartments in cities *(page 260)*

political machine an informal political group designed to gain and keep power *(page 261)*

graft getting money through dishonest or questionable means *(page 261)*

DRAWING FROM EXPERIENCE

Do you live in or have you visited a large city? What are some positive aspects of a city? What are some negative aspects?

The last section discussed immigration to the United States in the late 1800s. This section describes how the United States changed from a rural to an urban nation.

ORGANIZING YOUR THOUGHTS

Use the diagram below to help you take notes. A new kind of political system developed in cities to deal with problems there. Show how this system worked in the diagram below.

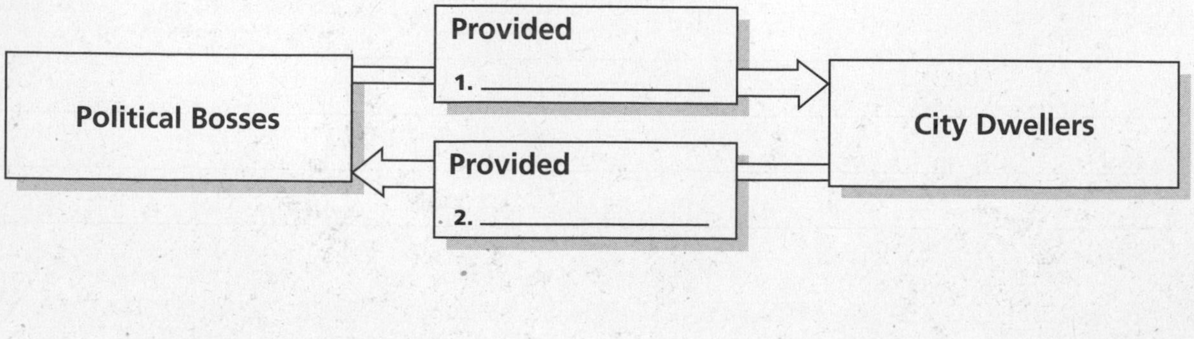

California History-Social Science Standards

11.1 Students analyze the significant events in the founding of the nation and its attempts to realize the philosophy of government described in the Declaration of Independence.

11.2 Students analyze the relationship among the rise of industrialization, large-scale rural-to-urban migration, and massive immigration from Southern and Eastern Europe.

11.3 Students analyze the role religion played in the founding of America, its lasting moral, social and political impacts, and issues regarding religious liberty.

Focuses on: 11.1.4, 11.2.1, 11.2.2, 11.2.3, 11.2.4, 11.3.3

Political Bosses

Provided
1. _____

Provided
2. _____

City Dwellers

The American Vision: Modern Times

Study Guide

Chapter 3, Section 3 *(continued)*

• Immigration *(page 255)*

More than half of all immigrants who came to the United States by 1900 were from eastern and southern Europe. They immigrated for a variety of reasons. Some came for jobs. Some came to avoid forced military service in their countries. Others, particularly Jews, came to avoid religious persecution.

Most immigrants who came to the United States booked passage in steerage, which was the most basic and cheapest accommodations on a steamship. After about two weeks, they arrived at Ellis Island. This was a tiny island in New York Harbor. Immigrants were required to pass a medical exam. They would generally pass through Ellis Island in about a day.

Many immigrants who passed inspection settled in cities such as New York, Chicago, Milwaukee, and Detroit. Immigrants in cities generally lived in neighborhoods that were separated into ethnic groups. Journalist Jacob Riis observed that New York City was filled with ethnic communities. There they spoke their native languages, worshiped in their churches or synagogues, and published their own newspapers.

Some immigrants did not stay in America. Some came just to make money and then return home. Those who adjusted well generally learned English quickly and adapted to the American culture. Those immigrants who had marketable skills or who settled among members of their own ethnic group also adjusted more easily to life in the United States.

In the mid-1800s, many Chinese immigrants arrived in the United States. Many came to escape the poverty and famine in their country. The discovery of gold in California in 1848 brought many Chinese immigrants there. A rebellion in China also led many Chinese to come to the United States. In addition, the demand for railroad workers on the transcontinental railroad increased Chinese immigration.

Chinese immigrants settled in western cities. They often worked as laborers, servants, or in skilled trades. Some worked as merchants.

In 1910 California opened a barracks on Angel Island to accommodate Asian immigrants, who were mostly young men. There, immigrants waited for their immigration to be processed. Their wait, in crowded conditions, sometimes lasted months.

The increase of immigration to the United States in the late 1800s led to increased feelings of **nativism.** This is a preference for native-born people and a desire to limit immigration. In the late 1800s, these feelings focused on eastern Europeans, Jews, and Asians.

Some nativists feared that the number of Catholics from Europe would take over the mostly Protestant United States. They feared that the Catholic Church would have too much power in the nation's government. Labor unions were against immigration because they believed that immigrants would work for low wages or work as strikebreakers.

Study Guide

Chapter 3, Section 3 (continued)

Some nativists formed anti-immigrant organizations. The American Protective Association worked to stop Catholic immigration. In the West, the Workingman's Party of California worked to stop Chinese immigration.

Concerns over unchecked immigration pushed Congress to create immigration limits. In 1882 a law banned convicts and the mentally disabled from coming to the United States. It placed a 50-cent head tax on each immigrant arriving in the United States. Congress also passed the Chinese Exclusion Act. This law banned Chinese immigration for 10 years. It also prevented the Chinese already in the country from becoming citizens. The Chinese in the United States protested the law. They pointed to the fact that laws did not ban European immigration. However, Congress renewed the law in 1892 and made it permanent in 1902. It did not repeal the Chinese Exclusion Act until 1943.

3. Why did some nativists fear immigration from Europe?

_____

_____

_____

_____

_____

- **Urbanization** (page 258)

By the 1890s, the urban population of the United States increased greatly. Most of the immigrants who arrived did not have the money to buy farms or the education to get high-paying jobs. They settled in the cities, where they worked for low wages in the factories. Even though the wages were low, the standard of living for most immigrants had improved. Farmers also moved to the cities looking for better-paying jobs. Cities offered running water and modern plumbing. It also had things to do, including museums and theaters.

As city populations increased, the demand for land increased its price. This induced people to begin building upward rather than outward. Tall, steel frame buildings called skyscrapers were constructed in the nation's cities.

Academic Vocabulary
induce: to cause a reaction in someone or something (p. 259)

Different kinds of transportation developed in the late 1800s to move the large numbers of people around the cities. At first cities used horsecars for transportation. These were railroad cars pulled by horses. Some cities, such as San Francisco, began using cable cars. They were pulled along tracks by underground cables. Some cities began using the electric trolley car. In large cities, congestion on streets became a problem. As a result, some cities built elevated railroads or subway systems.

Wealthy people, the middle class, and the working class lived in different parts of the cities. The wealthy lived in fashionable districts in the heart of the city, where they commissioned large, beautiful homes.

Academic Vocabulary
commission: to give authorization to perform a specific task (p. 260)

Study Guide

Chapter 3, Section 3 *(continued)*

Industrialization contributed to a growing middle class in the nation. The middle class included doctors, lawyers, engineers, and teachers. Many middle-class people moved from the heart of the cities to suburbs. Commuter rail lines helped to connect the suburbs to the cities.

The working class generally lived in **tenements,** or dark and crowded multi-family apartments, in the cities.

People living in cities in the late 1800s faced several problems. They faced the threat of crime, violence, disease, and pollution. Native-born Americans often blamed immigrants for the increase in crime and violence in the cities. Alcohol did contribute to the increase in violent crimes.

Improper ways of getting rid of sewage contaminated drinking water and caused diseases. Smoke from factory chimneys and soot from coal fires caused pollution.

A new kind of political system started in cities to deal with urban problems. The **political machine,** an informal political group that was designed to gain and keep power, became popular. People moving into cities needed jobs, housing, food, and police protection. Political machines led by party bosses provided these things in exchange for votes.

Party bosses controlled the cities' money. Machine politicians grew rich through fraud or **graft.** They got money through dishonest or questionable ways. For example, they accepted bribes from contractors in exchange for awarding the contractors with city contracts.

One of the most famous political machines was Tammany Hall in New York City. William M. Tweed was its famous corrupt party boss. City machines often controlled city services. For example, Thomas and James Pendergast, the political bosses in St. Louis, ran state and city politics from the 1890s until the 1930s. Although political machines were corrupt, they did provide necessary services to people living in the nation's cities.

4. How did the cities' political bosses grow wealthy?

_____

_____

Study Guide

Chapter 3, Section 4

For use with textbook pages 264–270

EARLY REFORMS IN A GILDED AGE

CONTENT VOCABULARY

individualism   the belief that anyone could be successful, regardless of background *(page 266)*

Social Darwinism   the idea that society progresses and becomes better because only the fittest people survive *(page 266)*

philanthropy   the using of one's wealth to further social progress *(page 267)*

settlement house   residences in poor neighborhoods in which middle-class people lived and helped poor people *(page 269)*

Americanization   the process of becoming knowledgeable about American culture *(page 270)*

DRAWING FROM EXPERIENCE

How do you and your family enjoy spending your leisure time? Does your community provide the activities that you enjoy participating in?

The last section described the growth of cities in the United States in the late 1800s. This section discusses changes in thinking and leisure activities in the United States in the late 1800s.

ORGANIZING YOUR THOUGHTS

Use the diagram below to help you take notes. Several philosophies and movements became popular in the United States in the late 1800s. List and describe them in the diagram.

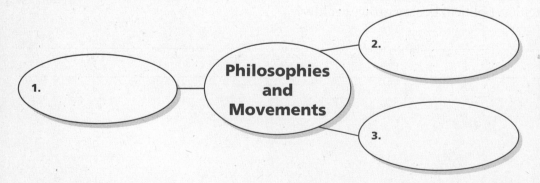

California History-Social Science Standards

11.1 Students analyze the significant events in the founding of the nation and its attempts to realize the philosophy of government described in the Declaration of Independence.

11.2 Students analyze the relationship among the rise of industrialization, large-scale rural-to-urban migration, and massive immigration from Southern and Eastern Europe.

11.3 Students analyze the role religion played in the founding of America, its lasting moral, social and political impacts, and issues regarding religious liberty.

Focuses on: 11.1.4, 11.2.3, 11.2.4, 11.2.7, 11.3.1, 11.3.2

Study Guide

Chapter 3, Section 4 *(continued)*

READ TO LEARN

- **The Gilded Age** *(page 265)*

The time in American history that begins about 1870 and ends around 1900 is often referred to as the Gilded Age. The term was the title of a novel by Mark Twain and Charles Warner. The time was one of new inventions, rapid industrial growth, growing cities, and wealthy people building huge mansions. The word *gilded* refers to something that is covered in gold only on the outside. Twain and Warner tried to point out that although things looked good on the outside, beneath the surface lay corruption, poverty, crime, and a huge difference in wealth between the rich and the poor.

The Gilded Age was a time of cultural change. One of the strongest beliefs of the time was the idea of **individualism.** Many people believed that no matter where they started in life, they could go as far as they were willing to go. Horatio Alger, an author, expressed the idea of individualism in his "rags-to-riches" novels. In these novels, a poor person generally arrived in a big city and became successful. The novels led many people to believe that they could overcome obstacles and become successful, too.

Another important idea of the Gilded Age was proposed by the philosopher Herbert Spencer. He applied the work of Charles Darwin to human society. Darwin said that plants and animals <u>evolved</u> through a process called natural selection. In this process, the species that cannot adapt to the environment in which they live gradually die out. Those that adapt survive. Spencer applied this idea to society. He said that society progressed because only the fittest people survived. His views became known as **Social Darwinism.** Those that shared these views were known as Social Darwinists. Industrial leaders quickly agreed with the theory. They believed themselves to be the fittest people, and therefore deserving of the wealth they had.

Academic Vocabulary
evolve: to change depending on your physical environment (p. 266)

Andrew Carnegie also agreed with the ideas of Social Darwinism. However, he also believed in a philosophy called the Gospel of Wealth. This philosophy said that wealthy people who profited from society owed it something in return. They should take part in **philanthropy**—using their wealth to further social progress. Carnegie donated millions of dollars to social causes.

A new movement known as realism became popular during the late 1800s. Realism attempted to show people realistically. Thomas Eakins and other realist painters often showed day-to-day activities, such as people swimming or surgeons operating.

Realist writers tried to show the world as it is. Mark Twain is one of the most famous of these writers. His novel *Adventures of Huckleberry Finn* included a setting, subject matter, characters, and style that were totally American. Writers such as Henry James and Edith Wharton realistically showed the lives of the upper class.

Study Guide

Chapter 3, Section 4 (continued)

With industrialization, many urban Americans in the late 1800s divided their lives into time at home and time at work. Industrialization also provided people with more money to spend on entertainment.

In many big cities, saloons played an important role in the life of male workers. Families in the late 1800s enjoyed their leisure time in amusement parks. Many people enjoyed watching professional boxing and baseball. Football also gained popularity. Many people enjoyed activities that involved physical exercise. Tennis, golf, and basketball became popular.

The theater provided other kinds of entertainment. Vaudeville, included animal acts, acrobats, gymnasts, and dancers. Ragtime music also became popular in the fast-paced cities. Its rhythms were based on the patterns of African American music.

4. What sports became popular in the United States in the late 1800s?

_____

_____

_____

- ## The Rebirth of Reform (page 267)

Many people in the United States in the late 1800s believed that many of the nation's problems could be solved only if Americans and the government had a role in regulating the economy and helping people who were needy.

In 1879 Henry George, a journalist, published *Progress and Poverty*. In it he wrote about the widening gap between the wealthy and the poor. Although most people did not agree with George's economic theory, he was one of the first to challenge the ideas of Social Darwinism and laissez-faire economics.

Lester Frank Ward also challenged the ideas of Social Darwinism. His ideas became known as Reform Darwinism. He believed people succeeded because they were able to cooperate, not because they were able to compete. He believed competition was wasteful. Ward believed that government and not competition in the marketplace could regulate the economy and cure poverty. Many people came to believe that the government should be more active in trying to solve society's problems.

Edward Bellamy published a book in 1888 that described life in the year 2000 as a perfect society. His ideas were a form of socialism and helped to shape reformers' beliefs.

A new style of writing known as naturalism became popular as a result of many of the criticisms of industrial society. Naturalists believed that some people were not successful because they had circumstances they could not control. Among the most famous naturalist writers were Stephen Crane, Frank Norris, Jack London, and Theodore Dreiser.

Study Guide

Chapter 3, Section 4 (continued)

Many people who criticized industrial society worked for reform. The Social Gospel movement tried to improve conditions in cities based on ideas in the Bible regarding charity and justice. Many supporters of the Social Gospel movement believed that competition caused many people to behave badly. The movement resulted in many churches taking on community <u>functions</u> designed to improve society.

<table>
<tr><td>Academic Vocabulary</td></tr>
<tr><td>function: a specific task performed by a person, object, or group (p. 269)</td></tr>
</table>

The Salvation Army provided help and religious counseling to poor people in the cities. The Young Men's Christian Association (YMCA) tried to help the urban poor by setting up Bible studies, citizenship activities, and group activities. YMCAs quickly spread throughout the country.

Some reformers believed it was their duty as Christians to improve conditions for the poor. One such reformer was Jane Addams. She started **settlement houses** in poor city neighborhoods. Middle class residents lived there and helped poor people, who were mostly immigrants. Addams started Hull House in Chicago. She inspired other people to establish settlement houses across the country.

The new industries that developed in the late 1800s needed workers who were trained and educated. As a result, the United States began to focus more on building schools in the late 1800s.

Public schools were especially important for immigrant children. It was there that they became Americanized, or knowledgeable about American culture. This **Americanization,** however, sometimes caused problems for immigrant children. Many parents worried that their children would forget their own cultural traditions.

Many people still did not have educational opportunities. Rural areas did not receive the same funds as urban schools. Many African Americans did not have equal educational opportunities. As a result, some started their own schools. Booker T. Washington was an important leader in this movement. He started the Tuskegee Institute in Alabama in 1881.

Colleges also increased in the late 1800s. This was partly due to the Morrill Land Grant Act. This law gave states federal land grants to start agricultural and mechanical colleges.

Educational opportunities for women also expanded in the late 1800s. The start of private women's colleges resulted in an increase in the opportunity for women to attend colleges.

Free libraries also made education available to people living in cities. Andrew Carnegie was a major supporter of public libraries, donating millions of dollars to building them.

5. Why did attending public schools sometimes create problems for immigrant children?

_____

_____

Study Guide

Chapter 3, Section 5

For use with textbook pages 271–281

POPULISM

CONTENT VOCABULARY

populism   the movement to increase farmers' political power and to work for legislation in their interest *(page 276)*

inflation   a decline in the value of money *(page 276)*

deflation   an increase in the value of money and a decrease in the level of prices *(page 276)*

graduated income tax   a tax that taxed higher earnings more heavily *(page 277)*

poll tax   a fee required to register to vote *(page 279)*

grandfather clause   a clause that allowed people to vote if their ancestors had voted in 1867 *(page 280)*

segregation   separation of the races *(page 280)*

Jim Crow laws   laws that enforced segregation *(page 280)*

DRAWING FROM EXPERIENCE

Have you ever visited a farm or know someone who owns one? What kind of work is done on a farm? What kind of problems do you think farmers face?

This section discusses why a new political party started in the 1890s.

ORGANIZING YOUR THOUGHTS

Use the diagram on the next page to help you take notes. Many farmers, frustrated with the lack of support for their issues from the two major political parties, supported the new People's Party. List the issues the People's Party ran on in the 1892 election.

> **California History-Social Science Standards**
>
> **11.1** Students analyze the significant events in the founding of the nation and its attempts to realize the philosophy of government described in the Declaration of Independence.
>
> **11.2** Students analyze the relationship among the rise of industrialization, large-scale rural-to-urban migration, and massive immigration from Southern and Eastern Europe.
>
> **11.10** Students analyze the development of federal civil rights and voting rights.
>
> **Focuses on:** 11.1.4, 11.2.4, 11.2.8, 11.10.2

People's Party Issues in 1892 Election

1.

2.

3.

Study Guide

Chapter 3, Section 5 (continued)

READ TO LEARN

- **Stalemate in Washington** *(page 272)*

Under the spoils system, or patronage, government jobs were given to those who supported the winning party in an election. When Rutherford B. Hayes became president, he tried to stop patronage. He appointed reformers to his cabinet and got rid of people who received their jobs through party bosses. Some Republicans, called Stalwarts, opposed Hayes's actions. They called Hayes and other Republican reformers "Halfbreeds."

In the 1880 presidential election, the Republicans nominated James Garfield, a Halfbreed, for president and Chester Arthur, a Stalwart, for vice president. They won, but President Garfield was assassinated a few months into his presidency.

In response, Congress passed the Pendleton Act in 1883. People applying for federal jobs had to pass an exam.

In the 1870s and 1880s the Republican Party had support from the North and the Midwest. The Democrats gained support from the South. They also had support from big cities, where large numbers of Catholics and immigrants lived. Republicans and Democrats were evenly divided and had to share power.

Between 1877 and 1896, the Democrats generally had more members in the House of Representatives, where each congressional district elected members directly. Republicans had more members in the Senate, because state legislatures chose senators and Republicans controlled a majority of state governments.

Most presidential elections during that time were very close. Twice during this time, a candidate lost the popular vote but won the election. Republicans won four of the six presidential elections between 1876 and 1896. However, the president had to deal with a House controlled by Democrats and a Senate controlled by Republicans who did not always agree with the president. In addition, at this time, local political bosses controlled the parties. With power divided almost equally between the two parties, Congress experienced deadlock on many issues.

In the 1884 presidential elections, Democrats nominated Grover Cleveland of New York. He had opposed Tammany Hall, the corrupt Democratic machine in New York City. The Republicans nominated James G. Blaine, a former Speaker of the House. The campaigns focused on the moral character of the candidates.

Some Republican reformers were unhappy with Blaine as the Republican candidate. They left the party and supported Cleveland. These reformers became known as Mugwumps. Cleveland won the election.

Study Guide

Chapter 3, Section 5 *(continued)*

Unrest among the nation's workers grew, and many strikes occurred. Americans were upset with the power of big business, particularly with the railroads. Some large corporations, such as Standard Oil, were able to negotiate rebates, or partial refunds, and lower their rates because of the large <u>volume</u> of goods they shipped. Those who did not ship large volumes had to pay much higher rates.

Congress responded in 1887 by passing the Interstate Commerce Act, which created the Interstate Commerce Commission. The law was the first to regulate interstate trade.

Tariffs were another issue facing the government. Many people believed that tariffs were no longer necessary to protect the nation's manufacturing because large American companies were now able to compete internationally. Democrats in the House passed tariff reductions. The Senate, however, rejected the bill in support of a high protective tariff.

The Republicans nominated Benjamin Harrison for president in 1888. He received large contributions from big businesses, which benefited from higher tariffs. Cleveland and the Democrats campaigned against high tariffs. Harrison lost the popular vote but won the electoral vote. After the election, Republicans controlled both the House and the Senate.

The Republicans addressed the tariff issue by passing the McKinley Tariff. This bill cut tobacco taxes and tariff rates on raw sugar while increasing rates on items such as textiles. The bill lowered federal revenue. The nation's budget surplus became a deficit.

To curb the power of trusts, Congress passed the Sherman Antitrust Act of 1890. However, the courts were responsible for enforcing this act and saw nothing in the law that would require big companies to change the way they did business. By the election of 1890, many people began to believe that the two political parties could not solve the nation's problems.

4. What was the effect of the Sherman Antitrust Act?

_____

_____

_____

_____

_____

Academic Vocabulary
volume: refers to a considerable amount (p. 274)

- **Populism** *(page 275)*

Populism was the movement to increase farmers' political power and to work to pass laws in their interest. Shortly after the Civil War, farmers produce more crops. The increase in crops led to lower prices. At the same time, high tariffs increased the price of manufactured goods farmers needed. This

Study Guide

Chapter 3, Section 5 (continued)

made it harder for farmers to sell their products overseas. Farmers also felt that they were being treated unfairly by both the banks from which they obtained their loans and from the railroads.

The farmers were concerned about the nation's money supply. To pay for the war, the United States had increased its money supply by issuing millions of dollars in greenbacks—paper currency that could not be exchanged for gold or silver coins. This increase in money supply without an increase in goods for sale led to **inflation**—a decline in the value of money. As the paper money lost its value, the prices of goods soared.

After the war, the United States had three types of currency—greenbacks, gold and silver coins, and bank notes backed by government bonds. The government stopped printing greenbacks to get inflation under control. It began paying off its bonds. Congress also decided to stop making silver into coins. As a result, the government did not have a large enough money supply to meet the needs of the economy. As the economy grew, **deflation**—or an increase in the value of money and a decrease in prices—began.

The farmers were particularly affected by deflation. They had to borrow money for seeds and supplies. With money in short supply, interest rates increased. This increased the amount of money that farmers owed. The falling prices due to deflation meant that farmers sold their crops for less. However, they still had to make the same loan payments. Farmers blamed the Eastern bankers for their condition. They believed that the bankers pressured Congress to reduce the money supply. Some farmers wanted the government to print more greenbacks to increase the money supply. Those who lived in the West, where silver mines were located, wanted the government to mint silver coins. Many farmers believed that the only way they could convince the government was to organize.

The first national farm organization was the Patrons of Husbandry. It was better known as the Grange. Many farmers joined the Grange to get help.

Grangers also pooled their resources and created cooperatives, which were marketing organizations that worked for the benefit of their members. Farmers could not charge more for their crops because there were so many farmers in competition. So when they joined a cooperative, farmers pooled their crops and held them off the market in order to force the price up. A cooperative could also work for better shipping rates from railroads.

The Grangers' strategies were not successful. The Grange's cooperatives failed because they were too small to influence prices. Also, Eastern businesses refused to deal with them because they believed that they were too much like unions.

By the late 1870s, a new organization known as the Farmers' Alliance began to form. The Alliance organized large cooperatives called exchanges in hopes of increasing farm prices while making loans to farmers at low interest rates. These exchanges had some success.

Study Guide

Chapter 3, Section 5 (continued)

However, overall the cooperatives failed. They were too small to affect world prices for farm goods. Soon, conflict started among members of the Alliance. Alliance members in the West wanted to form a new party and push for political reforms. They formed the People's Party, also known as the Populists. The party nominated candidates to run for Congress and the state legislature.

Most Southern members of the Alliance did not want to form a third party. They wanted the Democrats to keep control of the South. Instead, they wanted to produce a list of demands and promise to vote for candidates who supported the demands.

In 1890 the Farmers' Alliance met in Ocala, Florida, and set up the Ocala Demands. The demands were to help farmers decide whom to vote for in 1890. The demands called for the free coinage of silver, an end to tariffs and the national bank, regulation of the railroads, and direct election of senators instead of by state legislatures.

Republicans in Congress tried to discourage farmers from voting for Populists. The Sherman Silver Purchase Act of 1890 authorized the purchase of silver to put more money in circulation. It did little to help farmers.

Both the Southern and Western plans of the Alliance had worked. In the South, many Democratic governors and state legislators who were elected promised to support the demands of the Alliance. In the West, the People's Party did equally well.

Many southern members of the Alliance soon realized that they could not count on Democrats to work for their programs. Many broke with the Democrats and joined the People's Party. The party held its first national convention in Omaha, Nebraska, in July 1892. It nominated James B. Weaver to run for president. The Populists wanted the government to coin silver to increase the money supply. It wanted a **graduated income tax,** one that taxed higher earnings more heavily. The Populists also believed that the government should take a greater role in regulating big business. Although the Populists supported many of the positions that labor unions had, most urban workers continued to support the Democratic Party.

The Democratic Party nominated Grover Cleveland as their presidential candidate. He won easily. However, James Weaver did very well, winning four states and 22 electoral votes.

In 1893 the United States entered a serious economic crisis. Many railroad companies had expanded too quickly and were unable to repay their loans. They declared bankruptcy. The stock market crashed, and banks closed. By 1894 the economy was in a depression. As the nation's economy worsened, many foreign investors started cashing in their U.S. government bonds for gold. This left the government with a very small gold reserve. Gold was also being lost every time people exchanged silver for gold under the Sherman Silver Purchase Act. As a result, in 1893, President Cleveland asked Congress

Study Guide

Chapter 3, Section 5 *(continued)*

to repeal that law. His actions split the Democrats into two groups. The gold-bugs believed the American currency should be based only on gold. The silverites believed coining silver in unlimited quantities would solve the nation's economic problems.

In the 1896 presidential election, the Republicans supported a gold standard. The Populists hoped that pro-silver Democrats would vote for Populists. However, the Democrats nominated William Jennings Bryan, a supporter of silver, as their candidate. As a result, the Populists decided to support Bryan instead of nominating their own candidate.

Bryan ran an energetic campaign, traveling thousands of miles and making hundreds of speeches. Republicans knew that Bryan would be difficult to beat in the West and the South. They knew that they had to win in the Northeast and in the Midwest. They nominated William McKinley. Most urban workers and business leaders supported the Republicans. McKinley won the election.

In 1896 gold was discovered in Alaska and in Canada's Yukon Territory. This helped to increase the money supply without turning to silver. Credit became easier to get and the farmers' situation improved. In 1900 the United States officially adopted a gold-based currency.

When the silver issue died out, the Populists lost much of their energy. They had not been successful in helping the farmers or in regulating big business. However, some of the reforms that they wanted, such as the graduated income tax, came later.

5. From what parts of the country did Bryan and McKinley gain support during the 1896 presidential election?

_____

_____

_____

_____

• The Rise of Segregation *(page 279)*

After Reconstruction, many African Americans in the South lived in conditions that were similar to slavery. Although they were technically free, many could not escape poverty. Most African Americans were sharecroppers, or landless farmers who had to hand over a large part of their crops to the landlord to pay for rent and supplies. Because they were always in debt, many African Americans left farming to look for jobs or to claim homesteads in the West.

In 1879 thousands of African Americans migrated from the South to Kansas. They became known as Exodusters. Some African Americans did not move but joined with poor white farmers in the Farmers' Alliance. In 1886 a group of African Americans formed their own organization called the Colored

Study Guide

Chapter 3, Section 5 (continued)

Farmers' National Alliance. Many members joined the Populist Party when it formed in 1891. They hoped that by joining poor whites with poor African Americans, they could challenge the Democrats in the South.

The Democrats feared that if enough poor whites left the party and joined the African American Populists, that combination might become unbeatable. As a result, the Democrats began to appeal to racism. They warned whites that joining African Americans in the Populist Party would bring back "Black Republican" rule like that during Reconstruction. Democrats were also making it more difficult for African Americans to vote.

The Fifteenth Amendment said that states could not deny people the right to vote because of race or color. It did not, however, say that states could not require that citizens had to know how to read and write or had to own property in order to vote. Southern states began to use this loophole to prevent African Americans from voting.

Some Southern states began requiring that all citizens pay a $2 **poll tax**. Most poor African Americans could not afford to do so and were, therefore, not allowed to vote. Some states required that <u>prospective</u> voters had to prove that they could read and write. Many failed the test. Some African Americans who did know how to read and write failed because they were deliberately given complicated passages that few could understand. As a result of these restrictions, the number of African Americans registered to vote fell dramatically.

Election officials did not apply these laws as strictly to poor whites. Some states gave whites a break by introducing a **grandfather clause.** This allowed any man to vote if he had an ancestor who voted in 1867. The clause made almost all former enslaved Africans ineligible to vote.

African Americans faced discrimination in the North as well as in the South. They were often not allowed in public places used by whites. In the South, laws enforced **segregation,** or separation of the races. These laws were known as **Jim Crow laws.** The Civil Rights Act of 1875 prohibited keeping people out of public places and prohibited racial discrimination when selecting jurors. Whites challenged the law in both the North and the South. In 1883 the Supreme Court ruled that the Fourteenth Amendment said that "no state" could deny people equal protection under the laws. The Court said that private places and organizations could practice segregation.

After the ruling, Southern states passed laws that enforced segregation in all public places. Southern whites and African Americans could no longer ride in the same railroad cars or drink from the same drinking fountains. Restrooms and hotels were segregated. In 1892 an African American named Homer Plessy was arrested for riding in a railroad car that was designated for whites only. He challenged the law as being unconstitutional. Judge John H. Ferguson rejected that argument. In 1896 the Supreme Court ruled in *Plessy* v. *Ferguson* that the Louisiana law was constitutional. The ruling supported the idea of "separate but equal" facilities for African Americans. However,

Academic Vocabulary
prospective: to be likely to, or have intentions to, perform an act (p. 279)

Study Guide

Chapter 3, Section 5 *(continued)*

although facilities for African Americans were separate, they were almost always inferior to those for whites.

In addition to the Jim Crow laws, African Americans faced mob violence from whites. The incidences of lynchings—executions without proper court proceedings—by mobs increased. More than 80 percent of the lynchings happened in the South and most of the victims were African Americans.

In the 1890s, Ida B. Wells, an African American woman from Tennessee, started a campaign against lynching. She pointed out that greed was often behind racial violence.

Booker T. Washington believed that the way to stop discrimination was for African Americans to concentrate on economic goals rather than on political ones. He believed that African Americans should postpone the fight for civil rights and focus on education and vocations to prepare themselves economically for equality.

Other African Americans, such as W.E.B. Du Bois, challenged Washington's ideas. Du Bois pointed out that the civil rights of African Americans continued to be taken away even after they had educational and vocational training. He believed that the only way African Americans could achieve full equality was by demanding their rights, particularly voting rights.

6. How did the views of Booker T. Washington and W.E.B. Du Bois regarding the best way to solve discrimination differ?

_____

_____

_____

_____

_____

Study Guide

Chapter 4, Section 1

For use with textbook pages 294–299

THE IMPERIALIST VISION

CONTENT VOCABULARY

imperialism   the economic and political domination of a strong nation over other weaker nations *(page 295)*

protectorate   territory in which an imperial power allowed the local rulers to stay in control while protecting them from rebellion and invasion *(page 295)*

DRAWING FROM EXPERIENCE

Think of all the products you use every day. Are all the products made in the United States? What products are made in other parts of the world?

In this section, you will learn how and why the United States became an imperial power.

ORGANIZING YOUR THOUGHTS

Use the cause-and-effect diagram below to help you take notes. European nations in the late 1800s began expanding overseas. List the causes for this expansion.

Causes

1. _____

2. _____

3. _____

Effect

European nations began overseas expansion.

Study Guide

Chapter 4, Section 1 *(continued)*

READ TO LEARN

- **Building Support for Imperialism** *(page 295)*

   In the 1880s, many Americans wanted to make the United States a world power. At the time, several European nations were expanding overseas. This expansion became known as **imperialism.** It is the economic and political domination of a strong nation over other weaker nations.

   The Europeans began expanding for several reasons. By the late 1800s, high tariffs had helped to reduce trade between industrial countries. This led these countries to look overseas for markets for their products. The possibilities for investment in Europe had slowed. Most of the industries that needed to be built already had been. As a result, Europeans began investing in industries in other countries, especially in Africa and Asia. To protect their investments in these territories, the European countries began exercising control there. Some areas became colonies, while other areas became **protectorates.** In a protectorate, the imperial power allowed the local rulers to stay in control and protected them against rebellion or invasion. However, in exchange for the protection, the local rulers had to follow advice from Europeans on how to govern.

   The United States also became interested in expanding overseas. Before the late 1800s, the United States expanded by settling more territory in North America. With most of the frontier settled by the late 1800s, many Americans looked to develop overseas markets.

   Many Americans used the ideas of Social Darwinism—that the strongest nations would survive—to defend overseas expansion. Some took the idea even further, stating that English-speaking nations had superior character and systems of government and were therefore destined to control other nations. This idea became known as Anglo-Saxonism.

   4. Why did Americans become interested in expanding overseas in the late 1800s?

   _____

   _____

   _____

   _____

   _____

- **Expansion in the Pacific** *(page 296)*

   In the 1800s, many Americans began looking to expand across the Pacific Ocean. Business leaders wanted to trade with Japan and China. Japan's leaders believed that contact with the West would destroy Japanese culture. As a result, they allowed their nation to trade only with the Chinese and the Dutch.

Study Guide

Chapter 4, Section 1 (continued)

In 1852 President Franklin Pierce decided to force Japan to trade with the United States. He sent Commodore Matthew C. Perry to take a naval expedition to negotiate a treaty with Japan. Perry entered the Japanese waters with four American warships. The Japanese were impressed by American <u>technology</u> and power. They realized that they could not compete against modern Western technology. As a result, the Japanese opened two ports to American trade. They also decided to Westernize their country by starting their own industrial revolution. By the 1890s, the Japanese set out to build their own empire in Asia.

Academic Vocabulary
technology: the result of an improvement on an old or existing idea (p. 296)

In addition to being interested in China and Japan, Americans became interested in Hawaii. At first, missionaries settled there. Then American whaling ships operating in the North Pacific began using Hawaii as a base. Americans soon discovered that the soil and climate of Hawaii were suitable for growing sugarcane. By the mid-1800s, many sugarcane plantations had been started there. In 1875 the United States signed a treaty that exempted Hawaiian sugar from tariffs. This led to a boom in the Hawaiian sugar industry and wealth for the planters. In 1887 the planters pressured the Hawaiian king into signing a constitution that would limit the king's power but increase the planters' power. This angered the Hawaiian people.

When Congress passed the McKinley Tariff in 1890, it eliminated all taxes on sugar. However, it also gave subsidies to sugar producers in the United States. This meant that Hawaiian sugar was now more expensive than American sugar. This caused the sales of Hawaiian sugar to decrease and the Hawaiian economy to weaken.

In 1891 Queen Liliuokalani became the Hawaiian queen. She disliked the influence that Americans were gaining in Hawaii, and tried to create a new constitution that reestablished her authority as a ruler of the Hawaiian people. The planters responded by overthrowing the government and forcing the queen to give up her power. They then set up their own government and asked the United States to annex the islands.

5. How did American planters react to Queen Liliuokalani's attempt to reestablish her authority?

_____

_____

_____

_____

_____

_____

The American Vision: Modern Times

Study Guide

Chapter 4, Section 1 *(continued)*

- ## Relations With Latin America *(page 298)*

The United States also wanted to increase the sale of its products to Latin America. They wanted Europeans to see the United States as the dominant power in Latin America. In 1889 the United States invited the Latin American nations to a conference in Washington, D.C., to discuss ways in which the nations could work together to increase trade. The idea of working together became known as Pan-Americanism. The nations in the conference agreed to create an organization that worked to promote cooperation among the nations of the Western Hemisphere.

6. Why did the United States invite Latin American nations to a conference?

_____

_____

_____

_____

_____

- ## Building a Modern Navy *(page 299)*

In the late 1800s, the United States began taking a more assertive role in foreign affairs. The nation was more willing to risk war to defend its interests overseas. Many people, particularly Captain Alfred T. Mahan, believed that the United States needed a powerful navy. Mahan <u>published</u> a book arguing that a nation needed a large navy to protect its merchant ships and to defend its right to trade with other countries. Mahan also believed that building a large navy made it necessary for the United States to get territory for naval bases overseas.

Academic Vocabulary
published: having a document made available to the general public (p. 299)

In Congress, two senators, including Henry Cabot Lodge, pushed to build a strong navy. By the late 1890s, the Unites States was on its way to becoming one of the world's big naval powers.

7. What did Captain Alfred T. Mahan believe?

_____

_____

_____

_____

_____

The American Vision: Modern Times

Study Guide

Chapter 4, Section 2

For use with textbook pages 300–307

THE SPANISH-AMERICAN WAR

CONTENT VOCABULARY

yellow journalism   sensationalist reporting in which writers often exaggerate or make up stories to attract readers *(page 302)*

jingoism   an attitude of aggressive nationalism *(page 303)*

DRAWING FROM EXPERIENCE

What do you know about Cuba? What relationship does the United States have with Cuba today?

The last section explained the reasons the United States began expanding overseas. This section discusses the Spanish-American War and the results of the war.

> **California History-Social Science Standards**
>
> **11.4** Students trace the rise of the United States to its role as a world power in the twentieth century.
>
> **Focuses on:** 11.4.2

ORGANIZING YOUR THOUGHTS

Use the diagram below to help you take notes. After the Spanish-American War, the U.S. had to decide what to do with the Philippines. Describe the arguments for and against annexing the Philippines.

- 1.
- 2.
- **Arguments for Annexing the Philippines**
- 3.
- 5.
- 4.
- 6.
- 7.
- **Arguments Against Annexing the Philippines**
- 8.

Study Guide

Chapter 4, Section 2 *(continued)*

- ## The Coming of War *(page 301)*

On February 1898 the U.S.S. *Maine* blew up in the harbor in Havana, Cuba. No one is sure why it happened. Some experts believe that the ship's ammunition supply accidentally blew up. Others think a mine had exploded near the ship and had set off the ammunition. Many Americans blamed the explosion on Spain.

At the time, Cuba was fighting for independence from Spain. In 1878 the rebellion collapsed. Many rebels, including José Martí, fled to the United States. Martí lived in New York City and brought together many other Cuban exiles living in the United States. They raised money to buy weapons. They also trained their troops to prepare an invasion of Cuba.

By the 1890s, the United States and Cuba had become linked economically. The United States imported sugar from Cuba. Americans had invested millions of dollars in Cuba's railroads and sugar plantations. However, when the United States placed a tariff on imported sugar, the sale of Cuban sugar in the United States fell. The Cuban economy was devastated. Martí and his followers started a rebellion in February 1895. They took control of eastern Cuba and declared Cuba independent.

At first the United States government stayed neutral. However, many Americans supported the Cuban rebels. Americans were especially influenced by the gruesome stories of Spanish brutality that they read about in the newspapers. The *New York Journal*, published by William Randolph Hearst, and the *New York World*, published by Joseph Pulitzer, reported outrageous stories of how the Spanish were treating the Cubans. This sensational reporting of exaggerated and sometimes untrue stories written to attract readers became known as **yellow journalism.**

Although many stories were exaggerated, the Cubans did suffer under the Spanish. Cuban rebels carried out raids, burning plantations and sugar mills and destroying railroads. They knew that many Americans invested in the plantations and the railroads. They hoped that destroying this property would lead the United States to intervene in the war. The governor of Cuba, who was appointed by Spain, wanted to prevent Cuban villagers from helping the rebels. So he placed hundreds of thousands of villagers—men, women, and children—into reconcentration camps. Thousands died of starvation and disease in these camps. When Americans heard about this brutality, they called for American intervention on behalf of the Cubans.

President McKinley did not want the United States to get involved. He asked Spain if the United States could help negotiate an end to the problem. The Spanish government responded by removing the Spanish governor. They offered Cuba self-rule but only if it remained part of the Spanish empire. The Cubans refused, because they wanted full independence.

Study Guide

Chapter 4, Section 2 (continued)

In January 1898, people loyal to Spain rioted in Havana. President McKinley was worried that American citizens there might be attacked, so he sent the battleship *Maine* to Havana in case the Americans had to be evacuated. In February 1898, the *New York Journal* published a private letter that the Spanish ambassador to the United States had sent. The letter described McKinley as being weak. Many Americans were angry about the insult. Then the *Maine* exploded, and Americans quickly blamed Spain. Many young members of the president's political party held attitudes of aggressive nationalism, or **jingoism.** They pressured the president to declare war on Spain, which he did on April 11, 1898. On April 19, Congress declared Cuba independent. It demanded that Spain withdraw from Cuba and gave the president the authority to use armed forces. Spain then declared war on the United States.

9. How did American newspapers contribute to Americans' feelings against Spain?

_____

_____

_____

_____

_____

- **A War on Two Fronts** (*page 303*)

Spain was not prepared for war. However, the United States Navy was ready for war. A navy fleet blockaded Cuba. Another fleet in the Pacific was ordered to attack the Spanish fleet in the Philippines to prevent the fleet from attacking the United States. Under the command of Commodore George Dewey, the navy quickly overwhelmed the Spanish warships. Surprised by the quick victory, the U.S. army sent about 20,000 troops to the Philippines.

In the meantime, Filipinos were staging a rebellion against Spanish rule in the Philippines. The rebellion was led by Emilio Aguinaldo. At first Aguinaldo believed that the American troops would help him. However, he soon became suspicious of the Americans. The Americans quickly took Manila, the capital of the Philippines, from the Spanish. However, they refused to let the rebel troops into the city. They also refused to recognize Aguinaldo's rebel government. Hostility between the rebels and the Americans grew.

The U.S. army was not as ready for war as the navy was. The army did not have the <u>resources</u> necessary to train the volunteers. Training camps had unsanitary conditions, and many Americans died from disease. On June 14, 1898, about 17,000 soldiers landed in Cuba, in the city of Santiago. In addition to the troops, a volunteer cavalry regiment from the United States advanced into Santiago. They were a group of cowboys, miners, and law officers known as the "Rough Riders." Their commander was Leonard Wood, and the second in command was Theodore Roosevelt. He had resigned from the government to join the cavalry.

Academic Vocabulary
resource: materials used in the production process, such as money, people, land, wood, or steel (p. 303)

Study Guide

Chapter 4, Section 2 *(continued)*

The Rough Riders and the army troops defeated the Spanish in two battles. The victories panicked the Spanish commander in Santiago, who ordered the Spanish fleet in the harbor to leave. As the ships left the harbor, the American warships attacked them and sank every ship. The Spanish occupying Santiago surrendered. Soon American troops occupied the Spanish colony of Puerto Rico. On August 12, 1898, Spain and the United States agreed to a cease-fire.

10. Why did hostilities develop between Emilio Aguinaldo and the United States?

_____

_____

_____

_____

- **An American Empire is Born** *(page 305)*

After the war, Cuba obtained its freedom, and the United States annexed Guam and Puerto Rico. The question that remained was what to do with the Philippines. Some Americans pushed for annexing the Philippines. They believed that the Philippines would have economic and military benefits. They would also give the United States a naval base in Asia and a market for American goods. Some people believed it was America's duty to teach "less civilized" people how to live properly.

Some Americans opposed annexation. Some thought it would be too expensive to keep an empire. Others believed that cheap Filipino labor would drive down wages. Some believed that imperialism <u>violated</u> American principles.

The United States and Spain signed the Treaty of Paris on December 10, 1898. Under the treaty, Cuba became independent and the United States got Puerto Rico and Guam. The United States also agreed to pay $20 million to annex the Philippines. The United States now became an imperial power.

Aguinaldo viewed the annexation of the Philippines as an aggressive act. He ordered his troops to attack the American soldiers stationed in the Philippines. To fight the guerrillas, the United States army did some of the same things that the Spanish did in Cuba. They set up reconcentration camps to separate the guerrillas from the people who supported them. Thousands of Filipinos died in these camps.

In the meantime, William Howard Taft, the first U.S. civilian governor of the islands, tried to win over the people by introducing reforms. New bridges, railroads, and telegraph lines helped the economy. The United States helped set up a public school system. New health care policies <u>virtually</u> eliminated certain diseases. These reforms helped to decrease the Filipino hostility towards the United States. Filipino resistance ended by April 1902. Over the

Academic Vocabulary
violate: to go against a previously set standard (p. 306)

Academic Vocabulary
virtual: nearly or almost entirely (p. 306)

Study Guide

Chapter 4, Section 2 (continued)

years, the United States gave the Filipinos more control in governing their own country. It finally granted independence to the Philippines in 1946.

The United States had to figure out how to govern Puerto Rico. At first Congress made Puerto Rico an unincorporated territory. This meant that Puerto Ricans were not citizens and had no constitutional rights. It also meant that Congress could pass whatever laws it wanted for Puerto Rico.

Congress gradually gave Puerto Rico some self-government. Puerto Ricans were made citizens of the United States in 1917. In 1947 the island was given the right to elect its own governor. The debate over whether Puerto Rico should become a state, an independent country, or remain a Commonwealth of the United States continues today.

After the Spanish-American War, the United States set up a military government in Cuba. Many Americans did not support giving Cuba its independence. They believed that Cubans would not be able to govern themselves. Others believed that if it became independent, Cuba would be taken over by some other imperial power. President McKinley supported Cuban independence. However, he made sure that Cuba would remain tied to the United States. He allowed the Cubans to set up a new constitution, but he set up conditions. These conditions became known as the Platt Amendment. It said that Cuba could not make any treaty with another nation that would weaken its independence. Cuba could not allow a foreign power to get territory in Cuba. Cuba had to let the United States lease naval stations in Cuba. Cuba's debts had to stay low so that foreign countries would not try to invade it to get their payments. The United States had the right to intervene to protect Cuban independence.

The Cubans opposed the Platt Amendment. However, they did not want the United States to keep its military government there. So they added the amendment to their constitution. The Platt Amendment had in actuality made Cuba a protectorate of the United States.

11. Why did the Cubans agree to include the Platt Amendment in their constitution?

_____

_____

_____

_____

_____

_____

Study Guide

Chapter 4, Section 3

For use with textbook pages 310–315

NEW AMERICAN DIPLOMACY

CONTENT VOCABULARY

sphere of influence an area in a country where a foreign nation controlled economic development *(page 312)*

Open Door policy a policy in which all countries were allowed to trade in China *(page 313)*

dollar diplomacy President Taft's policy of influencing Latin American and Asian nations through American businesses rather than military force *(page 315)*

DRAWING FROM EXPERIENCE

What countries today are considered world powers? What do you think helps to make the United States a world power?

The last section discussed the lands acquired by the United States after the Spanish-American War. This section discusses the role of President Theodore Roosevelt's administration in foreign affairs.

California History-Social Science Standards

11.4 Students trace the rise of the United States to its role as a world power in the twentieth century.

Focuses on: 11.4.1, 11.4.2, 11.4.3, 11.4.4

ORGANIZING YOUR THOUGHTS

Use the chart below to help you take notes. President Roosevelt wanted to make the United States a world power. List the ways in which he attempted to do so.

Ways Roosevelt Helped Make the U.S. a World Power

1. _____

2. _____

3. _____

4. _____

Study Guide

Chapter 4, Section 3 (continued)

> **READ TO LEARN**

• Theodore Roosevelt's Rise to Power (page 311)

In the election of 1900, President McKinley once again ran against William Jennings Bryan. He asked Theodore Roosevelt to run as his vice president. McKinley won the election by a wide margin. On September 6, 1901, as President McKinley was making a public appearance in Buffalo, New York, he was shot by Leon Czolgosz, an anarchist who opposed all forms of government. McKinley died a few days later of his wounds. Theodore Roosevelt, just 42 years of age, became the youngest person ever to become president. Many Republicans chose Roosevelt to be McKinley's running mate because they hoped that the powerless position would quiet him down. Now they were worried about having a headstrong person in the White House.

Roosevelt's <u>exploits</u> during the Spanish-American War had enabled him to win the 1898 New York gubernatorial election. Roosevelt was an energetic president. Although often sick as a child, Roosevelt pushed himself to overcome his frailties. He became a marksman and an excellent horseback rider. He also boxed and wrestled. As president, Roosevelt believed in making the United States a world power.

Academic Vocabulary
exploit: an heroic act (p. 311)

5. What event made Theodore Roosevelt president of the United States?

_____

_____

_____

_____

• American Diplomacy in Asia (page 312)

By 1899 the United States had bases all across the Pacific Ocean and was a major power in Asia. The United States was very interested in developing trade in Asia. By 1900 American exports to China had quadrupled.

In 1894 China and Japan went to war over Korea, which was part of the Chinese empire. The United States expected China to win easily, but Japan easily defeated China. The peace treaty that ended the war gave Korea its independence. It also gave Japan a part of Manchuria. The defeat of China showed other nations that it was weaker than everyone thought.

Japan's increasing power worried Russia. They did not want Japan to have territory in Manchuria because it bordered Russia. The Russians forced Japan to return the part of Manchuria it got from China. Then Russia demanded that China lease that part of Manchuria to Russia instead. Leasing the territory meant that it would still belong to China but it would be under Russia's control. Then Germany, France, and Britain also wanted China to lease territory to them. Each part that was leased became the center of a **sphere of influence.**

    The American Vision: Modern Times

Study Guide

Chapter 4, Section 3 *(continued)*

This is an area where a foreign nation controlled economic development such as mining and railroad building.

The United States supported an **Open Door policy,** in which all countries would be allowed to trade with China. The United States Secretary of State John Hay called on all nations who had leaseholds in China to keep the Chinese ports open to ships of all nations.

In the meantime, secret Chinese societies were working to rid China of foreign control. One of these groups was the Boxers. In 1900 in the Boxer Rebellion, members of the organization seized foreign embassies in Beijing and killed more than 200 foreigners. An international force, including U.S. soldiers, crushed the rebellion. Some nations wanted to use the rebellion as an excuse to divide China among themselves. However, the country was never broken up into colonies, and the United States continued its trade with China.

President Roosevelt supported the Open Door policy. He did not want any single nation to monopolize trade there. For this reason, Roosevelt stepped in to negotiate a peace treaty between Japan and Russia in 1905 in Portsmouth, New Hampshire. He persuaded Russia to recognize the territories that Japan had gained. He persuaded Japan to stop fighting and to not try and gain more territory.

After the treaty, relations between Japan and the United States worsened. The two nations both looked to gain influence in Asia. Through several agreements, they agreed to respect each other's possessions and to uphold the Open Door policy in China. In 1907 President Roosevelt sent 16 battleships of the United States Navy, known as the "Great White Fleet," on a trip around the world to show the military power of the United States. The fleet made a stop in Japan, which increased the tensions between the two countries.

6. Why did President Roosevelt send the "Great White Fleet" on a trip around the world?

_____

_____

_____

_____

_____

_____

- **A Growing Presence in the Caribbean** *(page 313)*

   Roosevelt believed that if the United States displayed its power, it would make other nations think twice about fighting. He believed in the West African saying, "Speak softly and carry a big stick." He applied the "big stick" policy in the Caribbean. In 1903 Roosevelt purchased the Panama Canal Zone. He believed that a canal through Central America was important to American power in the world. It would save time and money in shipping.

Study Guide

Chapter 4, Section 3 *(continued)*

In 1901 the United States and Great Britain signed the Hay-Pauncefote Treaty. The treaty gave the United States the exclusive right to build and control a canal through Central America. The United States decided to build a canal through Panama. In 1903 Panama was still a part of Colombia. Secretary of State Hay offered Colombia $10 million and a yearly rent for the right to build a canal and control a strip of land on either side of it. The Colombian government refused the offer.

The Panamanians wanted the benefits of having a canal. They also did not want to be under Colombian control. As a result, <u>tensions</u> grew as Panamanian officials decided that the only way to get the canal was to declare independence from Colombia and make its own deal with the United States. A small army staged an uprising in Panama against Colombia. President Roosevelt sent ships to Panama to prevent Colombia from interfering. The United States recognized Panama's independence, and the two nations signed a treaty allowing the canal to be built. Protesters in the United States and in Latin America condemned the nation's actions. Roosevelt justified U.S. actions by stating that the canal shortened the distance from the Atlantic to the Pacific Ocean by about 8,000 nautical miles.

> **Academic Vocabulary**
>
> **tension:** unrest or strife over a situation (p. 314)

In 1904 President Roosevelt expanded his "big stick" diplomacy. In an address to Congress he declared the Roosevelt Corollary to the Monroe Doctrine. In it, he said that the United States would <u>intervene</u> in Latin American affairs when necessary to help keep the Western Hemisphere economically and politically stable.

> **Academic Vocabulary**
>
> **intervene:** to get involved in the affairs of another (p. 314)

The United States applied the Roosevelt Corollary in the Dominican Republic. The nation had fallen behind in paying its debts to European nations. In 1905 the United States took on the responsibility of collecting tariffs in the Dominican Republican. Latin American nations resented the extent of American involvement in the Caribbean. President William Howard Taft, Roosevelt's successor, continued Roosevelt's policies. Taft focused more on helping the region's industries than on military force. He believed that helping the industries would increase U.S. trade, increase American businesses' profits, and help get Latin American countries out of poverty. Taft's policy became known as **dollar diplomacy.**

7. Why did President Roosevelt want to build a canal across Panama?

_____

_____

_____

_____

_____

_____

Study Guide

Chapter 5, Section 1

For use with textbook pages 326–335

THE ROOTS OF PROGRESSIVISM

CONTENT VOCABULARY

progressivism   reform movement that believed the solution to social problems lay in a more active role on the part of government *(page 327)*

muckraker   journalist who investigated social conditions and political corruption *(page 328)*

commission plan   a system of city government in which a board of commissioners with expertise in city services hires specialists to run city departments *(page 329)*

direct primary   a party election in which all party members could vote for a candidate to run in the general election *(page 330)*

initiative   a reform that allowed a group of citizens to introduce legislation and required the legislature to vote on it *(page 330)*

referendum   a reform that allowed proposed legislation to be submitted to the voters for approval *(page 330)*

recall   a reform that allowed voters to demand a special election to remove an elected official from office before his or her term had expired *(page 330)*

suffrage   the right to vote *(page 330)*

temperance   the moderation or elimination of alcohol *(page 334)*

prohibition   laws banning the manufacture, sale, and consumption of alcohol *(page 334)*

socialism   the idea that the government should own and operate industry for the community as a whole *(page 335)*

DRAWING FROM EXPERIENCE

Imagine that you are a reporter for a newspaper. What issues do you think would be important for you to report on? Why would these issues be important for people in your community to be aware of?

In this section, you will learn about the development of the Progressive movement. You will also learn how progressives attempted to solve the nation's social problems.

California History-Social Science Standards

11.2 Students analyze the relationship among the rise of industrialization, large-scale rural-to-urban migration, and massive immigration from Southern and Eastern Europe.

11.5 Students analyze the major political, social, economic, technological, and cultural developments of the 1920s.

Focuses on: 11.2.9, 11.5.3, 11.5.4

Study Guide

Chapter 5, Section 1 *(continued)*

Use the diagram below to help you take notes. Progressives worked to reform several aspects of American society. Explain the reforms they made in each of the four areas listed.

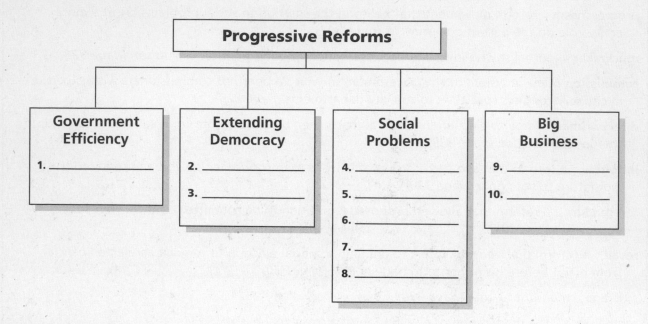

• The Rise of Progressivism *(page 327)*

The time in American history from about 1890 to 1920 is known as the Progressive Era. **Progressivism** was not a single political movement. It was a collection of ideas and views about how to fix the nation's problems.

Most progressives believed that industrialism and urbanization had caused many social problems. Although progressives focused on a variety of issues, they all believed that a more active role on the part of government was the solution to most of society's problems. Progressives belonged to both major political parties. Most were urban, educated middle-class Americans. Many worked as journalists, educators, and politicians.

Many progressives believed people could improve society because they had a strong faith in science and expertise. They believed that society could fix its problems by applying scientific principles to society.

Several journalists were the first to express Progressive ideas. These journalists, known as **muckrakers,** investigated social conditions and political corruption. They uncovered corruption in many areas. Some investigated the unfair practices of large American corporations. Ida Tarbell published articles about the practices of the Standard Oil Company. Some muckrakers investigated the

Study Guide

Chapter 5, Section 1 (continued)

government. Lincoln Steffens reported on vote stealing and other corrupt practices of political machines. Other muckrakers focused on social problems. Jacob Riis wrote about the poverty and disease that were part of many immigrant neighborhoods in New York City. The work of the muckrakers put pressure on politicians to start reforms.

11. What did most progressives believe was the cause of the nation's social problems?

_____

_____

_____

_____

- **Making Government Efficient** (page 328)

One group of progressives focused on making the government more efficient. These progressives took their ideas from business. They believed that businesses became efficient by applying the ideas of scientific management. Efficiency progressives believed that governing a modern city required experts, not politicians. In most cities, the mayor or city council chose the heads of the city's departments. These jobs generally went to political supporters and friends. These people often knew nothing about managing these departments.

Efficiency progressives wanted to replace this system with a **commission plan** or council-manager system of government. A board of commissioners or a city manager who had a background in city services would hire specialists to run city departments. Galveston, Texas, took on the commission system in 1901. Other cities soon followed.

12. From where did efficiency progressives get their ideas on how to run city government?

_____

_____

_____

_____

- **Democracy and Progressivism** (page 330)

Some progressives did not agree with efficiency progressives. They believed that society needed more democracy. They believed that elected officials should be more open to voters' concerns. Robert La Follette was the governor of Wisconsin. He used his office to oppose the way that political parties ran their conventions. At this time, party bosses controlled which candidates were chosen to run for office. La Follette pushed the state legislature to require each

Study Guide

Chapter 5, Section 1 *(continued)*

party to hold a **direct primary.** This is a party election in which all party members could vote for a candidate to run in the general election.

Progressives in other states pushed for similar changes. Three reforms were introduced. The **initiative** allowed a group of citizens to introduce <u>legislation</u> and require the legislature to vote on them. The **referendum** allowed proposed laws to be submitted to the voters for approval. The **recall** allowed voters to demand a special election to remove an elected official from office before his or her term had expired.

Another reform affected the federal government. This was the direct election of senators. The United States Constitution provided for each state legislature to elect two senators from that state. Often, political machines or trusts influenced the election of senators. The senators repaid them by awarding federal contracts and jobs. To stop this corruption, some progressives called for the direct election of senators by state voters. In 1913 Congress passed the Seventeenth Amendment, which provided for the direct election of senators.

> **Academic Vocabulary**
>
> **legislation:** a proposed law to be voted on by a governing body (p. 330)

13. What election reform did Robert La Follette introduce?

_____

_____

_____

_____

- ## The Suffrage Movement *(page 330)*

The first women's rights convention met in Seneca Falls, New York, in 1848. It was organized by Elizabeth Cady Stanton and Lucretia Mott. They believed that the top priority of the convention should be getting women the right to vote. The movement for gaining voting rights became known as the suffrage movement. **Suffrage** is the right to vote. Many progressives joined the woman suffrage movement.

When Congress introduced the Fourteenth and Fifteenth Amendments to the Constitution to protect voting rights of African Americans, some suffragists wanted the amendments worded to also give women the right to vote. The Republicans refused to do so. The debate over the Fourteenth and Fifteenth Amendments split the suffrage movement. One group, the National Woman Suffrage Association, was led by Cady Stanton and Susan B. Anthony. This group wanted Congress to pass a constitutional amendment to guarantee woman suffrage. The other group, the American Woman Suffrage Association, was led by Lucy Stone and Julia Ward Howe. This group believed that the best <u>strategy</u> was to convince state governments to give women the right to vote. The split made the movement less effective.

> **Academic Vocabulary**
>
> **strategy:** a plan or method for achieving a goal (p. 331)

In 1890 the two groups joined to form the National American Woman Suffrage Association (NAWSA). The organization had a slow start, partly

Study Guide

Chapter 5, Section 1 *(continued)*

because it was difficult to convince many women to become politically active. However, many women realized that they needed to have the right to vote to push for social reforms that they wanted passed. Many working-class women wanted the vote to push for labor laws that would protect women.

The suffrage movement began lobbying lawmakers and organizing marches. Alice Paul, who headed NAWSA's congressional committee, had organized a march in Washington, D.C. She wanted the march to push President Wilson to act on behalf of suffrage. Some people in NAWSA who wanted to work with the president opposed Paul's actions. Paul then left NAWSA and formed the National Woman's Party.

Carrie Chapman Catt became NAWSA's leader in 1915. She threw the organization's support behind Wilson in the 1916 presidential election. Although Wilson did not support a suffrage amendment, he supported the call for states to grant women the right to vote. As more people pushed for woman suffrage, Congress began to support a constitutional amendment. Finally, in June 1919, the Senate passed the Nineteenth Amendment. It was ratified by the states in 1920.

14. How did the National Woman Suffrage Association and the American Woman Suffrage Association differ regarding gaining suffrage for women?

_____

_____

_____

_____

_____

• Social Welfare Progressivism *(page 333)*

Many progressives focused on social problems. One problem involved child labor. In 1900 more than 1.7 million children under the age of 16 worked outside the home, often in unhealthy and unsafe conditions. Muckrakers described the harsh conditions for children working in coal mines. These reports convinced many states to pass laws that set a minimum age for employment. It set limits on child labor, such as maximum hours children could work. By the early 1900s, the number of child workers had decreased.

Working conditions were also difficult for adults. During the early 1900s, thousands of workers were injured or died on the job. They and their families received little compensation. Progressives and union leaders pushed states for workers' compensation laws. These laws set up insurance <u>funds</u> that were paid for by employers. Workers who were hurt on the job received payments from these funds.

Academic Vocabulary
funds: money that is set apart for a specific purpose (p. 334)

Study Guide

Chapter 5, Section 1 (continued)

Some progressives pushed for zoning laws. These laws divided a city into zones for specific uses. They regulated how land and buildings could be used. Building codes set minimum requirements for air, fire escapes, room size, and sanitation in tenements. Health codes required that restaurants keep a clean environment for their customers.

Some progressives believed that alcohol was responsible for many problems in society. Some employers believed that drinking hurt workers' effectiveness. Many Christians opposed drinking on moral grounds. All these concerns led to the start of the **temperance** movement. It <u>advocated</u> the moderation or elimination of alcohol.

Academic Vocabulary
advocate: to propose a certain position or viewpoint (p. 334)

Women were the main leaders of the temperance movement. In 1874 they formed the Women's Christian Temperance Union (WCTU). At first the movement worked to reduce alcohol consumption. Soon, however, it pushed for **prohibition,** or laws banning the making, sale, and consumption of alcohol.

15. What reforms did progressives work for regarding labor?

_____

_____

_____

_____

_____

- **Progressives Versus Big Business** (page 335)

Some progressives focused on regulating big business. They believed that too much wealth was owned by too few people. They were especially concerned about large trusts and holding companies. Progressives did not agree on how big business should be regulated. Some wanted the government to break up large corporations to restore competition. This led to the passage of the Sherman Antitrust Act in 1890. Other progressives pushed for the creation of agencies to regulate big companies and to prevent them from abusing their power. This led to the creation of the Interstate Commerce Commission in 1887.

Some progressives pushed for **socialism.** This is the idea that the government should own and operate industry for the community as a whole. They wanted the government to buy up companies that affected everyone, such as railroads and utilities. Many cities began to own and manage the local gas and water companies and set the price the consumers had to pay.

Socialism had gained some support at the national level. Eugene Debs, the leader of the American Socialist Party, won almost 1 million votes as the party's presidential candidate in the 1912 election. However, socialism never gained the support of more than a minority of the progressives. Most believed in America's free enterprise system.

Study Guide

Chapter 5, Section 1 *(continued)*

16. In what two ways did progressives believe big business should be regulated?

_____

_____

_____

_____

_____

Study Guide

Chapter 5, Section 2

For use with textbook pages 340–345

ROOSEVELT IN OFFICE

CONTENT VOCABULARY

arbitration   a settlement imposed by an outside party *(page 342)*

DRAWING FROM EXPERIENCE

How do you and your family know that the food you eat is safe? How does the government help to ensure that food is safe?

The last section discussed the development of the Progressive movement. This section discusses the administration of President Roosevelt and the Progressive programs he started.

ORGANIZING YOUR THOUGHTS

Use the chart below to help you take notes. Under President Roosevelt, the role of the federal government in solving social and economic problems expanded. Describe the federal government's role in each of the items listed in the chart.

Labor and business	1.
Consumer protection	2.
Conservation	3.

> **California History-Social Science Standards**
>
> **11.2** Students analyze the relationship among the rise of industrialization, large-scale rural-to-urban migration, and massive immigration from Southern and Eastern Europe.
>
> **Focuses on:** 11.2.1, 11.2.5, 11.2.9

READ TO LEARN

- **Roosevelt Revives the Presidency** *(page 341)*

President Theodore Roosevelt was a progressive. He believed that the government should become involved in the competing needs of various groups in American society. Roosevelt's reform programs became known as the Square Deal.

Roosevelt believed that large corporations were important and part of the reason for the nation's prosperity. However, he also believed that these corporations were hurting the public interest. During his first year in office, a fight began over the control of the Burlington Railroad. It involved the owners of two other railroad companies. The conflict almost <u>triggered</u> a financial crisis. Then the owners agreed to form a new holding company called Northern Securities.

> **Academic Vocabulary**
>
> **trigger:** an action that causes a greater reaction (p. 341)

Study Guide

Chapter 5, Section 2 (continued)

Many Americans and President Roosevelt became concerned about the formation of this company. Roosevelt decided that the holding company went against the Sherman Antitrust Act. He filed a lawsuit against Northern Securities. In 1904 the Supreme Court ruled that Northern Securities violated the Sherman Antitrust Act. This was a victory for Roosevelt, who was labeled as a "trustbuster" by newspapers.

President Roosevelt believed it was his job to stop conflicts between different groups in the nation. In 1902 the United Mine Workers (UMW) union had called a strike of miners who dug anthracite, or hard coal. The workers were demanding higher wages, fewer work hours, and recognition of their union. As the strike continued, coal prices increased. If the strike continued too long, the nation might have had a coal shortage that could shut down factories and keep people cold in the winter.

Roosevelt wanted the union and the owners to agree to **arbitration,** or a settlement imposed by an outside party. The union agreed, but the owners did not. The owners' refusal made Roosevelt and many Americans angry. Roosevelt threatened to have the army run the mines. The owners finally agreed to arbitration by a commission appointed by Roosevelt. By intervening in the dispute, Roosevelt had used presidential power in a new way.

Roosevelt believed that most trusts benefited the nation's economy. He did not want to break them up, but he did want to investigate them. In 1903 he convinced Congress to create the Department of Commerce and Labor. The department would include a special division called the Bureau of Corporations. Its job was to investigate corporations and report on them. Many corporations that were worried about antitrust lawsuits agreed to be investigated by the Bureau. However, they made a deal that if the bureau found anything wrong, the companies would be allowed to correct the problem without going to court. Only companies that refused to cooperate would be subject to antitrust lawsuits.

In 1906 Roosevelt pushed Congress to pass the Hepburn Act. It was designed to strengthen the Interstate Commerce Commission (ICC), which did not have enough authority to be effective. The Hepburn Act gave the ICC the power to set railroad rates to make sure that companies did not compete unfairly with each other. At first the railroads were suspicious of the ICC. However, by 1920 the ICC became a supporter of the railroads' interests and had started raising rates to ensure the railroads' profits.

4. What was President Roosevelt's view of big corporations?

_____

_____

_____

_____

_____

Study Guide

Chapter 5, Section 2 (continued)

• Consumer Protection and Conservation (page 344)

In the early 1900s, consumer protection had become an important <u>issue</u>. Some journalists had published articles that exposed the harmful practices of some industries. One journalist reported on the pharmaceutical industry. Many companies marketed medicines as cures for a variety of illnesses. These medicines were often little more than alcohol, colored water, and sugar. Consumers had no way of knowing what they were taking.

Many Americans became concerned about the food they ate. In 1906 Upton Sinclair published *The Jungle*. The book described the unsanitary conditions in the meatpacking industry. The book made consumers angry. President Roosevelt pushed for federal laws. Congress passed the Meat Inspection Act. It required federal inspection of meat and the Agriculture Department to set standards of cleanliness in meatpacking plants. The Pure Food and Drug Act banned the sale of impure or falsely labeled food and drugs.

President Roosevelt was especially influential in <u>environmental</u> conservation. Roosevelt saw that the nation's abundant natural resources were being used up. He urged people to conserve resources.

In 1902 Roosevelt supported the passage of the Newlands Reclamation Act. This law allowed the use of federal funds from the sale of public lands to be used to pay for irrigation and land development projects in the West.

Roosevelt also worked to preserve the nation's forests. He appointed Gifford Pinchot to head the United States Forest Service. Pinchot, like Roosevelt, believed in managing natural resources. He drew up regulations to control lumbering on federal lands. Roosevelt also helped to conserve natural resources by adding millions of acres of land as protected national forests. He established new national parks and federal wildlife reservations.

Roosevelt changed the role of the federal government. Americans came to believe that the federal government should help solve the nation's social and economic problems. Roosevelt also increased the power of the executive branch. More departments in the executive branch became involved in regulating different parts of the nation's life.

5. How did Americans' view of the federal government change during the Roosevelt administration?

_____

_____

_____

_____

Academic Vocabulary
issue: a matter of concern to a group of people (p. 344)

Academic Vocabulary
environmental: having to do with the environment; the complex system of plants, animals, water, and soil (p. 344)

Name _____ Date _____ Class _____

Study Guide

Chapter 5, Section 3

For use with textbook pages 348–351

THE TAFT ADMINISTRATION

CONTENT VOCABULARY

syndicate   a business group *(page 350)*

insubordination   disobedience *(page 350)*

DRAWING FROM EXPERIENCE

Have you ever visited a national park? What park was it? How would you describe your experiences there?

The last section discussed the domestic policies of President Roosevelt. This section discusses the policies of the Taft administration.

ORGANIZING YOUR THOUGHTS

Use the diagram below to help you take notes. President Taft faced several controversies with progressives during his administration. In the diagram, list the three major conflicts.

California History-Social Science Standards

11.2 Students analyze the relationship among the rise of industrialization, large-scale rural-to-urban migration, and massive immigration from Southern and Eastern Europe.

Focuses on: 11.2.9

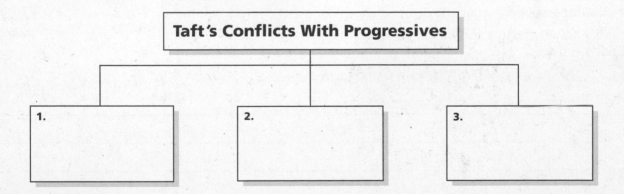

Taft's Conflicts With Progressives

1.

2.

3.

READ TO LEARN

• **Taft Becomes President** *(page 349)*

President Roosevelt supported Howard Taft as the Republican candidate in the 1908 presidential election. Taft and Roosevelt were very different people. Roosevelt was very <u>dynamic</u> and loved to be in the spotlight. He had grand ideas and <u>schemes</u> but left the details to others. Although Taft was a skilled administrator, he preferred to avoid conflict with others. Roosevelt acted

Academic Vocabulary

dynamic: the ability to grab the attention of an audience in order to express your goals (p. 349)

scheme: a plan of action (p. 349)

Study Guide

Chapter 5, Section 3 (continued)

quickly and decisively on issues. Taft preferred to respond slowly. His approach led to conflicts between him and other progressives.

One conflict had to do with tariffs. President Taft believed that high tariffs limited competition. He called Congress into special session to lower tariffs. To pass a new tariff, Taft needed the help of the Speaker of the House, Joseph G. Cannon. Progressives wanted to get rid of Cannon because he often blocked the laws they wanted. Taft disagreed. He pressured progressives to stop trying to unseat Cannon. In return, Cannon quickly pushed the tariff bill through the House of Representatives. However, the following year progressives joined with the Democrats and removed Cannon from power.

The progressives were also angry when the tariff bill went to the Senate. Republican Senator Aldrich, along with other conservative senators, wanted to keep high tariffs. The resulting bill was the Payne-Aldrich Tariff. The law hardly cut tariffs at all, and even raised them on some goods. Taft decided to accept the new tariff.

Taft's relationship with progressives grew worse after a controversy in 1909. Progressives had been unhappy with Taft's replacement of James Garfield, a conservationist, with Richard A. Ballinger as secretary of the interior. Ballinger was a conservative corporate lawyer. He tried to remove nearly a million acres of forests and mineral reserves from public lands and make them available for private development. Gifford Pinchot charged Ballinger with having plotted to turn over public lands in Alaska to a private **syndicate,** or business group, for profit. Taft dismissed the charges as groundless. Pinchot then leaked the story to the press. He asked Congress to investigate. Taft fired Pinchot for **insubordination,** or disobedience. Congress cleared Ballinger.

Taft's actions resulted in an easy Democratic victory in the 1910 congressional elections.

4. What were President Taft's views on tariffs?

_____

_____

_____

_____

_____

• **Taft's Progressive Reforms** (page 351)

Despite many of his problems, Taft had several successes. He was a big supporter of competition and brought more antitrust cases than did Roosevelt. Taft also <u>established</u> the Children's Bureau. This was a federal agency that investigated and publicized child labor problems.

Academic Vocabulary
establish: to create an organization or company (p. 351)

Study Guide

Chapter 5, Section 3 (continued)

Taft was a conservationist. His contributions in the area of conservation were at least equal to those of Roosevelt. Taft set up the Bureau of Mines to oversee the activities of mining companies. He expanded the national forests.

When Taft brought an antitrust suit against U.S. Steel, Roosevelt was upset. He believed that doing so would disturb the system of cooperation and regulation that he had arranged with big business. Roosevelt criticized Taft for his dealings with big business. After he broke with Taft, progressives convinced Roosevelt to run against Taft as the progressive candidate in the 1912 presidential election.

5. What led to the break between Roosevelt and President Taft?

_____

_____

_____

_____

Study Guide

Chapter 5, Section 4

For use with textbook pages 352–357

THE WILSON YEARS

CONTENT VOCABULARY

income tax   direct tax on the earnings of individuals and corporations *(page 355)*

unfair trade practices   business practices that unfairly limited competition *(page 355)*

DRAWING FROM EXPERIENCE

What are income taxes? Who pays them? How are they paid?

The last section described Progressive reforms and problems during the Taft administration. This section discusses Progressive reforms under President Wilson.

> **California History-Social Science Standards**
>
> **11.2** Students analyze the relationship among the rise of industrialization, large-scale rural-to-urban migration, and massive immigration from Southern and Eastern Europe.
>
> **Focuses on:** 11.2.1, 11.2.9

ORGANIZING YOUR THOUGHTS

Use the diagram below to help you take notes. Several Progressive reforms under President Wilson helped to regulate the economy. List these reforms in the diagram.

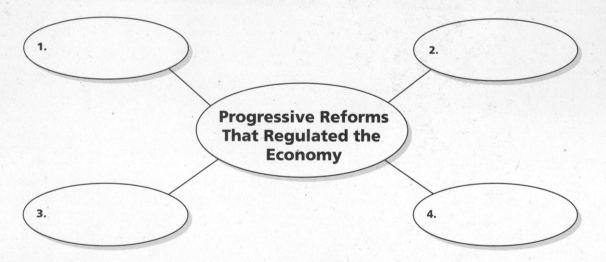

READ TO LEARN

- **The Election of 1912** *(page 353)*

Theodore Roosevelt was displeased with President Taft's performance. He did not believe that Taft lived up to Progressive ideals. So Roosevelt declared that he was willing to accept the Republican nomination for president in the 1912 election. At the Republican convention, conservative Republicans sup-

Study Guide

Chapter 5, Section 4 (continued)

ported Taft. Progressives supported Roosevelt. Roosevelt decided to leave the party and run as an independent candidate. He became the candidate for the newly formed Progressive Party, which was nicknamed the Bull Moose party. The election actually became a contest between Roosevelt and the Democratic candidate Woodrow Wilson.

Wilson was a progressive. As governor of New Jersey, he pushed through one Progressive law after another. Although Wilson and Roosevelt were both progressives, they approached reform differently. Roosevelt's programs became known as the New Nationalism. He favored regulating trusts, setting up laws to protect women and children in labor. He also wanted a federal trade commission to regulate industry.

Wilson's programs became known as the New Freedom. He believed that trusts were "regulated monopolies." He believed that Roosevelt's approach toward businesses gave the federal government too much power in the nation's economy. He believed that freedom in the economy was more important than efficiency.

Roosevelt and Taft split the Republican vote in the election, giving the presidency to Woodrow Wilson.

5. How did Roosevelt's and Wilson's views of trusts differ?

_____

_____

_____

_____

_____

• **Regulating the Economy** (page 354)

Wilson believed that the president should be as powerful as his <u>capacity</u> would allow. Shortly after becoming president, Wilson worked to get Congress to reduce tariffs. He believed that lowering tariffs would lead manufacturers to produce better products and to lower prices in order to be competitive with foreign goods. In 1913 Congress passed the Underwood Tariff. It lowered the average tariff on imported goods. Part of the Underwood Tariff Act included <u>levying</u> an **income tax,** or a direct tax on the earnings of individuals and corporations.

Since the 1800s, economic depressions had hit the United States. During those times many people lost their savings when small banks collapsed. The most recent economic crisis had occurred in 1907. To restore people's confidence in banks, Wilson proposed the creation of a Federal Reserve system. Under this system, banks would keep a portion of their deposits in a regional reserve bank. This would provide a cushion for these banks during an economic crisis. The

Academic Vocabulary
capacity: an individual's ability to perform a specific task (p. 354)

Academic Vocabulary
levy: to use legal authority in order to enforce or collect (p. 355)

Study Guide

Chapter 5, Section 4 *(continued)*

president would appoint a Board of Governors. The Board could set interest rates that the reserve banks charged other banks. It would control the amount of money in circulation. Congress approved this system by passing the Federal Reserve Act in 1913.

Wilson wanted to restore competition in the economy. He wanted to break up monopolies. However, once he became president, Wilson realized that it would be unrealistic to try and break up large companies. In 1914 Wilson asked Congress to create the Federal Trade Commission (FTC) to regulate American businesses. The commission could order companies to stop **unfair trade practices,** or business practices that unfairly limited competition. Progressives in Congress were not satisfied. They passed the Clayton Antitrust Act. The law banned businesses from charging different customers different prices for the same product. Manufacturers could no longer give discounts to those who bought a large volume of goods.

6. Why did President Wilson support the Federal Reserve system?

_____

_____

_____

_____

_____

_____

• Federal Aid and Social Welfare *(page 356)*

By 1914 Wilson believed that his reforms were complete. However, when Democrats suffered losses in the House of Representatives during the 1914 congressional elections, Wilson decided to support further reforms. He signed the Keating-Owen Child <u>Labor</u> Act, which banned the employment of children under the age of 14 in factories that made goods for interstate trade. He supported the Adamson Act, which set up an eight-hour workday for railroad workers. He supported the Federal Farm Loan Act to make long-term loans available to farmers.

> **Academic Vocabulary**
>
> **labor:** an action that produces a good or service (p. 356)

7. What program did President Wilson support to help farmers?

_____

_____

_____

_____

_____

Study Guide

Chapter 5, Section 4 *(continued)*

• **The Legacy of Progressivism** *(page 357)*

Academic Vocabulary

foundation: the basis on which an action or idea is maintained (p. 357)

Building on Roosevelt's <u>foundation</u>, Wilson expanded the role of the president and the federal government. Before the Progressive era, most Americans did not expect the government to pass laws to protect workers or to regulate businesses. By the end of the Progressive era, most Americans expected the government to play an active role. Through the passage of various programs, progressives did improve the quality of life of many people.

The Progressive movement, however, did not address issues facing African Americans. As a result, in 1905 W.E.B. Du Bois and other African American leaders met to demand full political rights for African Americans. The meeting eventually resulted in the beginning of the National Association for the Advancement of Colored People (NAACP) in 1909. African American leaders believed that voting was absolutely necessary to bring about an end to racial discrimination.

8. What group of people failed to benefit from Progressive reforms?

_____

_____

_____

_____

_____

Study Guide

Chapter 6, Section 1

For use with textbook pages 366–374

THE UNITED STATES ENTERS WORLD WAR I

CONTENT VOCABULARY

guerrillas   an armed band that carries out surprise attacks and sabotage rather than open warfare *(page 368)*

nationalism   an intense pride in one's homeland *(page 369)*

self-determination   the idea that people who belong to a nation should have their own country and government *(page 369)*

propaganda   information designed to influence opinion *(page 371)*

contraband   prohibited materials *(page 373)*

U-boat   German submarines *(page 373)*

DRAWING FROM EXPERIENCE

Do you think the United States should ever become involved in conflicts between foreign nations? Why or why not?

In this section, you will learn about American intervention in Mexico and the Caribbean. You will also learn what caused the United States to enter World War I.

> **California History-Social Science Standards**
>
> **11.4** Students trace the rise of the United States to its role as a world power in the twentieth century.
>
> **Focuses on:** 11.4.4, 11.4.5

ORGANIZING YOUR THOUGHTS

Use the cause-and-effect diagram below to help you take notes. Several factors caused conflicts among European nations by 1914. List these causes.

Causes   **Effect**

1. _____

2. _____ | Conflicts develop among European nations. |

3. _____

Study Guide

Chapter 6, Section 1 *(continued)*

READ TO LEARN

- **Woodrow Wilson's Diplomacy** *(page 367)*

President Wilson opposed imperialism. He did, however, believe that the United States should promote democracy. He believed that the <u>stability</u> of democracy was important to keep peace in the world. His beliefs were put to the test soon after he took office.

Academic Vocabulary
stability: being in a state of peace, free from social unrest (p. 367)

Mexico was ruled by dictator Porfirio Díaz from 1884 to 1911. He encouraged foreign investment to help build Mexico's industries. A few wealthy landowners controlled Mexican society. Most Mexicans were poor and landless. Eventually these people revolted against Díaz, who fled the country.

Francisco Madero replaced Díaz, but he proved to be an ineffective administrator. He was replaced by General Victoriano Huerta, who had Madero murdered. President Wilson was disgusted with Huerta's actions and refused to recognize the new government. He hoped that Huerta would be overthrown, so he allowed Americans to arm the groups within Mexico who opposed Huerta.

In April 1914, some American sailors visiting a Mexican city were arrested for entering a restricted area. Although they were released, their commander demanded an apology. The Mexicans refused. Wilson used this as an opportunity to overthrow Huerta and sent marines to take over the port of Veracruz. Anti-American riots followed this action. Venustiano Carranza, whose forces obtained arms from the United States, became the Mexican president.

Mexican forces opposed to Carranza were angry. They carried out raids into the United States. Pancho Villa led a group of **guerrillas,** or an armed band that carries out surprise attacks rather than open warfare, who burned the town of Columbus, New Mexico. They killed a number of Americans. Wilson sent troops into Mexico to find and capture Villa. They were unable to do so.

Many nations were critical of Wilson's actions in Mexico, which damaged U.S. foreign relations. However, in his first term Wilson sent the marines into Nicaragua, Haiti, and the Dominican Republic to try and set up governments that he hoped would be more democratic and stable than those that were there.

4. Why did President Wilson send marines into Nicaragua, Haiti, and the Dominican Republic?

_____

_____

_____

_____

_____

Study Guide

Chapter 6, Section 1 *(continued)*

• The Outbreak of World War I *(page 368)*

By 1914 conflicts among European nations led to the outbreak of war. In 1864 the German kingdom of Prussia started wars to unite the various German states into one nation. By 1871 Prussia succeeded in uniting Germany and setting up the German Empire. The Prussians attacked and defeated France and took a part of French territory along the German border. This action made France and Germany enemies. To protect itself, Germany signed an alliance with Austria-Hungary, an empire that controlled much of southeastern Europe, and with Italy. This alliance became known as the Triple Alliance.

The rise of Germany also upset Russia. It was afraid that Germany might expand into Russia. At the same time, Russia was a rival of Austria-Hungary. Many people living in Austria-Hungary were Slavs, who were the same ethnic group as the Russians. Russia and France found that they both opposed Germany and Austria-Hungary. So they signed the Franco-Russian Alliance.

In 1898 Germany began to build a navy. Great Britain, which had remained neutral up to this time, also started building up its navy. This naval race led to tensions between Germany and Britain. Britain then joined into an alliance with France and Russia, which became known as the Triple Entente.

Nationalism, or an intense <u>emphasis</u> on and pride in one's homeland, became a powerful idea in Europe by the late 1800s. It was one of the reasons for the conflicts among European countries. Each nation viewed the other nations as competitors. Many people were willing to go to war to expand their own nation. An important idea of nationalism is the right to **self-determination.** This is the idea that people who belong to a nation should have their own country and government. This idea led to problems in the Balkans, a region in southeastern Europe. The Ottoman Empire and the Austro-Hungarian Empire ruled the region. These empires were made up of different nations. In the 1800s, the different nations wanted their independence.

Among the groups wanting independence were the Serbs, Bosnians, Croats, and Slovenes. They all spoke similar languages. They called themselves the South Slavs, or Yugoslavs. The Serbs were the first to gain independence. They formed a nation between the Ottoman and Austro-Hungarian Empires and wanted to unite the South Slavs. Russia supported the Serbs. Austria-Hungary wanted to limit Serbia's growth. So it annexed Bosnia, which had been part of the Ottoman Empire. The Serbs were angry because they believed that Austria-Hungary did not want to let the Slavic people in its empire become independent.

In June 1914, the Archduke Franz Ferdinand, the heir to the Austro-Hungarian throne, visited Sarajevo, the capital of Bosnia. While there, he was assassinated by a Bosnian, who was a member of a Serbian nationalist group. Austria-Hungary blamed Serbia and wanted to attack it. However, the Austro-Hungarian government knew that attacking Serbia might trigger a war with its ally, Russia. So the Austrians asked its ally Germany for support. At the same

Academic Vocabulary
emphasis: a special importance given to an object or idea (p. 369)

Study Guide

Chapter 6, Section 1 *(continued)*

time, the Serbs counted on Russian support, who in turn counted on French support. On July 28, 1914, Austria declared war on Serbia. A few days later, Germany declared war on Russia and then on France. World War I had begun.

Germany planned on invading France and then on concentrating its efforts against Russia. However, it had to cross Belgium, which was neutral. The British promised to protect Belgium's neutrality. So when Germany crossed Belgium, Britain declared war on Germany. Those who were part of the Triple Entente were the Allies. It included France, Russia, Great Britain, and Italy. The Triple Alliance became the Central Powers and included Germany, Austria-Hungary, the Ottoman Empire, and Bulgaria.

The German troops advanced into France. However, they were surprised by the Russian invasion of Germany. As a result, the Germans had to pull some of their forces away from France to stop the Russians. The Allies took advantage of the situation by stopping the German advance at the Battle of the Marne, near Paris. Both sides became locked in a stalemate. The Germans and Austrians were more successful against the Russians. They swept across hundreds of miles of territory and took hundreds of thousands of prisoners.

5. What was Germany's early plan in fighting the war?

_____

_____

_____

_____

_____

• American Neutrality *(page 371)*

At the beginning of the war, President Wilson declared the United States neutral. However, many Americans supported one side or the other. Most Americans favored the Allies. Most of President Wilson's cabinet also supported the Allies. They believed that an Allied victory was necessary to keep the international balance of power.

The British worked to win U.S. support. They used **propaganda,** which is information designed to influence opinion. Britain also cut the transatlantic telegraph cable from Europe to the United States. This limited the news about the war mainly to British communications. Although many reports were exaggerated, enough Americans believed them to sway American support for the Allies.

Businesses also supported the Allies because they had ties with businesses in the Allied countries. American banks began to loan money to the Allies, investing in an Allied victory. If the Allies won, the money would be paid back. If the Allies lost, the money would be lost.

Study Guide

Chapter 6, Section 1 *(continued)*

6. What method did Britain use to gain American support?

_____

_____

_____

_____

_____

• Moving Toward War *(page 372)*

Although most Americans did not want to be involved in the war, several events eroded American neutrality and drew the United States into it. After the war began, the British navy blockaded Germany. The British stopped neutral ships to inspect them for **contraband,** or prohibited materials. The contraband included food.

Academic Vocabulary
erode: to wear away at something until it fades (p. 372)

To get around the blockade, Germany used submarines known as **U-boats.** In February 1915, it announced that it would sink without warning any ship located in the waters around Britain. People in the United States and in other countries were angry. Attacking civilian ships without warning was against international rules. The Germans said that many civilian ships were actually warships in disguise and that the U-boats would be at risk if they gave warning. In May 1915, the British passenger ship *Lusitania* entered the war zone after being warned by Germany. A German submarine fired on the ship, killing nearly 1,200 people. About 128 people were Americans.

President Wilson tried to stay out of the war. However, he did send notes to Germany insisting that it safeguard the lives of civilians in the war zones. After a U-boat shot at the French passenger ship *Sussex*, Wilson warned Germany to stop its submarine warfare or risk war with the United States. Germany was not interested in having the United States join the Allies in the war. In the Sussex Pledge, Germany promised to not sink any merchant ships without warning.

In January 1917, Arthur Zimmermann, a German official, instructed the German ambassador to Mexico to propose to Mexico that it ally itself with Germany in case of war between Germany and the United States. In return, Mexico would get back the territory that it once had in Texas, New Mexico, and Arizona. The British intercepted the Zimmermann telegram, which was leaked to American newspapers. Many Americans now believed that war with Germany was necessary. Then in February 1917, Germany again began unrestricted submarine warfare. Finally, after Germany sank six American merchant ships, Wilson asked Congress to declare war on Germany, which it did on April 6, 1917.

Study Guide

Chapter 6, Section 1 (continued)

7. What event led many Americans to call for war against Germany?

_____

_____

_____

_____

_____

Study Guide

Chapter 6, Section 2

For use with textbook pages 375–381

THE HOME FRONT

CONTENT VOCABULARY

conscription   forced military service *(page 376)*

victory garden   garden planted by Americans to raise their own vegetables *(page 378)*

espionage   spying to acquire secret government information *(page 380)*

DRAWING FROM EXPERIENCE

What do you think freedom of speech means? Do you think people should be allowed to say whatever they want whenever they want to? Explain your opinion.

The last section explained the reasons the United States entered World War I. This section describes the war effort at home.

> **California History-Social Science Standards**
>
> **11.4** Students trace the rise of the United States to its role as a world power in the twentieth century.
>
> **Focuses on:** 11.4.5

ORGANIZING YOUR THOUGHTS

Use the chart below to help you take notes. The United States government had to prepare for war in several areas. Identify the ways it prepared in each of the areas listed.

	How the Government Prepared
Building Up the Military	1.
Organizing the Economy	2.
Setting Up a Workforce	3.
Getting Public Support	4.

READ TO LEARN

- **Building Up the Military** *(page 376)*

When the United States entered the war, it did not have enough soldiers. Although many people volunteered, most officials believed that they would have to turn to **conscription,** or forced military service, also known as a <u>draft</u>. Many progressives believed that conscription was against democratic principles.

> **Academic Vocabulary**
>
> **draft:** to be selected at random for mandatory military service (p. 376)

Study Guide

Chapter 6, Section 2 (continued)

Congress, however, believed conscription was necessary. It set up a new system of conscription called selective service. It required all men between 21 and 30 to register for the draft. A lottery then randomly decided the order they were called to military service. Eventually about 2.8 million men were drafted. About 42,000 of the 400,000 African Americans who were drafted served in the war overseas. African American soldiers faced discrimination and prejudice in the army. They often served in racially segregated units that were almost always under the control of white officers. Despite this, many African Americans fought with distinction in the war. Two African American divisions fought in battles along the Western Front.

Women officially served in the armed forces for the first time in World War I. They served in non-combat positions. Women nurses served in both the army and the navy. With men serving in combat, the armed forces faced a shortage of clerical workers. The navy enlisted women to serve as clerical workers, radio operators, electricians, torpedo assemblers, and other occupations. The army, however, refused to enlist women. It hired women as temporary employees to fill clerical jobs. The only women to actually serve in the army were the army nurses.

5. Why did the United States use conscription during World War I?

_____

_____

_____

_____

_____

• Organizing Industry (page 377)

To get the economy ready for the war, Congress created special agencies. One of the first agencies was the War Industries Board (WIB). Its job was to coordinate the production of war materials. Bernard Baruch was in charge of the board. The WIB worked with business leaders. It told industries what they could and could not make.

The Food Administration was responsible for increasing the amount of food available for the armed forces, while decreasing the amount of food available for civilians. The government encouraged Americans to save food on their own such as by having Wheatless Mondays or Meatless Tuesdays. The government encouraged people to plant **victory gardens** to raise their own vegetables. This would leave more food for the troops. The government set high prices on wheat and other grains to increase farm production.

The Fuel Administration managed the use of coal and oil. To conserve energy, the government introduced daylight savings time. It also shortened workweeks for factories that did not make war materials.

Study Guide

Chapter 6, Section 2 (continued)

To raise money to pay for the war, Congress raised income tax rates. It placed new taxes on company profits and on the profits of arms factories. The government also borrowed money from the American people through Liberty Bonds and Victory Bonds. The government agreed to pay back the money with interest in a certain number of years.

6. How did the government attempt to get the money to pay for World War I?

_____

_____

_____

_____

_____

- **Mobilizing the Workforce** (page 378)

To prevent workers from striking, the government set up the National War Labor Board (NWLB). This agency mediated labor disputes that might otherwise lead to strikes. The NWLB pushed industry to give workers wage increases, an 8-hour workday, and the right to organize unions. In return, labor leaders agreed not to disrupt war production through strikes. Union membership increased.

Women's opportunities in the workforce increased during the war. Women took over jobs in industries that the men who were serving in the military had left. After the war, however, most women returned to their previous jobs or stopped working.

Many African Americans started working in factories that produced war materials. Many left the South and moved to factories in the North. This movement became known as the "Great Migration." It changed the racial makeup of cities such as Chicago, New York, Cleveland, and Detroit.

Many Mexicans left Mexico and <u>migrated</u> north. Some worked as farmers and ranchers in the Southwest. Others moved north to get wartime factory jobs. Mexican Americans often faced discrimination. They often settled in their own separate neighborhoods, where they could support each other.

Academic Vocabulary
migrate: to move from one location to another (p. 379)

7. Why did the government set up the National War Labor Board?

_____

_____

_____

_____

_____

Study Guide

Chapter 6, Section 2 *(continued)*

• Ensuring Public Support *(page 379)*

The government wanted to make sure that the public supported the war. It set up an agency called the Committee on Public Information (CPI) to do so. George Creel was the head of the agency. He hired advertisers, artists, authors, songwriters, entertainers, and others to sway public opinion in favor of the war. The CPI arranged for short patriotic talks at movie theaters and public gatherings. It hired thousands of "Four-Minute Men" to urge audiences to support the war in various ways.

The government passed laws to fight antiwar activities. The Espionage Act of 1917 provided for penalties and prison terms for anyone convicted of **espionage,** or spying to acquire secret government information. The law also provided for penalties for interfering with the war effort. The Sedition Act of 1918 made illegal any public expression of opposition to the war. In reality, it let officials prosecute anyone who criticized the government.

The fear of spies led to the mistreatment and persecution of German Americans. Things that were German came under suspicion. Some schools dropped the German language from its curriculums. Orchestras stopped playing music by German composers.

Other people also came under suspicion. They included radical labor activists and socialists. Newspaper ads urged people to report on any people who might be harming the war effort. Many people became concerned about the intolerance that was occurring in the country.

The courts, however, generally upheld the government's tactics. In *Schenck v. the United States,* the Supreme Court ruled that a person's freedom of speech could be curbed if the speech <u>constituted</u> a danger. The Court said that many things that could be said in peace time could be considered dangerous during war.

Academic Vocabulary
constitute: to cause something to be necessary (p. 381)

8. How did the Sedition Act of 1918 affect freedom of speech?

_____

_____

_____

_____

_____

_____

Study Guide

Chapter 6, Section 3

For use with textbook pages 384–389

A BLOODY CONFLICT

CONTENT VOCABULARY

convoy   group of merchant ships and troop transports *(page 387)*

armistice   a cease-fire *(page 388)*

reparations   payments for war damages *(page 389)*

DRAWING FROM EXPERIENCE

You have probably heard of the United Nations. Do you know what it does? Its forerunner was the League of Nations set up after World War I. The last section discussed the war effort at home during World War I. This section discusses the new technology used during the war and the treaty that ended the war.

> **California History-Social Science Standards**
>
> **11.4** Students trace the rise of the United States to its role as a world power in the twentieth century.
>
> **Focuses on:** 11.4.4

ORGANIZING YOUR THOUGHTS

The treaty ending World War I involved the Big Four. In the diagram, describe the major people involved and the major provisions of the treaty.

```
              ┌───────────────────────────────┐
              │   World War I Peace Talks      │
              └───────────────────────────────┘
              ┌───────────────┴───────────────┐
   ┌────────────────────┐          ┌────────────────────┐
   │  People Involved   │          │ Provisions of Treaty│
   │    (Big Four)      │          │                     │
   │                    │          │                     │
   │ 1. _____   │          │ 5. _____    │
   │                    │          │                     │
   │ 2. _____   │          │ 6. _____    │
   │                    │          │                     │
   │ 3. _____   │          │ 7. _____    │
   │                    │          │                     │
   │ 4. _____   │          │                     │
   └────────────────────┘          └────────────────────┘
```

READ TO LEARN

• **Combat in World War I** *(page 385)*

The ways used to fight wars changed during World War I. Troops began using the rapid-fire machine gun. They dug trenches to defend their lines against enemy attacks. On the Western Front, troops dug a <u>network</u> of trenches that stretched from the English Channel to the Swiss border. The space

> **Academic Vocabulary**
>
> **network:** an interconnected system (p. 385)

Study Guide

Chapter 6, Section 3 *(continued)*

between the opposing trenches became known as "no man's land." Soldiers from either side would race across no man's land and throw grenades into the opposing trenches. As they ran across, many were shot. In major battles, both sides sometimes lost hundreds of thousands of men.

Both sides developed new technologies. The Germans began using poison gas. The fumes caused vomiting, blindness, and suffocation. The Allies also began using poison gas, and gas masks became necessary equipment. The British introduced the tank, which could roll over barbed wire and trenches. Airplanes were first used in World War I. They were used at first to observe enemy activities. Then they were used to drop bombs. Later, machine guns were attached to airplanes, which took part in air battles.

8. What technology did the British introduce in World War I?

_____

_____

_____

_____

_____

• The Americans and Victory *(page 386)*

About 2 million American soldiers fought in World War I. Although they were mostly inexperienced, they boosted the morale of the Allied forces. The commander of the U.S. army was General John J. Pershing.

To avoid having troop ships sunk on their way to Europe, the admiral of the U.S. navy suggested that merchant ships and troop transports be gathered in groups, called **convoys.** Warships escorted the convoys. This system reduced the number of ships that were lost and made sure that American troops reached Europe safely.

In February 1917, riots broke out in Russia over the government's involvement in the war. Food and fuel was scarce. Russia's leader, Czar Nicholas II, stepped down from the throne. A temporary government took over. The government, however, was unable to <u>adequately</u> deal with the major problems, such as a lack of food, that the country faced.

The Bolsheviks, a group of Communists, soon wanted power in Russia. In November 1917, Vladimir Lenin, the leader of the Bolshevik Party, overthrew the Russian government and set up a Communist one. Lenin immediately pulled Russia out of the war. He signed the Treaty of Brest-Litovsk with Germany in March 1918. Under the treaty, Russia lost a great deal of land. The treaty also removed the German army from the remaining Russian lands. This helped Germany, which now was free to concentrate its troops on the Western Front.

Academic Vocabulary
adequately: to complete a task without going above or beyond what is required (p. 387)

Study Guide

Chapter 6, Section 3 (continued)

German troops now launched a massive attack and pushed deeply into Allied lines and almost reached Paris. American troops helped to stop the offensive by launching their own attack. American and French troops blocked the German drive on Paris. Germans tried to launch one last attack to take Paris, but American and French troops once again blocked the drive.

On September 16, 1918, American troops under General Pershing started a huge offensive against the Germans. By November, the Americans had destroyed the German defenses and pushed a hole in the German lines. Finally, on November 11, 1918, Germany signed an **armistice,** or cease-fire, that ended the war.

9. How did the Treaty of Brest-Litovsk affect Germany?

_____

_____

_____

_____

_____

- **A Flawed Peace** (page 388)

The peace conference started in January 1919, in Paris, France to try to resolve the issues arising from World War I. The main people involved were known as the Big Four, made up of the leaders of the Allied nations. They included President Wilson of the United States, Prime Minister David Lloyd George of Britain, Premier Georges Clemenceau of France, and Prime Minister Vittorio Orlando of Italy. Germany was not included.

President Wilson's plan for peace was known as the Fourteen Points. The fourteenth point called for the formation of an association of nations known as the League of Nations. The purpose of the League would be to help keep peace and prevent future wars. The other Allied governments did not support Wilson's plan. They believed that it was too easy on the Germans. The Treaty of Versailles weakened many of Wilson's proposals. Under the treaty, Germany had to disband its armed forces. It was forced to pay **reparations,** or war damages to the Allies, that amounted to $33 billion. That amount was more than Germany could afford to pay. Germany also had to accept blame for the outbreak of World War I and the destruction it caused.

The war led to the end of four empires: the Russian Empire, the Ottoman Empire, the German Empire, and the Austro-Hungarian Empire. Austria-Hungary was split into separate countries. In addition, nine new countries were established in Europe. The treaty did include Wilson's plan for the League of Nations.

Academic Vocabulary
resolve: to come to an agreement (p. 388)

Study Guide

Chapter 6, Section 3 *(continued)*

Many members of Congress opposed the Treaty of Versailles, particularly the League of Nations. They believed that it would force the United States to fight in many conflicts. Some senators, led by Henry Cabot Lodge, supported the League of Nations. However, they agreed to ratify the treaty only if some amendments were added to ensure that the United States could always act independently. Wilson wanted the Senate to ratify the treaty without any changes. So he took his case directly to the American people. The 8,000 miles of travel cost Wilson his health. He suffered a stroke, was bedridden, and isolated from his closest advisers.

The U.S. Senate refused to ratify the Treaty of Versailles. Instead, it signed treaties with each of the Central Powers. The League of Nations started without the United States.

10. Why did many Allied powers oppose President Wilson's plan for peace?

_____

_____

_____

_____

_____

Study Guide

Chapter 6, Section 4

For use with textbook pages 390–395

THE WAR'S IMPACT

CONTENT VOCABULARY

cost of living the cost of food, clothing, shelter, and other essentials that people need to survive *(page 391)*

general strike a strike that involves all workers in a certain location, not just workers in a particular industry *(page 391)*

deported to be expelled from a country *(page 394)*

DRAWING FROM EXPERIENCE

What do you think of when you hear the word "Communist"? What countries today have a Communist government? How do Americans today feel about communism?

The last section discussed the provisions of the treaty that ended World War I. This section discusses the effects of the war on the United States.

ORGANIZING YOUR THOUGHTS

Use the diagram below to help you take notes. The United States faced several problems after World War I. Identify these problems in the diagram.

> **California History-Social Science Standards**
>
> **11.4** Students trace the rise of the United States to its role as a world power in the twentieth century.

1.

2.

Problems After World War I

3.

4.

Study Guide

Chapter 6, Section 4 *(continued)*

• An Economy in Turmoil *(page 391)*

After the war ended, the United States government removed the controls it had placed on the economy during the war. People quickly bought goods that they were not able to buy during the war. Businesses increased their prices, which they could not do during the war. The result was inflation. It increased the **cost of living,** or the cost of food, clothing, shelter, and other items people need to survive.

Many businesses raised wages during the war. However, after the war the inflation wiped out most of the gains that workers had made. Workers wanted an increase in wages. Business owners, however, wanted to hold down wages to hold down their operating costs.

During the war, the number of workers in unions increased. After the war, unions were better organized than they were before the war and more ready to organize strikes. Business leaders were determined to break the unions. The situation resulted in a huge increase in strikes in 1919.

The first big strike took place in Seattle. It involved shipyard workers who wanted higher wages and shorter hours. Soon other workers joined the shipyard workers and organized a **general strike.** This is a strike that involves all workers living in a certain location, not just workers in a particular industry. The <u>widespread</u> strike paralyzed the city for several days. In the end, the strikers made no gains. The strike did worry many Americans because the general strike was a technique used by Communists and radical groups in Europe.

Academic Vocabulary
widespread: having influence on or affecting a large group (p. 392)

The Seattle strike was followed by a strike by police officers in Boston. Riots soon broke out in the city. Calvin Coolidge, the governor of Massachusetts, was forced to send in the National Guard. When the strikers returned to work, they were fired. The police commissioner hired a new police force instead.

One of the largest strikes was held by steelworkers. They went on strike against U.S. Steel for higher pay, shorter hours, and a recognition of their union. The company was determined to break the union. Many steelworkers were immigrants. The company blamed the strike on foreign radicals. It hired African Americans and Mexicans as replacement workers. The company was able to keep the steel mills operating. The strike failed and so did the union.

5. What did many workers in the United States in 1919 strike for?

_____

_____

_____

_____

Study Guide

Chapter 6, Section 4 (continued)

- ### Racial Unrest *(page 392)*

After the war, many soldiers returned to the United States looking for work. Many African Americans who moved north during the war were also looking for jobs and housing. Racism and frustration led to violence. In the summer of 1919, riots broke out in many Northern cities. The worst violence occurred in Chicago.

6. What led to race riots in many American cities in the United States in 1919?

_____

_____

_____

_____

_____

- ### The Red Scare *(page 393)*

The strikes in 1919 led many people to believe that Communists were trying to start a revolution in the United States. Many Americans were very angry with Russia when it withdrew from the war. Since the late 1800s, many Americans blamed immigrants for bringing Communist ideas into the United States. They also blamed immigrants for labor problems and violence. When Communists took control of Russia, Americans feared they would try to start revolutions in other places. Americans became especially fearful when the Soviet Union formed the Communist International. This was an organization that coordinated the activities of Communist parties in other countries.

As strikes started across the United States in 1919, the fear of Americans that Communists, or "Reds," would seize power led to a panic known as the Red Scare. Several incidents supported the panic. In June 1919, eight bombs in eight cities exploded within minutes of one another. One of these bombs damaged the home of United States Attorney General A. Mitchell Palmer. Although no one was ever caught, most people believed the bombings were the work of Communists trying to destroy the American way of life.

Attorney General Palmer set up a special division within the Justice Department. The General Intelligence Division was headed by J. Edgar Hoover, and it later became the Federal Bureau of Investigation (FBI). In the next few months, Palmer organized raids on several radical organizations, although no evidence pointed to any one group as the bombers. The <u>authorities</u> rounded up many immigrants and had them **deported,** or expelled from the country.

The Palmer raids were carried out without concern for people's civil rights. Homes were entered without search warrants. People were jailed indefinitely and not allowed to talk to their attorneys. Palmer was first praised for his

Academic Vocabulary
authorities: those who have control over determining and enforcing what is right or wrong (p. 394)

Study Guide

Chapter 6, Section 4 *(continued)*

work. However, when he failed to find any real evidence of a revolutionary conspiracy, his popularity faded. The Red Scare led to anti-immigrant feelings and a call for Congress to limit immigration.

7. How did the Palmer raids violate people's civil rights?

_____

_____

_____

_____

- **An End to Progressivism** *(page 395)*

By 1920 most Americans wanted an end to the unrest that overcame the country. In the 1920 election, the Democrats ran James M. Cox and Franklin D. Roosevelt. They ran on the ideals of progressivism. The Republicans ran Warren G. Harding. He called for a return to "normalcy" and a <u>restoration</u> of the simpler days before Progressive Era reforms. Many voters agreed with Harding, and he won by a landslide.

Academic Vocabulary
restoration: to rebuild something to resemble its original state (p. 395)

8. Why did Warren G. Harding win the presidential election in 1920?

_____

_____

_____

_____

Study Guide

Chapter 7, Section 1

For use with textbook pages 406–413

A CLASH OF VALUES

CONTENT VOCABULARY

anarchist   individual who opposes all forms of government *(page 407)*

eugenics   a false science that deals with the improvement of hereditary traits *(page 408)*

flapper   a young, dramatic, stylish, and unconventional woman *(page 410)*

evolution   theory that suggests that human beings had developed from lower forms of life over the course of millions of years *(page 411)*

creationism   Fundamentalist belief that God created the world as described in the Bible *(page 411)*

police powers   government's power to control people and property in the interest of public safety, health, welfare, and morals *(page 413)*

speakeasy   bar where people illegally purchased alcohol *(page 413)*

DRAWING FROM EXPERIENCE

How would you describe today's fashion style? What kinds of features make up this style?

In this section, you will learn about the increase in racism and nativism in the 1920s. You will also learn about the conflicts between traditional and modern values that shook the country.

ORGANIZING YOUR THOUGHTS

Use the diagram below to help you take notes. The 1920s saw the development of the new morality. List the ways the new morality showed itself.

California History-Social Science Standards

11.2 Students analyze the relationship among the rise of industrialization, large-scale rural-to-urban migration, and massive immigration from Southern and Eastern Europe.

11.3 Students analyze the role religion played in the founding of America, its lasting moral, social and political impacts, and issues regarding religious liberty.

11.5 Students analyze the major political, social, economic, technological, and cultural developments of the 1920s.

Focuses on: 11.2.3, 11.3.3, 11.5.2, 11.5.3, 11.5.4

Study Guide

Chapter 7, Section 1 (continued)

READ TO LEARN

- **Nativism Resurges** (page 407)

During the 1920s, anti-immigrant feelings increased in the United States, leading to increased feelings of racism and nativism. Many Americans viewed immigrants as a threat to the traditional American society. They believed that immigrants were taking jobs away from the millions of Americans who returned from the war.

In the 1920s, the majority of immigrants arrived from southern and eastern Europe. They faced ethnic and religious prejudices. The Sacco-Vanzetti case is an example of this discrimination. On April 15, 1920, two armed men killed two employees of a factory in Massachusetts and robbed the company of its payroll. Two Italian immigrants—Nicola Sacco and Bartolomeo Vanzetti— were arrested for the crime. Newspapers closely covered the case. They reported that the two immigrants were **anarchists,** those who opposed all forms of government. They also reported that Sacco owned a gun similar to the murder weapon. Although no one at the time knew whether the two men were guilty, many people concluded that they were guilty because they were Italian immigrants and anarchists. Other people believed that the case was an example of prejudice against people based on their ethnic origin. In July 1921, Sacco and Vanzetti were found guilty and sentenced to death. They were executed six years later, maintaining their innocence to the end.

Nativists used the idea of **eugenics** to boost their arguments against immigration. Eugenics is a false science that deals with the improvement of hereditary traits. It stressed that human inequalities were inherited. Eugenics boosted the nativists' idea that white Protestants from northern Europe who first came to America were the superior stock. People such as Woodrow Wilson supported this idea and lent support to racist theories.

One of the biggest movements to restrict immigration came from the Ku Klux Klan. After the Civil War, the Ku Klux Klan used violence to intimidate freed African Americans. After World War I, the Klan targeted immigrants, Catholics, Jews and other groups they believed did not represent traditional American values. Because of a large public campaign, Klan membership skyrocketed in the 1920s, spreading beyond the South and into Northern cities.

7. Why did nativist feelings increase in the 1920s?

_____

_____

_____

Study Guide

Chapter 7, Section 1 *(continued)*

- ## Controlling Immigration *(page 408)*

In 1921 Congress responded to the nativist demands to limit immigration with the Emergency Quota Act. The law set up a temporary quota system. The law limited the number of people admitted in a single year to 3 percent of the total number of people in any ethnic group already living in the United States as determined in the 1910 census. The provision discriminated against people from southern and eastern Europe. The National Origins Act, passed in 1924, made immigration restriction permanent. The law also changed the year residing to 1890. By moving the year back to 1890, it basically allowed immigration from northwestern Europe.

Immigrants were a <u>source</u> of cheap labor. The reduction in immigration caused a shortage of workers for agriculture, mining, and railroad work. Mexican immigrants filled some of these jobs. Mexican immigration started after the passage of the Newlands Reclamation Act. This law provided money for irrigation projects in the dry Southwest. The factory farms that started there needed large numbers of laborers. The quotas set up by the National Origins Act did not include natives of the Western Hemisphere. More than 600,000 Mexicans arrived in the United States between 1914 and the end of the 1920s.

> **Academic Vocabulary**
>
> **source:** the point at which something is provided (p. 408)

8. How did the Emergency Quota Act and the National Origins Act affect immigration?

_____

_____

_____

_____

_____

- ## The New Morality *(page 410)*

During the 1920s, a "new morality" took over the nation. The new morality challenged traditional ways of thinking and influenced various <u>aspects</u> of American society. It stressed youth and personal freedom. In the family, the new morality focused on the ideas of romance, pleasure, and friendship for a successful marriage. Work changed the relationships between men and women. In the 1920s, young single women began to work not just for wages for themselves and their family, but also as a way to break from parental authority and to establish their own personal identities.

> **Academic Vocabulary**
>
> **aspect:** refers to a portion of something with great influence or size (p. 410)

The automobile also played a part in the new morality. It gave America's young people more independence and made it easier for them to escape parental control and find new forms of entertainment with their friends.

Study Guide

Chapter 7, Section 1 (continued)

A new fashion look started in the 1920s. Women shortened their hair and wore silk stockings. Glamorous stage and screen stars became popular. A **flapper** was a young, dramatic, stylish, and unconventional woman. She smoked cigarettes and drank liquor. She also dressed in clothes considered too revealing at that time.

Many women in the 1920s looked for financial independence. They entered the workforce as salesclerks and secretaries. They made contributions in fields such as science, medicine, and literature.

9. What things did the new morality stress?

_____

_____

_____

_____

_____

- ### The Fundamentalist Movement (page 411)

Many Americans feared that the new morality, with its relaxed <u>ethics</u>, threatened traditional values and beliefs. These Americans believed that the nation was going through a moral decline. Many joined a religious movement known as Fundamentalism. This movement stressed the teachings of the Bible. Fundamentalists rejected the theory of **evolution,** which suggested that human beings had developed from lower forms of life over millions of years. Fundamentalists believed in **creationism,** that God created the world as described in the Bible.

Academic Vocabulary
ethic: a set of moral values to live by (p. 411)

Evolutionists and creationists eventually clashed. In 1925 Tennessee passed a law that prohibited the teaching of evolution. When John T. Scopes, a biology teacher, taught evolution in his high school in Dayton, Tennessee, he was arrested and put on trial. In the Scopes trial, William Jennings Bryan, a Fundamentalist, was the prosecutor. Clarence Darrow defended John Scopes. Scopes was found guilty and fined $100. The conviction was later overturned.

10. On what two theories did the Scopes trial focus?

_____

_____

_____

_____

_____

_____

Study Guide

Chapter 7, Section 1 *(continued)*

- **Prohibition** *(page 412)*

    Throughout the early 1900s, many people began supporting prohibition. Many believed that prohibition would reduce unemployment, domestic violence, and poverty. The Eighteenth Amendment, which took effect in January 1920, provided for prohibition. To enforce the amendment, Congress passed the National Prohibition Act, also known as the Volstead Act. Enforcing Prohibition became the job of the U.S. Treasury Department, which greatly expanded the federal government's **police powers.** This is a government's power to control people and property in the interest of public safety, health, welfare, and morals. The Treasury Department set up the Prohibition Unit to enforce Prohibition. It made hundreds of thousands of arrests. However, Americans ignored the law. They went to secret bars called **speakeasies,** where they could buy alcohol. Organized crime supplied and often ran these speakeasies, which were located all over the country.

    The huge profits that could be made from illegally selling liquor led to smuggling. Smugglers brought liquor into the United States from Canada and the Caribbean. Smuggling and the buying of liquor led to an illegal billion-dollar industry. Violence broke out in the streets as gangs fought to control the liquor trade. Crime became big business. Some gangsters made enough money and had enough power to corrupt local politicians. The Eighteenth Amendment was eventually repealed by the Twenty-first Amendment in 1933.

11. What was the purpose of the Eighteenth Amendment?

_____

_____

_____

_____

_____

Study Guide

Chapter 7, Section 2

For use with textbook pages 418–421

CULTURAL INNOVATIONS

CONTENT VOCABULARY

mass media   radio, movies, newspapers, and magazines aimed at a broad, popular audience
   (page 421)

DRAWING FROM EXPERIENCE

What do you think is the most popular form of entertainment in the United States today? What is the most popular form of entertainment among your classmates and friends?

The last section discussed the conflicts that developed in the 1920s between traditional and modern values. This section discusses the cultural trends of the 1920s.

> **California History-Social Science Standards**
>
> **11.5** Students analyze the major political, social, economic, technological, and cultural developments of the 1920s.
>
> **Focuses on:** 11.5.5, 11.5.6

ORGANIZING YOUR THOUGHTS

Use the diagram below to help you take notes. New forms of entertainment became popular in the United States in the 1920s. List these forms in the diagram.

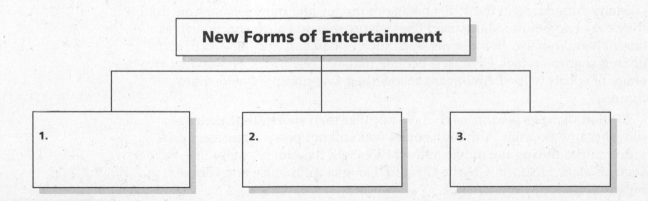

READ TO LEARN

• **Art and Literature** *(page 419)*

During the 1920s, American writers and artists searched for meaning in the <u>emerging</u> challenges of the modern world. Many artists, writers, and intellectuals gathered in Greenwich Village in Manhattan and Chicago's South Side. There they lived a Bohemian, or artistic and unconventional, way of life. The places helped free them from conforming to old ideas.

> **Academic Vocabulary**
>
> **emerge:** to be made known (p. 419)

Study Guide

Chapter 7, Section 2 (continued)

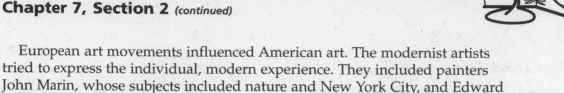

European art movements influenced American art. The modernist artists tried to express the individual, modern experience. They included painters John Marin, whose subjects included nature and New York City, and Edward Hopper, whose paintings used Realism and often showed isolated individuals.

Poets and writers of the 1920s used a <u>diverse</u> range of styles and subject matter. Carl Sandburg used common speech to glorify the Midwest. Edna St. Vincent Millay wrote about women's freedom and equality. Some poets, such as T.S. Eliot, wrote about the negative effects of modernism. Other writers of the 1920s included Ezra Pound, Amy Lowell, and William Carlos Williams. One of the most creative playwrights was Eugene O'Neill. He wrote about realistic characters in realistic, sometimes tragic, situations.

World War I affected many American novelists. They wrote about disillusionment with war and the myths of American heroes. Ernest Hemingway was one such writer. John Dos Passos criticized the capitalist culture. F. Scott Fitzgerald wrote about the emptiness of modern society.

Academic Vocabulary
diverse: being different from one another (p. 419)

4. What was the subject matter of many artists and writers in the 1920s?

_____

_____

_____

- **Popular Culture** (page 420)

Many Americans in the 1920s had more money and more leisure time than they ever had before. Many used their leisure time to watch sports such as baseball and boxing. Some sport stars, such as baseball star Babe Ruth and boxing champion Jack Dempsey, became national celebrities. Newspaper coverage of sports helped Americans follow their favorite sports and sports figures.

Motion pictures became even more popular than sports. Feature-length films became popular. Although sound was still not possible, theaters provided music during the movie and subtitles told the movie's story line. Actors such as Mary Pickford, Charlie Chaplin, Douglas Fairbanks, and Gloria Swanson became very famous.

Radio shows and music also became popular. Most radio stations in the 1920s played the popular music of the day. Radio shows also included classical music and comedy shows. In addition to entertaining, the **mass media**—radio, movies, newspapers, and magazines aimed at a broad, popular audience—helped to expand people's view of the world. It helped <u>unify</u> the nation and spread the new ideas of the time.

Academic Vocabulary
unify: to bring a group together with a similar goal or thought pattern (p. 421)

Study Guide

Chapter 7, Section 2 (continued)

5. How did the mass media change American society?

_____

_____

_____

_____

_____

_____

Study Guide

Chapter 7, Section 3

For use with textbook pages 426–431

AFRICAN AMERICAN CULTURE

CONTENT VOCABULARY

jazz   a style of music influenced by Dixieland music and ragtime *(page 428)*

blues   a soulful style of music that evolved from African American spirituals *(page 428)*

DRAWING FROM EXPERIENCE

What kinds of music do you enjoy listening to? How would you describe the music?

The last section described some cultural trends in the United States in the 1920s. This section describes some aspects of African American culture in the United States in the 1920s.

> **California History-Social Science Standards**
>
> **11.5** Students analyze the major political, social, economic, technological, and cultural developments of the 1920s.
>
> **Focuses on:** 11.5.2, 11.5.6

ORGANIZING YOUR THOUGHTS

Use the chart below to help you take notes. The Harlem Renaissance produced many African American writers, musicians, and actors. Identify them in the space available.

Writers	1.
	2.
	3.
Musicians	4.
	5.
Actors	6.
	7.

READ TO LEARN

- **The Harlem Renaissance** *(page 427)*

Many African Americans were part of the Great Migration, the movement from the rural South to the industrial North. They <u>sought</u> to escape segregation and to find opportunities to better their lives. As African American population increased in the large northern cities, so did nightclubs and music. This was particularly true in the New York City neighborhood of Harlem, which was the center for artistic development, racial pride, and a feeling of community. This flourishing of African American arts became known as the Harlem Renaissance.

> **Academic Vocabulary**
>
> **sought:** to have gone in search of change (p. 427)

132   ***The American Vision: Modern Times***

Study Guide

Chapter 7, Section 3 *(continued)*

One of the most important <u>authors</u> of the Harlem Renaissance was Claude McKay. His writing reflected defiance and a hatred of racism, two major characteristics of Harlem Renaissance writing. Another important writer of the Harlem Renaissance was Langston Hughes. He became a leading voice of the African American experience in the United States. Zora Neale Hurston wrote the first major stories about female African American characters.

Louis Armstrong introduced an improvisational form of **jazz.** This was a style of music influenced by Dixieland music and ragtime. Armstrong broke away from the New Orleans tradition of group playing to imaginative solo playing. He became the first great cornet and trumpet soloist in jazz music. Duke Ellington was also influenced by ragtime. He created his own sound using different combinations of instruments. Like other African American musicians, Ellington got his start at the Cotton Club. This was one of the most famous Harlem nightspots. Bessie Smith was famous for singing the **blues,** a soulful style of music that evolved from African American spirituals. Smith performed with many of the greatest jazz bands.

The theater also thrived during the Harlem Renaissance. Paul Robeson and Josephine Baker were two of the most famous theater performers of the time.

8. What was Harlem?

_____

_____

_____

_____

> **Academic Vocabulary**
>
> **author:** someone who creates original material (p. 428)

• African American Politics *(page 429)*

African Americans' political goals changed after World War I. As the number of African Americans increased in the North, their <u>impact</u> as a voting bloc increased. Most African Americans voted for Republicans. African Americans in Chicago elected Oscar DePriest, the first African American representative in Congress from a Northern state.

The National Association for the Advancement of Colored People (NAACP) worked against segregation and discrimination. It did so mainly by lobbying politicians and working through the courts. The NAACP lobbied against lynching throughout the 1920s and 1930s. It worked with organized labor and was successful in defeating the nomination of Judge John J. Parker to the U.S. Supreme Court. Parker was known for his racist and anti-labor positions.

While some people were fighting for integration, others were calling for African American separation from white society. One such person was Marcus Garvey. He founded the Universal Negro Improvement Association (UNIA). It was an organization that worked to promote black pride and unity. Garvey

> **Academic Vocabulary**
>
> **impact:** to make a lasting impression upon an individual or group (p. 430)

Study Guide

Chapter 7, Section 3 (continued)

believed that African Americans could gain economic and political power through education. He also believed African Americans should separate themselves from whites. Garvey told his followers that they would never find justice in the United States. He urged them to settle in Liberia, in Africa. Many African Americans distanced themselves from Garvey and his push for separation. Although Garvey was not successful in getting support for his movement, he did instill millions of African Americans with pride in their heritage. This feeling would eventually inspire the civil rights movement of the 1960s.

9. Why did Marcus Garvey call for African Americans to settle in Africa?

_____

_____

_____

_____

_____

Study Guide

Chapter 8, Section 1

For use with textbook pages 444–448

PRESIDENTIAL POLITICS

CONTENT VOCABULARY
normalcy   a reference to returning to a normal time *(page 445)*
immunity   freedom from prosecution *(page 446)*

DRAWING FROM EXPERIENCE

How would you describe the current president of the United States? What style of leadership does the president have? Do you think his style appeals to most Americans?

In this section, you will learn about the administration of President Harding. You will also learn about Calvin Coolidge's presidency.

ORGANIZING YOUR THOUGHTS

Use the chart below to help you take notes. President Harding's and President Coolidge's presidencies differed greatly. Describe some aspects of each in the chart.

> **California History-Social Science Standards**
>
> **11.2** Students analyze the relationship among the rise of industrialization, large-scale rural-to-urban migration, and massive immigration from Southern and Eastern Europe.
>
> **11.5** Students analyze the major political, social, economic, technological, and cultural developments of the 1920s.
>
> **Focuses on:** 11.2.9, 11.5.1

Harding's Presidency	Coolidge's Presidency
1.	4.
2.	5.
3.	6.

READ TO LEARN

- **The Harding Administration** *(page 445)*

Warren G. Harding was elected president in 1920. He ran on the campaign slogan to return to **normalcy,** or a return to "normal" life after the war. Harding was charming and well-liked. Harding thought that he lacked the

Study Guide

Chapter 8, Section 1 *(continued)*

intellect to be president, once stating "I should really be ashamed to <u>presume</u> myself fitted to reach out for a place of such responsibility." Although Harding appointed some distinguished people to cabinet posts, he also appointed many friends to cabinet positions and high-level jobs. These people became known as the Ohio Gang. Some members used their offices to sell government jobs or immunity from prosecution. They were involved in several scandals. One scandal broke in July 1923. At that time, President Harding was touring the West. During his trip, he became ill and died.

Academic Vocabulary
presume: to believe something without factual evidence (p. 445)

One of the scandals involved Harding's secretary of the interior, Albert B. Fall. He secretly allowed private companies to lease lands containing U.S. Navy oil reserves at Teapot Dome, Wyoming, and Elk Hills, California. He received bribes from these companies. The Senate investigated the Teapot Dome scandal, and Secretary Fall became the first cabinet member to go to prison.

Another scandal involved Attorney General Harry Daugherty, Harding's former campaign manager. This scandal involved a German-owned American company that the Americans took over during World War I. To buy the company, a German agent bribed a politician. A part of the bribe ended up in a bank account that Daugherty controlled. Daugherty refused to turn over bank files and testify under oath. He claimed **immunity,** or freedom from prosecution, because he said he had had confidential dealings with the president. Daugherty's attitude disgusted the new president, Calvin Coolidge. He demanded Daugherty's resignation.

7. What problems did President Harding face in his administration?

_____

_____

_____

_____

_____

_____

Study Guide

Chapter 8, Section 1 *(continued)*

• The Coolidge Administration *(page 447)*

President Coolidge tried to distance himself from the corruption of Harding's administration. He asked only the most capable cabinet members to stay on. Coolidge believed that the country would prosper if businesses prospered. He was determined that the government should interfere as little as possible with business. Coolidge restored <u>integrity</u> to the presidency. The nation prospered during his administration, and he easily won the Republican Party's nomination for president in 1924.

The Democrats were divided between supporters from the urban East and those from the rural South and West. As a result, they had a difficult time choosing a candidate. They finally agreed on John W. Davis of West Virginia.

Many people who did not want to choose between the Republican and the Democratic candidates left their parties to form a new Progressive Party. They nominated Robert M. La Follette as their presidential candidate, and he captured 16.6 <u>percent</u> of the popular vote. Coolidge won easily.

8. Why did some people form a new Progressive Party?

_____

_____

_____

_____

_____

Academic Vocabulary
integrity: a way of behaving that follows a strict moral code (p. 447)

Academic Vocabulary
percent: one part of one hundred (p. 448)

Study Guide

Chapter 8, Section 2

For use with textbook pages 449-455

A GROWING ECONOMY

CONTENT VOCABULARY

mass production   large-scale product manufacturing usually done by machinery *(page 450)*

assembly line   a manufacturing system that divided operations into simple tasks that unskilled workers could do *(page 450)*

welfare capitalism   situation in which companies allowed employees to buy stock, take part in profit sharing, and receive benefits *(page 454)*

open shop   a workplace where employees were not required to join a union *(page 454)*

DRAWING FROM EXPERIENCE

How important is the automobile today to American life? How important is it to your life?

The last section described the administrations of Presidents Harding and Coolidge. This section discusses the nation's economy in the 1920s.

ORGANIZING YOUR THOUGHTS

Use the diagram below to help you take notes. The automobile greatly changed American life in the 1920s. Explain how it did so in the diagram.

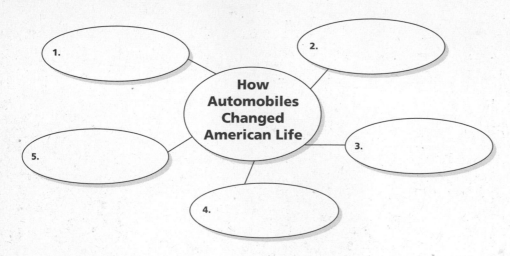

California History-Social Science Standards

11.2 Students analyze the relationship among the rise of industrialization, large-scale rural-to-urban migration, and massive immigration from Southern and Eastern Europe.

11.4 Students trace the rise of the United States to its role as a world power in the twentieth century.

11.5 Students analyze the major political, social, economic, technological, and cultural developments of the 1920s.

Focuses on: 11.2.1, 11.4.5, 11.5.1, 11.5.4, 11.5.6, 11.5.7

The American Vision: Modern Times

Study Guide

Chapter 8, Section 2 (continued)

READ TO LEARN

- ### The Rise of New Industries (page 450)

During the 1920s, the automobile became an important part of American life. During that time, Americans earned more money than ever before. The number of work hours decreased. The use of **mass production,** or large-scale product manufacturing usually done by machinery, made more products available. It also lowered the costs of the products. Innovation thrived and new industries emerged.

Carmaker Henry Ford used the **assembly line** to make cars. This system divided operations into simple tasks that unskilled workers could do. After Ford started using this system, the time it took to build a car decreased dramatically. Whereas in 1913, workers built a car in about 12 hours, by 1925 the assembly line built a car every 10 seconds. Ford's assembly-line product was the Model T. Using mass production to build cars helped to decrease the price of cars. In 1908 a Model T sold for about $850. By 1924 Model Ts sold for about $295.

The low prices for cars created a huge demand. By the mid-1920s, other corporations, such as General Motors and Chrysler, were competing with Ford. The automobile industry also led to the growth of other industries, such as plate glass, rubber, and steel.

Just as the automobile changed the way manufacturing was done, it also changed American life. The automobile created an increase in small businesses such as garages and gas stations. It brought people in rural areas closer to cities and city people closer to the country. It allowed people to live farther away from work. A new kind of worker, the auto commuter, developed. Many commuters lived in the suburbs and drove to work in the city.

With an increased income, consumers were also able to buy the many new products that came on the market. They bought items such as electric razors and frozen foods. They also bought labor-saving appliances such as electric irons, vacuum cleaners, refrigerators, and washing machines. Industries that made personal care items—such as mouthwash, deodorants, and cosmetics—became major industries in the 1920s.

The airline industry began to develop rapidly after the successful flight of the Wright brothers in 1903. Leading the way was Glenn Curtiss, an American who invented ailerons, which can be tilted to steer the plane.

By the 1920s, airplanes were used by the Post Office to deliver mail. In 1926 Congress passed the Air Commerce Act. The law provided federal aid for building airports. The idea of using airplanes for commercial flights received a boost in 1927, when former airmail pilot Charles Lindbergh made a solo flight across the Atlantic Ocean. Commercial flying became popular among American business executives in the 1920s.

Academic Vocabulary
innovation: a new idea or method (p. 450)

Academic Vocabulary
consumer: a person who buys what is produced by an economy (p. 451)

© by The McGraw-Hill Companies, Inc.

Study Guide

Chapter 8, Section 2 (continued)

Commercial radio also became popular in the 1920s. In 1926 the National Broadcasting Company (NBC) established a permanent network of stations to distribute daily programs. There were almost 700 stations across the country by 1927. The Federal Radio Commission had been set up to regulate these stations. Sales of radio sets soared. In 1928 the Columbia Broadcasting System (CBS) set up a coast-to-coast network of stations to compete with NBC. The two networks sold advertising time. They hired musicians, actors, and comedians to appear on their shows. In 1928 the stations provided complete coverage of the presidential election for the first time.

6. What was the effect of using mass production in making goods?

_____

_____

_____

_____

_____

- **The Consumer Society** (page 453)

The higher wages Americans earned in the 1920s allowed them to increase their buying power. The prosperity of the 1920s gave many Americans the confidence to go into debt to buy new goods. Before the 1920s, most Americans considered debt shameful. However, this attitude changed in the 1920s. Americans began believing that they could pay what they owed at a later time. Americans began buying items such as cars and furniture on credit.

One problem that many inventors faced was getting people to become aware of the invention. To get people to buy the new products, manufacturers turned to advertising. It became an important industry in the 1920s.

Many industries began creating modern organizational <u>structures</u> in what became known as the managerial revolution. Companies were divided into divisions with different functions, and these divisions needed managers to run them.

Unions in the 1920s lost membership and were not influential. This was due in large part because of anti-union activities of the employers. Employers supported the **open shop**—a workplace where employees were not required to join a union. Many companies also set up **welfare capitalism.** They allowed employees to buy stock, participate in profit sharing, and receive benefits such as medical care. These measures made unions seem unnecessary to many workers.

> **Academic Vocabulary**
>
> **structure:** a system of organization that arranges something large into smaller portions to create order (p. 454)

Study Guide

Chapter 8, Section 2 *(continued)*

7. How did manufacturers make people aware of their new products?

_____

_____

_____

_____

- ### The Farm Crisis Returns *(page 455)*

Farmers did not prosper in the 1920s. New technology allowed them to produce more. However, demand for the products did not increase, so farmers received lower prices for their goods.

During the war, the government encouraged farmers to produce more to fill the need for food in Europe. Many farmers went into debt to buy more land and machinery in order to grow more crops. The sales and prices were high, and farmers made money. After the war, Europeans began producing more farm products on their own. They no longer had the need for American products. Then in 1922, Congress passed the Fordney-McCumber Act. The law raised tariffs to protect American industries from foreign competition. However, Europeans reacted by not buying American agricultural products. American farmers could not sell their products overseas, and prices dropped.

Some members of Congress tried to help the American farmers sell their surplus products. They proposed that the government buy the crop surpluses and sell them abroad. They believed this would help farmers. Although Congress passed the bill, President Coolidge vetoed it. He believed that the bill would encourage farmers to produce even greater surpluses that the government would not be able to sell. As a result, American farmers stayed in recession throughout the 1920s.

8. Why did American farmers have difficulty selling their products overseas after World War I?

_____

_____

_____

_____

_____

_____

Study Guide

Chapter 8, Section 3

For use with textbook pages 456–459

THE POLICIES OF PROSPERITY

CONTENT VOCABULARY

supply-side economics the idea that the economy would grow by lowering taxes, which would increase spending and investing *(page 457)*

cooperative individualism an idea promoted by Herbert Hoover that encouraged manufacturers and distributors to form trade associations and voluntarily share information with the federal government *(page 458)*

isolationism philosophy that a nation should limit its involvement in international affairs *(page 458)*

moratorium a suspension of activity *(page 459)*

DRAWING FROM EXPERIENCE

How is the United States involved in the affairs of other nations? Do you think the United States could avoid being involved? Why do you think so?

The last section described the economic growth in the United States in the 1920s. This section discusses the economic policies of the government that contributed to the economic prosperity.

ORGANIZING YOUR THOUGHTS

Use the chart below to help you take notes. The United States continued to be involved in world affairs during the 1920s, signing several treaties. Explain the conditions of each of the treaties listed.

Treaty	Conditions of Treaty
Five-Power Naval Limitation Treaty	1.
Four-Power Treaty	2.
Nine-Power Treaty	3.
Kellogg-Briand Pact	4.

California History-Social Science Standards

11.4 Students trace the rise of the United States to its role as a world power in the twentieth century.

11.5 Students analyze the major political, social, economic, technological, and cultural developments of the 1920s.

Focuses on: 11.4.5, 11.4.6, 11.5.1

The American Vision: Modern Times

Study Guide

Chapter 8, Section 3 *(continued)*

• Promoting Prosperity *(page 457)*

Presidents Harding and Coolidge opposed government regulation of business. Secretary of the Treasury Andrew Mellon was important in developing much of the economic policy of the United States during the 1920s. He believed that the government should apply business <u>principles</u> to its operations. He reduced government spending and cut the federal budget. A major expense of the United States at that time was the interest on the national debt. The national debt had increased by 1920 because of World War I costs. Mellon refinanced the debt to lower the interest. He also persuaded the Federal Reserve to lower interest rates as well. These steps helped reduce the debt.

Academic Vocabulary
principle: a system of thinking that follows a strict set of rules (p. 457)

Mellon also worked to reduce tax rates. He believed that lowering taxes would allow businesses and consumers to spend and invest their extra money. This would cause the economy to grow. He believed that as the economy grew, Americans would earn more money and the government would actually collect more taxes at the lower rate than it would if the tax rates were kept high. This idea is known as **supply-side economics.** By 1928 Congress drastically lowered the tax rates.

In addition to Mellon's policies, other government programs also helped business. Secretary of Commerce Herbert Hoover tried to balance government regulation with his <u>philosophy</u> of **cooperative individualism.** This idea encouraged manufacturers and distributors to form trade associations, which would voluntarily share information with the government.

Academic Vocabulary
philosophy: the general beliefs, concepts or attitudes of an individual (p. 458)

5. What were two important policies of Andrew Mellon's economic program?

_____

_____

_____

_____

_____

_____

Study Guide

Chapter 8, Section 3 (continued)

• Trade and Arms Control (page 458)

Before World War I, the United States owed more money to foreign investors than foreigners owed the United States. This situation was <u>reversed</u> by the end of the war. By the 1920s, the United States was the world's dominant economic power.

Academic Vocabulary

reversed: for a situation to be completely changed (p. 458)

After World War I, most Americans favored **isolationism.** They did not want the United States to become involved in foreign affairs. The nation, however, was too interconnected with other countries, both politically and economically, to go back to isolationism.

After the war, the U.S. allies had a difficult time repaying their war debts. They claimed that the tariffs the American government placed on European goods closed the United States to European imports, which slowed down Europe's economic recovery. The United States argued that American taxpayers should not have to assume the debts of others. They argued that European nations received extra territory as a result of the war, whereas the United States had gained nothing. They also pointed out that European nations were receiving reparations, or huge cash payments that Germany was required to pay as punishment for causing the war. The payments, however, were crippling the German economy.

The United States wanted the European economies to be stable. It wanted Europeans to be able to buy American exports and to repay their debts. In 1924 Charles G. Dawes, an American banker, negotiated an agreement with France, Britain, and Germany. Under the agreement, American banks would loan money to Germany to help it meet their reparation payments. At the same time, Britain and France would accept less in reparations while paying more on their war debts. The plan, however, actually put Britain, France, and Germany deeper into debt to American banks.

After the war, the major powers became involved in a naval arms race. To stop the arms race, the United States asked the representatives of eight nations to Washington to discuss disarmament. Secretary of State Charles Evans Hughes proposed a 10-year **moratorium,** or pause, on the building of major new warships. He also proposed a list of warships for each country to destroy.

The conference resulted in three agreements. In the Five-Power Naval Limitation Treaty, Britain, France, Italy, Japan, and the United States basically agreed to Secretary Hughes's proposals. Under the Four-Power Treaty, the United States, Japan, France, and Britain recognized each country's island possessions in the Pacific. In the Nine-Power Treaty, all participating countries guaranteed China's independence.

The conference, however, did not place a limit on land forces. It angered Japan because it required the Japanese to keep a smaller navy than the United States or Great Britain.

Study Guide

Chapter 8, Section 3 *(continued)*

The success of the Washington Conference led to the belief that nations could work together to negotiate agreements to end war altogether. U.S. Secretary of State Frank Kellogg and French Foreign Minister Aristide Briand proposed a treaty that banned war. The United States and 14 other nations signed the Kellogg-Briand Pact on August 27, 1928. The treaty stated that all signing nations agreed to abandon war and negotiate disputes peacefully.

6. Why was it not possible for the United States to go back to a policy of isolationism after World War I?

_____

_____

_____

_____

_____

Study Guide

Chapter 9, Section 1

For use with textbook pages 468–473

CAUSES OF THE DEPRESSION

CONTENT VOCABULARY

stock market   a system for buying and selling shares of companies *(page 470)*

bull market   a long period of rising stock prices *(page 470)*

margin   a way of buying stocks by paying only a small percent of the price of the stock and taking a loan from a stockbroker to pay the rest *(page 470)*

margin call   a demand by a broker for the investor to repay the loan at once *(page 470)*

speculation   buying shares, betting that the stock market will continue to climb, and then selling the stock to make money quickly *(page 471)*

installment   monthly payment made on a high-cost item *(page 473)*

DRAWING FROM EXPERIENCE

How important is the stock market to the U.S. economy today? How do Americans participate in the stock market?

In this section, you will learn about the stock market in the 1920s. You will also learn about the causes of the Great Depression.

ORGANIZING YOUR THOUGHTS

Use the cause-and-effect diagram below to help you take notes. Several situations led to the stock market crash. List these causes below.

California History-Social Science Standards

11.5 Students analyze the major political, social, economic, technological, and cultural developments of the 1920s.

11.6 Students analyze the different explanations for the Great Depression and how the New Deal fundamentally changed the role of the federal government.

Focuses on: 11.5.1, 11.6.1, 11.6.2

Causes	Effect

1. _____

2. _____

3. _____

4. _____

5. _____

6. _____

Stock Market Crashes

Study Guide

Chapter 9, Section 1 (continued)

READ TO LEARN

- ### The Election of 1928 (page 469)

In the 1928 presidential election, Herbert Hoover ran as the Republican nominee. The Democrats nominated Alfred E. Smith. Several issues determined the election results. Hoover supported Prohibition. Smith opposed the ban. Hoover was a Quaker, and Smith was a Roman Catholic, the first one ever to be nominated for president. Many Protestants believed that if a Catholic were elected president, the Pope would rule the White House. This belief damaged Smith's candidacy. Hoover and the Republicans were also given credit for the nation's prosperity during the 1920s. As a result, Hoover won in a landslide victory.

7. How did religion play a part in the 1928 presidential election?

_____

_____

_____

_____

_____

- ### The Long Bull Market (page 470)

After the election, stock prices continued to increase. The **stock market** was started as a system for buying and selling shares of companies. The late 1920s saw a **bull market,** or a long period of rising stock prices. As a result, many Americans began <u>investing</u> heavily in stocks. As the bull market continued, many investors began buying stocks on **margin.** They made a small cash down payment on the stock, and took out a loan from a stockbroker to pay for the rest of the stock. The stockbroker earned a commission on the sale and interest on the loan. Buying on margin was safe as long as the stock prices kept rising. However, a decrease in prices became a problem. To protect the loan, the stockbroker could issue a **margin call.** This was a demand for the investor to repay the loan. If prices started falling, many investors had to sell their stock quickly in order to be able to repay their loans.

Academic Vocabulary
invest: to put money into a company in order to gain a future financial reward (p. 470)

Before the late 1920s, the prices that investors paid for stocks had to do with the company's profits. If the company's profits rose, the stock price rose. If earnings decreased, the value of the stock decreased. However, in the late 1920s, new investors would buy a company's stock without regard to a company's earnings. Buyers hoped to make a quick profit and practiced **speculation.** Instead of investing in the future of the companies whose stock they bought, they were betting that the stock market would continue to climb and then sell the stock quickly to make money.

Study Guide

Chapter 9, Section 1 *(continued)*

8. Why did many investors buy stocks on speculation in the late 1920s?

_____

_____

_____

_____

_____

- ### The Great Crash *(page 471)*

By mid-1929 the stock market was running out of new customers, and stock prices stopped rising. Investors began selling off their holdings and prices decreased. Other investors sold their shares to pay the interest on the loans they took out from brokers, and prices decreased even more. On October 29, 1929, which became known as Black Tuesday, stock prices took their steepest dive. By mid-November stock prices had dropped by over one-third. Some $30 billion was lost, a <u>sum</u> roughly equal to the total wages earned by Americans in 1929. The stock market crash did not cause the Great Depression, but it prevented the economy from surviving other weaknesses.

Academic Vocabulary
sum: a specified amount of money (p. 471)

Banks also suffered as a result of the stock market crash. Many banks had lent money to stock speculators. They also had invested depositors' money in the stock market in hopes of getting higher returns. When stock prices fell, many banks lost money on their investments, and speculators could not repay their loans. The banks had to cut back on the number of loans they made. As a result, many people were not able to borrow as much money as they once did.

Many banks were forced to close because of their losses. People who had deposits in these banks lost all their savings. Many Americans began withdrawing their deposits from banks because they feared that the banks would collapse. This run on the banks caused many banks to collapse.

9. Why did many banks collapse in 1929?

_____

_____

_____

_____

_____

Study Guide

Chapter 9, Section 1 *(continued)*

- ## The Roots of the Great Depression *(page 472)*

The stock market crash alone did not cause the Great Depression. Other reasons also contributed to it. One major reason was overproduction of manufactured goods. Most Americans did not have enough money to buy all the goods that were made. During the 1920s, many Americans bought high-cost items, such as refrigerators, on the **installment** plan. People made a down payment and paid the rest of the price in monthly installments. Some people reached a point where they had to reduce their purchases in order to pay their debts. When sales slowed, manufacturers cut production and laid off employees. The slowdown in one industry affected other industries. This kind of chain <u>reaction</u> put more and more Americans out of work.

Another reason for the Great Depression was the fact that Americans were not selling many goods to foreign countries. During the 1920s, banks earned more money by making loans to speculators than by lending to foreign companies so that they could buy American goods. As a result, foreign companies bought less from the United States. In 1930 Congress passed the Hawley-Smoot Tariff. It raised the tax on many imports. Although it protected American manufacturers from foreign competition, it also damaged American sales to foreign countries. Americans began buying fewer imports, which led foreign countries to buy fewer American goods. American companies and farmers were hurt by this situation. The high tariff deepened the Great Depression.

The actions of the Federal Reserve also contributed to the Great Depression. Instead of raising interest rates to stop speculation buying, the Federal Reserve lowered rates. These lower rates encouraged banks to make risky loans. Lower interest rates generally mean the economy is growing. By lowering interest rates, the Federal Reserve misled many business leaders. They believed the economy was still growing, so they borrowed more money to expand their production. This led to overproduction at a time when sales were decreasing. When the Depression finally came, the companies had to cut their costs and lay off their workers. The increased unemployment damaged the economy even more.

Academic Vocabulary
reaction: the response to a stimulus (p. 473)

10. How did the Hawley-Smoot Tariff contribute to the Great Depression?

_____

_____

_____

_____

_____

Study Guide

Chapter 9, Section 2

For use with textbook pages 474–479

LIFE DURING THE DEPRESSION

CONTENT VOCABULARY

bailiff   court official *(page 475)*

shantytown   community formed on unused or public lands by newly homeless people *(page 475)*

Hooverville   name given to shantytowns *(page 475)*

hobo   an unemployed individual who wandered around the country *(page 476)*

Dust Bowl   the dried-up lands of the Great Plains that resulted from a severe drought *(page 476)*

soap opera   daytime radio shows that were sponsored by the makers of laundry soaps
(page 478)

DRAWING FROM EXPERIENCE

What images come to mind when you hear the words *Great Depression?* Where do you think these images come from?

The last section explained the causes of the Great Depression. This section describes how the Great Depression affected Americans.

> **California History-Social Science Standards**
>
> **11.6** Students analyze the different explanations for the Great Depression and how the New Deal fundamentally changed the role of the federal government.
>
> **Focuses on:** 11.6.3

ORGANIZING YOUR THOUGHTS

Use the diagram below to help you take notes. Art during the 1930s reflected the Depression. Describe how it did so in the diagram.

```
                    Art Reflects Depression
        ┌──────────────────┬──────────────────┐
    Painting            Writing           Photography
    1.                  2.                4.

                        3.
```

The American Vision: Modern Times

Study Guide

Chapter 9, Section 2 (continued)

• The Depression Worsens (page 475)

The Depression grew worse during President Hoover's administration. Thousands of banks <u>suspended</u> operations. Thousands of companies went out of business. Millions of Americans were unemployed. Many of the unemployed went hungry. They joined bread lines with their old <u>colleagues</u> to receive a free handout of food. They lined up outside soup kitchens. These were private charities set up to give poor people a meal.

Many people could not afford to pay their rent or mortgage and lost their homes. Those who could not or would not move were given an eviction notice. Court officials called **bailiffs** threw them and their belongings in the street. Many of these homeless people put up shacks on unused or public lands, forming communities called **shantytowns** throughout the country. Many called the shantytowns **Hoovervilles,** because they blamed President Hoover for their problems.

Many homeless and unemployed people began to wander around the country. Known as **hobos,** they often sneaked rides on railroad cars to get from place to place.

In addition to the Depression, farmers soon faced a new problem. For a long time, farmers on the Great Plains had plowed the soil. They uprooted the grasses that held the soil's moisture and planted wheat. When crop prices decreased in the 1920s, however, Midwestern farmers left many of their fields unplanted. In 1932 the Great Plains experienced a severe drought. The unplanted soil turned to dust. Much of the Plains became a **Dust Bowl.** The winds blew the dry soil, blackening the sky for hundreds of miles. As the drought continued, the number of dust storms increased. Many families packed their belongings into old cars or trucks and headed west to California, to find better opportunities. There most remained homeless and in poverty.

5. Why did many farmers in the Great Plains leave their land in the 1930s and head west?

_____

_____

_____

_____

_____

• Escaping the Depression (page 477)

Americans turned to entertainment to escape their situation, if only for a little while. Many went to the movies. Most often, Americans would see people on the screen who were happier and richer than they were. Comedies provided

Academic Vocabulary
suspend: to temporarily stop an operation (p. 475)
colleague: a person who works in the same, or similar, profession (p. 478)

Study Guide

Chapter 9, Section 2 (continued)

people with a way to escape their daily fears. Many European actors, such as Marlene Dietrich and Greta Garbo, became superstars. Americans also enjoyed cartoons. Walt Disney produced the first feature-length animated film. Even films that focused on the serious side of life were generally optimistic.

Americans also listened to the radio. They listened to the news broadcasts. They also enjoyed different kinds of programs. One of the most popular heroes on the radio shows was the Lone Ranger. Short daytime dramas were also popular and provided people with escapes. Some of these dramas were sponsored by the makers of laundry soaps and were nicknamed **soap operas.** Talking about the lives of radio characters provided Americans with a common ground.

6. What part did movies and radio shows play in Americans' lives during the Great Depression?

_____

_____

_____

_____

_____

- **The Depression in Art** (page 479)

Art and literature in the 1930s showed what life was like in the Depression. Painters such as Grant Wood showed traditional American values, particularly those of rural Americans in the Midwest and the South.

Novelists such as John Steinbeck wrote about the lives of people in the Depression. In *The Grapes of Wrath*, Steinbeck told the story of an Oklahoma farm family who fled the Dust Bowl to find a better life in California.

Some writers during the Depression influenced literary style. In a <u>technique</u> known as stream of consciousness, William Faulkner showed what his characters were thinking and feeling even before they spoke.

Magazines became popular during the Depression. Magazine photographers traveled throughout the nation taking pictures of life around them. Many of these photographs were printed in magazines, which became very successful.

Academic Vocabulary
technique: a method of achieving a desired task (p. 479)

7. What was the subject of John Steinbeck's *The Grapes of Wrath*?

_____

_____

_____

Study Guide

Chapter 9, Section 3

For use with textbook pages 482–487

HOOVER RESPONDS

CONTENT VOCABULARY

public works   government-financed building projects *(page 483)*

relief   money that went directly to people in poverty *(page 485)*

foreclose   to take possession of by creditors *(page 486)*

DRAWING FROM EXPERIENCE

For what issues have groups of people in the United States held demonstrations or protests in recent years? What issues do you think are important enough to demonstrate for?

The last section described how the Great Depression affected Americans. This section explains how President Hoover attempted to end the Depression.

> **California History-Social Science Standards**
>
> **11.6** Students analyze the different explanations for the Great Depression and how the New Deal fundamentally changed the role of the federal government.
>
> **Focuses on:** 11.6.3

ORGANIZING YOUR THOUGHTS

Use the chart below to help you take notes. During the 1930s, the government proposed several programs to help end the Depression. Explain what each listed program was designed to do.

Programs	How They Attempted to End the Depression
public works	1.
National Credit Corporation	2.
Reconstruction Finance Corporation	3.
Emergency Relief and Construction Act	4.

Study Guide

Chapter 9, Section 3 (continued)

• Promoting Recovery (page 483)

Although President Hoover tried to persuade Americans that things would improve quickly, he was very worried about the economy. He organized a series of conferences with the heads of banks and other businesses, government officials, and labor.

At first Hoover received a pledge from business to keep factories open and to stop cutting wages. However, by 1931 they did not keep their pledges. Hoover then tried to increase **public works,** which are government-financed building projects. He hoped that the jobs these government projects would create would make up for the construction jobs lost in private business. The jobs made up for only a small part of the jobs that were lost in the private sector. The only way the public works would have created many new jobs would have been to increase government spending for the public works projects. If the government raised taxes to get the money, it would take money away from consumers and it would hurt the struggling businesses. If the government kept taxes low and spent more money than it collected in taxes, it would have to borrow the money it needed from banks. This would leave less money for businesses and consumers who needed loans. Hoover believed that this deficit spending would delay an economic recovery.

In the 1930 congressional elections, Americans blamed the Republican Party for the economic problems. As a result, the Republicans lost their majority in the House of Representatives and narrowly held on to it in the Senate.

> **Academic Vocabulary**
>
> **series:** a number of events that come one after another (p. 483)

5. Why did President Hoover propose the creation of public works projects?

_____

_____

_____

_____

_____

• Pumping Money Into the Economy (page 484)

Hoover wanted to make sure that banks could make loans to businesses so that they could start producing and rehire workers. He tried to persuade the Federal Reserve Board to put more money into circulation, but the board refused. Hoover then set up the National Credit Corporation (NCC) in 1931. This was a voluntary lending organization. Hoover persuaded a number of New York bankers to contribute to the organization to create a pool of money. Troubled banks could draw from this pool so they could continue lending money in their communities. The contributions made to the pool were not enough to help the nation.

> **Academic Vocabulary**
>
> **community:** people with common characteristics living in the same area (p. 485)
>
> **contribute:** to give to a common cause (p. 485)

Study Guide

Chapter 9, Section 3 (continued)

By 1932 Hoover decided that the only way to provide money for borrowers was for the government to lend it. He asked Congress to set up the Reconstruction Finance Corporation (RFC) to make loans to banks, railroads, and farming institutions. The RFC made millions of dollars worth of loans. However, it did not loan enough money to meet the needs. As a result, the economy continued to decline.

Hoover did not want the government to participate in **relief**—money that went directly to poor families. He believed that that was the job of state and local governments. These governments, however, were running out of money. By 1932 Congress passed the Emergency Relief and Construction Act, which provided loans to states for direct relief. This program was also too late to stop the continuing decline of the economy.

6. What was the purpose of the National Credit Corporation?

_____

_____

_____

_____

_____

• **In an Angry Mood** (page 485)

By 1931 Americans were getting increasingly upset about the bad economy. In December 1932, crowds began to form rallies and "hunger marches." One such group marched in Washington, D.C., demanding that the government feed the hungry and tax the wealthy.

Farmers also protested. Farm prices sank so low that most farmers could not pay their mortgages. Between 1930 and 1934, creditors foreclosed on almost one million farms. They took over the farms and forced the families off the farms. Some farmers began to destroy their crops, hoping that reducing the supply of crops would help raise prices.

To thank American soldiers for serving in World War I, Congress set up a $1,000 bonus for each veteran to be distributed in 1945. However, in 1931 Congress debated a bill that would authorize early payment of the bonuses. By 1932 the veterans, many of whom were homeless, were in need of the bonuses. About 1,000 veterans, named the Bonus Army, set off on a march to Washington to lobby Congress to pass the bill. They lived in Hoovervilles around the capital. The number of veterans grew in a few weeks to almost 15,000. President Hoover refused to meet with them. The Senate voted the new bonus bill down. Many veterans began to leave to return home. Some of the marchers, however, stayed on since they had no jobs. Some moved to unoccupied buildings.

Study Guide

Chapter 9, Section 3 *(continued)*

President Hoover ordered the police to clear the buildings. One police officer panicked and fired into a crowd. Two veterans were killed. The government of Washington, D.C., then called in the army. The soldiers were told to enforce the order to clear the veterans from the buildings. The soldiers used tear gas on the veterans and burned down their shacks. The press covered these events, and the pictures upset the public. These images and the Depression affected Americans' opinion of President Hoover.

7. Why did veterans march on Washington, D.C., in 1932?

_____

_____

_____

_____

_____

Study Guide

Chapter 10, Section 1

For use with textbook pages 498–507

ROOSEVELT TAKES OFFICE

CONTENT VOCABULARY

gold standard   a situation in which one ounce of gold equaled a set number of dollars *(page 500)*

bank holiday   the closing of banks before bank runs could put them out of business *(page 501)*

fireside chats   radio talks that President Roosevelt held with the American people to let them know what he hoped to accomplish *(page 502)*

DRAWING FROM EXPERIENCE

What do you think was the most important thing President Roosevelt had to do to help end the Depression? Why do you think so?

This section discusses the background of President Franklin Roosevelt and the programs he initiated in his first 100 days in office.

> **California History-Social Science Standards**
>
> **11.6** Students analyze the different explanations for the Great Depression and how the New Deal fundamentally changed the role of the federal government.
>
> **Focuses on:** 11.6.2, 11.6.4

ORGANIZING YOUR THOUGHTS

Use the diagram below to help you take notes. Congress passed several laws and set up programs to help various aspects of the U.S. economy. Identify the laws and programs that were to help each of the areas listed in the diagram.

New Deal

Banks and Stock Market	Farms and Industry	Debt Relief	Spending and Relief Programs
1. _____	4. _____	6. _____	8. _____
2. _____	5. _____	7. _____	9. _____
3. _____			

Study Guide

Chapter 10, Section 1 (continued)

READ TO LEARN

• Roosevelt Takes Office *(page 449)*

In the 1932 presidential election, many voters were against President Hoover, who was the Republican nominee. Democrats chose New York Governor Franklin Delano Roosevelt. Roosevelt's programs for ending the Depression became known as the New Deal.

Franklin Roosevelt was a distant cousin of President Theodore Roosevelt. He was born into a wealthy New York family. He was educated at Harvard University and Columbia Law School. After leaving law school, Roosevelt went into politics. He started as a senator in the New York legislature. He was the assistant secretary of the navy under President Wilson. He ran as the vice-presidential candidate in the 1920 election, which he lost. A year later, Roosevelt came down with polio, a paralyzing disease. While recovering from the disease, Roosevelt depended on his wife Eleanor to keep his name in the forefront in the New York Democratic Party. By the mid-1920s, Roosevelt returned to politics and became governor of New York. His policies made him a very popular governor. He cut taxes for farmers. He reduced rates charged by public utilities. In 1931 Roosevelt convinced the New York legislature to create an agency that would help unemployed New Yorkers. Roosevelt's popularity led to his nomination for president in the 1932 election. Roosevelt's optimism gave Americans hope during hard times and contrasted sharply with Hoover's <u>apparent</u> failure to do anything effective. He was elected in November 1932.

Between Roosevelt's election and his inauguration, unemployment continued to rise. Bank runs increased. Some of the bank runs happened because people were afraid that Roosevelt would get rid of the gold standard and lower the value of the dollar to fight the Depression. At that time, one ounce of gold was equal to a set number of dollars. To lower the value of the dollar, the United States would have to stop exchanging dollars for gold. Investors who had deposits in American banks decided to take their money out of the banks and exchange it for gold before it lost its value. By March 1933, more than 4,000 banks had collapsed. In 38 states, governors declared bank holidays. They closed the remaining banks before people could make a run on them and put them out of business.

Academic Vocabulary
apparent: appearing to be fact as far as can be understood (p. 499)

10. Why did many states declare bank holidays in 1933?

_____

_____

_____

Study Guide

Chapter 10, Section 1 *(continued)*

- ### The Hundred Days Begins *(page 501)*

Once Roosevelt came into office, he began sending bill after bill to Congress. Between March 9 and June 16, 1933, which came to be known as the Hundred Days, Congress passed 15 major laws to deal with the economy. All these programs became known as the First New Deal.

Roosevelt was willing to experiment and try several approaches to solve the economic problems. Lacking a strong political <u>ideology</u>, he asked for advice from people from a variety of backgrounds. He chose advisers who disagreed with each other so that he could hear several different viewpoints. Roosevelt alone made the final decision.

Roosevelt's advisers made up three major groups. One group favored the policies of Theodore Roosevelt. They believed that government and business should work together to manage the economy. A second group distrusted big business. They blamed business leaders for causing the Depression. They wanted the government to run important parts of the economy. A third group supported President Wilson's policies. They believed that large trusts were to blame for the Depression. They also believed that the government had to bring back competition to the economy. These advisers wanted Roosevelt to break up big companies to allow competition.

> **Academic Vocabulary**
>
> **ideology:** a system of thought that is held by an individual, group, or culture (p. 501)

11. What did the advisers who blamed business leaders for causing the Depression want the government to do?

_____

_____

- ### Fixing the Banks and the Stock Market *(page 502)*

President Roosevelt realized he had to quickly restore people's confidence in the banks. He declared a national bank holiday and then called a special session of Congress. On the day Congress met, the House of Representatives passed the Emergency Banking Relief Act. The Senate approved it the same evening and Roosevelt signed it into law. It said that federal officials would check the nation's banks and give licenses to those that were financially sound.

On March 12, President Roosevelt addressed the American public by radio. This was the first of many **fireside chats.** He used them to let the American people know what he was trying to accomplish. In his first chat, Roosevelt told the people that it would be safe for them to put their money back into the banks. The next day there were more bank deposits than bank withdrawals.

Roosevelt's advisers pushed for regulations for the banks and the stock market. Roosevelt agreed and supported the Securities Act of 1933 and the Glass-Steagall Banking Act. The Securities Act required that companies that sold stocks and bonds had to provide complete and truthful information to their investors. The next year, Congress set up the Securities and Exchange Commission. The agency was to regulate the stock market and prevent fraud.

Study Guide

Chapter 10, Section 1 (continued)

The Glass-Steagall Act separated commercial banking from investment banking. Commercial banks handle everyday transactions, such as taking deposits and cashing checks. Under the Glass-Steagall Act, these banks could not risk depositors' money by speculating on the stock market. The act also created the Federal Deposit Insurance Corporation (FDIC). It provided government insurance on bank deposits up to a certain amount.

12. How did President Roosevelt communicate with the American people about what he was trying to accomplish?

_____

_____

- **Managing Farms and Industry** *(page 503)*

President Roosevelt believed that farmers and businesses were suffering because prices were too low and production was too high. Several of Roosevelt's advisers wanted to set up federal agencies to manage the economy.

Farmers had been hurt badly by the Depression. To help them, Roosevelt announced plans for a new farm program. He asked Congress to pass the Agricultural Adjustment Act. It was based on the idea that prices for farm products were low because farmers grew too much food. Under this act, the government would pay farmers not to grow certain crops and certain livestock. This program was administered by the Agricultural Adjustment Administration (AAA).

Over the next two years, farmers took out millions of acres of land from production. They received more than $1 billion in support payments. The program reached its goal. Surpluses fell by 1936, and food prices rose. Farm income also rose. However, not all farmers benefited. The large commercial farmers who grew one crop benefited more than small farmers who grew several crops. In addition, thousands of poor tenant farmers became homeless when landlords took fields out of production.

In June 1933, Roosevelt and Congress enacted the National Industrial Recovery Act (NIRA). The law suspended antitrust laws. It allowed business, labor, and government to cooperate in setting up voluntary rules for each industry. The rules were known as codes of fair competition. They set prices, set up minimum wages, and limited factories to two shifts per day. This was done to spread production to as many firms as possible. Some codes shortened hours in the hope of creating more jobs. Another code guaranteed workers the right to form unions. The National Recovery Administration (NRA) ran the program. Those business owners who signed code agreements received signs displaying the NRA's symbol. People were urged to buy goods only from companies that displayed the signs.

Study Guide

Chapter 10, Section 1 *(continued)*

The NRA had few successes. Small companies complained that large companies wrote codes that favored themselves. Many companies disliked price fixing, which limited competition. Employers disliked the idea of workers' rights to form unions. The codes were also difficult to enforce, and many companies ignored them. Industrial production actually fell after the organization was set up. The Supreme Court ruled that the NRA was unconstitutional in 1935. However, public support for it was lost before that.

13. What were the effects of the Agricultural Adjustment Act?

_____

_____

_____

• **Providing Debt Relief** *(page 504)*

Some people believed that debt was standing in the way of an economic recovery. Income was falling, so people had to use much of their money to pay their debts. They had little left over to buy goods. Many people cut back on their spending in order to pay their mortgages. As a result, President Roosevelt introduced several programs to help Americans with their debts.

Roosevelt asked Congress to set up the Home Owners' Loan Corporation (HOLC). It bought the mortgages from many homeowners who were behind in their payments. It then restructured the payments with lower interest rates. The HOLC only helped those people who still had jobs. It foreclosed on the property of those who did not have jobs and could no longer pay their mortgages. However, the HOLC did help refinance one out of every five mortgages on private homes in the United States.

Congress also set up the Farm Credit Administration (FCA) to help farmers refinance their mortgages. The loans helped many farmers keep their land. However, giving loans to poor farmers meant that little money was left to loan to more efficient businesses in the economy.

14. What programs did Congress set up to help Americans pay their debts?

_____

_____

_____

• **Spending and Relief Programs** *(page 505)*

Although some of Roosevelt's advisers believed that low prices and debt caused the Great Depression, others believed that the <u>fundamental</u> cause was not buying enough to get the economy going. These advisers believed that the

Academic Vocabulary
fundamental: being of central importance (p. 505)

Study Guide

Chapter 10, Section 1 (continued)

best way to get out of the Depression was to find a way to provide money for people. To do this, Roosevelt asked Congress to set up government agencies that would organize work programs for the unemployed.

One such relief program was the Civilian Conservation Corps (CCC). Starting in 1933, it employed young men 18 to 25 years of age to work under the supervision of the national forestry service. They planted trees, fought fires, and built reservoirs. Men lived in camps near their work areas and earned about $30 a month. By the time the CCC closed down in 1942, it had provided outdoor work to about three million men.

Congress set up the Federal Emergency Relief Administration (FERA). This agency provided federal money to state and local agencies to pay for their relief projects. The Public Works Administration (PWA), set up in June 1933, was a federal relief agency. To put the many unemployed construction workers back to work, the PWA set up a series of construction projects. The projects included building and improving highways, dams, sewer systems, and waterworks. The PWA did not hire workers directly. Instead, it gave contracts to construction companies. The PWA did insist that contractors hire African Americans, thereby breaking down racial barriers in the construction industry.

The Civil Works Administration (CWA) hired workers directly and put them on the federal government's payroll. In the winter of 1933, the CWA had employed four million people. They built airports, roads, schools, and playgrounds. The CWA spent nearly $1 billion in just five months. Although the CWA helped many people get through the winter, President Roosevelt was concerned about how quickly it spent money. He did not want people to get used to the federal government providing them with jobs. As a result, he ordered the CWA to shut down and to fire the four million workers it had hired.

The programs of the New Deal did not restore the economy. However, they did inspire Americans with hope and restored their faith in the country.

15. How did the PWA hire workers?

_____

_____

_____

_____

_____

Study Guide

Chapter 10, Section 2

For use with textbook pages 510–517

THE SECOND NEW DEAL

CONTENT VOCABULARY

deficit spending   borrowing money to pay for programs *(page 511)*

binding arbitration   a process in a dispute in which a neutral party would listen to both sides and decide the issues *(page 515)*

sit-down strike   a protest action in which workers stopped working but refused to leave the factory *(page 515)*

DRAWING FROM EXPERIENCE

When you get your paycheck, some of the money you earn has been taken out for income tax. An additional amount has been removed for Social Security. President Roosevelt initiated the Social Security program. The last section discussed the programs set up under the First New Deal. This section discusses President Roosevelt's programs in the Second New Deal.

California History-Social Science Standards

11.6 Students analyze the different explanations for the Great Depression and how the New Deal fundamentally changed the role of the federal government.

Focuses on: 11.6.4, 11.6.5

ORGANIZING YOUR THOUGHTS

Use the diagram below to help you take notes. In 1935 President Roosevelt set up the Second New Deal—a series of new programs to help the economy recover. In the diagram, list the laws and programs in the Second New Deal and explain the purpose of each.

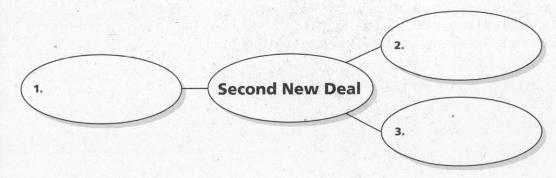

Study Guide

Chapter 10, Section 2 (continued)

- **Challenges to the New Deal** (page 511)

    After his first two years in office, Roosevelt had not been able to end the Depression. Opposition to his policies began to grow. People from both the right and the left of the political spectrum opposed them. The right opposed them because Roosevelt had begun **deficit spending** to pay for his programs. He ended the balanced budget and began borrowing money to pay for his programs. In 1934 anti-New Deal politicians and business leaders joined together to form the American Liberty League. They organized to oppose the New Deal.

    Challenges also came from the left, where people believed that Roosevelt had not gone far enough. They wanted the government to be involved even more in shifting wealth from the rich to middle-income and poor Americans. One of Roosevelt's biggest opponents was Huey Long, a senator from Louisiana. As governor of Louisiana, he had fought for the poor. He established a reputation for attacking the rich. Long's popularity increased. Many people believed that if Long ran for president, he would win several million votes. This would be enough to give Republicans the win.

    Another New Deal opponent from the left was Father Charles Coughlin, a Catholic priest in Detroit. He called for huge taxes on the wealthy. He established an organization that supported Huey Long.

    Dr. Francis Townsend was also an opponent from the left. He proposed that the federal government pay every citizen over age 60 a pension of $200 per month. Those who received the pension would have to spend their entire pension check each month. Townsend believed the plan would increase spending, remove people from the labor force, and free up jobs for the unemployed. Townsend's plan had many supporters, particularly the elderly. If his supporters joined the supporters of Long and Coughlin, there was a possibility that they would draw enough votes away from Roosevelt to stop him from being re-elected in 1936.

    4. Why did the left oppose President Roosevelt's policies?

    _____

    _____

    _____

    _____

    _____

The American Vision: Modern Times

Study Guide

Chapter 10, Section 2 *(continued)*

• Launching the Second New Deal *(page 513)*

President Roosevelt knew that he might lose political support from both the left and the right. He also knew that the New Deal had not improved the nation's economy. As a result, in 1935 he began a series of programs called the Second New Deal, which he hoped would provide an economic recovery.

In January 1935, Roosevelt asked Congress for funds to provide work relief and to increase jobs. Much of the money would be given to the Works Progress Administration (WPA), a new federal agency. Under the WPA, 8.5 million workers built miles of highways, roads, public buildings, and parks. The WPA also <u>financed</u> artists and writers. They created murals and sculptures to decorate the walls and halls of public buildings. Musicians set up city symphonies.

> **Academic Vocabulary**
>
> **finance:** to provide money for a project (p. 513)

Because of opposition to Roosevelt's programs, the bill that created the WPA did not pass in Congress until April 1935. Then in May 1935, the Supreme Court struck down the National Industrial Recovery Act. It ruled that the NIRA codes were unconstitutional. The President now knew that he had to introduce a new set of programs to get the voters' support. He called congressional leaders to the White House and told them they could not go home until Congress passed his new programs.

5. Why did the Supreme Court strike down the National Industrial Recovery Act?

_____

_____

_____

_____

_____

• The Rise of Industrial Unions *(page 514)*

When the Supreme Court ruled against the NIRA, it also struck down the part of the law that protected the right to form unions. President Roosevelt and others knew that the labor vote was important in the 1936 election. They also believed that unions could help end the Depression. They believed that higher union wages would let workers spend more money <u>thereby</u> boosting the economy. Opponents believed that high wages forced companies to charge higher prices and to hire fewer workers.

> **Academic Vocabulary**
>
> **thereby:** to be connected with or in reference to (p. 514)

In July 1935, Congress passed the National Labor Relations Act, also called the Wagner Act. It guaranteed workers the right to form unions and to collective bargaining. The law set up the National Labor Relations Board (NLRB). It organized factory elections by secret ballot to determine whether workers wanted a union. It also certified successful unions. The law set up a way that dissatisfied union members could take their complaints to **binding arbitration.** In this process, a neutral party would listen to both sides and decide the issues.

Study Guide

Chapter 10, Section 2 *(continued)*

By the mid-1930s, union activity increased. The United Mine Workers union began working with other unions to organize workers in industries where there were no unions. They formed the Committee for Industrial Organization (CIO) in 1935. The union set out to organize industrial unions. These unions included all workers in a particular industry—both skilled and unskilled. The CIO started by focusing on the steel and automobile industries, where workers were not yet organized.

When two union men were demoted at a General Motors (GM) plant in Cleveland, Ohio, 135 workers sat down and started a strike. They stopped working but refused to leave the factory. Then four days later the workers in the Flint, Michigan, plant started their own **sit-down strike.** Workers at other GM plants also went on strike.

Violence broke out in Flint between the police and striking workers. In the end, however, the company gave in and recognized the CIO's United Auto Workers (UAW). The UAW became one of the most powerful unions in the nation.

The United States Steel Corporation did not want to have the same experiences that GM had. It recognized the CIO's United Steelworkers of America. The union won a 40-hour workweek and a 10-percent pay raise.

By 1939 total union membership tripled. In 1938 the CIO changed its name to the Congress of Industrial Organizations. It became a federation of industrial unions.

6. What kind of union was the Committee for Industrial Organization?

_____

_____

_____

_____

_____

• **The Social Security Act** *(page 516)*

In August 1935, Congress passed the Social Security Act. Its goal was to provide some security for the elderly and for unemployed workers. Under this act, workers received benefits because they paid premiums. It also provided welfare payments to other needy people. The <u>crucial</u> part of Social Security was the monthly retirement benefit. People collected this benefit when they stopped working at age 65. Another part of Social Security was unemployment insurance, in which unemployed workers would receive a temporary income while looking for new jobs.

Academic Vocabulary
crucial: something considered important or essential (p. 516)

Study Guide

Chapter 10, Section 2 (continued)

Although Social Security helped many people, it left out farm and domestic workers. About 65 percent of all African American workers in the 1930s fell into these two groups of workers. However, Social Security set the principle that the federal government should be responsible for people who, through no fault of their own, were unable to work.

7. What was the goal of the Social Security Act?

_____

_____

_____

_____

_____

Study Guide

Chapter 10, Section 3

For use with textbook pages 520–525

THE NEW DEAL COALITION

CONTENT VOCABULARY

broker state   a government whose role includes mediating between competing groups
(page 525)

safety net   safeguards and relief programs that protected Americans against economic disasters
(page 525)

DRAWING FROM EXPERIENCE

How does the government today influence the nation's economy? What other areas is the government involved in?

The last section described the programs of the Second New Deal. This section describes how the New Deal affected Americans.

> **California History-Social Science Standards**
>
> **11.6** Students analyze the different explanations for the Great Depression and how the New Deal fundamentally changed the role of the federal government.
>
> **Focuses on:** 11.6.4, 11.6.5

ORGANIZING YOUR THOUGHTS

Use the chart below to help you take notes. Fewer New Deal programs were established during Roosevelt's second term. Describe the purpose of each of the programs listed in the chart.

National Housing Act	1.
Farm Security Administration	2.
Fair Labor Standards Act	3.

READ TO LEARN

- **Roosevelt's Second Term** *(page 521)*

By 1936 most African American voters had switched their support to the Democratic Party because of the New Deal. Roosevelt <u>demonstrated</u> his support of African Americans and women during his second term. Roosevelt appointed a number of African Americans to positions in his administration. He also tried to make sure that relief programs included African Americans. Roosevelt appointed the first woman to a cabinet position. Frances Perkins

> **Academic Vocabulary**
>
> **demonstrate:** to prove, or make clear, your beliefs (p. 521)

168

Study Guide

Chapter 10, Section 3 (continued)

became the Secretary of Labor. Roosevelt also appointed many women to lower-level jobs in the federal government.

In the 1936 election, the Republicans nominated Kansas Governor Alfred Landon. His campaign attacked the New Deal as violating the basic ideals of the American system. However, the New Deal was very popular with Americans. Roosevelt won the election by a landslide.

The Supreme Court saw some of the new Deal's programs as unconstitutional. It declared the Agricultural Adjustment Act unconstitutional in 1936. Other programs seemed likely to be struck down as well. Roosevelt was upset that a few justices might block his programs. He decided to change the balance of the Supreme Court. He sent a bill to Congress to increase the number of justices. If any justice had served for 10 years and did not retire within 6 months after reaching 70, the president could name an additional justice to the Court. This would allow Roosevelt to appoint as many as six new justices. This was referred to as the court-packing plan. Roosevelt's plan made it look as if he was trying to interfere with the separation of powers and with the Supreme Court's independence.

The issue split the Democratic Party. Southern Democrats feared that the plan would put justices on the Court who would overturn segregation. African Americans feared that a future president might pack the Court with justices who were against civil rights. Many Americans believed the plan would make the president too powerful.

Roosevelt's actions did seem to force the Supreme Court to back down. It upheld the Wagner Act and the Social Security Act as constitutional. The Senate quietly killed the court-packing bill. However, the plan hurt Roosevelt's reputation. It also encouraged conservative Democrats in Congress to work with Republicans to oppose further New Deal policies.

Roosevelt experienced another setback in late 1937, when unemployment dramatically increased. Roosevelt decided that although unemployment was high, it was time to balance the budget. He was concerned about too much debt, so he ordered the WPA and the PWA to be cut considerably. However, he cut spending just as the first Social Security payments removed $2 billion from the economy. As a result, the economy declined. By the end of 1937, two million people had been thrown out of work.

The recession led to a debate among Roosevelt's advisers about what to do. Secretary of the Treasury Henry Morgenthau wanted to balance the budget and cut spending. However, Harry Hopkins, the head of the WPA, and Harold Ickes, the head of the PWA, disagreed with Morgenthau. They wanted more government spending. They pointed to Keynesianism—a theory proposed by British economist John Maynard Keynes. This theory said that during a recession the government should spend heavily, even go into debt, in order to jump-start the economy. According to Keynesianism, Roosevelt did

Study Guide

Chapter 10, Section 3 (continued)

the wrong thing when he cut back programs in 1937. Many critics, however, said that the recession proved that people were becoming too dependent on government spending. Roosevelt was worried that they might be right. However, in 1938 he decided to ask Congress to provide more funds for the PWA and WPA.

4. What did supporters of Keynesianism believe President Roosevelt should do to stop the recession in 1937?

_____

_____

_____

_____

- **The Last New Deal Reforms** (page 523)

In his second term, President Roosevelt wanted to provide better housing for the poor. In 1937 the National Housing Act set up the United States Housing Authority. It received $500 million to subsidize loans for builders to buy blocks of slums and build low-cost housing.

Many tenant farmers were hurt when farmers were paid to take land out of production to increase food prices. Many tenant farmers left farming. To stop this, Congress set up the Farm Security Administration. It gave loans to tenants so they could buy farms.

The Fair Labor Standards Act of 1938 provided more protection for workers. It also abolished child labor and set up a 40-hour workweek to come into effect within three years.

In the congressional election of 1938, Republicans won many seats in Congress. Together with conservative Democrats, they began blocking New Deal legislation. By 1939 the New Deal era had ended.

5. How did the congressional elections of 1938 affect New Deal legislation?

_____

_____

_____

- **The Legacy of the New Deal** (page 525)

The New Deal resulted in business leaders, farmers, workers, and consumers all looking to government to protect their interests. The Supreme Court helped <u>enhance</u> the government's ability to take on this role through two rulings. The rulings increased federal power over the economy. It allowed

Academic Vocabulary
enhance: to improve or increase (p. 523)

Study Guide

Chapter 10, Section 3 *(continued)*

the government to <u>mediate</u> between competing groups. As a mediator, the New Deal set up what is called a **broker state,** or working out conflicts among different interests. It is a role that has continued to today.

The biggest change brought about by the New Deal was the Americans' view of government. The New Deal programs had created a kind of **safety net** for average Americans. Safeguards and relief programs protected them against economic disasters. By the time Roosevelt's administration ended, most Americans believed that the government had a duty to keep the safety net.

Academic Vocabulary
mediate: an attempt to resolve conflict between hostile people or groups (p. 525)

6. How did Supreme Court rulings affect the federal government?

_____

_____

_____

_____

_____

Study Guide

Chapter 11, Section 1

For use with textbook pages 536–541

AMERICA AND THE WORLD

CONTENT VOCABULARY

fascism   a kind of aggressive nationalism *(page 537)*

internationalism   the idea that trade between nations creates prosperity and helps to prevent war *(page 540)*

DRAWING FROM EXPERIENCE

What decision did the Treaty of Versailles, which ended World War I, make regarding the treatment of Germany? How do you think the decision affected Germany?

In this section, you will learn about the rise of dictatorships in Europe and Asia. You will also learn why Americans supported isolationism in the 1930s.

> **California History-Social Science Standards**
>
> **11.7** Students analyze America's participation in World War II.
>
> **Focuses on:** 11.7.1, 11.7.4

ORGANIZING YOUR THOUGHTS

Use the diagram below to help you take notes. Dictatorships were established in several countries after World War I. List the countries and the dictators in the diagram.

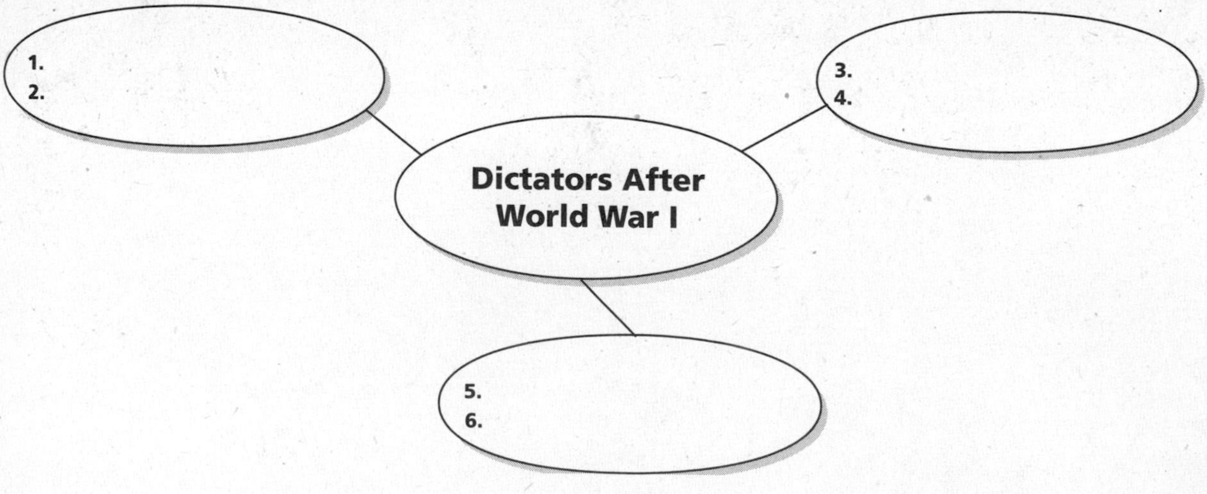

1.
2.

3.
4.

Dictators After World War I

5.
6.

Study Guide

Chapter 11, Section 1 *(continued)*

• The Rise of Dictators *(page 537)*

The terms of the peace treaty that ended World War I and the economic depression contributed to the rise of dictatorships in Europe and Asia. In Italy, Benito Mussolini founded Italy's Fascist Party. **Fascism** was a kind of aggressive nationalism. Fascists believed that the nation was more important than the individual. They believed that to be strong, a nation needed a strong government led by a dictator to <u>impose</u> order on society. Fascists also believed that a nation became strong by expanding its territory and building up its military. Fascists were anti-Communist. Many Europeans feared that Communists were trying to bring down their governments. Fascists played on these fears.

Academic Vocabulary
impose: to establish authority by force (p. 537)

Mussolini marched on Rome in 1922. He claimed that he was coming to defend Italy against a Communist revolution. Conservative leaders of the Italian parliament persuaded the king to appoint Mussolini as the premier and head of the government. Once Mussolini took over, he quickly set up a dictatorship. He was supported by business leaders, landowners, and the Roman Catholic Church.

After the Russian Revolution began in 1917, the Bolshevik Party, led by Vladimir Lenin, set up Communist governments throughout the Russian empire. They renamed these territories the Union of Soviet Socialist Republics (USSR). To control these territories, the Communists set up a one-party rule. They suppressed individual rights. They punished those who opposed them. Joseph Stalin became the Soviet leader by 1926, two years after Lenin died. Stalin started industrialization in the Soviet Union. He also caused the death of 8 to 10 million people who opposed the Communist policies.

In Germany, Adolf Hitler opposed communism. He admired Mussolini. He hated the Allies for their treatment of Germany after World War I. Germany's condition after the war led to the start of many new political parties. One such party was the National Socialist German Workers' Party, or the Nazi Party. The party was anti-Communist and nationalistic. Hitler was one of the first members of the party.

Hitler wrote his autobiography, entitled *Mein Kampf*, in which he called for the unification of all Germans under one government. He claimed that certain Germans, especially blond, blue-eyed ones, were part of a "master race" called Aryans. He believed these Germans needed more living space. Therefore, he wanted Germany to expand east into Poland and Russia. Hitler believed that the people of Eastern Europe were part of an inferior race. Hitler's prejudice was especially directed toward Jews. He believed that they were responsible for many of the world's, including Germany's, problems.

Hitler worked to have Nazis elected to Germany's parliament. Many Germans voted for Nazis, hoping that they might lead them out of the Great Depression that struck Germany. By 1932 the Nazis were the largest party in

Study Guide

Chapter 11, Section 1 (continued)

the German Parliament. Many German leaders supported Hitler and his nationalism. In 1933 they appointed him chancellor, or prime minister. After Hitler took office, he called for new elections. He ordered the police to crack down on the Communist Party and to intimidate voters. After the elections, the Nazi-dominated Parliament gave Hitler the powers of a dictator. Hitler then became president, which gave him control of the army.

In Japan, the economy was suffering. Japan had to import nearly all the resources it needed to make goods. The country did not make enough money from its exports to pay for the imports it needed. The Depression made the situation even worse. Many military leaders blamed the poor economy on the corrupt politicians. They believed that the only way for Japan to get the resources it needed was to seize territory. They looked to Manchuria, a province in northern China, which was rich in resources. A group of military officers decided to act alone and invade Manchuria. The prime minister of Japan wanted to end the invasion, but he was assassinated by Japanese officers. The Japanese military was now in control.

7. What situations in Germany and Japan led to the rise of dictatorships there?

_____

_____

_____

_____

_____

- ## America Turns to Neutrality (page 539)

After World War I, many Americans supported isolationism. They believed that the United States should stay out of international commitments that could bring the United States into a war. Support for isolationism became even stronger when many European nations announced that they could not repay money that they had borrowed during World War I. Then several books appeared, arguing that the arms manufacturers had tricked the United States into entering World War I. In 1934 Senator Gerald P. Nye of North Dakota had held hearings to <u>investigate</u> how involved the United States was. The Nye Committee investigated the huge profits that arms factories had made during the war. This gave the impression that these manufacturers did influence the United States to go to war. In response, Congress passed the Neutrality Act of 1935, which made it illegal for Americans to sell arms to any country at war.

The Spanish <u>Civil</u> War started in 1936. It was a conflict between the Communist government there and a group of Fascist rebels. The Soviet Union helped the Spanish government. Germany and Italy helped the Fascist rebels. In the same year, Germany and Italy signed an agreement to cooperate on

Academic Vocabulary
investigate: to systematically examine and make an official report (p. 540)
civil: relating to the citizens of a certain state or country (p. 540)

Study Guide

Chapter 11, Section 1 *(continued)*

several international issues. This relationship was referred to as the Rome-Berlin Axis. Japan joined Germany and Italy. The three nations became known as the Axis Powers.

The United States passed the Neutrality Act of 1937. It continued to ban the sale of arms. It also required that countries at war buy nonmilitary supplies on a "cash-and-carry" basis. Countries that needed supplies had to send their own ships to pick up the supplies, and they had to pay cash. The United States wanted to avoid a situation that had helped bring it into World War I.

President Roosevelt knew that ending the Depression was his first priority. However, he was not an isolationist. Instead, he supported **internationalism.** This was the belief that trade between nations creates prosperity and helps to prevent war. Roosevelt knew that isolationism was too strong to resist, however, so he did not veto the Neutrality Acts.

In July 1937, Japan launched a full-scale attack on China. Roosevelt decided to help the Chinese. Because neither China nor Japan had actually declared war, Roosevelt claimed that the Neutrality Act of 1937 did not apply. He ordered the sale of weapons to China. Yet Americans still wanted nothing to do with another war.

8. Why did President Roosevelt not veto the Neutrality Acts?

_____

_____

_____

_____

Study Guide

Chapter 11, Section 2

For use with textbook pages 542–548

WORLD WAR II BEGINS

CONTENT VOCABULARY

appeasement   giving concessions in exchange for peace *(page 544)*

blitzkrieg   lightning war *(page 545)*

DRAWING FROM EXPERIENCE

Why do you think many Americans wanted the United States to follow a policy of isolationism? Do you think that was possible when dictators came to power in several countries of the world? Why or why not?

The last section described the rise of dictatorships in Europe and Asia after World War I. This section discusses the events that led to the beginning of World War II.

California History-Social Science Standards
11.7 Students analyze America's participation in World War II.
Focuses on: 11.7.1, 11.7.4, 11.7.6

ORGANIZING YOUR THOUGHTS

Use the diagram below to help you take notes. Adolf Hitler made continuous demands for territory. Britain and France met some of the demands in an effort to avoid war. In the diagram, list Hitler's demands in the order in which they occurred, starting in 1937.

```
            Hitler's Demands
                  |
                  v
  1. _____

                  |
                  v
  2. _____

                  |
                  v
  3. _____
```

Study Guide

Chapter 11, Section 2 *(continued)*

READ TO LEARN

- ## "Peace in Our Time" *(page 543)*

European leaders did not try to stop Hitler. They thought that if they gave in to his demands, they would be able to avoid another war. They also thought that Hitler's idea that all German-speaking regions of Europe be united with Germany was reasonable. They also believed that if the Nazi <u>regime</u> received more territory, they would be more interested in peace.

Hitler wanted Austria and Czechoslovakia. He believed these territories would provide Germany with food and soldiers. Hitler threatened to invade Austria unless Austrian Nazis were given important government posts. The Austrian chancellor decided to put the possibility of Austrian unification with Germany to a vote. Hitler feared the results, so he sent troops into Austria and announced the *Anschluss,* or unification, of Austria and Germany.

Hitler then announced that he wanted an area of Czechoslovakia that had many German-speaking people. Unlike Austria, which had a common culture and language with Germany, people in Czechoslovakia spoke many different languages. <u>Furthermore</u>, Czechoslovakia was also allied with the Soviet Union and France. The Czechs resisted Germany's demands for a portion of their nation. To help stop another war, in September 1938, Britain, France, Italy, and Germany sent representatives to a meeting in Munich, Germany, to decide what to do about Czechoslovakia. At the meeting, Britain and France agreed to Hitler's demands. This policy became known as **appeasement,** or giving concessions in exchange for peace. They believed that if they gave Hitler what he wanted, war could be avoided. Germany violated the agreement in March 1939, when German troops marched into Czechoslovakia.

Hitler then demanded Poland. The British and French knew that appeasement had failed. In May 1939, Hitler ordered the German army to prepare to invade Poland. He then began negotiations with the USSR, because he did not want to have to fight the Soviets if he was going to have to fight Britain and France. In August 1939, Germany and the USSR signed the nonaggression pact. Britain and France believed that Hitler made the deal with the USSR to free himself to fight a war against them and Poland. They did not know that the nonaggression pact included a deal between Germany and the USSR to divide Poland between them.

Academic Vocabulary
regime: a form of government (p. 543)

Academic Vocabulary
furthermore: in addition (p. 543)

4. Why did Britain and France agree to a policy of appeasement toward Hitler?

_____

_____

_____

_____

_____

Study Guide

Chapter 11, Section 2 (continued)

- ### The War Begins (*page 544*)

Germany invaded Poland on September 1, 1939. It invaded Poland from the west, and the Soviets invaded it from the east. Hitler assumed that Britain and France would use appeasement toward him as they did before. However, on September 3, Britain and France declared war on Germany. World War II had started.

The Germans used a new type of warfare called **blitzkrieg,** or lightning war. This type of warfare used large numbers of tanks to break through and encircle enemy positions. In addition, waves of aircraft bombed enemy positions. Blitzkrieg depended on radios to coordinate tanks and aircraft. The Polish army was not able to defend itself against the German attack. By October 5, 1939, the Polish army had been defeated.

Countries in western Europe were waiting for the Germans to attack. After World War I, France had built a line of concrete bunkers and fortifications called the Maginot Line along the German border. Rather than attacking the Germans, the French waited behind the Maginot Line for the Germans to arrive.

After invading Poland, Germany attacked Norway and Denmark on April 9, 1940, and controlled both nations within a month. Hitler then turned his attention on France. He decided to go around the Maginot Line by starting a blitzkrieg against Belgium, the Netherlands, and Luxembourg. The British and French forces moved north into Belgium. The Germans, however, sent their troops through the mountains in Luxembourg and eastern Belgium. The French did not think the Germans could get their tanks through the mountains. As a result, they left few troops to defend that area. The Germans easily got through and moved west across northern France to the English Channel. The British and French forces could not move into France quickly enough. They were stuck in Belgium.

After the Allied troops were trapped in Belgium, Germans moved toward the English Channel. The Germans had captured all but one port, Dunkirk, in northern France near Belgium. As German forces moved close to Dunkirk, Hitler surprisingly ordered them to stop. This gave the British time to evacuate. About 850 ships headed to Dunkirk from England. By June 4, about 338,000 British and French troops had been evacuated. However, most of the British army's equipment remained at Dunkirk. This meant that it would almost be impossible to stop Hitler if he invaded Britain.

On June 22, 1940, France surrendered to Hitler. Germany then installed a puppet government in the town of Vichy, France, to govern France. The Germans believed it would be easy to take Britain.

Study Guide

Chapter 11, Section 2 *(continued)*

5. Why did the evacuation at Dunkirk make it almost impossible for Britain to defend itself against Hitler?

_____

_____

_____

_____

_____

- ### Britain Remains Defiant *(page 547)*

Hitler expected Britain to surrender just as France did. For British prime minister Winston Churchill, surrender was not an option. When Hitler realized that Britain would not surrender, he prepared to invade. Getting across the English Channel was a problem for Germany, however. Germany had few transport ships, so it would first have to defeat the British air force. In June 1940, the German air force, called the *Luftwaffe*, began to attack British ships in the English Channel. Then in August, Germany started an all-out air attack to destroy the British Royal Air Force. This battle lasted into October and became known as the Battle of Britain.

On August 23, German airplanes bombed London. This attack on civilians angered the British, who responded by bombing Berlin. Hitler responded by stopping the attacks on British military targets and concentrating them on London itself. Hitler wanted to terrorize the British people into surrendering. The British people did not do so and hid in the subways when the bombers appeared.

The British Royal Air Force was greatly outnumbered, but it had an advantage. It had developed the use of radar. As a result, the British were able to detect incoming German planes and to intercept them. They inflicted more damage on the Germans than they endured. On October 12, 1940, Hitler canceled his plans to invade Britain. He had not <u>anticipated</u> the bravery of the British people.

Academic Vocabulary
anticipate: to predict an action before it happens (p. 547)

6. What helped Britain prevent a German invasion?

_____

_____

_____

_____

_____

Study Guide

Chapter 11, Section 3

For use with textbook pages 549–555

THE HOLOCAUST

CONTENT VOCABULARY

Holocaust   the mass killing of Jews and other civilians carried out by the Nazi government before and during World War II *(page 550)*

concentration camps   detention centers set up by Nazis to which Jews were taken *(page 553)*

extermination camps   places attached to concentration camps in which Jews were executed in massive gas chambers *(page 554)*

DRAWING FROM EXPERIENCE

What is the Holocaust? Have you seen movies or read books about the Holocaust? What was the focus of the movie or the book?

The last section described the events that led to the beginning of World War II. This section discusses Germany's treatment of the Jews and the Holocaust.

> **California History-Social Science Standards**
>
> **11.7** Students analyze America's participation in World War II.
>
> **Focuses on:** 11.7.5, 11.7.6

ORGANIZING YOUR THOUGHTS

Use the chart below to help you take notes. Historians have considered several factors that could have led to an event such as the Holocaust to occur. List these factors in the chart.

Factors That Contributed to the Holocaust
1.
2.
3.
4.
5.
6.

Study Guide

Chapter 11, Section 3 (continued)

• Nazi Persecution of the Jews (page 550)

Millions of Jews suffered terrible persecutions before and during World War II. During the **Holocaust,** the catastrophe that devastated Europe's Jews, the Nazis killed nearly 6 million Jews. They also killed millions of other people from groups that they considered inferior. The Hebrew term for the Holocaust is Shoah, meaning "catastrophe." It is often used specifically to refer to the Nazi campaign to exterminate the Jews during World War II.

In Germany, the Nazis swiftly <u>implemented</u> the racial policies that Hitler had outlined in his book *Mein Kampf.* The Nazis persecuted anyone who opposed them, as well as disabled people, Gypsies, homosexuals, and Slavic peoples. However, their hatred focused most on the Jews. In September 1935, the Nazis set up the Nuremberg Laws. These took citizenship away from the Jewish Germans and banned marriage between Jews and other Germans. Another law defined a Jew as a person with at least one Jewish grandparent and did not allow Jews to hold public office or vote. Passports of Jews were marked with a red "J" to clearly identify them as Jewish. Jews were <u>prohibited</u> from working as journalists, farmers, teachers, lawyers, and doctors and from operating businesses. With no income, life became very difficult for Jews in Germany. Many Jews chose to stay in Germany during the early years of Nazi rule. They did not want to give up the lives they had built there.

On November 7, 1938, a Jewish refugee shot and killed a German diplomat in Paris. He was upset about the 10,000 Jews, including his father, being deported from Germany to Poland and wanted revenge. Hitler retaliated by staging attacks against the Jews. The night of November 9, 1938, saw anti-Jewish violence across Germany and Austria. The night came to be called *Kristallnacht*, or "night of broken glass." It was called that because broken glass littered the streets afterward. Many Jews were killed and hundreds were injured. After that night, the Gestapo, the government's secret police, arrested at least 20,000 wealthy Jews. They let them go only if they agreed to leave Germany and give up all their possessions.

Many Jews decided to leave Germany and flee to the United States. By 1939 about 350,000 Jews had escaped Germany. However, there was a backlog of visa applications from Jews trying to leave Germany. As a result, millions of Jews remained trapped in Nazi-dominated Europe.

Jewish immigration to the United States was hampered by several factors. Nazis did not allow Jews to take more than about four dollars out of Germany. Many countries refused to accept Jewish immigrants. The United States was reluctant to do so because laws prohibited immigration by people who might need financial assistance. Americans thought that this was true of the Jews because Germans forced them to leave their money and possessions behind. High unemployment rates in the United States made immigration

Academic Vocabulary

implement: to put into action (p. 550)

Academic Vocabulary

prohibit: to make illegal by an authority (p. 550)

Study Guide

Chapter 11, Section 3 *(continued)*

unpopular. Also, immigration quotas that set fixed quotas from each country were in place.

7. Why was the United States reluctant to accept Jewish immigrants?

_____

_____

_____

_____

_____

- **The Final Solution** *(page 553)*

In January 1942, Nazi leaders met at the Wannsee Conference to determine the "final solution of the Jewish question." The Nazis made plans to round up Jews from throughout Nazi-controlled Europe and take them to detention centers known as **concentration camps.** People in these camps would work as slave laborers until they died of exhaustion, disease, or malnutrition. The elderly, children, and the unhealthy would be sent to **extermination camps,** which were attached to concentration camps, to be executed in massive gas chambers.

The Nazis built concentration camps throughout Europe. One of the largest was Buchenwald, in Germany. Prisoners there worked 12-hour shifts as slave laborers in nearby factories. Hundreds died every month as a result of these horrible <u>methods</u>. The Nazis built extermination camps in several concentration camps, mostly in Poland. About 12,000 people were sometimes gassed in a single day at Auschwitz. About 1,300,000 of the 1,600,000 people who died at Auschwitz were Jews. The others included Poles, Gypsies, and Soviet prisoners-of-war.

Academic Vocabulary
method: to follow a plan of action in order to carry out a specific task (p. 554)

People continue to debate why and how the Holocaust could have happened. Most historians believe that several factors contributed to it. The German people felt they were harmed by the harsh treaty after World War I. Germany faced severe economic problems. Hitler had a strong hold on Germany. Germany did not have a strong tradition of representative government. Germans feared Hitler's secret police. Europe had a long history of anti-Jewish prejudice and discrimination.

8. What was the purpose of the Wannsee Conference?

_____

_____

_____

_____

Study Guide

Chapter 11, Section 4

For use with textbook pages 556–563

AMERICA ENTERS THE WAR

CONTENT VOCABULARY

hemispheric defense zone   the western half of the Atlantic which was declared part of the Western Hemisphere and therefore neutral *(page 560)*

strategic materials   materials important for fighting a war *(page 562)*

DRAWING FROM EXPERIENCE

Imagine that you are living in the United States in 1940. How do you think you would have felt about the nation becoming involved in the war overseas? Why?

The last section described Germany's treatment of the Jews and the Holocaust. This section discusses the events that led to the U.S. entry into World War II.

> **California History-Social Science Standards**
>
> **11.7** Students analyze America's participation in World War II.
>
> **Focuses on:** 11.7.1, 11.7.4

ORGANIZING YOUR THOUGHTS

Use the diagram below to help you take notes. President Roosevelt was determined to help Britain while keeping the United States neutral. List these ways in the diagram.

1.

2.

Ways to Provide Aid to Britain

4.

3.

Study Guide

Chapter 11, Section 4 *(continued)*

• FDR Supports England *(page 557)*

After Britain and France declared war on Germany, President Roosevelt declared the United States neutral. He wanted to help the two nations against Hitler, however. Roosevelt asked Congress to revise the Neutrality Acts. It had forbidden the sale of American weapons to any country at war. The revised law <u>eliminated</u> the ban on arms sales to nations at war as long as they paid cash and carried the arms away on their own ships.

Academic Vocabulary
eliminate: to get rid of (p. 557)

In May 1940, British Prime Minister Winston Churchill began asking President Roosevelt to give old American destroyers to Britain. Britain had lost most of its destroyers. It needed destroyers to protect its cargo ships from German submarines and to help prevent a German invasion of Britain. Roosevelt agreed to do so. He sent old American destroyers in exchange for the right to build American bases on British-controlled Newfoundland, Bermuda, and islands in the Caribbean.

5. What did the revised Neutrality Act provide?

_____

_____

_____

_____

• The Isolationist Debate *(page 558)*

By 1940 most Americans supported offering limited aid to the Allies. Yet there was a wide range of opinions. At one end was the Fight for Freedom Committee. It urged the repeal of all neutrality laws and stronger action against Germany. The Committee to defend America by Aiding the Allies pushed for increased American aid to the Allies but not military intervention.

Roosevelt's destroyers-for-bases deal led to the establishment of the America First Committee. This was an isolationist group that opposed any American intervention or aid to the Allies.

President Roosevelt decided to run for a third term as president. He believed that at this point, a change of leadership might not be in the country's best interest. During the 1940 campaign, Roosevelt called for a course between neutrality and intervention. He was re-elected by a wide margin.

6. Why did President Roosevelt decide to run for a third term as president?

_____

_____

Study Guide

Chapter 11, Section 4 (continued)

- **Edging Toward War** (page 559)

After he was re-elected, Roosevelt began to expand the nation's role in the war. He said that only Britain stood between the United States and a German attack. By December 1940, Britain had no funds left to fight Germany. President Roosevelt came up with a way to get around the cash-and-carry policy, which Britain could no longer meet. The Lend-Lease Act allowed the United States to lend or lease arms to any country that was considered vital to the defense of the United States. As a result, the United States could send weapons to Britain if Britain promised to return or pay rent for them after the war. Congress passed the Lend-Lease Act. Lend-lease aid eventually included aid to the Soviet Union as well. In June 1941, Hitler violated the Nazi-Soviet pact and started a massive invasion of the Soviet Union. Although Churchill detested communism, he promised to aid any nation that helped fight Nazism. Roosevelt supported Churchills's <u>policy</u>.

The United States faced the problem of how to get supplies and arms to Britain. German submarines were sinking ships in the Atlantic. Roosevelt could not order the navy to protect British ships because the United States was neutral. As a result, he set up the idea of a hemispheric defense zone. Roosevelt said that the entire western half of the Atlantic was part of the Western Hemisphere and was therefore neutral. He ordered the navy to patrol the western Atlantic and point out the location of German submarines to the British.

In August 1941, Roosevelt and Churchill met and agreed to the Atlantic Charter. The leaders agreed to a postwar world of democracy, nonaggression, free trade, economic advancement, and freedom of the seas. Then in early September a German U-boat fired on the American destroyer *Greer*. The destroyer had been radioing the U-boat's position to the British. Roosevelt ordered American ships to follow a shoot-on-sight policy toward German submarines. The Germans escalated hostilities. They torpedoed two American destroyers. One was the *Reuben James*. It sank, and 115 sailors died.

> **Academic Vocabulary**
>
> **policy:** a defined course of action that determines future response (p. 560)

7. What was the Lend-Lease Act?

_____

_____

_____

_____

_____

Study Guide

Chapter 11, Section 4 (continued)

- ### Japan Attacks the United States *(page 561)*

Academic Vocabulary

primary: first and
most important
(p. 562)

Roosevelt's <u>primary</u> goal between August 1939 and December 1941 was to help Britain and its allies defeat Germany. Much of the British navy was needed in Asia to protect British territory from an attack by the Japanese. However, Britain had to move many of its ships from Asia to the Atlantic to defend Britain against Germany. As a result, Roosevelt introduced policies to discourage the Japanese from attacking the British Empire. In July 1940, Congress passed the Export Control Act. The law gave Roosevelt the power to restrict the sale of **strategic materials** to other nations. These were materials that were important for fighting a war. Roosevelt blocked the sale of airplane fuel and scrap iron to Japan. This angered the Japanese, who signed an alliance with Germany and Italy and became a member of the Axis Powers.

By July 1941, Japan had sent troops to southern Indochina. This was a threat to the British Empire. Japan was now in a position to bomb Hong Kong and Singapore. Roosevelt responded by freezing Japanese assets in the United States. He reduced the amount of oil being shipped to Japan. He also sent General Douglas MacArthur to the Philippines to build up American defenses there. Roosevelt said the ban on oil would be lifted if Japan would leave Indochina and make peace with China.

The Japanese government appeared to be negotiating with the United States. The United States, however, had decoded Japanese communications that showed Japan was preparing to go to war against the United States. On November 27, 1941, American commanders at the Pearl Harbor naval base received a war warning from Washington. Pearl Harbor was thought to be too great a distance from Japan. Washington did not think that Japan would launch an attack from that distance.

On December 7, 1941, Japan launched a surprise attack on Pearl Harbor. Japan sank or damaged 21 ships of the U.S. Pacific Fleet. It also destroyed 188 airplanes, killed 2,403 Americans, and injured 1,178. The next day, Congress voted to declare war on Japan. On December 11, Germany and Italy both declared war on the United States.

8. What led Congress to declare war on Japan?

_____

_____

_____

_____

_____

Study Guide

Chapter 12, Section 1

For use with textbook pages 572–578

MOBILIZING FOR WAR

CONTENT VOCABULARY

cost-plus   type of government contract in which the government agreed to pay a company whatever it cost to make a product plus a guaranteed percentage of the costs as profit *(page 574)*

disfranchised   denied the right to vote *(page 577)*

DRAWING FROM EXPERIENCE

Imagine that you are living in the United States on December 7, 1941. How do you think you would have felt about the war after the Japanese attack on Pearl Harbor?

In this section, you will learn how the United States mobilized its economy to fight World War II. You will also learn what the nation did to create an army.

ORGANIZING YOUR THOUGHTS

Use the diagram below to help you take notes. Even before the attack on Pearl Harbor, the United States government mobilized the nation for war. List two ways it did so.

California History-Social Science Standards

11.7 Students analyze America's participation in World War II.

11.10 Students analyze the development of federal civil rights and voting rights.

11.11 Students analyze the major social problems and domestic policy issues in contemporary American society.

Focuses on: 11.7.3, 11.7.5, 11.7.6, 11.10.1, 11.11.3

```
                              1. _____
┌─────────────────┐          ┌──────────────────────────
│    Ways of      │──────────┤
│ Mobilizing for War│         │
└─────────────────┘          2. _____
```

Study Guide

Chapter 12, Section 1 (continued)

READ TO LEARN

• Converting the Economy (page 573)

Even before the attack on Pearl Harbor, the United States had begun to mobilize the economy. When the German blitzkrieg hit France, President Roosevelt declared a national emergency. He announced a plan to build 50,000 warplanes a year. Roosevelt and his advisers believed that the quickest way to mobilize the economy was to give industries an <u>incentive</u> to move quickly. Instead of asking companies to bid for contracts, the government signed **cost-plus** contracts. The government agreed to pay a company whatever it cost to make a product plus a guaranteed percentage of the costs as profit. Under this system, the more a company produced and the faster it did the work, the more money it would make. The system helped get things produced quickly.

To convince companies to switch their factories to make military goods, Congress gave the Reconstruction Finance Corporation (RFC) new authority. The government gave the agency permission to make loans to companies to help them cover the cost of converting to war production.

> | Academic Vocabulary |
> | --- |
> | **incentive:** something that motivates a person into action (p. 572) |

3. What was the effect of the cost-plus system on production?

_____

_____

_____

_____

_____

• American Industry Gets the Job Done (page 574)

By 1941 the nation's economy was only partially mobilized. Many companies were still producing consumer goods instead of military equipment. By the summer of 1942, however, most major industries had changed to war production. Automobile companies began to make trucks, jeeps, and tanks. They also made rifles, mines, helmets, and other pieces of military equipment. The Ford Company created an assembly line to build the B-24 bomber. By the end of the war, the company had built more than 8,600 aircraft.

Henry Kaiser's shipyards built ships. They were best known for making Liberty ships. These were the basic cargo ships used during the war. They were welded rather than riveted, making them cheap and easy to build and very hard to sink.

To make mobilization more efficient, President Roosevelt set up the War Production Board (WPB). This agency had the authority to set <u>priorities</u> and production goals. It also had the authority to control the distribution of raw materials and supplies. However, because military agencies continued to sign

> | Academic Vocabulary |
> | --- |
> | **priority:** a ranking of importance (p. 575) |

Study Guide

Chapter 12, Section 1 *(continued)*

contracts without <u>consulting</u> with the WPB, Roosevelt established the Office of War Mobilization to settle arguments between the different agencies.

4. What was the advantage of making welded rather than riveted ships?

_____

_____

_____

_____

Academic Vocabulary
consult: to ask for permission or advice (p. 575)

- **Building an Army** *(page 576)*

In addition to changing industries to war production, the country had to build up its military. After France surrendered to Germany, two members of Congress introduced the Selective Service and Training Act. This was a plan for the first peacetime draft in American history. Congress approved the draft in September 1940.

Draftees were sent to a reception center. There they were given a physical exam and shots. The draftees were then given uniforms, boots, and equipment. The clothing was labeled "G.I.," which meant "Government Issue." For this reason, American soldiers were called "GIs." Recruits were sent to basic training for eight weeks. There they learned how to handle weapons, read maps, and dig trenches. They also learned how to work as a team. Recruits came from all over the country. Training made them a unit.

Although training promoted unity, white recruits did not train alongside African Americans. The army was completely segregated. African Americans had separate barracks, mess halls, and recreational facilities. They were organized into their own military units. White officers were in command of them. Many military leaders did not want African American soldiers in combat. They assigned them to construction and supply units.

Some African Americans did not want to support the war. They noted that African Americans were segregated in the army and that lynchings continued. They also noted that African Americans were **disfranchised,** or denied their right to vote. Many African American leaders combined patriotism with protest. A leading African American newspaper in Pittsburgh started a "Double V" campaign. The paper argued that African Americans should join the war effort to achieve a double victory. This would be a victory over Hitler's racism and a victory over racism in the United States. President Roosevelt responded by ordering the military to begin recruiting African Americans and to put them into combat. He also appointed Colonel Benjamin O. Davis, the highest-ranking African American officer in the U.S. Army, to the rank of brigadier general.

Study Guide

Chapter 12, Section 1 (continued)

The army air force created an African American unit that trained in Tuskegee, Alabama. The fighter pilots became known as the Tuskegee Airmen. They were sent to the Mediterranean in April 1943, where the unit played an important role in a battle in Italy. African Americans also performed well in the army, receiving commendations for distinguished service. Although the military did not end all segregation during the war, it paved the way for President Truman's decision to fully integrate the military in 1948.

The army enlisted women for the first time during World War II, but they were banned from combat. Many women in the army had administrative and clerical jobs, freeing men for combat. The army set up the Women's Army Corps (WAC) in 1943. The Coast Guard, the navy, and marines set up their own women's organizations. In addition, thousands of women served as nurses in the army and navy.

5. How did women's role in the military change during World War II?

_____

_____

_____

_____

_____

Study Guide

Chapter 12, Section 2

For use with textbook pages 579–585

THE EARLY BATTLES

CONTENT VOCABULARY

periphery the edges *(page 583)*

convoy system a system in which cargo ships traveled in groups and were escorted by navy warships *(page 584)*

DRAWING FROM EXPERIENCE

Have you ever seen a movie about World War II? What was the movie about? How did it portray conditions during the war?

The last section described the ways that the United States mobilized for war. This section discusses the early battles of World War II.

> **California History-Social Science Standards**
>
> **11.7** Students analyze America's participation in World War II.
>
> **Focuses on:** 11.7.2, 11.7.3

ORGANIZING YOUR THOUGHTS

Use the chart below to help you take notes. Several battles occurred in the early years of World War II. Explain the result of each of the battles listed in the chart.

Battle	Result
Battle at Bataan Peninsula	1.
Battle of Midway	2.
Allied invasion of North Africa	3.
Battle of Stalingrad	4.

READ TO LEARN

• **Holding the Line Against Japan** *(page 580)*

Although the United States fleet at Pearl Harbor was badly damaged by the Japanese, American aircraft carriers were not. They were on a mission in the Pacific. Admiral Chester Nimitz, the commander of the United States Navy in the Pacific, was determined to use the carriers. However, after Pearl Harbor Nimitz could do little to stop Japanese advances into Southeast Asia. The

Study Guide

Chapter 12, Section 2 (continued)

Japanese attacked American airfields in the Philippines and landed troops in the islands.

The American and Filipino forces defending the Philippines were outnumbered. General Douglas MacArthur, their commander, decided to retreat to the Bataan Peninsula. They held off the Japanese for more than three months. However, a lack of supplies and disease took its toll. In April 1942, the defenders surrendered. By May the Philippines fell to the Japanese.

President Roosevelt wanted to bomb Tokyo. However, American planes could reach Tokyo only if an aircraft carrier brought them close enough. Japanese ships in the Pacific stopped carriers from getting close enough to launch their short-range bombers. In 1942 a military planner suggested using long-range B-25 bombers that could be launched from farther away. Although the B-25s could be launched from a carrier, they could not land on the carrier's short deck. As a result, after attacking Japan they would have to land in China.

President Roosevelt put Lieutenant Colonel James Doolittle in command of the mission. B-25s were loaded onto an aircraft carrier. On April 18, 1942, American bombs fell on Japan for the first time. Japanese leaders were horrified and changed their strategy. The commander of the Japanese fleet wanted to attack Midway Island. This was the last American base in the North Pacific west of Hawaii. He believed that attacking the base would bring the American fleet into battle. Then the Japanese fleet would destroy it. Japan also planned to attack New Guinea and cut American supply lines to Australia. Only three aircraft carriers were <u>assigned</u> to the mission; the rest were ordered to Midway.

Academic Vocabulary
assign: to appoint to a position or duty (p. 581)

The Japanese believed that launching two different attacks would work because they thought the United States would not know what Japan was doing. Japan did not know that the United States used a team of code breakers, based in Hawaii, who had already broken the Japanese Navy's secret code for conducting operations. The decoded messages alerted the United States that Japan would attack New Guinea. The United States sent two carriers to cut off the Japanese. Both sides started all-out air strikes against each other. The American attacks prevented the Japanese from landing in New Guinea. The American supply lines to Australia stayed open.

The code breakers also learned of the plan to attack Midway. Admiral Yamamoto <u>transmitted</u> the plans for the Midway attack by radio, using the same code the Americans had already cracked. Admiral Nimitz decided to ambush the Japanese fleet. He ordered carriers to move near Midway. When the Japanese aircraft flew near Midway, they were met with antiaircraft fire. Thirty-eight Japanese planes were shot down. As the Japanese were preparing a second wave of attacks on Midway, American aircraft attacked Japanese carriers. The American attacks greatly damaged the Japanese navy. The Japanese commander ordered the ships to retreat.

Academic Vocabulary
transmit: to send information through a medium such as radio or internet (p. 582)

Study Guide

Chapter 12, Section 2 *(continued)*

The Battle of Midway was a turning point in the war. The Japanese had lost four of its largest carriers. The Americans had stopped the Japanese advance in the Pacific. However, the battle killed 362 Americans and more than 3,000 Japanese.

5. How were Americans able to know about Japanese plans against the United States in the Pacific?

_____

_____

_____

_____

- ## Turning Back the German Army *(page 583)*

President Roosevelt wanted to get American troops into battle in Europe. British Prime Minister Churchill did not believe that the United States and Britain were ready for a full-scale invasion of Europe. He wanted to attack the **periphery,** or edges, of the German empire. Roosevelt agreed with Churchill and ordered the invasion of Morocco and Algeria. These were French territories indirectly under German control. This invasion gave the American army some experience and it did not involve a large number of troops. It also placed American troops in North Africa, where they could help the British fight Germans in Egypt. Egypt was important to Britain because of the Suez Canal. Most of Britain's empire used the canal to get supplies to Britain.

The American invasion of North Africa began on November 8, 1942, under the command of General Dwight D. Eisenhower. The German forces were under the command of General Erwin Rommel. The American forces in Morocco, led by General George Patton, quickly seized Casablanca. American forces in Algeria seized two cities there. British forces headed into Libya. When American forces advanced into western Tunisia, they fought the Germany army for the first time. The Americans were outfought. They suffered around 7,000 casualties. Eisenhower fired the general who led the attack and placed Patton in command. The American and British forces finally pushed the Germans back. In May 1943, the German forces in North Africa surrendered.

The war against German submarines in the Atlantic Ocean <u>intensified</u>. German submarines entered American coastal waters after Germany declared war on the United States. By August 1942, German submarines had sunk 360 American cargo ships. Because of the loss, the U.S. Navy decided to set up a **convoy system.** Under this system, cargo ships traveled in groups and were escorted by navy warships.

Academic Vocabulary
intensify: to become more frequent and powerful (p. 584)

Study Guide

Chapter 12, Section 2 *(continued)*

The German submarines sank more than 1.2 million tons of shipping in May and June 1942. At the same time, the United States and Britain built more than 1.1 million tons of new shipping. Soon, the United States was building more ships than German submarines managed to sink. American airplanes and warships also began to use new technology, such as radar and sonar, to pinpoint and attack submarines. Eventually the technology took its toll on German submarines. The Battle of the Atlantic turned in favor of the Allies.

Before the tide turned against Germany in the Atlantic, Hitler was confident that he would win the war. He decided to knock the Soviet Union out of the war. Hitler believed that the only way to defeat the Soviet Union was to destroy its economy. He ordered the German army to capture oil fields, industries, and farmlands. Stalingrad was the key city to attack. If Germany could capture Stalingrad, it would cut off the Soviets from the resources they needed to fight in the war. Soviet forces succeeded in surrounding Stalingrad and trapping thousands of German troops. When the battle ended, about 91,000 Germans surrendered. The Battle of Stalingrad was a major turning point in the war. It put the Germans on the defensive.

6. Why was the Battle of Stalingrad a turning point in the war?

_____

_____

_____

_____

_____

Study Guide

Chapter 12, Section 3

For use with textbook pages 586–593

LIFE ON THE HOME FRONT

CONTENT VOCABULARY

Sunbelt   a new industrial region, located in southern California and the Deep South *(page 589)*

rationing   limiting the availability of an item *(page 592)*

victory garden   a garden planted to produce more food for the war effort *(page 592)*

DRAWING FROM EXPERIENCE

During World War II, some local governments banned a certain style of dressing. Do you think a government should have the right to do that in certain circumstances? Why do you think so?

The last section discussed the early battles of World War II. This section describes the effect of the war on the home front.

ORGANIZING YOUR THOUGHTS

Use the diagram below to help you take notes. During World War II, the American people supported the war effort at home. Describe how they did so.

California History-Social Science Standards

11.7 Students analyze America's participation in World War II.

11.10 Students analyze the development of federal civil rights and voting rights.

11.11 Students analyze the major social problems and domestic policy issues in contemporary American society.

Focuses on: 11.7.3, 11.7.5, 11.7.6, 11.10.1, 11.10.4, 11.11.3

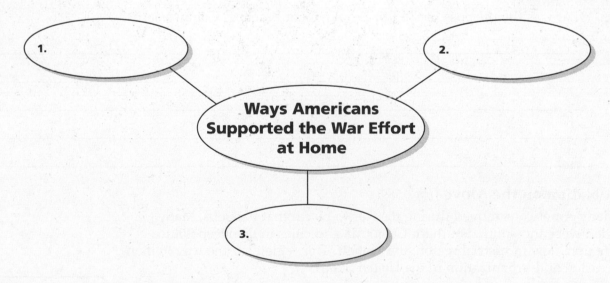

Study Guide

Chapter 12, Section 3 (continued)

READ TO LEARN

• **Women and Minorities Gain Ground** (page 587)

World War II changed American society at home. Before the war, most Americans believed married women should not work outside the home. However, the labor shortage during the war forced factories to hire married women to do the jobs that traditionally were done by men. "Rosie the Riveter" was the great symbol of the campaign to hire women. Images of Rosie appeared on posters and in newspaper ads. Although most women left the factories after the war, their work permanently changed Americans' perspectives about women in the workplace.

Many factories were willing to hire women but they did not want to hire African Americans. A. Philip Randolph, the head of the Brotherhood of Sleeping Car Porters—a major union for African American railroad workers—decided to do something. He told President Roosevelt that he was going to organize a march on Washington. Roosevelt responded by issuing an order saying that discrimination in hiring workers in defense industries would not be tolerated. Roosevelt created the Fair Employment Practices Commission to enforce the order. This was the first civil rights agency set up by the federal government since Reconstruction.

To help farmers in the Southwest overcome the labor shortage, the government started the Bracero Program in 1942. It arranged for Mexican farm-workers to help in the harvest. Migrant farmworkers became important to farming in the Southwest.

Academic Vocabulary
perspective: a way of looking at a situation that is unique to each individual (p. 587)

4. What was the purpose of the Fair Employment Practices Commission?

_____

_____

_____

_____

• **A Nation on the Move** (page 589)

Many Americans moved during the war to places that had jobs. Many headed west and south. Southern California and cities in the Deep South made up a new industrial region, the **Sunbelt.** This region led the way in manufacturing and urbanization in the United States.

Cities that had war industries had to deal with the problem of providing houses to the thousands of new workers. The federal government allocated $1.2 billion to build public housing and schools during the war. About two million people lived in government-built housing during the war.

Academic Vocabulary
allocate: to set apart for something specific (p. 589)

Study Guide

Chapter 12, Section 3 (continued)

During World War II, African Americans arrived in cities in the North and West in search of jobs. They were often met with intolerance that sometimes led to violence. The worst racial violence occurred in Detroit in June 1943. By the time it ended, 25 African Americans and 9 whites had been killed.

Wartime prejudice was evident in other areas of American society. In Los Angeles, racism against Mexican Americans and the fear of juvenile crime became linked because of the zoot suit. This was an overstuffed jacket that had wide lapels and reached to the knees. It also included baggy, pleated pants. Those who wore zoot suits often wore wide-brimmed hats and a long key chain. Many Americans considered the zoot suit unpatriotic. To save fabric for the war, many men wore a suit that had no vest or cuffs and included a short jacket with narrow lapels.

Many Mexican American teenagers in California wore the zoot suit. In June 1943, rumors spread that zoot suiters had attacked several sailors. Soldiers and sailors responded by attacking Mexican American teenagers in their neighborhoods in Los Angeles. The police did not stop the attacks, and the violence continued for days. The city of Los Angeles responded by banning zoot suits.

Hostility toward Mexican Americans did not stop them from joining the war effort. About 500,000 Hispanic Americans served in the American armed forces during the war.

After the attack on Pearl Harbor, many Americans turned their anger against Japanese Americans. Some attacked Japanese American businesses and homes. Some newspapers printed rumors about Japanese spies in the Japanese American community. Many people, including members of Congress, demanded that people of Japanese ancestry be removed from the West Coast. They believed that Japanese Americans would not remain loyal to the United States. No Japanese American was ever tried for spying. Japanese Americans served in the war. The all-Japanese 100th Battalion, later <u>integrated</u> into the 442nd Regimental Combat Team, was the most highly decorated unit in World War II. However, President Roosevelt signed an order that allowed the War Department to declare any part of the United States a military zone. The department declared most of the West Coast a military zone. People of Japanese ancestry were relocated to 10 internment camps. Some Japanese Americans protested the relocation. Fred Korematsu claimed that his rights were violated. He took his case to the Supreme Court. In December 1944, the Court ruled that the relocation was constitutional because it was based on military urgency, not on race. Afterward, the Court ruled that loyal American citizens could not be held against their will. In early 1945, the government began releasing the Japanese Americans from the camps.

Academic Vocabulary
integrate: to combine two previously separate things (p. 591)

5. How did racism and discrimination affect Japanese Americans during World War II?

_____

_____

_____

Study Guide

Chapter 12, Section 3 *(continued)*

- ### Daily Life in Wartime America *(page 591)*

President Roosevelt worried that mobilizing the economy might result in inflation. Wages and prices began to rise quickly during the war because of the demand for workers and raw materials. To stabilize this, Roosevelt set up the Office of Price Administration (OPA) and the Office of Economic Stabilization (OES). The agencies regulated wages and the price of products. They managed to keep inflation under control.

The War Labor Board tried to prevent labor strikes. Most unions pledged not to strike. The War Labor Board settled over 17,000 disputes by the end of the war.

The demand for raw materials and supplies created shortages. The OPA began **rationing,** or limiting the availability of, many consumer products to make sure that there were enough supplies for the military. Items such as meat and sugar were rationed. Households were given a book of ration coupons each month. When people bought foods, they also had to give enough coupon points to cover their purchases.

Americans volunteered to plant **victory gardens** to produce more food for the war effort. Land such as backyards, schoolyards, city parks, and empty lots were used for these gardens.

The government organized scrap drives for materials that were important to the war effort. These materials included spare rubber, tin, aluminum, and steel. They also included oils and fats, which were needed to make explosives.

The war cost more than $300 billion. To raise money, the government raised taxes, but the taxes covered less than half of the cost. The government issued bonds to raise the rest of the money. When Americans bought bonds, they were loaning money to the government. The government promised that the bonds could be cashed in at a future date for the price of the bond plus interest. The most common bonds were E bonds. Americans bought nearly $50 billion worth of war bonds. Banks and other financial institutions bought about $100 billion worth of bonds.

6. Why did the OPA introduce rationing during World War II?

_____

_____

_____

_____

_____

Study Guide

Chapter 12, Section 4

For use with textbook pages 598–605

PUSHING THE AXIS BACK

CONTENT VOCABULARY

amphtrac   an amphibious tractor *(page 603)*

kamikaze   type of attacks in which Japanese pilots would deliberately crash their planes into American ships *(page 605)*

DRAWING FROM EXPERIENCE

Do you know anyone who fought in or lived through World War II? What are their recollections about the battles fought during the war? How did they get information about the war?

The last section described the ways the war changed American society and the efforts of Americans on the home front. This section discusses how the Allied forces pushed back the Germans and the Japanese.

> **California History-Social Science Standards**
>
> **11.7** Students analyze America's participation in World War II.
>
> **Focuses on:** 11.7.2, 11.7.3, 11.7.4, 11.7.6

ORGANIZING YOUR THOUGHTS

Use the chart below to help you take notes. The Allies fought the Axis in Europe and in the Pacific. List the results of the battles that are listed in the chart.

Location of Battle	Outcome
Sicily	1.
Normandy	2.
Leyte Gulf	3.

READ TO LEARN

- **Striking Back at the Third Reich** *(page 599)*

To win the war, the Allies had to land their troops in Europe and on islands in the Pacific. To plan this, President Roosevelt met with Prime Minister Winston Churchill at the Casablanca Conference in Morocco. At this meeting, the two leaders decided to increase the bombing of Germany. The Allies also agreed to attack the Axis in Sicily. Churchill believed that the Italians would quit the war if Italy were invaded.

Study Guide

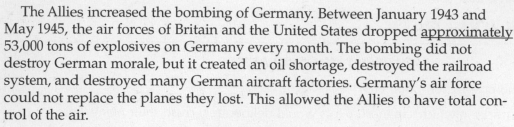

Chapter 12, Section 4 *(continued)*

The Allies increased the bombing of Germany. Between January 1943 and May 1945, the air forces of Britain and the United States dropped <u>approximately</u> 53,000 tons of explosives on Germany every month. The bombing did not destroy German morale, but it created an oil shortage, destroyed the railroad system, and destroyed many German aircraft factories. Germany's air force could not replace the planes they lost. This allowed the Allies to have total control of the air.

General Eisenhower was in charge of the invasion of Sicily. The invasion started on July 10, 1943. After the British and American troops came ashore, American tanks pushed through enemy lines and captured the western half of the island. The troops continued to move eastward and northward. By August 18, the Germans had left the island. The defeat of the Germans in Sicily caused the king of Italy to arrest Mussolini and to begin negotiating with the Allies for Italy's surrender. Hitler responded by taking control of northern Italy and putting Mussolini back in power.

To stop Allied advances, the Germans took up positions in some Italian towns. It took the Allies five months to break through the enemy lines. Fighting in Italy continued until May 2, 1945, causing more than 300,000 Allied casualties.

Roosevelt and Churchill met with Stalin in Tehran, Iran, in late 1943. The leaders reached several agreements. Stalin promised to attack the Germans when the Allies invaded France. They agreed that Germany would be broken up after the war. Stalin promised that after Germany was beaten, the Soviet Union would help the United States defeat Japan. Stalin also agreed to support an international organization to keep peace after the war.

4. What agreements were reached at the conference in Tehran?

_____

_____

_____

_____

_____

- **Landing in France** *(page 601)*

Roosevelt met with Churchill in Egypt to continue to plan the invasion of France. The <u>code</u> name for the invasion was Operation Overlord. Roosevelt selected General Eisenhower to be the commander of the invasion.

The Germans knew about the plans to invade France, so Hitler had fortified the coast. Hitler did not know when or where the invasion would take place, however. The Germans guessed that the Allies would land in Pas-de-Calais, an area of France closest to Britain. To make the Germans think they were

> **Academic Vocabulary**
>
> **approximately:** an estimation of a figure close to the actual figure (p. 599)

> **Academic Vocabulary**
>
> **code:** a signal or symbol used to represent something that is to be kept secret (p. 601)

Study Guide

Chapter 12, Section 4 *(continued)*

right, the Allies placed inflated rubber tanks and dummy landing craft along the coast across from Calais. The Germans were fooled. The Allies actually planned to land in Normandy.

By the spring of 1944, the invasion was ready to begin. It had to begin at night to hide the ships carrying the men and equipment across the English Channel. The invasion could take place in certain weather conditions. The best opportunity for invasion was June 5 to June 7, 1944. Eisenhower chose June 6, 1944. The date became known as D-Day. About 7,000 ships sailed for Normandy. About 23,000 paratroopers were dropped inland. Fighter-bombers dropped bombs up and down the coast. The beaches were given different code names. The landing on Utah Beach went smoothly, but Omaha Beach was a different story. The German attack was intense. General Omar Bradley, the commander of the American forces landing at Utah and Omaha, began to make plans to evacuate. American troops then began to knock out the German defenses. By the end of the day, more than 58,000 American troops then had landed at Omaha and Utah. The invasion was successful.

5. Why did the invasion of France have to begin at night?

_____

_____

_____

_____

_____

• Driving the Japanese Back *(page 603)*

At the same time that plans were in progress for the invasion of France, the United States was developing a plan to defeat Japan. It was a two-part plan. Admiral Nimitz would command the Pacific Fleet and would move through the central Pacific, hopping from one island to the next, closer and closer to Japan. The island-hopping plan started in the fall of 1943. The geography of the Pacific <u>posed</u> a problem, however. Many of the islands were coral reef atolls. This meant that the water over the coral reef was not always deep enough, and many ships ran aground. The troops had to wade in water, making them easy targets for the Japanese. Many were killed. One vehicle was able to cross the reef and deliver the troops to the beaches. It was the LVT, which was a boat with tank tracks. This amphibious tractor, or **amphtrac**, as it was nicknamed, had been invented in the late 1930s to rescue people in Florida swamps. The navy decided to buy about 200 of them in 1941.

The amphtracs were used in the attack on the Marshall Islands, where Americans suffered fewer casualties. The navy then attacked the Mariana Islands and captured them by August 1944.

> **Academic Vocabulary**
>
> **pose:** to act in a way as to require attention or consideration (p. 603)

Study Guide

Chapter 12, Section 4 (continued)

The second part of the plan to defeat Japan called for General MacArthur's troops to start their campaign in the southwest Pacific. It began with the invasion of Guadalcanal. MacArthur then captured the Japanese base on the north coast of New Guinea. To take back the Philippines, the United States put together a huge invasion force. In October 1944, about 700 ships with more than 160,000 troops sailed for Leyte Gulf in the Philippines. They began to land on the eastern side of the Philippines. The Japanese sent four aircraft carriers toward the Philippines from the north to stop the invasion. They secretly sent another fleet to the west. The American carriers headed north to stop the Japanese. The Japanese ships in the west raced through the Philippine Islands into Leyte Gulf and ambushed the American ships that were still there. The Battle of Leyte Gulf was the largest naval battle in history. It was the first time that the Japanese used **kamikaze** attacks. These were attacks in which pilots would deliberately crash their planes into American ships. They killed themselves but also inflicted huge damages. Just as the situation for the Americans looked hopeless, the Japanese commander ordered a retreat, because he believed that more American ships were on the way.

The campaign to take back the Philippines was long and difficult. MacArthur's troops did not capture Manila until March 1945. The city was left in ruins and more than 100,000 Filipino civilians were dead.

6. How did the geography of the Pacific affect American plans to defeat Japan?

_____

_____

_____

_____

_____

Study Guide

Chapter 12, Section 5

For use with textbook pages 608–617

THE WAR ENDS

CONTENT VOCABULARY

hedgerows   dirt walls, several feet thick and covered with shrubbery *(page 609)*

napalm   a kind of jellied gasoline *(page 613)*

charter   a constitution *(page 616)*

DRAWING FROM EXPERIENCE

What is the United Nations? Do you think the United Nations serves a necessary purpose? Why or why not?

The last section described how the Allies pushed back the German and Japanese forces. This section discusses the strategies the Allies used to defeat Germany and Japan.

California History-Social Science Standards

11.7 Students analyze America's participation in World War II.

11.9 Students analyze the U.S. foreign policy since World War II.

Focuses on: 11.7.2, 11.7.3, 11.7.5, 11.7.6, 11.7.7, 11.9.1

ORGANIZING YOUR THOUGHTS

Use the diagram below to help you take notes. Several events occurred during 1945—the last year of World War II. List the event that occurred on the date shown in each box.

1945

| February 19 |
| 1. _____ |

| April 1 |
| 2. _____ |

| April 12 |
| 3. _____ |

| April 25 |
| 4. _____ |

Study Guide

Chapter 12, Section 5 (continued)

May 8
5. _____

August 6
6. _____

August 9
7. _____

August 15
8. _____

READ TO LEARN

- ### The Third Reich Collapses *(page 609)*

The Allies knew that to defeat the Germans, they would need to move out of
Normandy, liberate France, and conquer Germany. D-Day was a success, but it
was just the beginning. The Germans surrounded many fields in Normandy
with **hedgerows,** or dirt walls that were several feet thick and covered in shrubbery. They helped Germans defend their positions. On July 25, 1944, American
bombers blew a hole in the German lines. This allowed American tanks to roll
through the gap. The Allies then liberated Paris on August 25, and three weeks
later American troops were within 20 miles of the German border.

Hitler decided to cut off Allied supplies that were coming through the port
of Antwerp, Belgium. The Germans caught the American defenders by surprise. As Germans moved west, their lines bulged outward, so the attack
became known as the Battle of the Bulge. Germans decided to capture the
town of Bastogne, where several roads met. American troops quickly moved
to the town before Germany did. The Germans surrounded the town and
demanded that the Americans surrender. The Americans refused. General
Eisenhower then ordered General Patton to rescue the surrounded Americans.
Patton hit the German lines, and Allied aircraft hit German fuel depots. The
German troops were forced to stop. The United States had won the Battle of
the Bulge. The Germans, who suffered 100,000 casualties, began to withdraw.
They had very little left to prevent the Allies from entering Germany.

At the same time the Allies fought to liberate France, the Soviets attacked
German troops in Russia. The Soviet troops had driven the Germans out of

Study Guide

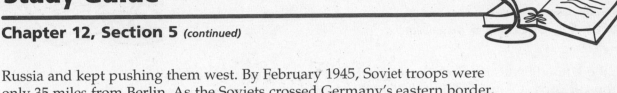

Chapter 12, Section 5 *(continued)*

Russia and kept pushing them west. By February 1945, Soviet troops were only 35 miles from Berlin. As the Soviets crossed Germany's eastern border, American forces attacked the western border. Before killing himself, Hitler chose Grand Admiral Karl Doenitz to be his <u>successor</u>. On May 7, 1945, Germany surrendered unconditionally. The next day, May 8, was proclaimed V-E Day, for "Victory in Europe."

> **Academic Vocabulary**
>
> **successor:** someone who takes the place of a ruler (p. 611)

9. What was the importance of the Allied victory at the Battle of the Bulge?

_____

_____

_____

_____

- ## Japan Is Defeated *(page 612)*

On April 12, 1945, President Roosevelt died after suffering a stroke. Vice President Harry S Truman became president. Truman had the responsibility of ending the war with Japan. In November 1944, Tokyo was bombed for the first time since 1942. The United States used B-29 bombers that traveled from the American bases in the Mariana Islands. The B-29s kept missing their targets because Japan was too far away. By the time the bombers reached Japan, they did not have enough fuel to fix their navigational <u>errors</u>. American planners decided that they needed to capture an island closer to Japan, where the bombers could refuel. They decided to invade Iwo Jima.

> **Academic Vocabulary**
>
> **error:** a misjudgment or miscalculation (p. 612)

Iwo Jima was located halfway between Japan and the Mariana Islands. Although the location was perfect, the geography of the island was rugged. Also, the Japanese had built a network of concrete bunkers that were connected by miles of tunnels. The U.S. Marines landed on Iwo Jima on February 19, 1945. The Japanese began firing on them. More than 6,800 marines were killed before the island was captured.

As American engineers were preparing airfields in Iwo Jima, General Curtis LeMay, commander of the B-29s in the Marianas, decided to change plans. To help the B-29s hit their targets, he ordered them to drop bombs filled with **napalm,** a kind of jellied gasoline. The bombs would not just explode, but they would also set fires. Even if the bombs missed their targets, the fire would spread to the targets. Using firebombs was controversial because they killed civilians. Yet LeMay believed it was the only way to destroy Japan's war production quickly. By the end of June 1945, six of Japan's most important industrial cities had been firebombed. Half of their urban area was destroyed.

Despite the firebombings, Japan was not ready to surrender. American leaders believed that Japan would not surrender until Japan had been invaded. To

Study Guide

Chapter 12, Section 5 (continued)

do so, the United States needed a base near Japan to store supplies and build up troops. It chose Okinawa, located 350 miles from Japan. American troops landed on Okinawa on April 1, 1945. The Japanese positioned themselves on the island's rugged mountains. American troops had to fight their way up the mountains as the Japanese fired on them. More than 12,000 Americans died during the fighting. On June 22, 1945, the troops finally captured Okinawa.

After Okinawa was captured, the Japanese emperor urged the government to surrender. Many Japanese leaders were willing to do so but only with the condition that the emperor would stay in power. Americans opposed that because they blamed the emperor for the war. President Truman was <u>reluctant</u> to go against public opinion. He also knew that the United States had a new weapon that it could use to force unconditional surrender.

<table>
<tr><td>Academic Vocabulary</td></tr>
<tr><td>reluctant: not willing (p. 614)</td></tr>
</table>

In 1941 a scientific committee set up by President Roosevelt met with British scientists who were working on an atomic bomb. The research convinced Roosevelt to begin a program to build an atomic bomb. The program was code-named the Manhattan Project. In 1942 two physicists—Leo Szilard and Enrico Fermi—built the world's first nuclear reactor at the University of Chicago. General Leslie R. Groves, the head of the Manhattan Project, organized a group of engineers and scientists to build an atomic bomb at a secret laboratory in Los Alamos, New Mexico. On July 16, 1945, they detonated the world's first atomic bomb.

American officials debated how to use the bomb. Some opposed it because it would kill civilians. Some wanted to warn the Japanese about the bomb and to tell them that they could keep the emperor if they surrendered. Truman's advisers told him that the United States would experience huge casualties if the United States invaded Japan. Truman believed that he should use every weapon available to save American lives.

Truman ordered the military to drop the atomic bomb. On August 6, 1945, a bomber named the *Enola Gay* dropped an atomic bomb on Hiroshima, an important industrial city. The bomb destroyed about 63 percent of the city. It killed between 80,000 and 120,000 people instantly, and thousands more died later. Then on August 9, the Soviet Union declared war on Japan. On the same day, the United States dropped an atomic bomb on Nagasaki. Between 35,000 and 74,000 people were killed. Japan surrendered on August 15, **V-J Day.** World War II had ended.

10. Why did President Truman decide to use the atomic bomb against Japan?

_____

_____

_____

_____

_____

The American Vision: Modern Times

Study Guide

Chapter 12, Section 5 (continued)

- ### Building a New World (page 616)

Even before the war ended, President Roosevelt wanted to ensure that a world war would not happen again. In 1944 he took part in a meeting at Dumbarton Oaks Estate in Washington, D.C., with delegates from 39 countries to discuss a new international political organization, which was to be called the United Nations (UN). On April 25, 1945, representatives from 50 countries met in San Francisco to organize the United Nations. The United Nations would have a General Assembly, where every nation would have one vote. It would have a Security Council with 11 member. Five members would be permanent: Britain, France, China, the Soviet Union, and the United States. The five members would have veto power. The members at the San Francisco meeting also designed the **charter,** or constitution, of the United Nations. The General Assembly was given the power to vote on resolutions and to choose the non-permanent members of the Security Council. The Security Council was responsible for international peace and security.

In August 1945, the United States, Britain, France, and the Soviet Union created the International Military Tribunal (IMT). At the Nuremberg trials, the IMT tried German leaders suspected of committing war crimes. Many of these leaders were executed. Several Japanese leaders were also tried and executed.

11. Why did President Roosevelt want to establish an international organization?

_____

_____

_____

_____

_____

Study Guide

Chapter 13, Section 1

For use with textbook pages 626–631

ORIGINS OF THE COLD WAR

CONTENT VOCABULARY

Cold War   a period of confrontation and competition between the United States and the Soviet Union *(page 627)*

iron curtain   the separation of the Communist nations of Eastern Europe from the West *(page 631)*

DRAWING FROM EXPERIENCE

What was the Cold War? What have you heard about it and why did it end?

In this section, you will learn why tensions between the Soviet Union and the United States increased after World War II. You will also learn about Stalin's foreign policy after the war.

ORGANIZING YOUR THOUGHTS

Use the diagram below to help you take notes. The Yalta and Potsdam Conferences were held to determine the postwar world. List the decisions of the two conferences in the diagram.

California History-Social Science Standards
11.4 Students trace the rise of the United States to its role as a world power in the twentieth century.
11.7 Students analyze America's participation in World War II.
11.9 Students analyze the U.S. foreign policy since World War II.
Focuses on: 11.4.6, 11.7.4, 11.9.1, 11.9.2, 11.9.3, 11.9.4

Decisions at Yalta Conference

1. _____

2. _____

3. _____

Decisions at Potsdam Conference

4. _____

5. _____

Study Guide

Chapter 13, Section 1 *(continued)*

READ TO LEARN

- **A Clash of Interests** *(page 627)*

After World War II, the relations between the United States and the Soviet Union became more and more strained. This led to an era of confrontation and competition that lasted from 1946 to 1990. It was known as the **Cold War.** The tensions existed because the two countries had different goals. The Soviet Union was concerned about its security because Germany had invaded it twice in 30 years. The Soviet Union wanted to keep Germany weak to make sure it did not invade again. The Soviet Union wanted to control the countries between it and Germany. The Soviets also believed that communism was a superior system that would eventually replace capitalism. They wanted communism to spread to other nations. Believing that capitalism would try to destroy communism, Soviet leaders became suspicious of capitalist nations.

The United States focused on economic problems. President Roosevelt and his advisers believed that economic growth was important to keeping peace in the world. They believed that world trade would lead to economic prosperity. The American leaders wanted to promote democracy throughout the world. They believed that democratic nations were more stable and less likely to go to war. They also believed that the free enterprise system was the best <u>route</u> to prosperity.

Academic Vocabulary
route: a specific course of action (p. 628)

6. Why were Soviet leaders suspicious of capitalist nations?

_____

_____

_____

_____

_____

- **The Yalta Conference** *(page 628)*

In February 1945, before the war was finally over, Roosevelt, Churchill, and Stalin met at Yalta, a resort in the Soviet Union, to plan the postwar world. The first issue was Poland. When Germany invaded Poland in 1939, the Polish government leaders had fled to Britain. When the Soviet Union liberated Poland from German control, they wanted Polish Communists to set up a new government. As a result, two governments—Communist and non-Communist—claimed the right to govern Poland. Churchill and Roosevelt wanted the Poles to choose their own government. Stalin, however, believed that Poland should be Communist to make the Soviet Union more secure against Germany. Churchill and Roosevelt compromised by recognizing the Polish government that the Soviets set up. Stalin agreed to include members

Study Guide

Chapter 13, Section 1 *(continued)*

of the old Polish government and to allow free elections in Poland as soon as possible.

Roosevelt, Churchill, and Stalin agreed to issue the Declaration of Liberated Europe. It declared the right of all people to choose the kind of government they wanted to live under. They also promised to create <u>temporary</u> governments that represented "all democratic <u>elements</u>." The meeting then focused on Germany. The three leaders agreed to divide Germany into four zones, with Great Britain, the United States, the Soviet Union, and France each controlling one zone. The four countries would also divide the city of Berlin. Stalin wanted Germany to pay heavy reparations. Roosevelt insisted that reparations should be based on Germany's ability to pay. He also argued that Germany pay reparations with trade goods and products instead of cash. The Allies would be allowed to take machinery and other equipment from Germany as reparations. The question of German reparations would contribute to tensions between the United States and the Soviet Union.

Two weeks after the meeting at Yalta, the Soviet Union pressured Romania into installing a Communist government. The United States accused the Soviet Union of going against the Declaration of Liberated Europe. The Soviet Union also did not allow free elections to be held in Poland. President Roosevelt informed the Soviets that their actions were not acceptable. Eleven days later, President Roosevelt died, and Harry S Truman became president.

7. What was the Declaration of Liberated Europe?

_____

_____

_____

_____

• Truman Takes Control *(page 629)*

Truman was suspicious of Stalin. He was also strongly anticommunist. He did not want to appease Stalin. He demanded that Stalin hold free elections as he promised at Yalta. Truman finally met Stalin in July 1945, at a conference at Potsdam, which was located near Berlin. They met to work out a deal on Germany. Truman and his advisers believed that unless Germany's economy was revived, the rest of Europe would never recover. Truman also believed that if Germany's economy stayed weak, the country might turn to communism. Stalin and his advisers wanted reparations from Germany. They believed that Germany had devastated the Soviet Union and should pay.

To solve the problem of reparations, Truman suggested that the Soviet Union take its reparations from its zone. The Soviets opposed this because

> **Academic Vocabulary**
>
> **temporary:** lasting only for a short time (p. 629)
>
> **element:** the simplest principles of a system of thought or philosophy (p. 629)

Study Guide

Chapter 13, Section 1 *(continued)*

their zone was mostly agricultural and could not provide the reparations the Soviets needed. Truman responded by offering Stalin a small amount of German industrial equipment from the other zones. He also accepted the new German-Polish border the Soviets had set up. Stalin did not like Truman's proposal. He suspected that the Americans were trying to limit reparations to keep the Soviet Union weak. In the end, the Soviet Union had no choice but to accept the deal. However, the Potsdam conference was another event that increased tensions between the Soviet Union and the United States.

The Soviets refused to commit to uphold the Declaration of Liberated Europe. Pro-Soviet Communist governments would eventually be established in Poland, Romania, Bulgaria, Hungary, and Czechoslovakia. These countries of Eastern Europe came to be called satellite nations. They had their own governments and were not under the direct control of the Soviet Union. However, they had to remain Communist and friendly to the Soviet Union. Churchill called the Communist takeover in Eastern Europe the creation of the **iron curtain,** separating the Communist nations of Eastern Europe from the West.

8. Why did President Truman not want to place harsh reparations on Germany?

_____

_____

_____

_____

_____

_____

The American Vision: Modern Times

Study Guide

Chapter 13, Section 2

For use with textbook pages 632–639

THE EARLY COLD WAR YEARS

CONTENT VOCABULARY

containment   the policy of keeping communism within its present territory through the use of diplomatic, economic, and military actions *(page 633)*

limited war   a war fought to achieve a limited objective such as containing communism *(page 639)*

DRAWING FROM EXPERIENCE

Do you think communism is a threat to the United States today? Why or why not?

The last section described the growing tensions between the Soviet Union and the United States. This section discusses how the United States attempted to contain communism.

ORGANIZING YOUR THOUGHTS

Use the diagram below to help you take notes. The Soviet Union and the United States responded to various events during the Cold War. List their responses to the events listed in the diagram.

Event
Germany divided into West Germany and East Germany

Soviet Response
1. _____
2. _____

Event
Korean War

U.S. Response
3. _____
4. _____
5. _____
6. _____

California History-Social Science Standards

11.4 Students trace the rise of the United States to its role as a world power in the twentieth century.

11.7 Students analyze America's participation in World War II.

11.8 Students analyze the economic boom and social transformation of post–World War II America.

11.9 Students analyze the U.S. foreign policy since World War II.

Focuses on: 11.4.6, 11.7.8, 11.8.5, 11.9.1, 11.9.2, 11.9.3

Study Guide

Chapter 13, Section 2 (continued)

READ TO LEARN

• Containing Communism (page 633)

Both Britain and the United States urged the Soviet Union to hold free elections in Eastern Europe. The Soviets refused to do so. The United States asked the American Embassy in Moscow to explain Soviet behavior. Diplomat George Kennan explained his views of Soviet goals. He believed that Communists were in a historical struggle against capitalism and that it was impossible to reach any permanent settlement with them. Kennan believed that the Soviet system had several economic and political weaknesses. He believed that if the United States could keep the Soviets from increasing their power, then eventually the Soviet system would fall apart. Kennan's suggestions led to the rise of the policy of **containment.** The policy called for keeping communism within its present territory through the use of diplomatic, economic, and military actions.

A crisis in Iran seemed to show that Kennan's ideas were right. During World War II, the United States had put troops into southern Iran while Soviet troops were in northern Iran to ensure a supply line from the Persian Gulf. After the war, the Soviet Union did not withdraw as promised. Instead, Stalin demanded access to Iran's oil supplies. The Soviets also helped Communists in northern Iran set up a separate government. The United States demanded that the Soviet Union withdraw. The pressure worked, and the Soviet Union withdrew.

Stalin then turned to Turkey. The Soviet Union wanted to control the straits of the Dardanelles, which was an important route from Black Sea ports to the Mediterranean. It demanded that Turkey share control of this route with the Soviet Union. The United States saw this as a way for the Soviet Union to control the Middle East. The United States sent aircraft carriers into the eastern Mediterranean. In the meantime, Britain tried to help Greece in its fight against Communists there. However, helping Greece was too much for Britain's economy. As a result, in March 1947, Truman went before Congress to ask for funds to fight the Soviets in Turkey and in Greece. His speech became known as the Truman Doctrine. It pledged that the United States would fight communism worldwide.

The European economy was in ruins after the war. In June 1947, Secretary of State George C. Marshall set up the Marshall Plan, which would give European nations American aid to rebuild their economies. Marshall offered the aid to all nations that planned a recovery program. The Soviet Union and its satellite nations rejected the offer. The Soviet Union developed its own economic program. The Marshall Plan put billions of dollars worth of supplies and food into Western Europe. It weakened the appeal of communism there. It also opened new markets for trade.

Study Guide

Chapter 13, Section 2 *(continued)*

7. What was the purpose of the Marshall Plan?

_____

_____

_____

_____

_____

- ### The Berlin Crisis *(page 634)*

The dispute between the Soviet Union and the United States over Germany almost led to war. By 1948 the United States believed that the Soviets were trying to undermine Germany's economy. As a result, the United States, Great Britain, and France announced that they were combining their zones in Germany and allowing the Germans to have their own government. They also combined their zones in Berlin and made West Berlin a part of the new German nation. It was called the Federal Republic of Germany and became known as West Germany. The Soviet zone became known as East Germany.

The Soviets were angry. They cut all road and rail traffic to West Berlin. They also set up a blockade of the city. They wanted to force the Americans to change Germany's status. President Truman had to keep West Berlin going without pushing the Soviets to war. As a result, he ordered the Berlin airlift. Cargo planes supplied the people in Berlin with food and other supplies. The airlift continued for eleven months. Stalin finally lifted the blockade.

The blockade convinced many Americans that the Soviets were trying to conquer other nations. They began supporting the idea of America becoming part of a <u>mutual</u> military alliance with Western Europe. An agreement had been reached that created NATO, the North Atlantic Treaty Organization. It was made up of 12 countries, including the United States. The members agreed to help any member who was attacked. A few years later, NATO allowed West Germany to join the alliance. The Soviets responded by setting up its own alliance in Eastern Europe, which became known as the Warsaw Pact.

Academic Vocabulary
mutual: to share a common goal and take on equal responsibility (p. 635)

8. How did the Soviet Union respond to the establishment of West Germany and West Berlin?

_____

_____

_____

_____

_____

Study Guide

Chapter 13, Section 2 *(continued)*

• The Cold War Spreads to East Asia *(page 636)*

The Cold War eventually spread to Asia. In China, Mao Zedong had led Communist forces against Chiang Kai-shek's Nationalist government since the 1920s. The two sides stopped the conflict during World War II in order to stop Japanese occupation. After World War II ended, the two groups resumed their fighting. To stop the spread of communism in Asia, the United States sent Chiang money. However, the Communists captured Beijing, the Chinese capital, and moved southward. The United States discontinued aid to the Chinese Nationalists, who left mainland China for the island of Taiwan. In 1949 the Communists set up the People's Republic of China.

In the same year, the Soviet Union announced that it had tested its first atomic weapon. In 1950 it signed a treaty of alliance with China. Western nations feared that China and the Soviet Union would support Communist revolutions in other parts of the world. The United States set up formal relations with the Nationalists in Taiwan and helped the Nationalists <u>retain</u> their U.N. seat. It helped keep Communist China out of the United Nations.

Academic Vocabulary
retain: to keep control or possession (p. 637)

The United States changed is policy toward Japan. After World War II, General Douglas MacArthur took charge of occupied Japan. He wanted to introduce democracy there. The United States encouraged economic recovery in Japan. It saw Japan as a way to defend Asia against communism.

9. Why did the United States change its policy toward Japan after World War II?

_____

_____

_____

_____

_____

• The Korean War *(page 637)*

Academic Vocabulary
parallel: an imaginary line that circles the earth's surface to mark latitude (p. 638)

After the war, the Allies divided Korea at the 38th <u>parallel</u>. The Soviets controlled the north, and the United States controlled the south. A Communist government was set up in the north, and an American-backed government was set up in the south. The Soviets gave military aid to North Korea, which built up a huge army. This army invaded South Korea on June 25, 1950.

President Truman saw the invasion of South Korea as a test of the containment policy. He asked the United Nations for troops to help the American troops. General MacArthur led the American troops. In September 1950, MacArthur ordered an invasion that took the North Korean troops by surprise. Within weeks, they retreated back across the 38th parallel. The Communist Chinese saw the UN troops as a threat and ordered them to

The American Vision: Modern Times

Study Guide

Chapter 13, Section 2 (continued)

retreat. Their warnings were ignored and they started a massive attack. They were able to drive the UN forces back across the 38th parallel.

General MacArthur wanted to expand the war into China. He criticized President Truman for wanting a **limited war,** a war fought to achieve a limited objective such as containing communism. President Truman fired MacArthur. He chose General Matthew Ridgway to replace him. By mid-1951, the Korean War had settled into small bloody battles. An armistice was not signed until July 1953. More than 35,000 Americans died in the war.

After the Korean War, the United States began a military buildup. Until then, the United States believed that it had to focus on Europe to contain communism. Now it also focused militarily on Asia. Defense agreements were signed with Japan, South Korea, Taiwan, the Philippines, and Australia. The United States also began providing aid to the French forces fighting Communists in Vietnam.

10. How did the Korean War change the United States's view of containment?

_____

_____

_____

_____

_____

Study Guide

Chapter 13, Section 3

For use with textbook pages 642–649

THE COLD WAR AND AMERICAN SOCIETY

CONTENT VOCABULARY

subversion   an effort to secretly weaken a society and overthrow its government *(page 643)*

perjury   lying under oath *(page 644)*

censure   formal disapproval *(page 648)*

fallout   the radiation left over after a nuclear blast *(page 649)*

fallout shelter   shelter built to protect against fallout *(page 649)*

DRAWING FROM EXPERIENCE

Does your school conduct practice drills for what to do in certain emergencies? What are the emergencies for which you have these drills?

The last section explained the steps the United States took to contain communism abroad. This section describes how the fear of communism affected Americans at home.

ORGANIZING YOUR THOUGHTS

Use the diagram below to help you take notes. In the United States, people's fear of communism resulted in the Red Scare. In the diagram, list the government's responses to the Red Scare.

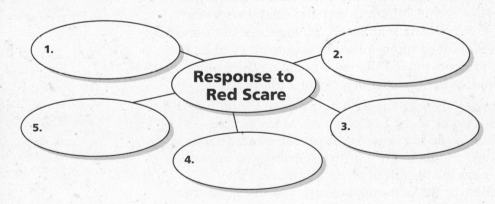

> **California History-Social Science Standards**
>
> **11.8** Students analyze the economic boom and social transformation of post–World War II America.
>
> **11.9** Students analyze the U.S. foreign policy since World War II.
>
> **Focuses on:** 11.8.7, 11.8.8, 11.9.3, 11.9.4

Study Guide

Chapter 13, Section 3 *(continued)*

READ TO LEARN

- **A New Red Scare** *(page 643)*

During the 1950s, people in the United States began to fear that the Communists were trying to take over the world. This fear, the Red Scare, began in September 1945, when a clerk working in the Soviet Embassy in Canada defected. He had documents that showed that the Soviet Union was trying to infiltrate organizations and government agencies in Canada and the United States. The Soviet Union was trying to find information about the atomic bomb.

The search for spies soon turned into a general fear of Communist **subversion.** In 1947 President Truman set up a loyalty review program to screen all federal employees. This action seemed to <u>confirm</u> fears that Communists had infiltrated the government. More than 6 million federal employees were screened for their loyalty. People became suspects simply for reading certain books or belonging to various groups. Thousands were subject to intense FBI investigations.

Academic Vocabulary
confirm: to give assurance of validity (p. 643)

J. Edgar Hoover, the FBI Director, wanted to go further than screening federal employees. He went before the House Un-American Activities Committee (HUAC) to urge the committee to hold public hearings on Communist subversion. FBI agents were sent to infiltrate groups suspected of subversion. They also wiretapped thousands of telephones.

In 1948 Whittaker Chambers, a *Time* magazine editor, testified before HUAC that several government officials, including Alger Hiss, had been Communists or spies at that time. Chambers claimed that Hiss, who had served in President Roosevelt's administration, had given him secrets from the State Department. Hiss denied being a member of the Communist Party, and he denied knowing Chambers. The committee continued hearings to determine who was lying. Hiss admitted that he had met Chambers in the 1930s. He then sued Chambers, claiming that his accusations were unfounded. To defend himself, Chambers showed copies of secret documents that he had hidden. He believed the documents proved that he was telling the truth. A jury agreed with him. It convicted Hiss of **perjury,** or lying under oath.

Another spy case had to do with accusations that American Communists had sold secrets of the atomic bomb to the Soviet Union. Many people believed that the Soviet Union could not have developed an atomic bomb in 1949 without this help. In 1950 testimony by a British scientist that he sent information to the Soviet Union led the FBI to arrest Julius and Ethel Rosenberg, who were members of the Communist Party, and to charge them with passing on atomic secrets. Although the Rosenbergs denied the charges, they were condemned to death and executed in June 1953. Their guilt was debated by many Americans. Future investigation and documents, however, provided strong evidence that they were guilty.

Study Guide

Chapter 13, Section 3 *(continued)*

The Red Scare spread beyond the federal government. State and local governments, universities, businesses, and unions began looking for Communists. Some universities required their faculty members to take loyalty oaths. The Taft-Hartley Act required that union leaders take loyalty oaths.

6. Why did President Truman set up the loyalty review program?

_____

_____

_____

_____

_____

- **"A Conspiracy So Immense"** *(page 646)*

After the Soviet Union tested an atomic bomb in 1949 and China fell to communism, many Americans feared that the United States was losing the Cold War. Many believed that Communists had infiltrated the government and were unnoticed. Then in February 1950, Wisconsin Senator Joseph R. McCarthy made a statement that he had a list of 205 Communists in the State Department. McCarthy never actually produced the list, but he accused many politicians and military officials of being Communists or leaning toward communism.

Senator Pat McCarran declared that "world communism has as its <u>sole</u> purpose the establishment of a totalitarian dictatorship in America."

Academic Vocabulary
sole: single, having no other (p. 646)

In 1950 the United States passed the McCarran Act. The law required all Communist organizations to provide the government with their records. It also required that in a national emergency, Communists and Communist sympathizers could be arrested. Truman did not believe that people should be punished for their beliefs, so he vetoed the bill. Congress overrode it.

In 1952 McCarthy became chairman of the Senate subcommittee on investigations. He used his position to force government officials to testify about so-called Communist influences. McCarthy turned the investigation into a witch hunt. His investigations were based on weak evidence and irrational fears. His method of destroying reputations with unfounded charges became known as McCarthyism. McCarthy would badger witnesses and then refuse to accept their answers. His methods left a sense of suspicion about the witness that was often interpreted as guilt.

In 1954 McCarthy began targeting the United States Army. The army's own investigation found no spies. McCarthy then brought his investigation to the television. Millions of Americans watched as McCarthy bullied witnesses. His popularity began to decrease. Finally, people began to challenge McCarthy and his methods. In 1954 the Senate passed a vote for **censure,** or formal disapproval, against McCarthy. McCarthy's influence was gone, and he faded from public view.

Study Guide

Chapter 13, Section 3 *(continued)*

7. What led many Americans in 1949 to believe the United States was losing the Cold War and that Communist infiltration was the reason for it?

_____

_____

_____

_____

_____

• Life During the Early Cold War *(page 648)*

The fear of communism dominated everyday life in the United States in the 1950s. Americans were upset when the Soviet Union tested the more powerful hydrogen bomb. They got ready for a surprise Soviet attack. They set up special areas as bomb shelters. Students practiced bomb drills, although experts warned that these measures would not have protected people from <u>nuclear</u> radiation. They pointed out that in a nuclear bomb blast, many people would die not only from the blast itself but also from **fallout,** or the radiation left over after a blast. To protect themselves, some people built **fallout shelters** in their yards. They stocked these shelters with food.

The fear of communism influenced American movies and fiction. Many movies focused on FBI activities in espionage cases. Novels described the effects of nuclear war.

Academic Vocabulary
nuclear: a weapon whose power comes from a chain reaction of uranium or plutonium atoms (p. 648)

8. How did Americans in the 1950s get ready for a surprise Soviet attack?

_____

_____

_____

_____

_____

Study Guide

Chapter 13, Section 4

For use with textbook pages 650–657

EISENHOWER'S POLICIES

CONTENT VOCABULARY

massive retaliation   the policy of threatening Communist states with nuclear war if the state tried to take territory by force *(page 652)*

brinkmanship   the willingness to go to the brink of war to force the other side to back down *(page 653)*

covert   hidden *(page 654)*

developing nation   nation with a primarily agricultural economy *(page 654)*

military-industrial complex   the relationship between the military establishment and the defense industry *(page 657)*

DRAWING FROM EXPERIENCE

What do you think of when you hear the term *CIA?* What does the CIA do? Do you think the CIA is important in today's world? Why?

The last section described American reaction to the threat of communism. This section discusses President Eisenhower's plans to contain communism.

ORGANIZING YOUR THOUGHTS

Use the diagram below to help you take notes. President Eisenhower used the policy of brinkmanship in dealing with Cold War conflicts. List three ways he used this policy.

California History-Social Science Standards

11.8 Students analyze the economic boom and social transformation of post–World War II America.

11.9 Students analyze the U.S. foreign policy since World War II.

Focuses on: 11.8.4, 11.8.5, 11.8.7, 11.9.2, 11.9.3, 11.9.4, 11.9.6

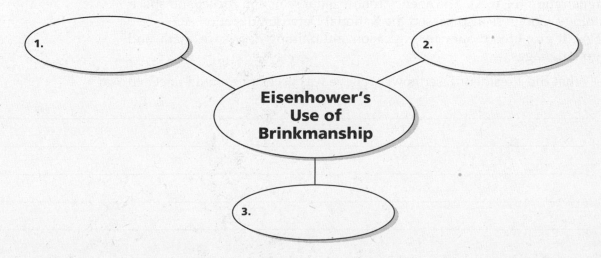

1.

2.

Eisenhower's Use of Brinkmanship

3.

Study Guide

Chapter 13, Section 4 *(continued)*

READ TO LEARN

• **Eisenhower's "New Look"** *(page 651)*

In the 1952 presidential election, the Democrats nominated Adlai Stevenson, the governor of Illinois. The Republicans nominated General Dwight D. Eisenhower. Americans wanted a leader who they believed would lead the nation through the Cold War. Eisenhower won in a landslide.

Eisenhower believed that both a strong military and a strong economy were essential to win the Cold War. He also believed that preparing for a large-scale conventional war would cost too much money. Therefore, he believed that instead of a large-scale army, the United States had to be prepared to use atomic weapons.

Eisenhower believed that the United States could not contain communism through a series of small wars, such as the Korean War. He believed that it had to prevent such wars from happening in the first place. The best way to do this was to threaten to use nuclear weapons if a Communist state tried to take a territory by force. This policy became known as **massive retaliation.** It allowed Eisenhower to cut military spending by billions of dollars. He cut back the army but increased the nation's nuclear weapons.

The new policy required new technology. The Air Force developed huge bombers that could fly across the continent and drop nuclear bombs anywhere in the world. Eisenhower also began to develop intercontinental ballistic missiles (ICBMs) that could deliver bombs anywhere in the world. He also began developing submarines that could launch nuclear missiles.

On October 4, 1957, the Soviets launched *Sputnik,* the first artificial satellite to orbit the earth. Many Americans saw that as a sign that the United States was falling behind the Soviet Union in missile technology and in scientific research. In response, Congress set up the National Aeronautics and Space Administration (NASA). The agency conducted research in rocket and space technology. Congress also passed the National Defense Education Act (NDEA). It provided money for education and training in science, math, and foreign languages.

4. What did President Eisenhower believe was necessary to win the Cold War?

_____

_____

_____

_____

_____

The American Vision: Modern Times

Study Guide

Chapter 13, Section 4 *(continued)*

- **Brinkmanship In Action** *(page 652)*

Eisenhower supported the policy of **brinkmanship,** the willingness to go to the brink of war to force the other side to back down. Secretary of State John Foster Dulles, the <u>dominant</u> figure in foreign affairs, strongly defended the policy. Some thought the policy was too dangerous. However, Eisenhower used the threat of nuclear war to try to end the Korean War. He believed that the war was costing too many lives. So he threatened China with a nuclear attack. The threat seemed to work, because in July 1953, an armistice was signed. The line between the two sides became the border between North Korea and South Korea. A demilitarized zone (DMZ) separated them.

After the Korean War ended, problems arose over Taiwan. In 1954 China threatened to take two islands from Taiwan. Eisenhower asked Congress to authorize the use of force to defend Taiwan. He then warned the Chinese that if they invaded Taiwan, they would be confronted by American naval forces. Eisenhower also hinted that a nuclear attack was also possible. China backed down.

In 1955 problems developed in the Middle East. Eisenhower wanted to prevent Arab nations from siding with the Soviet Union. He offered Egypt financial help to build a dam on the Nile River. Egypt accepted the offer. Congress, however, did not agree to provide financial aid because Egypt had bought weapons from Communist Czechoslovakia. A week later, Egypt gained control of the Suez Canal from the Anglo-French company that controlled it. Egypt wanted to use the profits from the canal to pay for the dam. In response, in October 1956, British and French troops invaded Egypt. The action upset President Eisenhower. The conflict became worse when the Soviet Union threatened to attack France and Britain and to send troops to help Egypt. Again, Eisenhower threatened a nuclear attack. Britain and France called off the invasion. Other Arab nations soon began accepting Soviet aid.

> **Academic Vocabulary**
>
> **dominant:** one that takes control over all others (p. 652)

5. How did President Eisenhower use brinkmanship to end the conflict in Korea?

_____

_____

_____

_____

_____

- **Fighting Communism Covertly** *(page 654)*

President Eisenhower knew that brinkmanship would not work all the time. He knew it would not work to prevent Communists from starting revolutions within countries. To prevent revolutions, Eisenhower used **covert,** or hidden, operations that were run by the Central Intelligence Agency (CIA).

Study Guide

Chapter 13, Section 4 *(continued)*

Many of these operations took place in **developing nations,** or nations with economies that depended primarily on agriculture. Many of these nations blamed American capitalism for their problems, and they looked to the Soviet Union as a model to industrialize their economy. American leaders feared that these countries would side with the Soviet Union or stage a Communist revolution. To prevent this, President Eisenhower offered financial aid to some of these nations. In nations where the Communist threat was stronger, the CIA used covert operations to overthrow anti-American leaders. They then replaced them with pro-American leaders.

Covert operations worked in Iran. There the prime minister was ready to make an oil deal with the Soviet Union. He moved against the pro-American Shah of Iran, who was forced to leave Iran. CIA agents organized street riots in Iran and arranged a coup to oust the prime minister and to return the Shah to power.

Covert operations also worked in Guatemala. The president of Guatemala had won the election with the support of the Soviet Union. His reform program took over large <u>estates</u>, including one owned by an America-owned company. Guatemala received weapons from Communist Czechoslovakia. The CIA then armed and trained the Guatemalan opposition. The CIA-trained forces then invaded Guatemala, and the pro-Communist president left office.

> **Academic Vocabulary**
>
> **estate:** a large amount of land, usually containing a large house (p. 655)

Sometimes covert operations did not work. After Stalin died, Nikita Khrushchev became the Soviet leader. He delivered a secret speech to Soviet leaders in which he attacked Stalin's policies. The CIA obtained a copy of the speech and had it broadcasted in Eastern Europe. In June 1956, riots started in Eastern Europe. A full-scale uprising developed in Hungary. Khrushchev, though willing to tolerate greater freedom in Eastern Europe, never meant to <u>imply</u> that he would tolerate an end to communism there. Soviet troops moved into Budapest, the capital, and crushed the uprising.

> **Academic Vocabulary**
>
> **imply:** to express indirectly (p. 655)

6. In what two countries were covert operations successful in preventing Communist revolutions?

_____

_____

_____

_____

_____

- **Continuing Tensions** *(page 656)*

In 1958 Khrushchev demanded that the United States, Great Britain, and France remove their troops from West Germany. The United States rejected the demands and threatened to use military force if the Soviets threatened Berlin. The Soviets backed down. To try to improve relations, Eisenhower asked

The American Vision: Modern Times

Study Guide

Chapter 13, Section 4 (continued)

Khrushchev to visit the United States. The two leaders met and agreed to hold a meeting in Paris in 1960. However, shortly before the meeting was to begin, the Soviet Union shot down an American U-2 spy plane. Khrushchev responded by breaking off the meeting.

President Eisenhower left office in January 1961. He delivered a farewell address to the nation. In it, he pointed out the new relationship that had developed between the military and the defense industry. He warned Americans against the influence of this **military-industrial complex.**

7. Why did Khrushchev break off the Paris meeting with President Eisenhower scheduled in 1960?

_____

_____

_____

_____

_____

Study Guide

Chapter 14, Section 1

For use with textbook pages 666–671

TRUMAN AND EISENHOWER

CONTENT VOCABULARY

closed shop   the practice of forcing business owners to hire only union members *(page 667)*

right-to-work law   law which outlawed union shops *(page 667)*

union shop   shops in which new workers were required to join the union *(page 667)*

featherbedding   the practice of limiting work output in order to create more jobs *(page 667)*

dynamic conservatism   the policy of balancing economic conservatism with some activism *(page 670)*

DRAWING FROM EXPERIENCE

What kinds of roadways does your community have? How important are they to you, your family, and your community?

In this section, you will learn about President Truman's domestic policy. You will also learn about President Eisenhower's domestic policy.

ORGANIZING YOUR THOUGHTS

Use the diagram below to help you take notes. President Eisenhower's policies regarding the role of the federal government were conservative, but he also believed in activism. Describe the ways President Eisenhower showed conservatism and the ways he showed activism.

> **California History-Social Science Standards**
>
> **11.8** Students analyze the economic boom and social transformation of post–World War II America.
>
> **11.10** Students analyze the development of federal civil rights and voting rights.
>
> **11.11** Students analyze the major social problems and domestic policy issues in contemporary American society.
>
> **Focuses on:** 11.8.3, 11.8.4, 11.10.1, 11.11.2

Ways of Showing Conservatism

1.

2.

3.

4.

Ways of Showing Activism

5.

6.

Study Guide

Chapter 14, Section 1 *(continued)*

READ TO LEARN

- ## Return to a Peacetime Economy *(page 667)*

After the war ended, the United States economy continued to grow. Consumer spending helped this growth. Americans, who lived with shortages throughout the war, were eager to buy the luxury goods that they had wanted. The economy also got a boost from the Servicemen's Readjustment Act, which was popularly called the GI Bill. It provided loans to veterans to help them buy homes, start businesses, or go to college.

The large demand for goods led to higher prices. This led to growing inflation. As the cost of living increased, so did labor unrests. Strikes occurred in the automobile, steel, and mining industries.

The labor unrests and inflation caused many people to call for a change in leadership. In the 1946 congressional elections, Republicans took control of both houses of Congress. The new Congress set out to decrease the power of unions. They proposed the Taft-Hartley Act. It outlawed the **closed shop,** or the practice of forcing business owners to hire only union members. The law allowed the states to pass **right-to-work laws,** which outlawed **union shops,** or shops in which new workers were required to join the union. The law also prohibited **featherbedding,** or the practice of limiting work output in order to create more jobs. President Truman vetoed the bill. Congress overrode the veto and passed the Taft-Hartley Act in 1947, <u>restraining</u> union activities. Labor leaders were upset, saying that the law had done away with many of the gains that unions had made since 1933.

Academic Vocabulary
restrain: to keep under control, or limit freedom (p. 668)

7. Why did Congress pass the Taft-Hartley Act?

_____

_____

_____

_____

_____

- ## Truman's Domestic Program *(page 668)*

Although Republicans controlled Congress, President Truman continued to work to push his programs through Congress. He wanted to expand Social Security benefits, increase the minimum wage, set up long-range environmental and public works, and set up a system of national health insurance. Truman also asked Congress to pass a civil rights bill that would protect African Americans' right to vote and make lynching a federal crime. He issued an executive order that banned discrimination in federal employment. It also ended segregation in the armed forces. However, many of Truman's

Study Guide

Chapter 14, Section 1 (continued)

suggested programs were shut down by a coalition of Republicans and Southern Democrats in Congress.

Many people did not think that President Truman would win the 1948 election. The Democratic Party itself was divided over whom to nominate. Southern Democrats formed a new party and nominated Strom Thurmond. The liberal members of the Democratic Party formed a new Progressive Party and nominated Henry A. Wallace. The Republican nominee was the popular New York Governor Thomas Dewey. Most newspaper writers believed that Dewey would win by a landslide.

Truman believed he could win. He waged an energetic campaign, traveling more than 20,000 miles. He blamed the Republican Congress, referring to it as the "Do-Nothing Congress," for refusing to pass his programs. His claims were not exactly true. Congress did pass many parts of his foreign-policy programs, such as the Marshall Plan. However, these programs did not affect Americans directly, and his "do-nothing" claims seemed to stick. Truman won by a narrow margin in a surprising victory. In addition, the Democrats had regained control of both houses of Congress.

Truman continued to work for passage of his programs. He said that all Americans had the right to expect a fair deal from the government. The Fair Deal became the name of Truman's programs. Congress passed some aspects of the Fair Deal. It increased the minimum wage and approved an expansion of Social Security benefits. Congress also passed the National Housing Act, which provided funding for the building of low-income housing and long-term rent <u>subsidies</u>. Congress refused to pass national health insurance or civil rights laws.

Academic Vocabulary
subsidy: money granted by the government to achieve a specific goal that is beneficial to society (p. 670)

8. What were the results of the 1948 election?

_____

_____

- ## The Eisenhower Years (page 670)

Harry Truman did not run for re-election in 1952. The Republicans nominated General Dwight Eisenhower for president and Richard Nixon for vice president. The Democrats nominated Illinois governor Adlai Stevenson. Eisenhower won in a landslide. The Republicans had a majority in the House, while the Senate was evenly divided between Democrats and Republicans.

President Eisenhower's political beliefs fell between conservative and liberal. He believed in **dynamic conservatism,** which meant balancing economic conservatism with some activism.

Eisenhower's conservatism showed itself in several ways. He appointed several business leaders to his cabinet. Following their advice, Eisenhower ended government price and rent controls. Many conservatives had viewed

The American Vision: Modern Times

Study Guide

Chapter 14, Section 1 (continued)

these controls as unnecessary federal control over business. Eisenhower cut government aid to public housing. He limited the federal government's aid to businesses by abolishing the Reconstruction Finance Corporation (RFC), which had lent money to banks and other large businesses. He cut the amount of money allocated for the Tennessee Valley Authority (TVA), another Depression-era agency.

Eisenhower showed his activist side. To provide more travel routes for the rapidly increasing number of cars, Eisenhower asked Congress to pass the Federal Highway Act. This was the largest public works program in American history. The act called for the building of more than 40,000 miles of interstate highway. He also authorized the building of the Great Lakes-St. Lawrence Seaway. It connected the Great Lakes with the Atlantic Ocean.

Although Eisenhower wanted to limit the federal government's role in the economy, he did agree to extend the Social Security system. He also extended unemployment compensation and increased the minimum wage. By the time Eisenhower won the presidential campaign in 1956, the nation had successfully completed the transition from a wartime to a peacetime economy.

Academic Vocabulary
transition: passing from one circumstance to another (p. 671)

9. What was the purpose of the Federal Highway Act?

_____

_____

_____

_____

_____

Name _____ Date _____ Class _____

Study Guide

Chapter 14, Section 2

For use with textbook pages 674–679

THE AFFLUENT SOCIETY

CONTENT VOCABULARY

white-collar kind of jobs that do not involve physical labor in industry *(page 675)*

blue-collar kind of jobs that involve physical labor *(page 675)*

multinational corporation large corporation that expanded overseas *(page 675)*

franchise a business in which a person owns and runs one or several stores of a chain operation *(page 676)*

baby boom the time between 1945 and 1961, when more than 65 million children were born *(page 677)*

DRAWING FROM EXPERIENCE

How do you decide what brand of clothes or other products to buy? How does advertising affect your choices?

The last section described the domestic policies of Presidents Truman and Eisenhower. This section discusses the effects of the nation's economic boom on Americans.

ORGANIZING YOUR THOUGHTS

Use the diagram below to help you take notes. Several technological changes occurred in the United States in the 1950s. Identify these advances in the diagram.

California History-Social Science Standards

11.8 Students analyze the economic boom and social transformation of post–World War II America.

11.10 Students analyze the development of federal civil rights and voting rights.

11.11 Students analyze the major social problems and domestic policy issues in contemporary American society.

Focuses on: 11.8.1, 11.8.7, 11.10.7, 11.11.3, 11.11.7

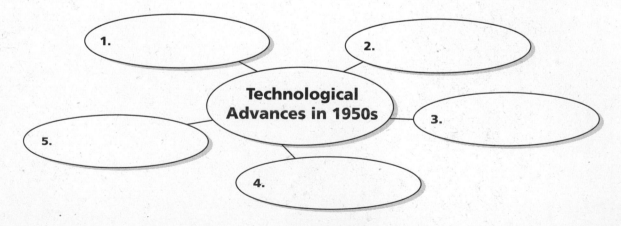

The American Vision: Modern Times

Study Guide

Chapter 14, Section 2 (continued)

READ TO LEARN

• **American Abundance** (page 675)

In 1958 economist John Kenneth Galbraith published *The Affluent Society*. In it he claimed that the economic prosperity that the nation was experiencing was a new phenomenon. He believed that the United States had created an economy of abundance. New business techniques and improved technology helped the nation make an abundance of goods and services for its people. This allowed the people to have a higher standard of living than they ever thought possible.

Galbraith's observation seemed to be true. Between 1940 and 1960, income tripled for many Americans. They produced more than they could use. More people than ever before owned their own homes. Accompanying the country's economic growth were dramatic changes in work environments. Fewer farmers and laborers were needed to provide food and goods. As a result, more Americans were working in **white-collar** jobs, such as those in sales and management. In 1956 white-collar workers outnumbered **blue-collar** workers, or those who perform physical labor in industry.

Academic Vocabulary
accompany: to be associated with (p. 675)

Many white-collar workers worked for large corporations. Some of these corporations expanded overseas. These **multinational corporations** were located closer to raw materials and benefited from a cheaper labor pool. This made the companies more competitive. The number of **franchises** increased in the 1950s. These are businesses in which a person owns and runs one or several stores of a chain operation. The owners of franchises demanded that their franchises have the same look and style.

Academic Vocabulary
benefit: to be useful or profitable (p. 675)

Many corporate leaders also expected their employees to conform. They generally did not want their employees to be independent thinkers. Sociologist David Riesman criticized this approach. In his 1950 book, *The Lonely Crowd*, he argued that the individual who judged himself on the basis of his own values was now becoming an individual who was more concerned with winning the approval of the corporation or the community.

In the 1950s, part of fitting in included owning the same new products as everyone else. Having more income available to them, Americans bought luxury items such as swimming pools, refrigerators, and air conditioners.

Advertising became more sophisticated in the 1950s. It became a major industry. Many manufacturers used new techniques to sell their products. The purpose of advertising was to influence Americans to choose among brands of goods that were basically the same. The advertisers aimed their ads on people who had money to spend. Most of these people lived in the growing suburbs. One of the earliest of these new suburbs was Levittown, New York. The suburbs included hundreds of mass-produced, similar-looking homes. Thousands of people rushed to buy the inexpensive homes.

Study Guide

Chapter 14, Section 2 *(continued)*

Most new homes in the 1950s were built in the suburbs. The number of people living in suburbs doubled. Unlike city life, life in the suburbs provided people with access to the countryside. Being able to afford a house was easier in the 1950s. This was due to the low-interest loans offered by the GI Bill. In addition, the government offered tax deductions for home mortgage interest payments and property taxes. For many Americans, the suburbs symbolized the American dream. However, some critics viewed all the identical-looking communities as a sign of conformity.

6. Why did housing become more affordable in the 1950s?

_____

_____

_____

_____

_____

• **The 1950s Family** *(page 677)*

In the 1950s, the American family was changing. The birthrate increased greatly after World War II. The time between 1945 and 1961, when more than 65 million children were born, was known as the **baby boom.** There were several causes for the baby boom. Couples who postponed marriage during World War II and the Korean War could now marry and begin their families. The government encouraged having children by offering GI benefits for home purchases. Advertising sang the praises of pregnancy and large families.

During the 1950s, many women focused on establishing families and staying home to care for them. This discouraged many women from getting jobs. Magazine ads encouraged women to stay at home. However, despite the push for women to only be homemakers, the number of women who had jobs outside the home increased during the 1950s.

7. What factors contributed to the baby boom?

_____

_____

_____

_____

_____

Study Guide

Chapter 14, Section 2 *(continued)*

• **Technological Breakthroughs** *(page 678)*

Several important scientific advances occurred in the 1950s. American physicists developed the transistor, a tiny device that <u>generated</u> electric signals and made it possible to miniaturize radios and calculators. The device made it possible to miniaturize radios and calculators. In 1946 scientists also developed one of the nation's earliest computers to make military calculations. Several years later, a newer model was developed. This computer handled business data. The computer allowed people to work more quickly and efficiently. This provided Americans in the 1950s with more free time for leisure activities.

Medical advances included antibiotics to fight infections and new drugs to fight cancer, diabetes, and heart disease. New surgical techniques were also developed. Polio, however, continued to puzzle researchers. In the 1940s and 1950s a powerful polio epidemic swept the United States. The disease particularly targeted the young, causing crippling and death. In 1952 58,000 cases of polio were reported. Then Jonas Salk developed an injectable vaccine that prevented polio. In 1955 the vaccine became available to the public. The number of polio cases dropped dramatically. Albert Sabin then developed an oral vaccine for polio. In the following years, the threat of polio almost completely disappeared.

After the Soviet Union launched *Sputnik*, the United States hurried to catch up. On January 31, 1958, the United States launched its own satellite. At the same time, engineers were building smoother and faster commercial planes.

8. What was the effect of Jonas Salk's polio vaccine?

_____

_____

_____

_____

_____

Study Guide

Chapter 14, Section 3

For use with textbook pages 680–685

POPULAR CULTURE OF THE 1950S

CONTENT VOCABULARY

generation gap   a cultural separation between children and their parents *(page 684)*

DRAWING FROM EXPERIENCE

Are television and movies important parts of your leisure activities? What kinds of television programs and movies do you enjoy the most? Why?

The last section discussed the ways Americans were affected by the economic boom. This section describes popular culture in the United States in the 1950s.

> **California History-Social Science Standards**
>
> **11.8** Students analyze the economic boom and social transformation of post–World War II America.
>
> **Focuses on:** 11.8.8

ORGANIZING YOUR THOUGHTS

Use the cause-and-effect diagram below to help you take notes. Rock 'n' roll had an impact on American society in the 1950s. List its effects in the diagram.

Cause   **Effects**

| Rock 'n' Roll | — | 1. _____ |
| | | 2. _____ |

READ TO LEARN

• **The New Mass Media** *(page 681)*

By the end of the 1950s, the television was a popular household item. By 1957 there were about 40 million television sets in use. By the late 1950s, television was an important source of information. Television advertising, which paid for the programming, led to a growing market for new products. One critic referred to television programs as "a <u>device</u> to keep the advertisements and commercials from bumping loudly together." Television programs included comedy, action and adventure, and variety-style entertainment. Many early television comedy shows were based on old radio shows.

> **Academic Vocabulary**
>
> **device:** a scheme meant to deceive (p. 681)

Study Guide

Chapter 14, Section 3 (continued)

Americans enjoyed action shows such as *The Lone Ranger* and *Dragnet*. Variety shows such as Ed Sullivan's *Toast of the Town* and quiz shows such as *The $64,000 Question* were popular. In 1956 Charles Van Doren, a contestant on the quiz show *Twenty-One*, won $129,000 during his time on the show. People soon found out, however, that Van Doren, like many other contestants, received the answers to questions in advance. Van Doren admitted his role to a congressional committee in 1959. Many quiz shows left the air after the scandal.

Television's popularity forced the other forms of mass media to innovate in order to keep their audiences. The film business suffered in the 1950s with the growing popularity of television. Hollywood tried to make films more exciting. Movies such as *The Ten Commandments* and *Around the World in 80 Days* were shown on large screens. Although these kinds of movies were expensive to make, they made up their cost by attracting many people and making large profits. Most films, like most television shows, conformed with the times. Very few showed strong-minded women. African Americans were usually shown in stereotypical roles such as servants or sidekicks to white heroes.

Television also took away radio listeners. As a result, the radio industry had to find ways to draw listeners. Many radios began to broadcast recorded music, news, and talk shows. They also presented shows for specific audiences. As a result of these changes, radio stations survived and prospered.

3. What types of programs did television show in the 1950s?

_____

_____

_____

_____

_____

• The New Youth Culture *(page 683)*

In the 1950s, some of the nation's youth rebelled against middle-class suburban values, particularly conformity. They turned to new and unconventional styles of music and literature. In 1951 a white disc jockey named Alan Freed introduced African American rhythm and blues records to white radio stations. Soon white artists began making music that was based on African American rhythms and sounds. This form of music was rock 'n' roll. It became wildly popular with the nation's teenagers. Teens bought the latest hits from such as artists as Buddy Holly and Chuck Berry. Elvis Presley became the first rock 'n' roll hero. By 1956 Presley had a record deal, a movie contract, and public appearances on several television shows.

Study Guide

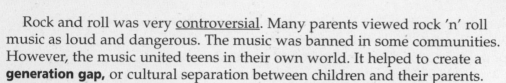

Chapter 14, Section 3 *(continued)*

Rock and roll was very <u>controversial</u>. Many parents viewed rock 'n' roll music as loud and dangerous. The music was banned in some communities. However, the music united teens in their own world. It helped to create a **generation gap,** or cultural separation between children and their parents.

In the 1950s, a group of white artists who called themselves the beats focused on a values gap in the United States. They lived unconventional lives away from a culture they hated. Beat poets, writers, and artists criticized the conformity of American life and the emptiness of popular culture. Jack Kerouac published *On the Road* in 1957. Although shocking to some, the book became a classic in modern American literature.

> | Academic Vocabulary |
> | --- |
> | **controversial:** something that causes opposing views to be debated (p. 683) |

4. What contributed to a generation gap in the 1950s?

_____

_____

_____

_____

_____

• African American Entertainers *(page 685)*

During the 1950s, African American entertainers tried to find acceptance. Television tended to shut them out. African American rock 'n' roll singers such as Little Richard had more luck in gaining acceptance. In the late 1950s, African American women's groups also became popular. At the same time that African American entertainers attempted to gain acceptance, the African American community attempted to gain equality and opportunities.

5. What did African American entertainers try to do in the 1950s?

_____

_____

_____

_____

_____

Study Guide

Chapter 14, Section 4

For use with textbook pages 688–693

THE OTHER SIDE OF AMERICAN LIFE

CONTENT VOCABULARY

poverty line   a figure the government set to reflect the minimum income required to support a family *(page 689)*

urban renewal   type of program that tried to eliminate poverty by tearing down slums and building high-rise buildings for poor residents *(page 689)*

termination policy   government plan that withdrew all official recognition of the Native American groups as legal entities and made them subject to the same laws as white citizens *(page 691)*

juvenile delinquency   antisocial or criminal behavior of young people *(page 692)*

DRAWING FROM EXPERIENCE

Do you think poverty is a problem in the United States today? Do you think it is a problem in other countries? What things do you think contribute to poverty?

The last section described popular culture in the United States in the 1950s. This section discusses the reasons many groups in the United States lived in poverty in the 1950s.

ORGANIZING YOUR THOUGHTS

Use the chart below to help you take notes. Many groups of people in the United States did not enjoy economic prosperity. Identify these groups in the chart below.

California History-Social Science Standards
11.8 Students analyze the economic boom and social transformation of post–World War II America.
11.10 Students analyze the development of federal civil rights and voting rights.
Focuses on: 11.8.2, 11.8.4, 11.10.1

Groups Living in Poverty in the 1950s
1.
2.
3.
4.

Study Guide

Chapter 14, Section 4 (continued)

READ TO LEARN

- **Poverty Amidst Prosperity** (page 689)

Although many Americans benefited from the economic boom in the 1950s, about 30 million Americans still lived below the **poverty line** by 1959. This is a figure the government set to reflect the minimum income required to support a family. Most Americans assumed that everyone in the nation was prosperous. However, writer Michael Harrington wrote a book in 1962 that reported on poverty in the United States. His book, *The Other America*, showed Americans the rundown communities of the country.

The poor in the United States included many different groups. Poverty was most obvious in the nation's urban centers. As white people moved to the suburbs, the inner cities became home to poorer minority groups. Sometimes government efforts to help made things worse. For example, during the 1950s, **urban renewal** programs tried to eliminate poverty by tearing down slums and building new high-rise buildings for poor residents. These high-rises resulted in crowded conditions and violence. The government also ended up encouraging residents to remain in poverty by evicting them from the projects as soon as they earned any money.

Many residents of the inner cities were African Americans. This was due in part to the northward migration of about 3 million African Americans between 1940 and 1960. Many moved to northern cities to find jobs and to escape racial intimidation. Life was not much better in northern cities, however. Fewer and fewer jobs became available as many factories moved to the suburbs. Racial discrimination in schools, housing, and in hiring in the North kept African Americans in the inner cities poor. Poverty and racial discrimination also deprived African Americans of other things, such as proper medical care. One correspondent wrote, "It is not an <u>abstraction</u> to us that the average [African American] has a life expectancy of five to ten years less than the average white." Several African American groups, such as the NAACP, pushed for greater equality and economic opportunity for African Americans. They had few successes.

Academic Vocabulary
abstraction: an idea that is difficult for some to understand (p. 690)

Hispanics in the United States also faced poverty. In the 1940s and the 1950s, nearly 5 million Mexicans immigrated to the United States to help fill the nation's farm labor needs through the Bracero program. Those who worked on large farms throughout the country worked long hours for little pay in horrible conditions. Away from the farms, many Mexican families lived in small shacks.

By the mid-1900s, Native Americans made up the poorest group in the nation. After World War II, the United States government started a program to bring Native Americans into mainstream society, whether they wanted to or not. Under a plan known as the **termination policy,** the federal government withdrew all official recognition of the Native American groups as legal entities and made them subject to the same laws as white citizens. The government also helped move Native Americans off the reservations to cities such as Minneapolis. The termination policy deepened the poverty of many Native Americans.

Study Guide

Chapter 14, Section 4 *(continued)*

Poverty was not limited to minorities. It also affected white families of Appalachia. During the 1950s, about a million people left Appalachia to start a better life in the cities. They left behind the elderly and other residents. Many people in Appalachia were suffering from poor nutrition. The region had few doctors. Schooling in Appalachia was considered worse than that in the inner cities.

5. What was the result of urban renewal programs?

_____

_____

_____

_____

_____

• Juvenile Delinquency *(page 692)*

Another problem facing the nation was **juvenile delinquency,** or antisocial or criminal behavior of young people. Juvenile crime rose by 45 percent between 1948 and 1953. Car thefts by juveniles increased. In addition, more young people belonged to street gangs and committed muggings and even murder. Experts blamed juvenile delinquency on a number of things. They blamed it on factors such as poverty, television, racism, and a rising divorce rate. Some critics claimed that young people were rebelling against <u>conformity</u>. Some blamed a lack of discipline. Delinquency existed across class and racial lines. Although most teens were not involved in crime or drugs, the public tended to stereotype all young people as juvenile delinquents.

Academic Vocabulary
conformity: a change in a way that fits a standard or authority (p. 692)

Many parents in the 1950s were concerned over the educational system in the United States. With many baby boomers becoming school age in the 1950s, the number of children in school increased by 13 million. School districts had to build new school buildings and hire new teachers. However, there were shortages of both. The launch of *Sputnik* by the Soviet Union made many Americans believe that schools lacked <u>technical</u> education. As a result, efforts were made to improve math and science education in schools.

Academic Vocabulary
technical: to have special understanding of mechanical or scientific knowledge (p. 693)

6. What caused concerns about the educational system in the United States in the 1950s?

_____

_____

_____

_____

_____

_____

Study Guide

Chapter 15, Section 1

For use with textbook pages 704–711

THE NEW FRONTIER

CONTENT VOCABULARY

missile gap   the United States's lag behind the Soviet Union in weaponry *(page 706)*

reapportionment   the way in which states draw up political districts based on changes in population *(page 710)*

due process   the idea that the law may not treat individuals unfairly or unreasonably and that courts must follow proper procedures when trying cases *(page 710)*

DRAWING FROM EXPERIENCE

Have you seen police detective shows on television? What do police officers do when they arrest a suspect? Why do they do that?

In this section, you will learn about President Kennedy's economic policies. You will also learn why Congress did not support many of Kennedy's domestic programs.

ORGANIZING YOUR THOUGHTS

Use the chart below to help you take notes. The Supreme Court in the early 1960s helped to determine national policy through several of its rulings. Describe the Court decision in each of the rulings listed in the chart.

California History-Social Science Standards

11.8 Students analyze the economic boom and social transformation of post–World War II America.

11.10 Students analyze the development of federal civil rights and voting rights.

11.11 Students analyze the major social problems and domestic policy issues in contemporary American society.

Focuses on: 11.8.4, 11.10.2, 11.10.7, 11.11.2, 11.11.3

Court Case	Court Ruling
Reynolds v. *Sims*	1.
Mapp v. *Ohio*	2.
Gideon v. *Wainwright*	3.
Escobedo v. *Illinois*	4.

Study Guide

Chapter 15, Section 1 (continued)

READ TO LEARN

• The Election of 1960 (page 705)

Television played an important part in the 1960 presidential election. This was the first election in which a majority of voters used the <u>medium</u> of television as a voting tool. The Democrats nominated John F. Kennedy, and the Republicans nominated Richard M. Nixon. Both parties spent money on television ads.

The main issues in the campaign were the economy and the Cold War. The candidates had few differences regarding these issues. Kennedy believed that the Soviets were a serious threat to the United States. He was concerned about a possible **"missile gap,"** in which the United States lagged behind the Soviet Union in weaponry. Nixon argued that the United States was on the right track. He warned that enacting the Democrats' policies would increase inflation. Kennedy faced a religious issue. The United States had never had a Catholic president. Kennedy faced the issue by pointing out that in the United States, separation of church and state was absolute.

The four televised presidential debates influenced the outcome of the campaign. Kennedy won by a narrow margin.

5. How did television affect the 1960 presidential election?

_____

_____

_____

• The Kennedy Mystique (page 706)

President Kennedy was very popular with the American people. His looks, glamorous wife Jacqueline, and their children led to constant coverage by the media. Newspeople followed the family everywhere. Kennedy used the media well. He was the first to have his press conferences televised. He also inspired many of his staff.

6. How did Americans react to President Kennedy?

_____

_____

_____

• Success and Setback on the Domestic Front (page 707)

President Kennedy was not popular with all Americans. Congress also was less taken with him. After Kennedy became president, he sent a legislative package to Congress. His domestic programs became known as the New Frontier. Kennedy wanted to increase aid to education, provide health insurance

Academic Vocabulary
medium: a means of conveying information, communication, or entertainment (p. 705)

The American Vision: Modern Times

Study Guide

Chapter 15, Section 1 *(continued)*

to the elderly, and create a Department of Urban Affairs. Convincing Congress to pass the legislation was not easy.

Kennedy was not able to push through many of his domestic programs. Because Kennedy had won by such a narrow margin, he was not helpful in getting many Democrats elected to Congress. As a result, lawmakers found it easy to look out for their own interests instead of considering the interests of the president. Republicans and conservative Southern Democrats believed that the New Frontier was too costly. They also opposed an increase of federal power.

Although Kennedy was unsuccessful in getting Congress to pass many of his programs, he was successful in passing some economic programs. The American economy had slowed by the end of the 1950s. Unemployment was high and the growth rate of the gross national product was low. To boost the economy, Kennedy pushed Roosevelt's strategy of deficit spending. Kennedy convinced Congress to spend more on defense and space exploration. This spending did create more jobs and stimulate the economy. Kennedy also wanted to boost the economy by increasing business production. His administration also asked businesses to keep prices down and to hold down pay increases.

Labor unions in the steel industry agreed to lower their demands for wage increases. In 1962, however, several steel companies raised prices. The president threatened to buy cheaper steel from foreign companies. The steel companies backed down and cut their prices.

To get the economy moving, Kennedy followed supply-side ideas. He pushed for a cut in tax rates, hoping this would give businesses more money to expand and create new jobs. Congress defeated the tax cut because many members feared it would cause inflation. Kennedy did get Congress to increase the minimum wage. He provided about $400 million to distressed areas. A Housing Act created a home-building and slum clearance program.

A number of women held important positions in Kennedy's administration. In 1961 Kennedy created a Presidential Commission on the Status of Women. It called for federal action against gender discrimination and the right of women to equally paid employment. Kennedy issued an executive order that ended gender discrimination in the federal civil service. In 1963 he signed the Equal Pay Act for women.

7. Why did many members of Congress oppose the programs of the New Frontier?

_____

_____

_____

_____

_____

Study Guide

Chapter 15, Section 1 (continued)

• **Warren Court Reforms** (page 709)

In 1953 President Eisenhower nominated Earl Warren to be the Chief Justice of the United States. The Warren Court was an active one, helping shape national policy by taking a stand on several issues. An important decision of the Warren Court had to do with **reapportionment,** or the way in which states draw up political districts based on changes in population. By 1960 more people <u>resided</u> in urban rather than rural areas. Many states had not changed their electoral districts to match this change, however. For example, in Tennessee a rural district with about 2,300 voters had one representative in the state legislature, while a city district with about 133 times more voters had only seven representatives. Some people in Tennessee decided to challenge this system in the courts. The case eventually reached the Supreme Court. In *Reynolds* v. *Sims,* the Supreme Court ruled that the current apportionment system in many states was not constitutional. The ruling required that state legislatures reapportion their electoral districts so that citizens' votes would have equal weight. This decision shifted political power throughout the country from rural, often conservative, areas to urban, often more liberal, areas.

The Supreme Court began to use the Fourteenth Amendment to apply the Bill of Rights to the states. The Bill of Rights originally applied to the federal government. Many states had their own bill of rights. The Fourteenth Amendment said that no state could deprive an individual of rights with **due process.** This means that the law may not treat individuals unfairly, or <u>arbitrarily</u>, or unreasonably and that courts must follow proper procedures and rules when trying cases. Due process makes sure that all people are treated the same by the courts. In several cases, the Supreme Court ruled that using due process meant that the federal bill of rights applied to the states.

In *Mapp* v. *Ohio,* the Supreme Court ruled that state courts could not use evidence that was obtained illegally. In *Gideon* v. *Wainwright,* it ruled that a defendant in a state court had the right to a lawyer, regardless of his ability to pay. In *Escobedo* v. *Illinois,* the Court ruled that a suspect has to have access to a lawyer and had to be informed of the right to remain silent before being questioned by the police. In *Miranda* v. *Arizona,* the justices ruled that authorities had to give suspects a four-part warning that included their right to remain silent and their right to a lawyer. These warnings are known as the Miranda rights. The rulings received mixed reactions. Some believed the Court favored criminals, whereas others believed the rulings promoted the rights of all citizens.

The Supreme Court also ruled on the relationship between church and state. In *Engel* v. *Vitale,* the Court ruled that states could not require prayers to be said in state public schools. In *Abington School District* v. *Schempp,* state-mandated Bible readings in public schools were not disallowed.

8. What effect did the Warren Court have on the United States?

_____

_____

> **Academic Vocabulary**
>
> **reside:** to live in a particular location (p. 710)

> **Academic Vocabulary**
>
> **arbitrary:** based on individual preference or convenience and not dependent on standards (p. 710)

© by The McGraw-Hill Companies, Inc.

The American Vision: Modern Times

Study Guide

Chapter 15, Section 2

For use with textbook pages 714–719

JFK AND THE COLD WAR

CONTENT VOCABULARY

flexible response   the policy of allowing conventional troops and weapons to be used against Communist movements *(page 715)*

space race   vying for dominance of space to increase competitive positions on Earth *(page 716)*

DRAWING FROM EXPERIENCE

Have you heard of the Peace Corps? What do you think is the purpose of the Peace Corps? Would you be interested in joining it? Why or why not?

The last section described President Kennedy's domestic programs. This section discusses the ways President Kennedy dealt with Cold War challenges.

ORGANIZING YOUR THOUGHTS

Use the diagram below to help you take notes. President Kennedy faced several crises that were the result of the Cold War. List these crises in the diagram.

California History-Social Science Standards

11.8 Students analyze the economic boom and social transformation of post–World War II America.

11.9 Students analyze the U.S. foreign policy since World War II.

Focuses on: 11.8.5, 11.8.7, 11.9.3

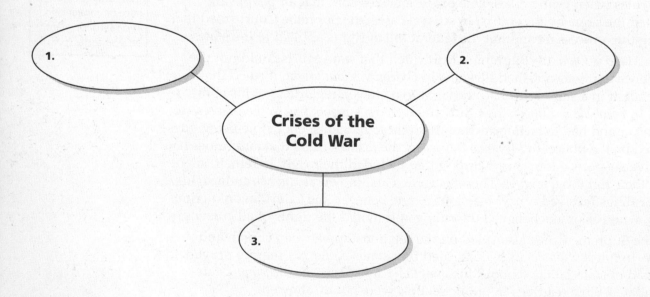

The American Vision: Modern Times

Study Guide

Chapter 15, Section 2 *(continued)*

- **Kennedy Confronts Global Challenges** *(page 715)*

Kennedy believed that Eisenhower depended too much on nuclear weapons, which could only be used in extreme situations. Kennedy wanted to allow for a **flexible response,** in which conventional troops and weapons could be used against Communist movements. To do this, Kennedy supported the Special Forces. This was a small army unit that was created to deal with guerrilla warfare.

Kennedy wanted to improve relations in Latin America. Many governments in Latin America were controlled by a wealthy few, whereas most of the people lived in poverty. In some of these countries, left-wing movements tried to overthrow their governments. The United States generally supported the existing governments in order to prevent the Communist movements from being successful. Poor Latin Americans resented the United States.

To improve relations between Latin America and the United States, President Kennedy proposed an Alliance for Progress. This was a series of cooperative aid projects with Latin American governments. The United States promised $20 billion to help Latin American countries set up better schools, housing, health care, and fairer land distribution. Some countries benefited from the aid. In other countries, the government leaders used the money to keep themselves in power.

President Kennedy also set up the Peace Corps to help fight poverty in less developed nations. It was an organization that sent young Americans to do humanitarian services in less developed nations. Volunteers were trained and then spent two years in a nation that had requested help. Their work included building roads, training medical technicians, and laying out sewage systems. The Peace Corps is still active today.

In 1961, the Soviet Union was the first nation to successfully launch a human being into orbit around the earth. Kennedy worried that Soviet space successes would affect the outcome of the Cold War. Both nations started a **space race,** the vying for dominance of space to increase their competitive positions on Earth. Kennedy challenged the U.S. government and the nation's industry to safely land a human on the moon. The challenge was met in July 1969, demonstrating America's technological superiority.

4. What was the purpose of the Alliance for Progress?

_____

_____

_____

_____

Study Guide

Chapter 15, Section 2 *(continued)*

- ### Crises of the Cold War *(page 717)*

President Kennedy faced several crises in the Cold War. The first one started in Cuba. Fidel Castro had overthrown the Cuban dictator in 1959. He immediately established ties with the Soviet Union. He <u>instituted</u> drastic land reforms and took over foreign-owned businesses, many of which were American. The Communists were now very close to the United States. The United States was concerned that the Communists would set up a base in Cuba from which to spread their beliefs throughout the Western Hemisphere. President Eisenhower authorized the Central Intelligence Agency (CIA) to train and arm Cuban exiles and to invade the island. The United States hoped that the invasion would start an uprising in Cuba against Castro.

Shortly after Kennedy became president, Kennedy's advisers approved the invasion plan. On April 17, 1961, armed Cuban exiles landed at the Bay of Pigs, on the south coast of Cuba. The invasion failed. It showed that the United States had tried to overthrow a neighbor's government. It made the United States look weak.

Shortly after the failed invasion, Kennedy faced another problem. Kennedy met with Soviet leader Khrushchev in Austria in June 1961. Khrushchev wanted to keep the Germans from moving out of Communist East Germany into West Berlin. He wanted Western countries to recognize East Germany. He also wanted the United States, Britain, and France to leave Berlin. Kennedy refused. Khrushchev responded by building the Berlin Wall, a visible <u>symbol</u> of the Cold War. It stopped movement between the Soviet part of the city and the rest of the city. Guards along the wall shot at many of those trying to escape from the East.

The most frightening crisis happened in 1962, and it dealt with Cuba. The United States had learned that Soviet technicians and equipment had arrived in Cuba. They also learned that a military buildup was in progress. On October 22, 1962, President Kennedy told the American people that photos taken by spy planes showed that the Soviet Union had placed long-range missiles in Cuba. These posed a serious threat to the United States. Kennedy ordered a naval blockade to stop the Soviet Union from delivering more missiles. He warned that if the Soviet Union launched missiles on the United States, he would respond against the Soviet Union. However, work on the missile sites continued.

The leaders of the two countries started secret negotiations. They reached an agreement on October 18. Kennedy agreed not to invade Cuba and to remove U.S. missiles from Turkey. The Soviet Union agreed to remove their missiles from Cuba.

The Cuban missile crisis brought the world close to nuclear war. It made both the Soviet Union and the United States face the consequences of a nuclear war. As a result, both countries worked to lessen tensions. They agreed to a treaty to ban the testing of nuclear weapons in the atmosphere.

Academic Vocabulary
institute: to initiate or establish something (p. 717)

Academic Vocabulary
symbol: something that stands for or suggests something else (p. 718)

The American Vision: Modern Times

Study Guide

Chapter 15, Section 2 *(continued)*

5. What were the results of the Cuban missile crisis?

_____

_____

_____

_____

_____

• **The Death of a President** *(page 718)*

On November 22, 1963, President Kennedy and his wife traveled to Texas to make some political appearances. As the presidential motorcade rode through Dallas, President Kennedy was shot. He was pronounced dead at a local hospital. Lee Harvey Oswald, the man accused of killing Kennedy, was shot to death two days later while in police custody. In 1964 the Warren Commission, a national commission headed by Chief Justice Warren, concluded that Oswald acted alone. However, theories about a conspiracy to kill the president have continued.

The United States and the world mourned the loss of President Kennedy. Although he served as president for only about 1,000 days, he left a lasting impression on most Americans.

> **Academic Vocabulary**
>
> **theory:** a hypothesis meant for argument or investigation (p. 719)

6. What did the Warren Commission conclude?

_____

_____

_____

_____

_____

Name _____ Date _____ Class _____

Study Guide

Chapter 15, Section 3

For use with textbook pages 722–729

THE GREAT SOCIETY

CONTENT VOCABULARY

consensus   general agreement *(page 724)*

war on poverty   a program announced by President Johnson to fight poverty in the United States *(page 725)*

DRAWING FROM EXPERIENCE

Do you think poverty is a problem in the United States today? How, if at all, do you think the government should help reduce poverty? Why do you think so?

The last section described the events in foreign affairs during the Kennedy administration. This section discusses the domestic programs of President Johnson.

ORGANIZING YOUR THOUGHTS

Use the chart below to help you take notes. President Johnson's Great Society set up several new programs. Describe what each of the listed programs provides.

Program	What It Does
Medicare	1.
Medicaid	2.
Project Head Start	3.
VISTA	4.

California History-Social Science Standards

11.8 Students analyze the economic boom and social transformation of post–World War II America.

11.11 Students analyze the major social problems and domestic policy issues in contemporary American society.

Focuses on: 11.8.4, 11.11.1, 11.11.2, 11.11.6, 11.11.7

READ TO LEARN

- **Johnson Takes the Reins** *(page 723)*

Michael Harrington's book, *The Other America*, showed that many Americans lived in poverty in the United States. As a result, both President Kennedy and Kennedy's successor, President Lyndon Johnson, made the elimination of poverty a major goal.

Study Guide

Chapter 15, Section 3 (continued)

After President Kennedy's death, President Johnson knew that he had to reassure the nation that he could hold it together. He went before Congress and urged the nation to move on.

Johnson's leadership style was quite different from that of President Kennedy. He had developed his style through long years of public service. He had 26 years in Congress, serving in both the House and the Senate. He had also served as vice president. He had a reputation as a person who got things done. His tactics became known as the "Johnson treatment." He used "mimicry, humor, and the genius of <u>analogy</u>," among other things, to get his way. He always tried to find **consensus,** or general agreement.

President Johnson pushed a number of Kennedy's programs through Congress. He won passage of a major civil rights bill and an anti-poverty program. Johnson had known poverty firsthand. He believed that a government should try to improve its citizens' lives. In his State of the Union address to Congress in 1964, Johnson announced that he was declaring a **"war on poverty in America."** Congress set up the Office of Economic Opportunity (OEO), which worked to create jobs and fight poverty.

The Great Society also set up programs that were aimed at creating jobs and strengthening education. VISTA (Volunteers in Service to America) was a kind of domestic Peace Corps. The program put young people to work in poor school districts.

In the 1964 election, President Johnson's Republican opponent was Barry Goldwater, a senator from Arizona. Johnson won in a landslide.

> **Academic Vocabulary**
>
> **analogy:** something that is common between two seemingly uncommon things (p. 724)

5. What was the war on poverty?

_____

_____

_____

_____

• The Great Society (page 726)

President Johnson began working on the Great Society, a package of programs that Johnson hoped would move beyond the <u>confines</u> of government supplying material things. This was Johnson's plan for building a better society for all. During his administration, the civil rights movement had achieved many of its goals through the Civil Rights Act of 1964. The Voting Rights Act of 1965 ensured African Americans the right to vote.

Johnson's goals were achieved for a variety of reasons. The civil rights movement had brought the concerns of African Americans to the forefront. The economy was strong, so people did not see why poverty could not be greatly reduced.

> **Academic Vocabulary**
>
> **confine:** to enclose or restrain (p. 726)

Study Guide

Chapter 15, Section 3 *(continued)*

More than 60 of Johnson's programs were passed between 1965 and 1968. Among these were Medicare and Medicaid. Medicare was a health insurance program for the elderly. Medicaid financed health care for people on welfare. Great Society programs also supported education. The Elementary and Secondary Education Act of 1965 provided millions of dollars to public and private schools for books and special education materials. Project Head Start was an education program directed at disadvantaged preschool children.

Johnson also wanted to help the nation's deteriorating inner cities. He urged Congress to pass legislation to address this problem. One law created a new cabinet agency, the Department of Housing and Urban Development. It was headed by Robert Weaver, the first African American to serve in a cabinet. Other laws provided federal funding to many cities for programs such as transportation, health care, and housing. Still other laws provided billions of dollars to build houses for low- and middle-income people.

One law passed during the Great Society affected the makeup of the American population. The Immigration Reform Act of 1965 kept a strict limit on the number of immigrants admitted to the United States each year. However, it eliminated the national origins system, which gave preference to immigrants from northern Europe. The new law allowed immigrants from all parts of Europe, and Asia and Africa.

6. How did the Immigration Reform Act of 1965 change the makeup of the American population?

_____

_____

_____

_____

_____

- **Legacy of the Great Society** *(page 728)*

The Great Society programs had improved the lives of many Americans, but people have debated the Great Society's success. The programs had been established quickly. Some of them did not work as well as people had hoped. The programs were often difficult to evaluate. Some criticized Great Society programs because they believed that the federal government had become too involved in people's lives. The programs sometimes lacked funds. The programs were expensive, and when money was needed for the Vietnam War, many of these programs suffered.

Some Great Society programs remain today. They include Medicare, Medicaid, and Project Head Start. They also include two cabinet agencies—the Department of Transportation and the Department of Housing and Urban Development (HUD).

Study Guide

Chapter 15, Section 3 (continued)

The Great Society also produced questions. They included questions about how the government can help disadvantaged citizens and how much the government should help a society without interfering with the private <u>sector</u>.

Academic Vocabulary
sector: a subdivision of society based on economic or political lines (p. 729)

7. What Great Society programs continue today?

_____

_____

_____

_____

_____

Study Guide

Chapter 16, Section 1

For use with textbook pages 740–747

THE MOVEMENT BEGINS

CONTENT VOCABULARY

separate-but-equal doctrine that said laws segregating African Americans were allowed as long as equal facilities were provided for them *(page 741)*

de facto segregation segregation by custom and tradition *(page 741)*

sit-ins form of protest in which protesters refused to leave segregated places *(page 742)*

DRAWING FROM EXPERIENCE

What do the words *segregation* and *integration* mean? How were they an issue in United States history? Are they an issue today?

In this section, you will learn how the civil rights movement began. You will also learn how the federal government's role in enforcing civil rights changed.

California History-Social Science Standards

11.10 Students analyze the development of federal civil rights and voting rights.

Focuses on: 11.10.2, 11.10.3, 11.10.4, 11.10.5, 11.10.6

ORGANIZING YOUR THOUGHTS

Use the chart below to help you take notes. Several African American organizations worked to ensure civil rights for African Americans. Describe the work of each of these organizations.

Organization	Work of Organization
NAACP	1.
CORE	2.
SCLC	3.

READ TO LEARN

- **The Origins of the Movement** *(page 741)*

On December 1, 1955, Rosa Parks boarded a bus in Montgomery, Alabama, on her way home from work. Buses there at that time reserved the front section for whites and the back section for African Americans. Parks took a seat right behind the white section. When she was asked to give up her seat to a white man who was standing, she refused. She was arrested. She challenged

Study Guide

Chapter 16, Section 1 *(continued)*

bus segregation in court. After her arrest, African Americans in Montgomery started a boycott of the bus system. In the next few years, boycotts and protests started across the nation. African Americans had decided it was time to demand equal rights.

The Supreme Court's 1896 decision in *Plessy* v. *Ferguson* set up a **separate-but-equal** policy. Laws that segregated African Americans were allowed as long as equal facilities were provided for them. After this decision, laws segregating African Americans became common. These Jim Crow laws segregated buses, schools, and restaurants. Signs saying "Whites Only" or "Colored" appeared on entrances to many places. Jim Crow laws were common in the South, but segregation also existed in other places. Areas that did not have segregation laws, such as in many places in the North, often had **de facto segregation,** or segregation by custom and tradition.

Since 1909, the National Association for the Advancement of Colored People (NAACP) had supported court cases that had to do with overturning segregation. It was successful in some cases. In addition to these successes, African Americans began experiencing more political power. Before World War I, most African Americans lived in the South, where they were not allowed to vote. Through the Great Migration, many African Americans arrived in Northern cities, where they were allowed to vote. Northern politicians began seeking their vote and listening to their concerns. During the Great Depression, many African Americans voted for President Franklin Roosevelt. Their votes made the Democratic Party in the North stronger. Their votes also forced the Democratic Party to pay attention to civil rights.

African Americans began using their political power to demand more rights. In 1942 James Farmer and George Houser started the Congress of Racial Equality (CORE). Members of the organization began using **sit-ins,** a form of protest. They used the sit-in strategy to integrate restaurants. If the restaurants would not serve them, they sat down and refused to leave. Through sit-ins, CORE successfully integrated many restaurants and other public facilities in several Northern cities.

4. How did CORE successfully integrate many public facilities in some Northern cities?

_____

_____

_____

_____

_____

Study Guide

Chapter 16, Section 1 *(continued)*

• The Civil Rights Movement Begins *(page 742)*

The chief counsel of the NAACP from 1939 to 1961 was African American attorney Thurgood Marshall. He focused his attention on desegregating public schools. In 1954 the Supreme Court heard cases regarding segregation in schools. One case involved Linda Brown. She was a young African American girl who was denied admission to her neighborhood school in Topeka, Kansas, because of her race. Together with the NAACP, her parents sued the Topeka school board. In May 1954, the Supreme Court ruled in the case of *Brown* v. *Board of Education of Topeka, Kansas,* that segregation in public schools was "<u>inherently</u> unequal" and unconstitutional. It also ruled that segregation violated the equal protection clause of the Fourteenth Amendment. This decision reversed the decision in *Plessy* v. *Ferguson.* The *Brown* v. *Board of Education* ruling signaled to African Americans that it was time to challenge other forms of segregation. The ruling made many white Southerners more determined to defend segregation. Many resisted the Supreme Court's ruling and kept their schools segregated for many more years.

Academic Vocabulary
inherent: to be characteristic of something by nature or habit (p. 743)

It was during the conflict over the *Brown* v. *Board of Education* case that Rosa Parks decided to challenge the segregation of the bus system in Montgomery. African Americans supported the decision by boycotting the buses. The boycott was a success. Several African American leaders formed the Montgomery Improvement Association to negotiate with city leaders to end segregation. They elected the young minister Martin Luther King, Jr., to lead the organization. A powerful speaker, King believed that the way to end segregation and racism was through nonviolent passive resistance. This approach was based on the philosophy of the Indian leader Mohandas Gandhi. He had used nonviolent resistance in his struggle against British rule in India. Both Gandhi and King urged followers to disobey unjust laws.

African Americans in Montgomery continued their boycott for more than a year. Rosa Parks's lawsuit led to a Supreme Court ruling in 1956. The Court ruled that Alabama's laws requiring segregation on buses were unconstitutional.

5. What technique did Martin Luther King, Jr., believe would be most effective in ending segregation?

_____

_____

_____

_____

_____

Study Guide

Chapter 16, Section 1 *(continued)*

• African American Churches *(page 745)*

Martin Luther King, Jr., was not the only minister to take part in the Montgomery boycott. Many of the leaders were African American ministers. African American churches in Montgomery were important to the success of the boycott. The churches were used for planning and protest meetings. The churches also organized many volunteers for <u>specific</u> civil rights campaigns. Led by King, African American ministers set up the Southern Christian Leadership Conference (SCLC) in 1957. The organization worked to do away with segregation in American society and to encourage African Americans to <u>register</u> to vote. Martin Luther King, Jr., became the SCLC's first president. The organization challenged segregation of public transportation, housing, and public accommodations.

Academic Vocabulary
specific: to be referred to as belonging to a particular category (p. 745)
register: to file personal information in order to become eligible for an official event (p. 746)

6. What did the Southern Christian Leadership Conference work toward?

_____

_____

_____

_____

• Eisenhower and Civil Rights *(page 746)*

Although President Eisenhower personally opposed segregation, he disagreed with those who wanted to end it through protests and court rulings. He believed that segregation should end gradually. With the nation involved in the Cold War, Eisenhower feared that challenging white Southerners on segregation would divide the nation at a time when the nation needed to pull together.

Although Eisenhower believed the Supreme Court decision in *Brown* v. *Board of Education* was wrong, he believed the federal government had the duty to uphold the decision. In September 1957, the Little Rock, Arkansas, school board won a court order to admit nine African American students to Central High, a school with 2,000 white students. The governor of Arkansas ordered troops from the Arkansas National Guard to prevent the African American students from entering the school. A mob of white people joined the troops to prevent the students from entering the school. Eisenhower could not allow the governor to challenge the federal government. The governor removed the National Guard troops, but he did not take action to stop the mob of whites. They came close to capturing the terrified black students. Eisenhower became impatient with the mob violence. He ordered the United States Army to send troops to Little Rock. The troops encircled the school. A few hours later, the African American students arrived in an army station wagon and walked into the school. The troops stayed at the school for the rest of the school year.

Study Guide

Chapter 16, Section 1 *(continued)*

In the same year that the Little Rock violence took place, Congress passed the Civil Rights Act of 1957. It was intended to protect the right of African Americans to vote. It was an important step in involving the federal government into the civil rights debate. The law created a civil rights division within the Department of Justice. It also created the United States Commission on Civil Rights to investigate instances in which the right to vote was denied.

7. Why did President Eisenhower send the United States Army to Little Rock, Arkansas, in 1957?

_____

_____

_____

_____

_____

_____

Study Guide

Chapter 16, Section 2

For use with textbook pages 748–756

CHALLENGING SEGREGATION

CONTENT VOCABULARY

Freedom Riders   teams of African Americans and white Americans who traveled through the South to draw attention to the South's refusal to integrate bus terminals *(page 750)*

filibuster   a tactic in which senators take turns speaking and refuse to stop the debate and allow a bill to come to a vote *(page 754)*

cloture   a motion which cuts off debate and forces a vote *(page 754)*

poll tax   a fee that had to be paid in order to vote *(page 755)*

DRAWING FROM EXPERIENCE

What do you think of when you hear the words *civil rights?* What are your civil rights? How are they protected?

The last section discussed the beginnings of the civil rights movement. This section discusses the expansion of the movement.

ORGANIZING YOUR THOUGHTS

Use the diagram below to help you take notes. President Kennedy attempted to support the civil rights movement in several ways. Describe these ways in the diagram.

California History-Social Science Standards

11.10 Students analyze the development of federal civil rights and voting rights.

11.11 Students analyze the major social problems and domestic policy issues in contemporary American society.

Focuses on: 11.10.4, 11.10.5, 11.10.6, 11.11.2

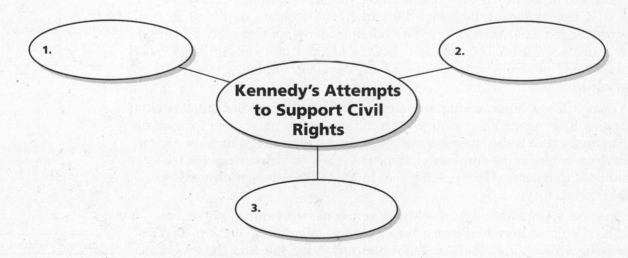

Study Guide

Chapter 16, Section 2 (continued)

READ TO LEARN

- ## The Sit-In Movement (page 749)

The sit-in strategies to end segregation spread to several cities. Many African American college students joined the sit-in movement. Students like Jesse Jackson saw the sit-in as a way for students to take things into their own hands. At first, the leaders of the NAACP and the SCLC were concerned about the sit-ins. They feared that the students might not remain nonviolent if they were provoked. The students did remain peaceful, despite being punched, kicked, and beaten by bystanders. The students' behavior attracted the nation's attention.

4. What group of people did the sit-in movement draw?

_____

_____

_____

_____

_____

- ## SNCC (page 750)

As the sit-ins spread, student leaders realized that they needed to create an organization of their own. Ella Baker, the executive director of the SCLC, invited student leaders to a convention in Raleigh, North Carolina, where she urged them to start their own organization instead of joining SCLC or the NAACP. The students established the Student Nonviolent Coordinating Committee (SNCC). Marion Barry, a student leader who later served as the mayor of Washington, D.C., became SNCC's first chairperson. Although most of the SNCC members were African American college students, many whites also joined.

The SNCC was instrumental in desegregating public facilities in many communities. The organization realized that the civil rights movement focused on urban areas. As a result, members of SNCC began working to register African American voters in the rural areas of the Deep South. Three members who attempted to register African Americans in Mississippi were murdered by local officials there.

One SNCC organizer, a former sharecropper named Fannie Lou Hamer, had been evicted from her farm after registering to vote. She was arrested in Mississippi for urging other African Americans to register, and she was beaten by the police. She then helped organize the Mississippi Freedom Democratic Party. She challenged the <u>legality</u> of the segregated Democratic Party at the 1964 Democratic National Convention.

> **Academic Vocabulary**
>
> **legality:** a requirement to follow a specific law (p. 750)

The American Vision: Modern Times

Study Guide

Chapter 16, Section 2 (continued)

5. Where did the SNCC focus its efforts?

_____

_____

_____

_____

_____

• **The Freedom Riders** (page 750)

In 1961 James Farmer, the leader of CORE, asked groups of African Americans and white Americans to travel into the South to draw attention to the South's segregation of bus terminals. These groups became known as **Freedom Riders.** When buses carrying Freedom Riders arrived at various cities in the South, white mobs attacked them. In Birmingham, Freedom Riders leaving the bus were viciously beaten by a gang of young men. Later evidence showed that the head of police in Birmingham had contacted the local Ku Klux Klan and had told them he wanted the Freedom Riders beaten. The violence in Alabama shocked many Americans. President John F. Kennedy, who took office four months before the violence took place, decided he had to do something to get the violence under control.

6. What was the goal of the Freedom Riders?

_____

_____

_____

_____

_____

• **John F. Kennedy and Civil Rights** (page 751)

In his campaign, John Kennedy promised to support the civil rights movement if he was elected president. African Americans overwhelmingly voted for him. At first, Kennedy was as cautious as Eisenhower on civil rights. He knew he needed the support of Southern senators to get some other programs he wanted passed. However, Kennedy did name about 40 African Americans to high-level positions in the federal government. He appointed Thurgood Marshall to an Appeals Court in New York. This position, the highest judicial position yet <u>attained</u> by an African American, was one level below the United States Supreme Court. Kennedy also set up the Committee on Equal Employment Opportunity (CEEO). Its purpose was to stop the federal

Academic Vocabulary
attain: to gain possession of something (p. 751)

Study Guide

Chapter 16, Section 2 *(continued)*

government from discriminating against African Americans when hiring and promoting people.

President Kennedy was reluctant to challenge Southern Democrats in Congress. He allowed the Justice Department, which was led by his brother Robert F. Kennedy, to support the civil rights movement. Robert Kennedy helped African Americans register to vote by having the Justice Department file lawsuits throughout the South.

After the Freedom Riders were attacked in Alabama, Kennedy urged them to stop the rides. They refused to do so and planned to head into Mississippi on their next trip. To stop the violence, President Kennedy made a deal with a senator from Mississippi. Kennedy told the senator that if he used his influence to prevent violence, he would not object if the Mississippi police arrested the Freedom Riders. The senator kept the deal. The cost of bailing the Freedom Riders out of jail used up most of CORE's funds. Thurgood Marshall offered money from the NAACP's Legal Defense Fund to keep the rides going.

When President Kennedy realized that the Freedom Riders were still active, he ordered the Interstate Commerce Commission to tighten its regulations against segregated bus terminals. Robert Kennedy ordered the Justice Department to take legal action against Southern cities that continued to segregate bus terminals. All these actions were successful. By late 1962, segregation on interstate travel had come to an end.

At the same time that the Freedom Riders were trying to desegregate bus terminals, people continued to work to integrate public schools. In early 1961, African American James Meredith applied to the University of Mississippi. At that time, the university had avoided obeying the Supreme Court ruling that ended segregated education. In September 1962, Meredith tried to register at the university. He was blocked from entering by the governor of Mississippi. President Kennedy sent 500 federal marshals to escort Meredith. A white mob attacked the campus and a riot started. The fighting continued throughout the night. Many marshals were wounded. Kennedy then ordered the Army to send troops to the campus. For the rest of the school year, Meredith attended classes at the university under federal guard.

Martin Luther King, Jr., and other civil rights leaders were frustrated over the events in Mississippi. They were disappointed that the president did not push for a new civil rights law. When the Cuban missile crisis began in October 1962, foreign policy took priority over civil rights issues. King observed that the federal government intervened in civil rights issues only when violence occurred. As a result, King ordered demonstrations in Birmingham, Alabama, knowing that it would likely lead to violence. He believed that it was the only way to get Kennedy to actively support civil rights.

Shortly after the protests in Birmingham began, King was arrested. After he was released, the protests grew again. The local authorities ordered the police to use clubs, police dogs, and high-pressure fire hoses on the demonstrators.

Study Guide

Chapter 16, Section 2 *(continued)*

Millions of Americans watched the violence on television. President Kennedy
was worried that the government was losing control, so he ordered his aides
to prepare a new civil rights bill.

7. Why was President Kennedy cautious about pushing for civil rights?

_____

_____

_____

_____

_____

- ## The Civil Rights Act of 1964 *(page 753)*

In June 1963, Alabama governor George Wallace stood in front of the
University of Alabama's admissions office to stop two African Americans
from enrolling. Federal marshals ordered him to move. President Kennedy
took that opportunity to present his civil rights bill.

Martin Luther King, Jr., realized that Kennedy would have a difficult time
pushing his civil rights bill through Congress. He decided to support a massive
march on Washington. On August 28, 1963, more than 200,000 demonstrators gathered peacefully at the nation's capital. Dr. King delivered his powerful "I Have a Dream" speech, in which he presented his dream of freedom
and equality for all Americans. The march on Washington had built support for
Kennedy's civil rights bill. However, opponents in Congress continued to do
what they could to slow the bill down. The bill would have an especially difficult time passing in the Senate. Senators are allowed to speak for as long as they
like when a bill is being debated. The Senate is not allowed to vote on a bill
until all the senators have finished speaking. A **filibuster** is when a small group
of senators take turns speaking and refuse to stop the debate and allow a bill to
come to a vote. Today a filibuster can be stopped if at least three-fifths of the
senators vote for **cloture,** a motion which cuts off debate and forces a vote.

African Americans became even more worried that the civil rights bill
would never pass when President Kennedy was assassinated in November
1963. President Johnson, however, committed himself to getting Kennedy's civil
rights bill passed. On July 2, 1964, President Johnson signed the Civil Rights
Act of 1964 into law. This was the most <u>comprehensive</u> civil rights law enacted
by Congress. The law gave Congress the power to outlaw segregation in most
public places. It gave citizens equal access to facilities such as restaurants,
parks, and theaters. The law gave the attorney general more power to bring
lawsuits to force schools to desegregate. It also set up the Equal Employment
Opportunity Commission (EEOC). This agency was set up to oversee the ban
on job discrimination by race, religion, gender, and national origin.

Academic Vocabulary
comprehensive: to cover a broad range of topics (p. 755)

Study Guide

Chapter 16, Section 2 *(continued)*

8. Why did Martin Luther King, Jr., support a march on Washington?

_____

_____

_____

_____

- ## The Struggle for Voting Rights *(page 755)*

The Civil Rights Act of 1964 did little to guarantee the right to vote. The Twenty-fourth Amendment, ratified in 1964, helped somewhat by abolishing **poll taxes,** or fees paid in order to vote in national elections. The SNCC and SCLC increased their voter registration drives in the South. Those that tried to register African American voters were often attacked and beaten. Some were murdered. Civil rights leaders, including Martin Luther King, Jr., decided that a new law was necessary to protect African American voting rights. They decided to start their campaign in Selma, Alabama. The sheriff of that city prevented African Americans from registering to vote by deputizing and arming many white citizens. They terrorized and attacked the demonstrators. Approximately 2,000 African Americans were arrested by Selma's sheriff.

To keep the pressure on the president and Congress to act, Dr. King and other SNCC activists organized a march from Selma to Montgomery. It began on March 7, 1965. As protesters approached the bridge that led out of Selma, the sheriff ordered them to break up. While the marchers knelt in prayer, state troopers and the deputized citizens rushed the demonstrators. The attack left more than 70 African Americans hospitalized and many more injured. The nation was shocked as it saw the brutality on television. President Johnson was furious. He came before Congress to present a new voting rights law.

In August 1965, Congress passed the Voting Rights Act of 1965. It ordered federal examiners to register qualified voters. It got rid of discriminatory practices such as literacy tests. By the end of 1965, almost 250,000 new African American voters had registered to vote. The number of African American elected officials in the South also increased. With the passage of the Voting Rights Act, the civil rights movement had achieved its two goals. Segregation had been banned, and laws were in place to prevent discrimination and protect voting rights.

9. What was the purpose of the march from Selma to Montgomery?

_____

_____

_____

_____

Study Guide

Chapter 16, Section 3

For use with textbook pages 757–763

NEW ISSUES

CONTENT VOCABULARY

racism   prejudice or discrimination toward someone because of his or her race *(page 758)*

black power   a movement that called for African American control of the social, political, and economic direction of the struggle for equality and stressed pride in the African American cultural group *(page 760)*

DRAWING FROM EXPERIENCE

Do you think the civil rights movement is active today? What kinds of issues do you think still need to be addressed? Why do you think so?

The last section described the political gains made by the civil rights movement. This section discusses the efforts of the civil rights movement to gain economic equality for African Americans.

ORGANIZING YOUR THOUGHTS

Use the diagram below to help you take notes. African Americans faced many economic problems even after civil rights laws had been passed. In the diagram, list those problems and describe the Kerner Commission and its results.

California History-Social Science Standards

11.10 Students analyze the development of federal civil rights and voting rights.

11.11 Students analyze the major social problems and domestic policy issues in contemporary American society.

Focuses on: 11.10.4, 11.11.7

Problems Facing Urban African Americans

1. _____

2. _____

3. _____

4. _____

5. _____

Kerner Commission Appointed to:

6.

Results of Kerner Commission:

7.

Study Guide

Chapter 16, Section 3 (continued)

READ TO LEARN

• Problems Facing Urban African Americans *(page 758)*

Although several civil rights laws had been passed by the 1960s, **racism,** or prejudice or discrimination toward someone because of his or her race, was still common in the United States. In 1965 the majority of African Americans lived in large cities. Many had moved from the South to cities in the North and West, where they faced the same prejudice and discrimination that they did in the South. Many whites refused to live with African Americans in the same neighborhoods. Landlords refused to rent to African Americans. Those African Americans who moved into cities were often trapped by poverty in the inner city. Whites moved to the suburbs. Many African Americans were <u>channeled</u> into low-paying jobs. In 1965 only 15 percent of African Americans held professional or clerical jobs, compared to 44 percent of whites. Half of all African American families lived in poverty.

> **Academic Vocabulary**
>
> **channel:** to force through a preexisting pathway (p. 758)

Poor neighborhoods in the nation's cities were dirty and overcrowded. Crime rates were high. These kinds of problems existed in all poor neighborhoods. A greater proportion of African Americans lived in poverty, so a greater percentage of their neighborhoods faced these problems. The African Americans who lived in poverty were aware of the gains made by the civil rights movement. They were also aware that the gains did not address their problems, which were social and economic. Their anger at the situation erupted into violence.

A race riot broke out in Watts, an African American neighborhood in Los Angeles. Allegations of police brutality had started the riots, which lasted six days. Thousands of National Guard troops and law officers were needed to bring back order. Rioters burned and looted entire neighborhoods. Thirty-four people were killed and hundreds were injured.

Race riots broke out in other cities. The worst riot occurred in Detroit in 1967. The United States Army had to send in tanks and armed soldiers to bring an end to the riot. More than 1,300 buildings were damaged.

President Johnson appointed the National Advisory Commission on Civil Disorders to study the causes of the riots. Governor Otto Kerner of Illinois headed the Commission. The Kerner Commission studied the problem. It agreed with what many African American leaders had been saying for years. The Commission blamed white society and white racism for most of the problems in the inner city. The Commission recommended that two million new jobs and six million new housing units be created in the inner city. However, at the time, the United States was spending massive amounts of money on the Vietnam War. As a result, the report of the Kerner Commission produced no changes for African Americans.

Study Guide

Chapter 16, Section 3 (continued)

8. On what did the Kerner Commission blame the problems of the inner city?

_____

_____

_____

_____

_____

• **The Shift to Economic Rights** (page 759)

By the mid-1960s, some African American leaders were critical of Martin Luther King's nonviolent strategies. They believed the strategies were not successful in improving the economic <u>status</u> of African Americans. As a result, Dr. King began to focus on economic issues. In 1965 Dr. King was invited to Chicago by a group of community organizations that worked to improve conditions for the poor in Chicago. To call attention to the poor housing conditions that many African Americans faced, Dr. King and his wife moved into a slum apartment. He hoped to work with local leaders to improve economic conditions for African Americans in poor neighborhoods. The so-called Chicago Movement was unsuccessful.

When Dr. King led a march through a Chicago suburb to demonstrate the need for open housing, he was met with angry white mobs like those he met in the South. Mayor Richard Daley ordered the police to protect the marchers. He then met with Dr. King and suggested a program to clean up the slums. Under the plan, mortgages and rental property would be available to everyone regardless of race. However, very little changed.

Academic Vocabulary
status: the condition of something relative to what is normal (p. 760)

9. Why were some civil rights leaders critical of King's nonviolent strategies?

_____

_____

_____

_____

_____

• **Black Power** (page 760)

Dr. King's failure in Chicago seemed to show many African Americans that nonviolence could not change their economic problems. Many young African Americans living in poverty in urban areas began to turn away from King's movement. They turned to more aggressive forms of protest. African Americans began to place less emphasis on interracial cooperation. Many

Study Guide

Chapter 16, Section 3 *(continued)*

young African Americans called for **black power.** A few believed that the term meant that self-defense, even violence, were acceptable when defending one's freedom. Most African Americans, including Stokely Carmichael, the leader of the SNCC in 1966, believed black power meant that African Americans should control the social, political, and economic directions of the struggle for equality. It meant <u>psychological</u> as well as social equality. Black power stressed pride in African American culture. It rejected cultural assimilation, or the philosophy of incorporating different racial or cultural groups into the dominant society. Black power was very popular in the poor urban neighborhoods where many African Americans lived.

Academic Vocabulary
psychological: relating to one's mental perception (p. 761)

By the early 1960s, a man named Malcolm X became the symbol of black power. As a young man, Malcolm X was convicted of burglary and sent to prison. There he began to educate himself and joined the Nation of Islam, or Black Muslims. The group was led by Elijah Muhammad. The Black Muslims did not hold the same beliefs as Muslims. The Black Muslims believed that African Americans should separate themselves from whites and form their own communities.

The Black Muslims viewed themselves as a nation. They tried to make themselves self-sufficient. They ran their own businesses and published their own newspaper. Malcolm X was a dynamic speaker. He gained national attention for the Nation of Islam.

By 1964 Malcolm X had broken with the Black Muslims. He was upset with the scandals involving the Nation of Islam's leader. Malcolm X visited the Muslim holy city in Saudi Arabia. There he saw many different races worshipping together. He started to believe that an integrated society was possible. After he left the Nation of Islam, Malcolm X continued to criticize the organization and Elijah Muhammad. In February 1965, members of the Nation of Islam killed Malcolm X while he was giving a speech in New York. Malcolm X's speeches pointed out to African Americans that although they were victims in the past, they did not have to continue being victimized. He encouraged African Americans to believe in their ability to make their own way in the world.

Malcolm X's ideas continued to influence a new generation of militant African American leaders. One group, the Black Panthers, preached black power, black nationalism and economic self-sufficiency. The Black Panthers believed a revolution was necessary. They urged African Americans to arm themselves and confront white society to force whites to grant them equal rights.

Study Guide

Chapter 16, Section 3 *(continued)*

10. What did the Black Muslims believe African Americans should do regarding white society?

_____

_____

_____

_____

_____

- ## The Assassination of Martin Luther King, Jr. *(page 762)*

By the late 1960s, the civil rights movement was divided into competing organizations that were at odds with one another. The call by some African Americans for violent action angered some white supporters of the civil rights movement.

In 1968 Dr. Martin Luther King, Jr., went to Memphis, Tennessee, to support a strike of African American sanitation workers. On April 4, 1968, King was assassinated as he stood on his hotel balcony. The assassination touched off riots in more than 100 cities. After Dr. King's death, Congress passed the Civil Rights Act of 1968. The law banned discrimination in the sale and rental of housing. After Dr. King's death, the civil rights movement continued but lacked the vision that Dr. King had given it.

11. What happened to the civil rights movement by the late 1960s?

_____

_____

_____

_____

_____

_____

Study Guide

Chapter 17, Section 1

For use with textbook pages 772–776

THE UNITED STATES FOCUSES ON VIETNAM

CONTENT VOCABULARY

domino theory   the belief that if Vietnam fell to communism, so would the other Southeast Asian nations *(page 775)*

guerrillas   irregular troops who usually blend into the civilian population and are often difficult for regular armies to fight *(page 775)*

DRAWING FROM EXPERIENCE

Where is Vietnam located? What do you know about the country? From where did your information about the nation come?

In this section, you will learn about the nationalist movement in Vietnam. You will also learn why the United States became involved in Vietnam.

California History-Social Science Standards

11.9 Students analyze the U.S. foreign policy since World War II.

Focuses on: 11.9.2, 11.9.3

ORGANIZING YOUR THOUGHTS

Use the diagram below to help you take notes. The Geneva Accords negotiated the end of the conflict between France and Vietnam. List the results of the negotiations in the diagram.

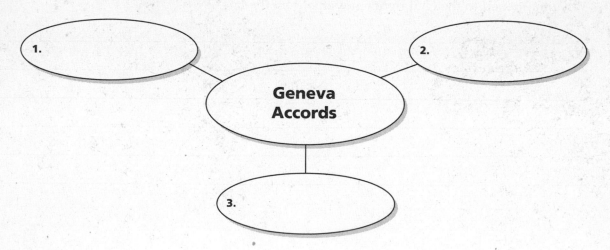

Study Guide

Chapter 17, Section 1 *(continued)*

READ TO LEARN

- ## Early American Involvement in Vietnam *(page 773)*

Vietnam had often been ruled by foreign powers. China controlled it off and on for hundreds of years. From the late 1800s until World War II, France ruled Vietnam and neighboring Laos and Cambodia. This <u>region</u> became known as French Indochina. Japan took power in Vietnam during World War II.

By the early 1900s, nationalism spread through Vietnam. Several political parties pushed for independence from France. One of the leaders of the movement was Ho Chi Minh. In 1930 he helped start the Indochinese Communist Party and worked to overthrow French rule. In 1941, after Japan had taken control of Vietnam, Ho organized a nationalist group called the Vietminh. The group's goal was to get rid of the Japanese forces. The United States sent military aid to the Vietminh.

When Japan was defeated in August 1945, it gave up control of Indochina. Ho announced that Vietnam was an independent nation. France, however, did not want to see Vietnam independent. It wanted to regain its colonial empire in Southeast Asia. France sent troops to Vietnam in 1946 and drove the Vietminh's forces into hiding in the countryside. By 1949 France had set up a new government in Vietnam. The Vietminh fought against the French and slowly increased their control over large areas of the countryside. As fighting increased, France asked the United States for help.

The request put the United States in a difficult position. The United States had opposed colonialism. It urged the Dutch to give up their holdings in Indonesia. It supported the British decision to grant India independence. However, the conflict over Vietnam also included the issue of communism. The United States did not think that France should control Vietnam. At the same time, it did not want Vietnam to be Communist.

President Truman decided to help France for two reasons: the fall of China to communism and the Korean War. President Eisenhower continued to support the French against the Vietminh. Eisenhower defended the U.S. policy in Vietnam by stressing the **domino theory.** This was a belief that if Vietnam fell to communism, the other Southeast nations would also.

Academic Vocabulary

region: a division of land based on geographic or political boundaries (p. 773)

4. How did President Eisenhower defend the U.S. policy in Vietnam?

_____

_____

_____

_____

_____

© by The McGraw-Hill Companies, Inc.

Study Guide

Chapter 17, Section 1 *(continued)*

• The Vietminh Drive Out the French *(page 774)*

The Vietminh military tactics frustrated the French. The Vietminh used the tactics of **guerrillas,** or irregular troops who usually blend into the civilian population and are often difficult for regular armies to fight.

In 1954 French troops <u>occupied</u> the Vietnamese town of Dien Bien Phu. They hoped to interfere with the Vietminh's supply lines. Soon after, a large Vietminh force surrounded the town and began bombarding it. On May 7, 1954, the French forces at Dien Bien Phu fell to the Vietminh. The French decided to withdraw from Indochina.

Negotiations to end the conflict took place in Geneva, Switzerland. The Geneva Accords temporarily divided Vietnam into North Vietnam and South Vietnam. Ho Chi Minh and the Vietminh controlled North Vietnam. A pro-Western regime controlled South Vietnam. Elections were to be held in 1956 to reunite the country under a single government.

The United States stepped in and became the <u>principal</u> protector of the new government in South Vietnam. Its leader was Ngo Dinh Diem, who was anti-Communist. When the time came to hold elections in 1956, Diem refused. Eisenhower supported Diem, and the United States increased military and economic aid to South Vietnam. Tensions between the North and South increased.

> **Academic Vocabulary**
>
> **occupy:** to take control or possession of a location (p. 775)

> **Academic Vocabulary**
>
> **principal:** an important or influential concept (p. 776)

5. What was the significance of the battle of Dien Bien Phu?

_____

_____

_____

_____

_____

Study Guide

Chapter 17, Section 2

For use with textbook pages 777–783

GOING TO WAR IN VIETNAM

CONTENT VOCABULARY

napalm   a jellied gasoline that explodes on contact *(page 782)*

Agent Orange   a chemical that strips leaves from trees and shrubs *(page 782)*

DRAWING FROM EXPERIENCE

Have you seen any movies or read any books about the Vietnam War? How did the movie or book depict it? What conditions did American troops face there?

The last section described the French involvement in Vietnam. This section discusses how the United States became militarily involved in Vietnam.

California History-Social Science Standards

11.8 Students analyze the economic boom and social transformation of post–World War II America.

11.9 Students analyze the U.S. foreign policy since World War II.

Focuses on: 11.8.5, 11.9.3

ORGANIZING YOUR THOUGHTS

Use the cause-and-effect diagram below to help you take notes. Identify the causes or the effects of the events listed.

Cause	Effect
1. _____ 2. _____	The power of the Vietcong increased.
Congress passes the Gulf of Tonkin Resolution.	3. _____
President Johnson refuses to invade North Vietnam for fear of China's involvement.	4. _____

Study Guide

Chapter 17, Section 2 *(continued)*

READ TO LEARN

- **American Involvement Deepens** *(page 778)*

After Diem refused to hold national elections, Ho Chi Minh began an armed struggle to reunify the nation. He and his followers organized a new guerrilla army, which became known as the Vietcong. After fighting began between the Vietcong and South Vietnam's forces, President Eisenhower increased American aid and sent military advisers to train South Vietnam's army. However, the Vietcong's power increased. This was partly due to the fact that many Vietnamese were against Diem's government. It was also due to the Vietcong's use of terror. The Vietcong had killed thousands of government officials and gained control of much of the countryside. Diem looked increasingly to the United States for help.

President Kennedy's <u>administration</u> continued to support South Vietnam, seeing it as an important part of fighting communism. He increased military aid and sent more advisers. The United States believed that the Vietcong were so popular because Diem's government was corrupt and unpopular. They urged him to introduce more democratic reforms. He introduced some, but they had little effect. Diem, a Catholic, was also unpopular because he discriminated against Buddhism, which was one of the most practiced religions in Vietnam. When he banned traditional religious flags for Buddha's birthday, Buddhists protested. Diem's police killed 9 people and injured 14 others. In one of the demonstrations, a Buddhist monk set himself on fire. The photograph of this appeared on television and in newspapers around the world. It clearly showed the opposition to Diem.

When Henry Cabot Lodge arrived in Vietnam as American ambassador in August 1963, he found out that several Vietnamese generals were plotting to overthrow Diem. Lodge told them that the United States was sympathetic to their cause. The generals overthrew Diem and executed him. Although Diem was unpopular, he was a good administrator. After his death, the government became even more unstable. This forced the United States to become even more involved as it tried to prop up the weak South Vietnamese government. <u>Coincidentally</u>, shortly after Diem's death, President Kennedy was assassinated. The conflict in Vietnam fell to President Johnson.

5. Why did the Vietcong's power increase?

_____

_____

_____

_____

_____

> **Academic Vocabulary**
>
> **administration:** a group of people meant to advise and assist the president (p. 778)

> **Academic Vocabulary**
>
> **coincidental:** when two related things occur at the same time (p. 779)

Study Guide

Chapter 17, Section 2 (continued)

• Johnson and Vietnam (page 779)

President Johnson was determined to stop South Vietnam from becoming Communist. Johnson also knew that many Republicans blamed the Democrats for losing China to communism. As a result, he did not want to be blamed for losing Vietnam to communism.

On August 2, 1964, President Johnson announced that North Vietnamese torpedo boats had fired on two American destroyers in the Gulf of Tonkin. He insisted that the attack was unprovoked. He ordered American aircraft to attack North Vietnamese ships. Johnson did not reveal that American warships had been helping South Vietnam in spying and raids on North Vietnam.

Johnson asked Congress for authorization to use force to defend American forces. On August 7, 1964, Congress passed the Gulf of Tonkin Resolution. It essentially handed over war powers to the president. Shortly afterward, the Vietcong began to attack American bases where U.S. advisers were stationed. In February 1965, after one Vietcong attack in which 7 Americans were killed and more than 100 were wounded, President Johnson ordered American aircraft to strike North Vietnam. Most Americans approved of Johnson's actions. His advisers, including Secretary of Defense Robert McNamara and National Security Adviser McGeorge Bundy, also approved. Some, however, warned that if the United States got too involved in Vietnam, it might be difficult to get out.

In March 1965, Johnson increased American involvement. He switched from using individual air strikes to a <u>sustained</u> bombing campaign, which was named Operation Rolling Thunder. Johnson also ordered the first combat troops into Vietnam. They fought alongside the South Vietnamese troops against the Vietcong.

Academic Vocabulary
sustain: to ensure the persistence of an action (p. 781)

6. How did American involvement in Vietnam change after March 1965?

_____

_____

_____

_____

_____

• A Bloody Stalemate Emerges (page 781)

By 1966 more than 300,000 American soldiers were fighting in Vietnam. Americans believed that with such a large fighting force, the United States was destined to win. Not having this kind of power, the Vietcong used ambushes and hit-and-run tactics. The Vietcong also blended into the population in the cities and countryside and then vanished. To counter these tactics,

Study Guide

Chapter 17, Section 2 (continued)

American troops tried to find enemy troops and bomb their positions. They hoped to destroy their supply lines and force them out in the open.

American troops also wanted to get rid of the Vietcong's ability to hide in the thick jungles by destroying the landscape. American planes dropped **napalm,** a jellied gasoline that explodes on contact. They also used **Agent Orange,** a chemical that strips leaves from trees and shrubs. The chemical destroyed farmland and forests.

American military leaders believed that continuous bombing and killing of many Vietcong would destroy the enemy's morale and make them surrender. However, the guerrillas had no intention of surrendering. Although the Vietcong were made up of many South Vietnamese, North Vietnam supported them with arms and advisers. Later, North Vietnam began sending its own army to South Vietnam. They sent the supplies by a network of paths that went through Cambodia and Laos. The paths bypassed the border between North Vietnam and South Vietnam. The network was known as the Ho Chi Minh trail. North Vietnam received its supplies from the Soviet Union and China. President Johnson refused to order an invasion of North Vietnam because he feared an attack would bring China into the war. This policy made it difficult to win the war. Instead of conquering enemy troops, American troops followed a strategy of defeating the enemy forces by slowly wearing them down.

Although American planes killed as many as 220,000 Vietnamese between 1965 and 1967, the Vietcong showed no signs of surrendering. American casualties also increased, with more than 6,700 American soldiers killed by the end of 1966.

7. Why did President Johnson refuse to order an invasion of North Vietnam?

_____

_____

_____

_____

_____

Study Guide

Chapter 17, Section 3

For use with textbook pages 786–791

VIETNAM DIVIDES THE NATION

CONTENT VOCABULARY

credibility gap   a lack of belief in government reports regarding the Vietnam War *(page 787)*

teach-in   an informal discussion held between college faculty and students about issues relating to the war and the reasons for opposing it *(page 788)*

doves   those who wanted the United States to withdraw from the Vietnam War *(page 789)*

hawks   those who wanted the United States to stay and fight *(page 789)*

DRAWING FROM EXPERIENCE

Imagine that you are an American living in the United States during the Vietnam War. Would you have supported or opposed the war? Why?

The last section described the U.S. military involvement in Vietnam. This section discusses how the Vietnam War led to a division between supporters and opponents of the war.

ORGANIZING YOUR THOUGHTS

Use the diagram below to help you take notes. The year 1968 was a very critical year in the nation's history. Identify the events of that year in the diagram.

California History-Social Science Standards

11.9 Students analyze the U.S. foreign policy since World War II.

11.10 Students analyze the development of federal civil rights and voting rights.

Focuses on: 11.9.3, 11.9.4, 11.10.4

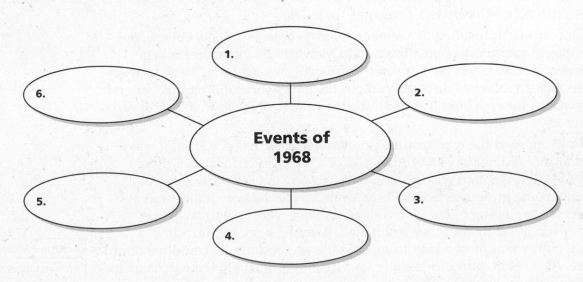

Study Guide

Chapter 17, Section 3 *(continued)*

• A Growing Credibility Gap *(page 787)*

Opposition to the Vietnam War grew in the United States in the late 1960s. One of the main reasons for the increased opposition was that many Americans were suspicious of the government's truthfulness about the war. In 1967 General William Westmoreland, the American commander in South Vietnam, reported that the United States was near victory. However, daily media accounts, particularly on television, showed images of wounded and dead Americans. These <u>contradictory</u> images made Americans doubt the optimistic government reports. Many Americans believed a **credibility gap** had developed. Congress also grew uncertain about the war. The Senate Foreign Relations committee held hearings on Vietnam. The committee called in Secretary of State Dean Rusk and other presidential advisers to explain the war program.

Academic Vocabulary
contradict: to do the opposite of what is expected (p. 787)

7. What led to a credibility gap in the United States in the late 1960s?

_____

_____

_____

_____

_____

• An Antiwar Movement Emerges *(page 788)*

As more Americans died in Vietnam, many people, especially college students, began to protest against the war. In March 1965, a group of college teachers and students at the University of Michigan joined together in a **teach-in.** This was an informal discussion about the issues surrounding the war and their reasons for opposing it. Soon teach-ins were being held in other college campuses.

People opposed the war for different reasons. Some believed that it was a civil war that did not have anything to do with the United States. Others believed South Vietnam was a corrupt democracy, and supporting it was immoral. Some protesters believed the United States had an unfair draft system. At the beginning of the war, college students were able to postpone military service until after they graduated. A young person from a low-income family was more likely to serve in the war because he could not afford college. As a result, minorities made up a <u>disproportionately</u> large percentage of the soldiers in Vietnam. The high number of African Americans and poor Americans dying in Vietnam angered African American leaders. In April 1967, Martin Luther King, Jr., publicly condemned the war.

Academic Vocabulary
proportion: a measurement of equality between two ratios (p. 788)

The American Vision: Modern Times

Study Guide

Chapter 17, Section 3 *(continued)*

As the war continued, more people were drafted. Many draftees refused to go. Some fled the country, moving to Canada or other nations. Others stayed and went to prison rather than fight in a war they opposed. In 1969 the government issued a lottery system for the draft. Only those who had low lottery numbers were drafted.

Demonstrators against the war were not only college students. In October 1967, a rally at the Lincoln Memorial drew tens of thousands of protesters. Although the antiwar protesters were a vocal group, a majority of people in early 1968 supported President Johnson's determination to keep fighting. The nation seemed to be divided into two groups. Those who wanted the United States to withdraw from Vietnam were known as **doves.** Those who wanted the United States to stay and fight became known as **hawks.**

8. Why did minorities make up a large percentage of the soldiers in Vietnam?

_____

_____

_____

_____

_____

• 1968: The Pivotal Year *(page 789)*

On January 30, 1968, the Vietcong and North Vietnamese launched a huge surprise attack during the Tet, the Vietnamese New Year. It was called the Tet offensive. The guerrilla fighters attacked all American airbases in South Vietnam and most of the nation's major cities. After about a month of fighting, the American and South Vietnamese soldiers fended off the enemy troops, who suffered heavy losses.

However, the North Vietnamese scored a major political victory. Americans were shocked that the North Vietnamese, who were supposedly near defeat, could launch such a huge attack. General Westmoreland called for additional troops. This seemed to indicate to Americans that the United States could not win the war. In addition, the media criticized the military effort. The media also indicated that the United States could not win the war.

After the Tet offensive, President Johnson's approval rating fell drastically. As a result, in March 1968, Johnson announced that he would not run for re-election in 1968. Even before his announcement, Democrats began looking for an <u>alternative</u> candidate to nominate. Eugene McCarthy, a dove, announced his candidacy in November 1967. Senator Robert Kennedy also announced his candidacy.

> **Academic Vocabulary**
>
> **alternative:** something that is different from what is normal (p. 790)

Study Guide

Chapter 17, Section 3 (continued)

In April 1968, Dr. Martin Luther King, Jr., was shot and killed. This led to riots in several major cities. Then in June 1968, Senator Robert Kennedy was shot and killed just after winning California's Democratic primary. Violence continued in 1968 with a clash between police and protesters at the Democratic National Convention in Chicago. Protesters demanded that the Democrats adopt an antiwar platform.

The delegates to the convention chose Hubert Humphrey, President Johnson's vice president, as their presidential nominee. At the same time, the protesters and police began fighting in a park near the convention hall. A riot broke out on the streets of downtown Chicago.

The violence associated with the Democratic Party worked to the benefit of the Republican presidential candidate, Richard Nixon. It also encouraged a third candidate, Governor George Wallace of Alabama, to run as an independent. Nixon promised to unify the nation and to restore law and order. He also announced that he had a plan to end the Vietnam War. Nixon defeated Humphrey by a slim margin.

9. Why did President Johnson not run for re-election in 1968?

_____

_____

_____

_____

_____

Study Guide

Chapter 17, Section 4

For use with textbook pages 792–797

THE WAR WINDS DOWN

CONTENT VOCABULARY

linkage   the policy of improving relations with the Soviet Union and China to persuade them to reduce their assistance to North Vietnam *(page 793)*

DRAWING FROM EXPERIENCE

What memories do your parents or grandparents have of the Vietnam War? How do they think the war affected the country?

The last section described the division in the United States over the Vietnam War. This section discusses the events that led to the withdrawal of the United States from Vietnam.

California History-Social Science Standards

11.9 Students analyze the U.S. foreign policy since World War II.

Focuses on: 11.9.3, 11.9.4

ORGANIZING YOUR THOUGHTS

Use the diagram below to help you take notes. List the effects of the war on South Vietnam and on the United States in the diagram.

Study Guide

Chapter 17, Section 4 (continued)

READ TO LEARN

• Nixon Moves to End the War *(page 793)*

President Nixon appointed Henry Kissinger as special assistant for national security affairs. Kissinger was given authority to use diplomacy to end U.S. involvement in the Vietnam War. Kissinger started a policy called **linkage,** which meant improving relations with the Soviet Union and China to persuade them to cut back their assistance to North Vietnam. Kissinger also resumed negotiations with North Vietnam. In August 1969, he started secret talks with Le Duc Tho, a North Vietnamese negotiator, about the <u>ultimate</u> fate of South Vietnam. The talks went on for four years. In the meantime, President Nixon began cutting back on the number of troops in Vietnam. He set up a plan called Vietnamization. It called for a gradual withdrawal of American troops and for the South Vietnamese army to take over more of the fighting. Nixon did not view the troop withdrawal as surrender. He wanted to keep America's strength in Vietnam during negotiations. To do this, Nixon increased air strikes against North Vietnam. He also ordered the bombing of the Vietcong in Cambodia.

Academic Vocabulary
ultimate: the greatest or most intense characteristic of something (p. 793)

8. Why did Henry Kissinger set up the policy of linkage?

_____

_____

_____

_____

_____

• Turmoil at Home Continues *(page 793)*

Protests and violence continued in the United States after Nixon became president. In November 1969, the American media reported that in the spring of 1968, an American platoon under the command of Lieutenant William Calley had massacred more than 200 unarmed South Vietnamese civilians in My Lai. Most of the victims were old men, women, and children. Calley went to prison for his role. The My Lai massacre increased the feelings among many Americans that the war was brutal and senseless. These feelings were strongest among the younger <u>generation</u>.

Academic Vocabulary
generation: a classification of people who share the same experience throughout their lives (p. 794)

In April 1970, Nixon announced that American troops had invaded Cambodia to destroy Vietcong military bases there. Many Americans viewed this action as enlarging the war. More protests occurred. At Kent State University in May 1970, Ohio National Guard soldiers fired on students without an order to do so. They killed four students. Two African American students were killed ten days later at a demonstration at Jackson State College in Mississippi.

Study Guide

Chapter 17, Section 4 (continued)

Members of Congress were upset with the president for not notifying them of his plan to invade Cambodia. In December 1970, Congress repealed the Gulf of Tonkin Resolution. Then in 1971, Daniel Ellsberg, a former Defense Department worker, leaked the Pentagon Papers to the *New York Times*. The documents showed that many government officials during the Johnson administration had privately questioned the war while publicly defending it. The documents also showed how various administrations deceived Congress, the media, and the public about the situation in Vietnam. They showed that the government had not been honest with the American people.

9. How did Congress respond to Nixon's invasion of Cambodia?

_____

_____

_____

_____

• The United States Pulls Out of Vietnam (page 795)

By 1971 a majority of Americans wanted to end the Vietnam War. In October 1972, Henry Kissinger announced that peace was near. In the 1972 presidential election, the Democrats nominated Senator George McGovern, a critic of the war. However, many Americans were tired of protesters and elected Nixon in a landslide.

Soon after the presidential election, in mid-December 1972, peace talks broke down. South Vietnam refused to agree to any plan in which North Vietnamese troops were left in South Vietnam. The next day Nixon began massive bombing raids to force North Vietnam to return to negotiations. They finally agreed. South Vietnam gave in to U.S. pressure and allowed North Viet-namese troops to remain in the South. On January 27, 1973, an agreement was signed to end the war. The United States agreed to withdraw its troops. Both sides agreed to an exchange of prisoners of war. The United States's direct involvement in Vietnam had ended.

In March 1975, shortly after the United States pulled out the last of its troops, North Vietnam started a full-scale invasion of South Vietnam. South Vietnam asked the United States for help. President Nixon had promised such help during the negotiations. However, he had resigned following the Watergate scandal. President Ford asked Congress for funds to help South Vietnam, but Congress refused to do so. On April 30, 1975, North Vietnam captured Saigon, the capital of South Vietnam. It united Vietnam under Communist rule and renamed Saigon Ho Chi Minh City.

Study Guide

Chapter 17, Section 4 *(continued)*

10. What happened after the United States troops left Vietnam?

_____

_____

_____

_____

_____

- **The Legacy of Vietnam** *(page 796)*

The Vietnam War left lasting effects on the United States. It had cost more than $170 billion. It resulted in the deaths of about 58,000 Americans and in the injuries of more than 300,000. In Vietnam, about one million North and South Vietnamese had died. The war had a psychological impact on many American soldiers. Many Americans considered the war a defeat. As a result, the sacrifices made by many veterans were left unrecognized. There were few welcome-home parades for American soldiers. The war continued for many American families whose relatives were prisoners of war or missing in action.

In 1973 Congress passed the War Powers Act. This was an attempt to set limits on the power of the president. The law required the president to inform Congress of any commitment of troops within 48 hours. It also required the president to withdraw troops in 60 to 90 days unless Congress <u>explicitly</u> approved the troop commitment.

Academic Vocabulary
explicit: to express without confusion of intent (p. 797)

After the Vietnam War, many Americans became more reluctant to involve the United States in the affairs of other nations. The Vietnam War also increased Americans' cynicism about their government. Many believed that the government had misled them.

11. How were the veterans of the Vietnam War often treated on their return home?

_____

_____

_____

_____

_____

_____

Study Guide

Chapter 18, Section 1

For use with textbook pages 806–812

THE STUDENT MOVEMENT AND THE COUNTERCULTURE

CONTENT VOCABULARY

counterculture   youth who adopted alternative ways of life *(page 809)*

communes   group living arrangements in which members shared everything and worked together *(page 809)*

DRAWING FROM EXPERIENCE

What image comes to mind when you hear the word "hippie"? From where have these images come?

In this section, you will learn about the youth movement in the United States. You will also learn how the youth movement affected the nation's culture.

ORGANIZING YOUR THOUGHTS

Use the diagram below to help you take notes. The counterculture affected American society in several ways. Describe these ways in the diagram.

California History-Social Science Standards

11.3 Students analyze the role religion played in the founding of America, its lasting moral, social and political impacts, and issues regarding religious liberty.

11.9 Students analyze the U.S. foreign policy since World War II.

Focuses on: 11.3.4, 11.9.4

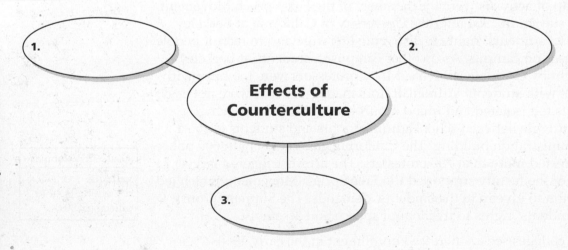

Effects of Counterculture

1.

2.

3.

Study Guide

Chapter 18, Section 1 *(continued)*

READ TO LEARN

• The Growth of the Youth Movement *(page 807)*

The 1960s saw the rise of a youth movement. The movement challenged American politics and society. Although the nation enjoyed economic prosperity in the 1950s, this prosperity did not affect everyone. The writers and artists of the "beat" movement criticized American society. The nuclear arms race made many young people in the United States uneasy about the future. This unease led many young people to become involved in social causes, such as the civil rights movement.

Because of the baby boom, the early 1960s saw an increase in the number of young people enrolled in college. The economic boom of the 1950s allowed more families to be able to afford college. Young people in college were able to meet and bond with others who shared their feelings and concerns. As a result, protest movements were loudest on college campuses.

A group of college students was concerned about the injustices that it saw in the nation's politics and society. The members of this group believed that a few wealthy people controlled politics. One organization of this group was the Students for a Democratic Society (SDS). It set its views in a 1962 declaration known as the Port Huron Statement, written largely by Tom Hayden. He was the editor of the University of Michigan's student newspaper. The declaration called for an end to apathy and for citizens to stop accepting a country that was run by big corporations and big government. SDS groups protested the Vietnam War. They also focused on issues such as poverty and racism.

Another group of activists were the members of the Free Speech Movement. The movement started in 1964 after the University of California at Berkeley decided to restrict students' rights to distribute literature and to recruit people for political causes on campus. As on other campuses, students at Berkeley were often taught by graduate students. Many professors were too busy with research to meet with students. Administrators made rules that were not easy to obey. Students felt isolated and found a purpose in the Free Speech Movement. A struggle between school administrators and students led to a sit-in at the administration building. The California governor sent in 600 police officers who arrested more than 700 protesters. The arrests triggered larger protests. Much of the faculty supported the Free Speech Movement, which led the administration to give in to the students' demands. The Supreme Court <u>validated</u> the students' rights to freedom of speech and assembly.

> **Academic Vocabulary**
>
> **validate:** to make something legal or official (p. 809)

4. Why did colleges see an increased enrollment in the early 1960s?

_____

_____

_____

_____

Study Guide

Chapter 18, Section 1 *(continued)*

• The Counterculture *(page 809)*

In the 1960s, thousands of mostly white middle- and upper-class youths created an alternative lifestyle. They became known as the **counterculture.** They were commonly called "hippies." The hippies rebelled against the dominant culture in the United States. They rejected <u>rationality</u> and traditional middle-class values. The counterculture had an ideal of a society that was freer and full of love and empathy. As the movement grew larger, however, the newcomers did not understand the original ideas of the counterculture. For these people, what mattered were the outward signs such as long hair, shabby jeans, and the use of drugs.

Many hippies left home and lived together with other young people in **communes.** These were group living arrangements in which members shared everything and worked together. A popular hippie destination in the mid-1960s was the Haight-Ashbury district in San Francisco.

Many members of the counterculture looked to various beliefs ranging from astrology to Eastern religions and new forms of Christianity. Some religious groups centered around authoritarian leaders who controlled the lives of the group members. Parents accused religious sects of using mind-control techniques on their children. Two such new religious groups in the 1960s were the Unification Church and the Hare Krishna movement.

The counterculture began to deteriorate after a few years. Many young people of the counterculture gradually returned to mainstream society.

5. What did members of the counterculture rebel against?

_____

_____

_____

_____

_____

> **Academic Vocabulary**
>
> **rational:** the ability to use reason (p. 809)

• Impact of the Counterculture *(page 811)*

The counterculture did change American life. It changed the fashion industry, which took its cues from the young men and women. Clothing became more colorful and more comfortable. Ethnic clothing became popular. Beads imitated Native American costumes. Tie-dyed shirts borrowed techniques from India and Africa. Longer hair on men and more individual clothes for both men and women became generally accepted. Clothing of the counterculture soon became mainstream.

During the 1960s, there was less distinction between traditional art and popular art, or pop art. Pop art <u>derived</u> its subject matter from parts of the popular culture, such as photographs and advertisements.

> **Academic Vocabulary**
>
> **derive:** to gain something from a specific source (p. 811)

Study Guide

Chapter 18, Section 1 (continued)

Counterculture music became part of the mainstream. The Beatles were one of the most famous of the counterculture musicians. They inspired many other rock 'n' roll groups both in Great Britain and in the United States. The lyrics of much of the counterculture music spoke to the fears of the young people and to the widening gap between them and their parents. Electrically amplified instruments changed the sound of the new music. A master of the new guitar sound was Jimi Hendrix. Thousands of people got together to celebrate the new music at rock festivals such as Woodstock, in New York, and Altamont, in California. The style of dancing had also changed. People danced individually without a partner and were surrounded by other people who danced alone.

6. How did the counterculture change fashion in the United States?

_____

_____

_____

_____

_____

Study Guide

Chapter 18, Section 2

For use with textbook pages 813–819

THE FEMINIST MOVEMENT

CONTENT VOCABULARY

feminism   the belief that men and women should be equal politically, economically, and socially *(page 814)*

Title IX   part of a law that prohibited federally funded schools from discriminating against girls and young women in all aspects of their operations *(page 817)*

DRAWING FROM EXPERIENCE

What issues do you think women face today? How do you think these issues are being addressed?

The last section described the effect of the youth movement in the United States. This section discusses the achievements of the women's movement in the United States.

ORGANIZING YOUR THOUGHTS

Use the chart below to help you take notes. The women's movement in the 1960s addressed several issues. Identify these issues in the chart.

California History-Social Science Standards

11.10 Students analyze the development of federal civil rights and voting rights.

11.11 Students analyze the major social problems and domestic policy issues in contemporary American society.

Focuses on: 11.10.7, 11.11.3, 11.11.7

Issues Addressed by the Women's Movement

1.
2.
3.
4.

Study Guide

Chapter 18, Section 2 *(continued)*

READ TO LEARN

- **A Weakened Women's Movement** *(page 814)*

By the early 1960s, many women in the United States became dissatisfied with their roles as homemakers. Those women who worked outside the home recognized that they received lower pay and fewer opportunities than men. The situation led to the start of a new feminist movement in the 1960s. Since the adoption of the Nineteenth Amendment in 1920, **feminism,** or the belief that men and women should be equal politically, economically, and socially, had been an issue. Soon after the Nineteenth Amendment was passed, the women's movement split into two groups. One group was the League of Women Voters. It worked to promote laws to protect women and children, such as limiting the hours they could work. Another group was the National Woman's Party (NWP). This group opposed protective laws for women. Instead, the NWP persuaded some members of Congress to introduce the first Equal Rights Amendment. The amendment was to forbid federal, state, and local laws from discriminating on the basis of <u>gender</u>. However, Congress ignored the proposed amendment.

During World War II, women became an <u>integral</u> part of the nation's workforce. When the war ended, many women lost their jobs to the men who returned home. However, many women gradually reentered the labor force. By 1960 they made up almost 40 percent of the nation's workforce.

Academic Vocabulary
gender: term applied to the characteristics of a male or female (p. 814)
integral: a part of something that has complete importance to the whole (p. 814)

5. What situation led to the development of a new feminist movement in the 1960s?

_____

_____

_____

_____

- **The Women's Movement Reawakens** *(page 815)*

By the 1960s, many women were resentful of being discriminated against because of gender. This was particularly true in the workforce, where women worked at lower-paying jobs. Women also had a better understanding of their unequal status from their work in the civil rights and antiwar movements. Very often women in these movements were not part of any policy decisions. This awareness led to a new feminist movement across the United States. It was part of the 1960s pursuit for rights.

The women's movement came to life as a result of the mass protest of ordinary women and the President's Commission on the Status of Women. President Kennedy appointed the commission to study the status of women in

Study Guide

Chapter 18, Section 2 *(continued)*

the United States. The commission's report pointed to the problems of women in the workplace. It helped put together a network of feminist activists who lobbied Congress for women's laws. In 1963 they won the passage of the Equal Pay Act. The law outlawed paying men more than women for the same job. Congress also added a measure to the 1964 Civil Rights Act. It was called Title VII and it outlawed <u>bias</u> by private employers on the basis of race, religion, national origin, and gender. The Equal Employment Opportunity Commission (EEOC) was a federal agency set up to administer these laws. However, even this commission still held on to the belief that jobs should be distinguished by gender.

> **Academic Vocabulary**
>
> **bias:** the presence of prejudice within someone's judgment (p. 815)

Many people date the start of the new women's movement from the publication in 1963 of *The Feminine Mystique* by Betty Friedan. Friedan had interviewed women who had graduated with her from college and found that many of them felt unfulfilled, despite having everything they could want in life. The book became a bestseller and allowed many women to share their feelings and build a base for a nationwide movement.

In June 1966, Friedan and others began considering the need for women to form a national organization. This led to the start of the National Organization for Women (NOW). The organization demanded greater educational opportunities for women. It focused on helping women in the workplace. They fought against the practice of paying women less than men for the same work. The organization pushed for the passage of the Equal Rights Amendment. It also published its own magazine, *Ms.* The editor of the magazine was Gloria Steinem, one of the leading figures of NOW.

6. What do many people date as the start of the new women's movement in the United States in the mid-1960s?

_____

_____

_____

_____

_____

• **Successes and Failures** *(page 816)*

A major accomplishment of the women's movement was gaining greater equality for women in education. Leaders of the movement pushed lawmakers to pass federal laws banning discrimination in education. In 1972 Congress passed a collection of laws known as the Educational Amendments. One part of these laws was **Title IX.** It prohibited federally funded schools from discriminating against girls and young women in all aspects of their operations.

Study Guide

Chapter 18, Section 2 *(continued)*

An important goal for many women was the repeal of laws against abortion. Until 1973, the right to regulate abortion was given to the states. In that year, the Supreme Court ruled in *Roe* v. *Wade* that state governments could not regulate abortion during the first three months of pregnancy. This was interpreted as being within a woman's constitutional right to privacy. The decision led to the rise of the right-to-life movement. Members of this movement considered abortion an absolute wrong and wanted it to be banned.

In 1972 Congress passed the Equal Rights Amendment (ERA). Under this amendment, protection against discrimination on the basis of gender would become part of the Constitution if 38 states ratified it. Opposition to the ERA had been growing. Many people saw it as a threat to traditional values. Some women opposed it because they feared that it would take away the legal rights of wives. A vocal opponent of the ERA was Phyllis Schlafly. She organized the nationwide Stop-ERA campaign. She argued that the ERA would take away many of the rights that women already had, such as alimony after a divorce. The ERA failed to be ratified by three votes, and it finally failed in 1982.

7. What was the significance of Title IX?

_____

_____

_____

_____

_____

_____

Study Guide

Chapter 18, Section 3

For use with textbook pages 824–831

NEW APPROACHES TO CIVIL RIGHTS

CONTENT VOCABULARY

affirmative action   a policy that called for companies and institutions doing business with the federal government to actively recruit African American employees *(page 825)*

busing   the transporting of children to schools outside their neighborhoods to gain greater racial balance *(page 826)*

bilingualism   the practice of teaching immigrant students in their own language while they also learned English *(page 829)*

DRAWING FROM EXPERIENCE

What methods do groups in the United States today use to urge the government to address issues that are important to them? What methods do you think are most effective? Why?

The last section discussed the achievements of the women's movement in the United States. This section discusses the ways that minority groups sought to increase their civil rights.

ORGANIZING YOUR THOUGHTS

Use the diagram below to help you take notes. In the late 1960s and 1970s, minority groups formed organizations to increase their civil rights. Describe the work of each of the organizations listed in the diagram.

> **California History-Social Science Standards**
>
> **11.6** Students analyze the different explanations for the Great Depression and how the New Deal fundamentally changed the role of the federal government.
>
> **11.9** Students analyze the U.S. foreign policy since World War II.
>
> **11.10** Students analyze the development of federal civil rights and voting rights.
>
> **11.11** Students analyze the major social problems and domestic policy issues in contemporary American society.
>
> **Focuses on:** 11.6.5, 11.9.7, 11.10.2, 11.10.4, 11.10.5, 11.11.1

Work of Minority Organizations

Congressional Black Caucus	United Farm Workers	*La Raza Unida*	American Indian Movement
1. _____	2. _____	3. _____	4. _____

Study Guide

Chapter 18, Section 3 (continued)

• Fighting for Greater Opportunity (page 825)

By the late 1960s, laws banned racial discrimination. However, most African Americans saw little improvement in their daily lives. Getting good jobs and a good education was difficult. As a result, civil rights leaders began focusing on these issues. They looked to **affirmative action.** It called for companies and institutions doing business with the <u>federal</u> government to actively recruit African American employees. This would be enforced through federal laws and with the hope that this would lead to improved social and economic conditions for African Americans. In Atlanta, Mayor Maynard Jackson, an African American, opened bidding for the expansion of the city's airport more widely to minority companies. As a result, small and minority companies <u>contracted</u> 25 percent of all airport construction work.

Critics of affirmative action called it "reverse discrimination." In 1974 an application to the University of California Medical School by a white applicant named Allan Bakke was turned down. Bakke found out that slots had been set aside for minorities, some of whom had scored lower than Bakke on their exams. He sued the school, arguing that the school discriminated against him because of his race. In 1978 the Supreme Court ruled that the university did violate Bakke's rights. However, it also ruled that schools could use racial criteria for admission as long as they did not use fixed quotas.

Civil rights leaders also worked for educational improvements. Even after the Supreme Court ruling in *Brown* v. *Board of Education of Topeka, Kansas,* many schools in the 1960s remained segregated. Since children normally went to neighborhood schools, segregation in the schools reflected the racial segregation of neighborhoods. As a result, a number of local governments started a policy known as **busing,** or transporting children to schools outside their neighborhoods to gain greater racial balance. The Supreme Court ruled that busing was constitutional. Many whites, however, opposed busing. Many took their children out of public schools. By 1976 African Americans and other minorities made up the majority of Boston's public school students.

African Americans found new political leaders. One leader was Jesse Jackson. Jackson was an activist during the civil rights movement. He continued working to improve the economic and political situation of African Americans. He founded People United to Save Humanity (PUSH). The organization's goal was to register voters, develop African American businesses, and improve educational opportunities.

African Americans gained influence in Congress. In 1971 African American members of Congress formed the Congressional Black Caucus. It was organized to better represent the legislative concerns of African Americans. It promoted African American interests in areas such as health care and economics.

Academic Vocabulary
federal: refers to a strong central government (p. 825)

Academic Vocabulary
contract: a binding legal document between two parties (p. 825)

Study Guide

Chapter 18, Section 3 *(continued)*

5. What was the purpose of busing?

_____

_____

_____

_____

- ## Hispanic Americans Organize *(page 828)*

Hispanics in the 1960s also worked to gain greater rights. Hispanics came to the United States from different places and for different reasons. Hispanics, like other immigrant groups, experienced prejudice and a lack of access to proper housing and employment. Encouraged by the civil rights movement, they began to organize a protest movement.

Hispanics began working to win rights for farmworkers. Most Mexican American farmworkers earned little money and had few benefits. In the early 1960s, César Chávez and Dolores Huerta organized two groups that fought for the rights of farmworkers. They staged successful protests and a nation-wide boycott against California grape growers. In 1966 Chávez and Huerta merged their organizations into the United Farm Workers (UFW). They continued their boycott until 1970, when the grape growers agreed to a contract to raise wages and improve working conditions.

Hispanic Americans also became more politically active. In 1969 a new political party called *La Raza Unida* was organized. The group mobilized Mexican American voters to support programs that called for job-training programs and greater access to financial institutions. Another issue that both Hispanic students and political leaders worked for was **bilingualism.** This is the practice of teaching immigrant students in their own language while they also learned English. Congress responded by passing the Bilingual Education Act in 1968. Some American voters opposed bilingual education because they believed that it made it more difficult for a child to adjust to American culture. The U.S. Supreme Court ruled in favor of bilingualism in 1974.

6. For what did César Chávez work?

_____

_____

_____

_____

Study Guide

Chapter 18, Section 3 *(continued)*

- **Native Americans Raise Their Voices** *(page 829)*

Native Americans suffered many injustices. Their unemployment rate was 10 times the national rate. Unemployment was especially high on reservation lands. More than half of Native Americans lived on these lands. Life expectancy for Native Americans was about seven years below the national average. In the late 1960s and 1970s, many Native Americans began to organize to improve these conditions.

Native Americans called for better economic opportunities on reservations. Many wanted greater independence from the mainstream society in the United States. In 1968 Congress passed the Indian Civil Rights Act. The law <u>guaranteed</u> Native Americans on reservations the protection of the Bill of Rights. It also recognized local reservation law. Some Native Americans believed the government was not doing enough. They formed more militant groups such as the American Indian Movement (AIM). In February 1973, members of AIM occupied the town of Wounded Knee, where federal troops had killed around 150 Sioux in 1890. The AIM members demanded changes in the way the reservations were run. They also wanted the government to honor its treaty obligations to Native Americans. A clash occurred between the Native Americans and the FBI. Two Native Americans were killed and several people were wounded. The takeover ended a short time later.

> **Academic Vocabulary**
>
> **guarantee:** a statement of assurance (p. 830)

The Native American movement did have some successes. In 1975 Congress passed the Indian Self-Determination and Educational Assistance Act. The law increased funds for Native American education. It increased the role of Native Americans in administering federal programs. By working through the courts, Native Americans won a number of land and water rights that they worked for. They have also developed businesses on reservations, which are operated under the laws of the reservation.

7. What did the Indian Civil Rights Act provide?

_____

_____

_____

_____

_____

_____

Study Guide

Chapter 18, Section 4

For use with textbook pages 832–837

SAVING THE EARTH

CONTENT VOCABULARY

smog   fog made heavier and darker by smoke and chemical fumes *(page 834)*

fossil fuels   coal, oil, and natural gas *(page 835)*

DRAWING FROM EXPERIENCE

What steps does your local government take to protect your community's environment? What actions do you and your family take?

The last section described the ways that minority groups sought to increase their civil rights. This section discusses the beginnings of the environmental movement and the consumer movement.

ORGANIZING YOUR THOUGHTS

Use the cause-and-effect diagram below to help you take notes. Several incidents in the 1960s and 1970s had a great effect on the nation's environment. List the effects in the diagram.

California History-Social Science Standards
11.8 Students analyze the economic boom and social transformation of post–World War II America.
11.11 Students analyze the major social problems and domestic policy issues in contemporary American society.
Focuses on: 11.8.6, 11.11.5, 11.11.7

Cause	**Effect**
Rachel Carson wrote *Silent Spring*.	1. _____
Congress passed several pieces of environmental legislation.	2. _____
The Three Mile Island accident occurred.	3. _____
Ralph Nader wrote *Unsafe at Any Speed*.	4. _____

Study Guide

Chapter 18, Section 4 *(continued)*

• The Beginnings of Environmentalism *(page 833)*

In the 1960s and 1970s, many Americans began to look more closely at the effects of industrialism on the environment. They were alarmed at what they found. The United States seemed to have little concern for the environment. Pesticides had damaged a wide range of wildlife. Pollution had damaged the air and the water. Nuclear energy was used more and more. In her book *Silent Spring,* Rachel Carson wrote of the danger in the increasing use of pesticides, particularly DDT. She wrote that although pesticides killed insect populations, they also killed birds, fish, and other animals. Carson's book became one of the most powerful books of the 1960s. It sold nearly half a million copies within six months of its <u>publication</u>. Many Americans took Carson's warnings seriously. They began to focus on environmental issues. <u>Nonetheless</u>, the chemical industry began an intense campaign to discredit Carson.

> **Academic Vocabulary**
>
> **publication:** a manuscript that has been printed and distributed (p. 834)
>
> **nonetheless:** expresses a view regardless of the circumstances surrounding it (p. 834)

5. What effect did Rachel Carson's book have on many Americans?

_____

_____

_____

• The Environmental Movement *(page 834)*

By the late 1960s, environmental problems existed in every region of the nation. Acres of forestland were being cut down in the Northwest. **Smog,** or fog made heavier and darker by smoke and chemical fumes, covered many cities. Pollution and garbage had caused the death of nearly all the fish in Lake Erie. Many people believed it was time to take action to protect the environment.

The environmental movement began officially in April 1970. That month the nation held the first Earth Day. It was a day devoted to addressing environmental issues. Millions of Americans participated in some way to show environmental awareness. After Earth Day, many people formed local environmental groups. Organizations such as the Sierra Club and the Wilderness Society became well-known. The federal government soon became involved with environmental issues. In 1970 the Environmental Protection Agency was established. Its job was to set and enforce pollution standards. The agency also coordinated anti-pollution activities with state and local governments. The Clean Air Act set up air emissions standards for factories and automobiles. The Clean Water Act limited the amount of pollutants that could be discharged into the nation's lakes and rivers. The Endangered Species Act set up measures for saving threatened animal species. Eventually, these laws improved the condition of the nation's environment.

Study Guide

Chapter 18, Section 4 *(continued)*

In the 1970s, people living in the Love Canal—a housing development near Niagara Falls, New York—noticed a high rate of health problems in their community. The problems included nerve damage, blood diseases, and cancer. The people learned that their community was located on top of an old toxic waste dump. The hazardous materials in the dump had leaked into the ground. The people of Love Canal demanded that the government address the problem. After they made the problem known to the entire nation, the state relocated about 200 families. In 1980 President Carter declared the Love Canal a federal disaster area. He moved the 600 remaining families to new locations. The Love Canal residents sued the company that created the dumpsite. They settled the case for $20 million. The site was cleaned up and homes above the dumping ground were burned.

During the 1970s, many Americans were concerned over the growth of nuclear power. Those who supported the use of nuclear power claimed it was a cleaner and less expensive alternative to **fossil fuels,** such as coal, oil, or natural gas. Those who opposed the use of nuclear power warned of the risks that nuclear energy posed, particularly the <u>consequences</u> of radiation accidentally released into the air. On March 28, 1979, one of the reactors at the Three Mile Island nuclear facility outside Harrisburg, Pennsylvania, overheated. Later, low levels of radiation escaped from the reactor. Nearby residents were evacuated. Others left on their own. Citizens staged protests. The reactor was closed down and the leak was sealed. The Three Mile Island accident left many people doubtful about the safety of nuclear energy. The doubts continue today.

Academic Vocabulary
consequence: the positive or negative result of an action (p. 835)

6. What effect did the accident at Three Mile Island have on Americans?

_____

_____

_____

_____

• The Consumer Movement *(page 836)*

Many Americans in the 1960s and 1970s began questioning the quality and safety of many new technological products. Some people began to demand government involvement in setting up a consumer policy to ensure product safety and accurate information about products that consumers were buying. The most famous personality in the new consumer movement was Ralph Nader. In the 1960s, he began noticing a high number of deaths from automobile accidents. He researched the problem and presented his findings in a book titled *Unsafe at Any Speed*. The book charged that car manufacturers put style and cost ahead of safety. Nader's work helped to get Congress to pass

Study Guide

Chapter 18, Section 4 *(continued)*

the National Traffic and Motor Vehicle Safety Act in 1966. The law set manda-
tory standards and established a system for notifying car owners about
defects. Carmakers had to incorporate safety standards into their car designs.
Nader was also successful in getting laws passed that regulated products such
as dangerous toys and unsafe meat and poultry.

7. How did Congress respond to Ralph Nader's findings regarding automobile safety?

_____

_____

Study Guide

Chapter 19, Section 1

For use with textbook pages 850–856

THE NIXON ADMINISTRATION

CONTENT VOCABULARY

revenue sharing   bills that granted federal funds to state and local agencies to use as they saw fit *(page 853)*

impound   refuse to release *(page 853)*

détente   the relaxation of tensions between the United States and its two major Communist rivals *(page 855)*

summit   high-level diplomatic meeting *(page 855)*

DRAWING FROM EXPERIENCE

What kinds of problems did the United States face at the end of President Johnson's administration? Which problem do you think would be the most important one for the next president to address?

In this section, you will learn about President Nixon's domestic policy, You will also learn about his foreign policy.

ORGANIZING YOUR THOUGHTS

Use the diagram below to help you take notes. President Nixon's foreign policy was one of détente. List some of the results of détente in the diagram.

> **California History-Social Science Standards**
>
> **11.8** Students analyze the economic boom and social transformation of post–World War II America.
>
> **11.9** Students analyze the U.S. foreign policy since World War II.
>
> **11.11** Students analyze the major social problems and domestic policy issues in contemporary American society.
>
> **Focuses on:** 11.8.4, 11.9.3, 11.11.2, 11.11.6, 11.11.7

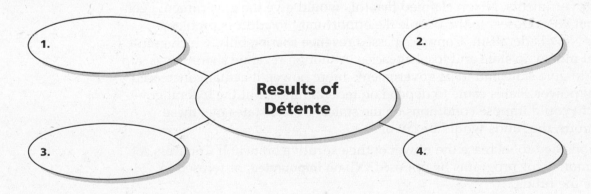

1.

2.

Results of Détente

3.

4.

The American Vision: Modern Times

Study Guide

Chapter 19, Section 1 *(continued)*

READ TO LEARN

• Appealing to Middle America *(page 851)*

In the late 1960s, many Americans longed for the violence in the nation to stop. The Republican candidate for president in 1968, Richard Nixon, appealed to these Americans. Nixon promised peace in Vietnam, law and order, and a return to more conservative values. Hubert Humphrey was the Democratic presidential candidate. George Wallace was the third-party candidate. Nixon won the election.

An important reason for Nixon's victory was the support he received in the South. Nixon gained support by promising several things. He promised to appoint only conservatives to the federal courts and to appoint a Southerner to the Supreme Court. He promised to oppose court-ordered busing and to choose a vice presidential candidate acceptable to the South. Nixon chose Spiro Agnew, who was from Maryland. Nixon's promises paid off. On election day, Nixon carried several southern states. After his victory, Nixon set out to bring more Southerners to the Republican Party. This effort became known as the Southern strategy. Nixon made good on his promises and took steps to slow desegregation.

Nixon set out to deliver on his promise to restore law and order. He targeted the antiwar protesters. Nixon also went against the Supreme Court rulings that expanded the rights of accused criminals. He openly criticized the rulings and Chief Justice Earl Warren. When Warren resigned after Nixon took office, Nixon replaced him with a conservative judge, Warren Burger. The Burger Court did not reverse the rulings on the rights of criminal suspects, but it did refuse to expand those rights.

Nixon's domestic policies became known as New Federalism. It called for getting rid of several federal programs and giving more control to state and local governments. Nixon claimed that this would give the government agencies that were closest to the people the opportunity to address problems. Under New Federalism, Congress passed **revenue sharing** bills, which granted federal money to state and local agencies. Although revenue sharing was supposed to give state and local governments more power, it actually increased federal power. States came to depend on federal funds, but the federal government could impose conditions on the states. Unless states met these conditions, the funds would be cut off.

Nixon tried to increase the power of the executive branch. If Congress set aside money for programs he opposed, Nixon **impounded,** or refused to release the funds.

President Nixon wanted to reform the nation's welfare system. Both Republicans and Democrats criticized the program. Many argued that the program was set up in such a way that it was better for poor people to apply for benefits rather than taking low-paying jobs. To replace this program, in 1969

Study Guide

Chapter 19, Section 1 *(continued)*

Nixon proposed the Family Assistance Plan. It gave needy families $1,600 per year. That amount could be <u>supplemented</u> by outside earnings. The House of Representatives approved the plan in 1970. However, it was defeated in the Senate.

Academic Vocabulary
supplement: an addition to something meant to make it complete (p. 853)

5. What did President Nixon do to keep his promise of restoring law and order?

_____

_____

_____

- **Nixon's Foreign Policy** *(page 854)*

President Nixon was more interested in foreign affairs than in domestic ones. He chose Henry Kissinger as his national security adviser. He took the lead in helping Nixon shape his foreign policy.

Both Nixon and Kissinger believed that the United States would have to gradually withdraw from Vietnam. Both rejected the <u>notion</u> that the nation's policy against communism was too soft. They wanted to contain communism, but they believed that negotiation was a better way to achieve the goal. As a result, they began friendlier relations with China and the Soviet Union.

Academic Vocabulary
notion: a theory based upon experience (p. 854)

Kissinger and Nixon developed an approach called **détente,** or relaxation of tensions between the United States and its two major Communist rivals— China and the Soviet Union. Nixon claimed that the United States had to build a better relationship with the two countries in order to lessen the <u>potential</u> of a nuclear war.

Academic Vocabulary
potential: something that contains the possibility of becoming actual (p. 855)

In 1972 Nixon made a historic visit to China. Leaders of both nations agreed to set up more normal relations between their countries. Nixon believed that relaxing tensions with China would encourage the Soviet Union to do so. Shortly after negotiations with China took place, the Soviets proposed a **summit,** or high-level diplomatic meeting, to be held between the United States and the Soviet Union. During the summit, the two countries signed the first Strategic Arms Limitation Treaty, or SALT I. This was a plan to limit nuclear arms. The two nations also agreed to increase trade and to exchange scientific information.

6. What was the purpose of SALT I?

_____

_____

_____

_____

Study Guide

Chapter 19, Section 2

For use with textbook pages 857–862

THE WATERGATE SCANDAL

CONTENT VOCABULARY

executive privilege   the principle that White House conversations should remain confidential to protect national security *(page 861)*

impeach   official charges of presidential misconduct *(page 862)*

DRAWING FROM EXPERIENCE

What does the term *Watergate* mean to you? Whom did the Watergate scandal involve? How do you know about the Watergate scandal?

The last section discussed the domestic and foreign policies of President Nixon. This section discusses the events that led to the Watergate scandal and the effects of the scandal.

> **California History-Social Science Standards**
>
> **11.11** Students analyze the major social problems and domestic policy issues in contemporary American society.
>
> **Focuses on:** 11.11.4

ORGANIZING YOUR THOUGHTS

Use the cause-and-effect diagram below to help you take notes. The Watergate crisis affected Congress and the American people. List these effects in the diagram.

Cause		Effects
		1.
Watergate Crisis		2.
		3.

READ TO LEARN

• **The Roots of Watergate** *(page 858)*

President Nixon's administration became involved in what became known as Watergate. It was an attempt by members of Nixon's administration to cover up its involvement in the break-in at the Democratic National Committee (DNC) headquarters at the Watergate apartment-office complex. Although the scandal began with the burglary, many experts <u>attribute</u> the scandal in large part to the character of Richard Nixon. He had suffered several political defeats during his career and had to fight hard to win the

> **Academic Vocabulary**
>
> **attribute:** to describe an effect by applying a cause (p. 858)

302

Study Guide

Chapter 19, Section 2 *(continued)*

presidential election in 1968. Over the years, he had grown defensive and secretive. Nixon became president when the United States was still in turmoil over the Vietnam War. He viewed protesters as people out to bring down his administration. He even developed an "enemies list" of people he considered a threat to his presidency.

Nixon was expected to win the 1972 presidential election. His approval rating was high, particularly for his foreign policy in China and the Soviet Union. However, the Vietnam War was continuing. Nixon and his advisers also remembered that he won the 1968 election by a slim margin. As a result, his team tried to <u>obtain</u> an edge in every way they could. This included spying on the opposition, spreading rumors, and stealing information from the Democratic Party's headquarters. Five Nixon supporters broke into the party's office. As the burglars were at work on June 17, 1972, a security guard found a piece of tape holding a door lock. He took the tape off, but when he returned he found that it had been replaced. He called the police, who arrested the men.

One of the burglars, James McCord, was a member of the Committee for the Re-election of the President (CRP). As questions came up about the White House connection to the burglary, the cover-up began. Members of the administration destroyed documents and gave false testimony to investigators. Although President Nixon may not have ordered the break-in, he did order the cover-up. Members of the administration asked the CIA to stop the FBI from asking about the source of the money paid to the burglars. They argued that such an investigation would threaten national security. At the same time, the White House denied any involvement in the break-in. Most Americans believed the denial and re-elected Nixon in the November 1972 election. He won by one of the largest margins in history.

> **Academic Vocabulary**
>
> **obtain:** to gain possession of (p. 859)

4. Why did members of Nixon's administration order a break-in into the Democratic Party's headquarters?

_____

_____

_____

_____

• The Cover-Up Unravels *(page 859)*

The Watergate burglars went on trial in 1973. James McCord agreed to cooperate with the grand jury investigation and with the Senate's Select Committee on Presidential Campaign Activities. Senator Sam J. Ervin headed the committee. Many confessions came forward after McCord's testimony.

A major confession came from John Dean, the counsel to the president. In June 1973, Dean testified that former Attorney General John Mitchell had

Study Guide

Chapter 19, Section 2 *(continued)*

ordered the Watergate break-in and that Nixon had played an active role in covering it up. The Nixon administration denied the charges. The committee then tried to determine who was telling the truth. Then on July 16, White House aide Alexander Butterfield testified that Nixon had ordered a taping system installed in the White House to record conversations. The committee believed that the tapes would tell them what they needed to know.

Everyone wanted the tapes. However, President Nixon claimed **executive privilege.** This is the principle that White House conversations should remain confidential to protect national security. He refused to give up the tapes. Archibald Cox, a special prosecutor appointed by the president to handle the Watergate cases, took Nixon to court in October 1973, to force him to give up the tapes. Nixon ordered Attorney General Elliot Richardson to fire Cox. He refused to do so and resigned in protest. Finally, Solicitor General Robert Bork fired Cox. The incident damaged Nixon's reputation with the public.

Also in the fall of 1973, Vice President Spiro Agnew was forced to resign because he had taken bribes from state contractors while he was governor of Maryland and while he was serving in Washington. Gerald Ford, the Republican leader of the House of Representatives, became the new vice president.

President Nixon appointed a new special prosecutor, Leon Jaworski, who also wanted the president's tapes. In April 1974, Nixon released edited notes of the tapes that he believed proved his innocence. However, investigators did not believe so and wanted the unedited tapes. In July the Supreme Court ruled that the president had to turn over the tapes themselves, not just the transcripts.

A few days later, the House Judiciary Committee voted to **impeach** Nixon, or officially charge him with presidential misconduct. The committee charged that Nixon had obstructed justice in the Watergate cover-up. The next step was for the entire House of Representatives to vote whether or not to impeach.

Investigators also found evidence against the president. One of the tapes showed that on June 23, 1972, just a few days after the burglary, Nixon had ordered the CIA to stop the FBI's investigation of the break-in. Nixon's impeachment and conviction by the Senate now seemed <u>inevitable</u>. As a result, on August 9, 1974, Nixon resigned his office. Gerald Ford became president.

Academic Vocabulary
inevitable: impossible to stop from occurring (p. 861)

5. Why was John Dean's testimony in the Watergate investigation significant?

_____

_____

_____

_____

_____

Study Guide

Chapter 19, Section 2 (continued)

• The Impact of Watergate (page 861)

After the Watergate crisis, Congress passed a number of laws to limit the power of the executive branch and to get a greater balance of power in government. The Federal Campaign Act Amendments limited campaign contributions, and it set up an independent agency to administer stricter election laws. The Ethics in Government Act required that high government officials in all three branches of government provide financial disclosures.

Watergate made many Americans distrust their public officials. Other Americans saw Watergate as proof that no person in the United States is above the law.

6. Why did Congress pass several laws after the Watergate crisis?

_____

_____

_____

_____

_____

Study Guide

Chapter 19, Section 3

For use with textbook pages 863–870

FORD AND CARTER

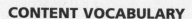

CONTENT VOCABULARY

inflation   a rise in the cost of goods *(page 864)*

embargo   a stoppage of shipping *(page 865)*

stagflation   a combination of rising prices and economic stagnation *(page 865)*

DRAWING FROM EXPERIENCE

What are the major sources of energy in the United States today? Do you think conserving energy is an issue today? What steps do you and your family take to conserve energy?

The last section discussed the Watergate scandal. This section discusses the administrations of Presidents Ford and Carter.

ORGANIZING YOUR THOUGHTS

Use the chart below to help you take notes. Both President Ford and President Carter faced foreign policy issues. List these issues in the chart.

Foreign Policy Issues Under President Ford	Foreign Policy Issues Under President Carter
1.	3.
2.	4.
	5.
	6.

California History-Social Science Standards

11.9 Students analyze the U.S. foreign policy since World War II.

11.11 Students analyze the major social problems and domestic policy issues in contemporary American society.

Focuses on: 11.9.3, 11.9.6, 11.11.2, 11.11.4

The American Vision: Modern Times

Study Guide

Chapter 19, Section 3 (continued)

• The Economic Crisis of the 1970s *(page 864)*

The United States had enjoyed a strong economy during the 1950s and 1960s, which many Americans had come to assume was the <u>norm</u>. This was due in large part because the United States had easy access to raw materials and had a strong manufacturing industry at home. These conditions had changed in the 1970s.

The economic problems had started under President Johnson. During the Vietnam War, he increased government deficit spending to pay for the war and to set up Great Society programs. This led to **inflation,** or a rise in the cost of goods. The rising cost of raw materials was another cause of inflation.

The rising cost of oil greatly affected the nation's economy. The United States became dependent on imports from the Middle East and Africa. In the early 1970s, the Organization of Petroleum Exporting Countries (OPEC) decided to use oil as an economic and political weapon. In 1973 a war went on between Israel and its Arab neighbors. U.S. support of Israel made American relations with the Arab nations tense. OPEC decided that its members would **embargo,** or stop shipping, oil to countries that supported Israel. This included the United States. OPEC also raised the price of oil by 70 percent and then by 130 percent. As a result, the United States had its first fuel shortage since World War II.

OPEC ended the embargo a few months after it began. However, oil prices continued to rise. The rapid increase in prices rapidly increased inflation. Americans were paying high prices for gasoline and home heating. As a result, they had little money to spend on other goods. The economy then went into a recession.

By the 1970s, the United States manufacturing industry faced international competition. Many manufacturing plants in the United States were not as new as those in Japan and Europe. These changes forced many factories to close and many people to be unemployed. In the early 1970s, Nixon faced a new economic problem called **stagflation.** This was a combination of rising prices and economic stagnation. Many economists did not think that inflation and recession could exist at the same time. As a result, they did not know what economic policies the government should set up.

Nixon decided to focus on controlling inflation. The government cut spending and raised taxes. However, Congress and the American people opposed the idea of a tax hike. Nixon then tried to get the Federal Reserve to raise interest rates. He hoped that this would reduce consumer spending and possibly curb inflation. This plan failed. Nixon then placed a 90-day freeze on all wages and prices. This plan also failed. When Nixon resigned, the inflation rate remained high and the unemployment rate was increasing.

> **Academic Vocabulary**
>
> **norm:** a standard by which people live (p. 864)

Study Guide

Chapter 19, Section 3 (continued)

7. Why was it difficult for economists to set up a policy to deal with stagflation?

_____

_____

_____

• Ford Takes Over (page 866)

President Ford, who <u>acknowledged</u> his undynamic personality, nonetheless attempted to restore American faith in its government leaders. He granted a full pardon to Richard Nixon, hoping to bring that chapter of the nation's history to an end. He believed that doing so was in the public interest. Nixon's pardon was severely criticized. Ford's popularity plunged soon after the pardon.

By 1975 the economy of the United States was the worst it had been since the Great Depression. Unemployment was at nearly nine percent. Ford pushed for voluntary controls of wages and prices to help stop inflation. His plan became known as WIN—Whip Inflation Now. The plan, however, failed. Ford then tried reducing government spending and establishing higher interest rates to curb inflation. This plan also failed. At the same time that Ford was trying to improve the economy, he also tried to balance the budget and keep taxes low.

Ford continued Nixon's foreign policy. Kissinger remained the secretary of state and continued the policy of détente. In 1975 Ford and the leaders of NATO and the Warsaw Pact signed the Helsinki Accords. They agreed to recognize the borders of Eastern Europe set up at the end of World War II. The Soviets promised to uphold basic human rights. Ford also faced problems in Southeast Asia. Cambodia seized the *Mayaguez*, an American cargo ship traveling near its shores. Cambodia said that the ship had been on an intelligence-gathering mission. Ford sent U.S. Marines to get the ship back.

In 1976 Americans were unsure of the future. Rising inflation and unemployment forced many Americans to change their lifestyle. The United States also faced instability in foreign affairs. As the 1976 presidential election approached, Americans hoped for a leader who could meet these challenges. The Republicans nominated Gerald Ford. He ran against the Democratic candidate Jimmy Carter. Carter's image as a moral and upstanding person attracted many voters. Carter won the election by a narrow margin.

Academic Vocabulary
acknowledge: to recognize or admit to (p. 866)

8. What was the public reaction to President Ford's pardon of Richard Nixon?

_____

_____

_____

Study Guide

Chapter 19, Section 3 (continued)

Academic Vocabulary
devote: to assign for a specific task (p. 867)

• **Carter Battles the Economic Crisis** (page 867)

Carter <u>devoted</u> much of his time to trying to fix the economy. Carter decided to deal with the economy by increasing government spending and cutting taxes. When inflation rose in 1978, he changed his mind. He tried to lower inflation by reducing the money supply and raising interest rates. His plans, however, were unsuccessful.

Carter believed that the nation's most serious problem was its dependence on foreign oil. He proposed a national energy program to conserve oil and to push for the use of coal and renewable energy sources such as solar power. He also wanted Congress to create the Department of Energy. Carter also asked Americans to reduce the amount of energy they used. Many people ignored the request.

Many business leaders wanted President Carter to deregulate the oil industry. These regulations limited the oil companies from passing on OPEC price increases to American consumers. As a result, oil companies had a difficult time making a profit. They then did not have enough money to invest in new oil wells at home. These regulations and increased OPEC oil prices contributed to the energy crisis on the 1970s. Carter agreed on deregulation, but he insisted on a profit tax so that oil companies would not overcharge consumers. The profit tax, however, did not free up money to find new sources of oil. Carter's plan to solve the energy problem did not work.

Many people have suggested that President Carter's lack of leadership and his inability to work with Congress caused his difficulties in solving the nation's economic problems. Carter reached out to Congress, so Congress blocked many of his energy proposals. Carter also did not develop a theme for his administration. By 1979 Carter's popularity had dropped.

9. What did President Carter believe was the nation's most serious problem?

_____

_____

_____

_____

• **Carter's Foreign Policy** (page 868)

President Carter's foreign policy was more clearly defined than his domestic policy. He believed that the United States had to be honest and truthful in dealing with other nations. In Latin America, Carter moved to give control of the Panama Canal to the Panamanians on December 31, 1999. Carter pointed to the Soviet Union as being a violator of human rights. He spoke against the Soviet practice of imprisoning people who protested against the government.

Study Guide

Chapter 19, Section 3 *(continued)*

When the Soviet Union invaded Afghanistan in December 1979, Carter placed an embargo on the sale of grain to the Soviet Union. He also led a boycott of the 1980 Summer Olympic Games, which were held in Moscow. Under Carter, détente practically came to an end.

Carter's greatest success in foreign affairs had to do with the Middle East. In 1978 Carter helped set up a peace treaty between Israel and Egypt known as the Camp David Accords. It was signed in 1979 and marked the first step in achieving peace in the region. A few months after the treaty, Carter faced conflict in Iran. The United States had supported Iran's ruler, the Shah, because Iran was a major oil supplier. Iran was also a buffer against Soviet expansion in the Middle East. However, the Shah was unpopular with Iranians. He was repressive and tried to introduce Western ways that went against traditional Islamic ways. In January 1979, Iranian protesters forced the Shah to leave. They declared an Islamic republic, headed by religious leader Ayatollah Khomeini. The new government distrusted the United States because of its support of the Shah. In November 1979, revolutionaries seized the American embassy in Tehran and held 52 American hostages.

President Carter tried unsuccessfully to negotiate for the hostages' release. In April 1980, he approved a daring military rescue mission, which failed and resulted in the death of eight American servicemen. The hostage crisis continued into the fall. Carter's failure to gain the release of the hostages contributed to his loss to Ronald Reagan in the 1980 presidential election. Negotiations for the hostage release continued until Carter's last day in office. After 444 days in captivity, the hostages were released on January 20, 1981, the day of Reagan's inauguration.

10. What was President Carter's greatest success in foreign affairs?

_____

_____

_____

_____

_____

_____

Study Guide

Chapter 19, Section 4

For use with textbook pages 871–875

THE "ME" DECADE: LIFE IN THE 1970S

CONTENT VOCABULARY

guru mystical leader *(page 873)*

transcendental meditation a religious movement started by Maharishi Mahesh Yogi that suggested daily meditation and the silent repetition of spiritual mantras *(page 873)*

disco dance music with a loud and persistent beat that became popular in the 1970s *(page 874)*

DRAWING FROM EXPERIENCE

What kind of music is popular today? Who are your favorite musical groups? What makes them your favorites?

The last section discussed the domestic and foreign policies of Presidents Ford and Carter. This section discusses the cultural changes in the United States in the 1970s.

ORGANIZING YOUR THOUGHTS

Use the diagram below to help you take notes. Several fads became popular during the 1970s. List these fads in the diagram.

California History-Social Science Standards

11.3 Students analyze the role religion played in the founding of America, its lasting moral, social and political impacts, and issues regarding religious liberty.

11.8 Students analyze the economic boom and social transformation of post–World War II America.

11.10 Students analyze the development of federal civil rights and voting rights.

11.11 Students analyze the major social problems and domestic policy issues in contemporary American society.

Focuses on: 11.3.4, 11.8.8, 11.10.7, 11.11.3

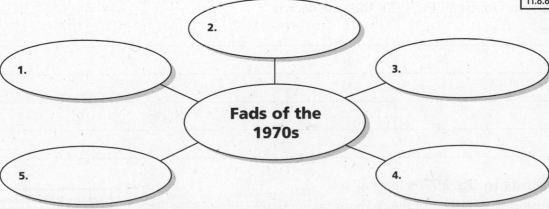

Study Guide

Chapter 19, Section 4 (continued)

READ TO LEARN

- **The Search for Fulfillment** *(page 872)*

Most Americans in the 1970s believed that the United States would move beyond the Watergate scandal and the effects of the Vietnam War. Americans found ways to cope with the tense times. Writer Tom Wolfe named the 1970s the "me decade." He was referring to the idea that many Americans looked inward. They became self-absorbed and looked for greater individual satisfaction.

Some young people moved away from their parents' traditional religions. They looked for fulfillment in secular movements and activities that made up the New Age movement. Followers of this movement believed that people were responsible for and capable of things such as self-healing. They believed that spirituality could be found in common practices, not just in traditional churchgoing. They tried activities such as yoga to gain spiritual awareness and <u>mental</u> health.

Many Americans who were dissatisfied with traditional religions joined new religions, which were often referred to as cults. Some new wave religions started in Asia and focused on the teachings of **gurus,** or mystical leaders. A well-known guru was Maharishi Mahesh Yogi. He moved from India to the United States, where he led a religious movement known as **transcendental meditation.** It preached daily meditation. Followers believed that if all people on Earth converted to transcendental meditation, the world would enjoy peace.

The search for fulfillment affected American families. By the 1970s, more women had joined the workforce. Women aged 25 to 34 had the largest annual percentage growth in the number of people joining the workforce between 1970 and 1980. These changes led to changes in family life. Americans were having smaller families. Parents and children were spending less time together. The divorce rate doubled.

> | Academic Vocabulary |
> | --- |
> | **mental:** having to do with mind and its thought processes (p. 872) |

6. Why did Tom Wolfe call the 1970s the "me decade"?

_____

_____

_____

_____

_____

- **Cultural Trends in the 1970s** *(page 873)*

Popular entertainment reflected the changes taking place in the 1970s. The subjects of television programs had changed from earlier years. *The Mary Tyler Moore Show,* for example, was a situation comedy that <u>denoted</u> the experiences

> | Academic Vocabulary |
> | --- |
> | **denote:** to make reference to (p. 875) |

Study Guide

Chapter 19, Section 4 *(continued)*

of an unmarried woman with a meaningful career. *All in the Family* took risks by addressing uncomfortable social issues, such as racism. The program featured a bigoted Archie Bunker, who argued with his liberal family members and neighbors about various social issues. It provided viewers with a way to examine their own feelings about issues such as racism. Other innovative programs included *Good Times.* This program focused on an African American family struggling to raise their children in a low-income housing development in Chicago.

The hard-driving rock of the 1960s moved to a softer sound in the 1970s. Music became less political. The 1970s saw the rise of **disco** music. Discotheques, which played dance music with a loud and persistent beat, attracted many fans. Disco music reflected the "me generation." It allowed the people dancing to be more important than the actual music. Disco music reached its peak after the 1977 movie *Saturday Night Fever.* The soundtrack from the movie sold millions of copies and led to the increase of disco openings throughout the country.

In addition to disco, other fads swept the nation in the 1970s. Many Americans began wearing T-shirts with personalized messages. Teens enjoyed skateboarding. Drivers began using citizen band ("CB") radios in their vehicles. This radio system allowed drivers to communicate with each other over a two-way frequency. Drivers adopted their own CB name and talked to each other using CB code words. Fitness was another trend in the 1970s. Americans turned to exercise to improve the way they felt and looked. Aerobics became popular because it provided a way to stay fit while having fun and <u>interacting</u> with others. Running also became a popular way to stay fit.

Academic Vocabulary
interact: to act on or communicate with one another (p. 875)

7. How did television programs change during the 1970s?

_____

_____

_____

_____

_____

_____

_____

Study Guide

Chapter 20, Section 1

For use with textbook pages 886–891

THE NEW CONSERVATISM

CONTENT VOCABULARY

liberal   a person who believes in government intervention in economic matters but not in social ones *(page 887)*

conservative   a person who believes that government should not interfere in the nation's economy and that religious commitment could best address issues of morality *(page 887)*

televangelists   Christian evangelicals who reached a nationwide audience through television *(page 891)*

DRAWING FROM EXPERIENCE

What do you think of when you hear the terms *liberal* and *conservative*? Do you consider yourself a liberal or a conservative? Why?

In this section, you will learn about the conservative shift in the United States in the 1980s. You will also learn about the effect of population shifts on the nation.

ORGANIZING YOUR THOUGHTS

Use the chart below to help you take notes. Conservatives and liberals had different views. List these views in the chart.

California History-Social Science Standards

11.3 Students analyze the role religion played in the founding of America, its lasting moral, social and political impacts, and issues regarding religious liberty.

11.8 Students analyze the economic boom and social transformation of post–World War II America.

11.9 Students analyze the U.S. foreign policy since World War II.

11.11 Students analyze the major social problems and domestic policy issues in contemporary American society.

Focuses on: 11.3.2, 11.8.6, 11.9.4, 11.11.7

Liberal Views	Conservative Views
1.	5.
2.	6.
3.	7.
4.	8.

The American Vision: Modern Times

Study Guide

Chapter 20, Section 1 (continued)

READ TO LEARN

- **Conservatism and Liberalism** (page 887)

Liberal politics dominated the United States for much of the 1900s. Conservative ideas gained strength during the 1980s. People who call themselves **liberals** believe that the government should regulate the economy and help disadvantaged people. Liberals do not believe the government should make any attempts to regulate social behavior. They believe that economic inequality is the basis of most social problems.

Conservatives distrust the power of the government. They believe that government regulation of the economy weakens the economy. Conservatives believe that most social problems result from issues of morality. They believe that, in most <u>instances</u>, these issues are best solved through commitment to a religious faith.

Academic Vocabulary
instance: a specific occurrence or example (p. 888)

9. How do liberal and conservative views regarding the government's role in the economy differ?

_____

_____

_____

_____

_____

- **Conservatism Revives** (page 888)

Conservative ideas gained support after World War II for two main reasons. First, some Americans believed that the government's role in the economy was leading the United States toward communism. The second reason had to do with the fact that many Americans viewed the Cold War in religious terms. Communism rejected religion and stressed material things. To Americans with a deep religious faith, the struggle against communism was a struggle between good and evil. As a result, many Americans turned away from liberalism, which stressed economic welfare. These Americans began to turn to conservatism.

A conservative named William F. Buckley founded a new conservative magazine called *National Review.* It helped to renew conservative ideas in the United States. Conservatives began to push their ideas and demand a greater role in the decision making of the Republican Party. By 1964 the conservative movement became influential enough in the Republican Party to get conservative Barry Goldwater nominated for president.

Study Guide

Chapter 20, Section 1 (continued)

10. What was the effect of William F. Buckley's magazine *National Review*?

_____

_____

_____

_____

- **Conservatism Gains Support** *(page 888)*

The events of the 1960s and 1970s convinced many Americans to support conservatism. In the 1950s and early 1960s, conservative Americans generally split their votes between Republicans and Democrats. The South and West were generally more conservative than other parts of the country. Southern conservatives generally voted for Democrats, while Western conservatives generally voted for Republicans. This meant that whichever party won the heavily-populated liberal Northeast vote, would win the election.

During World War II, many Americans moved south and west to get jobs in the war factories. The movement to the South and West, which was known as the Sunbelt, continued after the war. Americans who moved to the Sunbelt began looking at government differently than people living in the Northeast.

Industry in the Northeast began to decline. As a result, the region had many unemployed people and congested and polluted cities. Many Americans in the region looked to the federal government to help them solve their problems. Americans who lived in the Sunbelt opposed taxes and federal regulations that might interfere with growth in the region. In the 1964 presidential election, many Southerners began to agree with Goldwater that the federal government was becoming too strong. For the first time since Reconstruction, many Southerners voted Republican. That showed the Republican Party that the way to get Southern votes was to support conservative policies. Americans living in the West also opposed the environmental regulations of the federal government that limited ranching or controlled water use. By 1980 the population of the Sunbelt was greater than that of the Northeast. This gave the conservative regions of the country more influence in shaping policy.

During the 1960s and 1970s, many Americans moved to the suburbs to escape the chaos of the cities. However, their lifestyle there was in danger. The rising inflation had caused the buying power of middle-class Americans to decrease. Many Americans resented the high taxes they had to pay for Great Society programs while their economic conditions worsened. Anti-tax movements sprang up all over the country. Many middle-class Americans began to believe the conservative argument that the government had become too big.

The American Vision: Modern Times

Study Guide

Chapter 20, Section 1 *(continued)*

Some Americans were attracted to conservatism because they were afraid that Americans had lost touch with traditional values. The Supreme Court ruling in *Roe* v. *Wade*, which established abortion as a constitutional right, upset many conservative Americans. The feminist movement upset conservatives, who saw the movement as an attack on the traditional family. Religious conservatives included people from many different faiths. However, the largest group belonged to evangelical Protestant Christians. Evangelicals believe that they are saved from their sins through conversion, which they refer to as being "born again."

A religious revival began in the United States after World War II. Protestant ministers such as Billy Graham built huge followings. By the late 1970s, many Americans described themselves as "born again." Evangelicals owned newspapers, magazines, and television networks. Ministers known as **televangelists** were able to reach large audiences throughout the nation through television. Jerry Falwell, a televangelist, founded a movement that he called the *"Moral Majority."* The Moral Majority set up a network of ministers to register new voters to back conservative candidates. By 1980 the movement had formed a conservative coalition of voters.

11. How were televangelists able to reach large audiences to spread their conservative ideas?

_____

_____

_____

_____

_____

Study Guide

Chapter 20, Section 2

For use with textbook pages 892–899

THE REAGAN YEARS

CONTENT VOCABULARY

supply-side economics   the economic idea that cutting taxes would boost businesses and provide more money for consumers to spend *(page 895)*

budget deficit   the amount by which expenditures exceed income *(page 895)*

contras   anti-Sandinista guerrilla forces in Nicaragua *(page 898)*

DRAWING FROM EXPERIENCE

What are today's concerns about the nation's economy? How are these concerns affecting the American people?

The last section described the conservative shift in the United States. This section discusses the administration of Ronald Reagan.

ORGANIZING YOUR THOUGHTS

Use the diagram below to help you take notes. President Reagan's foreign policy became known as the Reagan Doctrine. It called for the United States to support guerrilla groups who were fighting to overthrow Communist or pro-Soviet governments. Describe the instances in which the Reagan Doctrine was applied.

> **California History-Social Science Standards**
>
> **11.8** Students analyze the economic boom and social transformation of post–World War II America.
>
> **11.9** Students analyze the U.S. foreign policy since World War II.
>
> **11.10** Students analyze the development of federal civil rights and voting rights.
>
> **Focuses on:** 11.8.4, 11.9.4, 11.9.5, 11.9.6, 11.11.2

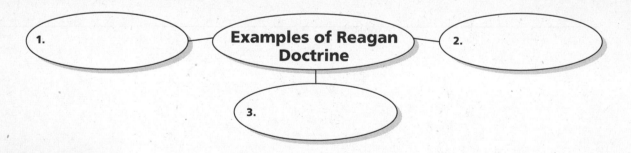

1. _____

Examples of Reagan Doctrine

2. _____

3. _____

READ TO LEARN

- **The Road to the White House** *(page 893)*

Ronald Reagan started out as an actor. For 25 years, he made more than 50 movies. In 1947 Reagan became president of the Screen Actors Guild, which was the actors' union. As the head of the union, he testified about communism in Hollywood before the House Un-American Activities Committee. In 1954 Reagan became the host of a television program called *General Electric.*

Study Guide

Chapter 20, Section 2 *(continued)*

He was also a motivational speaker for the company. He traveled across the country speaking to workers and managers. As he did so, he became more and more conservative. He heard stories from Americans about high taxes and how government regulations made it impossible for them to get ahead.

In 1964 Barry Goldwater asked Reagan to speak on behalf of Goldwater's presidential campaign. Reagan's speech impressed several wealthy people from California. They convinced Reagan to run for governor of California, and he won. In 1980 he was the Republican candidate for president. Reagan promised to cut taxes and increase defense spending. He called for a constitutional amendment banning abortion. His position on issues won the support of conservatives. Reagan won the election. The Republicans also gained control of the Senate.

4. What did Ronald Reagan call for in his presidential campaign?

_____

_____

_____

_____

_____

- **Reagan's Domestic Policies** *(page 894)*

Reagan's first priority was the nation's economy. The economy was experiencing high unemployment and high inflation at the same time. Economists were puzzled about this because the two things were not supposed to occur at the same time. Economists offered two different ideas for fixing the economy. One group believed that the biggest problem was inflation, caused by too much money in circulation. They believed that raising interest rates was the solution. Another group of economists supported **supply-side economics.** They believed that the economy was weak because taxes were too high. They believed that cutting taxes would help businesses use the extra money to make new investments. They believed that this would allow businesses to grow and create new jobs. This would in turn result in more goods for consumers, who would have more money to spend.

Reagan decided to combine the ideas of the two groups of economists. He urged the Federal Reserve to raise interest rates and he asked Congress to pass a tax cut. Critics called this economic approach Reaganomics, or "trickle down economics." Cutting tax rates would increase the **budget deficit,** the amount by which expenditures <u>exceed</u> income. To control the deficit, Reagan suggested cuts for social programs, such as welfare benefits. Although Congress fought the cuts, they eventually passed them. Reagan realized that he would never get Congress to cut spending enough to balance the budget.

Academic Vocabulary
exceed: to go beyond what is required (p. 895)

Study Guide

Chapter 20, Section 2 *(continued)*

As a result, he decided that cutting taxes and building up the military were more important than balancing the budget.

Reagan believed that government regulations were another cause for the nation's economic problems. After becoming president, he eliminated price controls for oil and gasoline, and energy prices fell. Other deregulation followed. It included deregulating the airline industry, which led to lower fares. Reagan's Secretary of the Interior, James Watt, angered environmentalists when he increased the amount of public land that corporations could use for oil drilling, mining, and logging.

The economy began to recover in 1983. The median income of American families rose by 15 percent by 1989. Millions of new businesses and new jobs were created. The unemployment rate had fallen to about 5.5 percent.

President Reagan applied his conservative ideas to the judicial branch. He wanted judges on the Supreme Court who followed the original intent of the Constitution. He nominated Sandra Day O'Connor to be the first woman on the Supreme Court. In 1986 Reagan chose conservative William Rehnquist to be the Chief Justice. He also nominated other conservative justices.

The growing economy made Reagan very popular at the time of the 1984 presidential election. Democrats nominated former vice president Walter Mondale as their presidential candidate. He chose Representative Geraldine Ferraro as his running mate. She was the first woman to run for vice president for a major party. Reagan won in a landslide.

5. What did President Reagan do to control the increasing budget deficit?

_____

_____

_____

_____

- **Reagan Builds Up the Military** *(page 896)*

Reagan did not follow containment or détente in his foreign policy. He viewed the Soviet Union as evil and he believed that the United States should not negotiate with it. Reagan believed that the United States had to use strength in dealing with the Soviet Union. As a result, he started a huge military buildup. This buildup increased the federal budget deficit even more. Reagan had hoped that as the economy grew, there would be an increase in the amount of taxes collected. Although the amount of taxes the government collected did rise, it was not enough to <u>offset</u> the rising deficit. Congress was not willing to cut other programs. Reagan's defense spending pushed the annual budget deficit from $80 billion to over $200 billion.

Academic Vocabulary
offset: to counteract an effect (p. 897)

Study Guide

Chapter 20, Section 2 *(continued)*

6. Why did Reagan start a huge military buildup in the 1980s?

_____

_____

_____

_____

- **The Reagan Doctrine** *(page 897)*

In addition to building up the military, Reagan believed that the United States should support guerrilla groups who were fighting to overthrow Communist or pro-Soviet governments. This policy became known as the Reagan Doctrine. In December 1979, the Soviet Union invaded Afghanistan to support a Soviet-backed government. The Soviets fought a large Afghan resistance movement. In a <u>visible</u> example of the Reagan Doctrine, the United States sent money to assist the resistance. The Soviets found themselves trapped in Afghanistan, just as the United States was in Vietnam. The war became unpopular with the Soviets. The Soviet Union agreed to withdraw in 1988.

Academic Vocabulary
visible: what can be seen (p. 897)

In Nicaragua, rebels known as the Sandinistas had overthrown a pro-American dictator. They set up a socialist government, and accepted Soviet aid. The Reagan administration began secretly arming anti-Sandinista forces known as the **contras.**

When Congress learned of this, it banned future arming of the contras. Individuals in Reagan's administration, however, continued to illegally support them. These officials secretly sold weapons to Iran in exchange for the release of American hostages being held in the Middle East. The profits from the arms sales were then sent to the contras. News of the Iran-Contra scandal broke in November 1986. A major figure in the scandal was Marine Colonel Oliver North. He was an aide to the National Security Council. North and other officials testified before Congress that they had covered up the illegal actions. President Reagan had approved the sale of arms to Iran. However, the congressional investigation determined that Reagan did not know about the profits from the sales being sent to the contras.

7. What was the Reagan Doctrine?

_____

_____

_____

_____

© by The McGraw-Hill Companies, Inc.

Study Guide

Chapter 20, Section 2 *(continued)*

- ### New Approaches to Arms Control *(page 898)*

President Reagan decided to position nuclear missiles in Western Europe to counter Soviet missiles in Eastern Europe. This action resulted in thousands of protesters pushing for a stop to the positioning of new nuclear missiles. Reagan agreed to remove American missiles if the Soviet Union agreed to remove its missiles. Reagan also suggested Strategic Arms Reduction talks (START) to reduce the number of missiles on both sides. The Soviets refused and walked out of the talks.

Reagan disagreed with the idea that as long as both the United States and the Soviet Union could both destroy each other with nuclear weapons, they would be afraid to use them. He believed that such an idea was immoral because it depended on the threat to kill many people. Also, there was no way to defend the United States if that kind of war did begin. In March 1983, Reagan proposed the Strategic Defense Initiative (SDI). This plan called for developing weapons that could destroy incoming missiles.

In 1985 Mikhail Gorbachev became the leader of the Soviet Union. He agreed to resume arms control talks. He did not think that the Soviet Union's economy could afford an arms race with the United States. Although at first the two leaders disagreed on many issues, by 1987 Reagan was convinced that Gorbachev wanted to reform the Soviet Union and end the arms race. The two leaders signed the Intermediate-Range Nuclear Forces (INF) Treaty. It called for the destruction of nuclear weapons. The treaty marked the beginning of the end of the Cold War. Gorbachev introduced economic and political reforms in the Soviet Union that led to the end of communism in Eastern Europe and in the Soviet Union.

8. What were the provisions of the INF Treaty and why was it important?

_____

_____

_____

_____

_____

Study Guide

Chapter 20, Section 3

For use with textbook pages 902–909

LIFE IN THE 1980S

CONTENT VOCABULARY

yuppies   young urban professionals *(page 903)*

space shuttle   a reusable spacecraft *(page 907)*

space stations   orbiting platforms where continuous observation of the universe could take place *(page 908)*

DRAWING FROM EXPERIENCE

What kind of space exploration is the United States doing today? Do you think space exploration is important? Why or why not?

The last section discussed the domestic and foreign policies of President Reagan. This section discusses the reasons for renewed activism in the United States in the 1980s.

ORGANIZING YOUR THOUGHTS

Use the diagram below to help you take notes. The United States dealt with several social problems in the 1980s. Identify these problems in the diagram.

California History-Social Science Standards

11.8 Students analyze the economic boom and social transformation of post–World War II America.

11.10 Students analyze the development of federal civil rights and voting rights.

11.11 Students analyze the major social problems and domestic policy issues in contemporary American society.

Focuses on: 11.8.7, 11.8.8, 11.10.7, 11.11.3, 11.11.5, 11.11.7

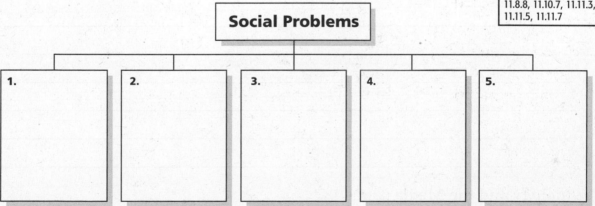

Social Problems

| 1. | 2. | 3. | 4. | 5. |

Study Guide

Chapter 20, Section 3 *(continued)*

• A Decade of Indulgence *(page 903)*

The media portrayed the 1980s as a decade focused on wealth. After the economy revived, news stories described many young brokers and investors making multimillion-dollar deals as the value of real estate and stocks soared. The young moneymakers were referred to by journalists as **yuppies,** from "young urban professionals." Many worked in law or finance. They rewarded themselves by buying luxury items and eating in upscale restaurants.

The economic growth and focus on <u>accumulating</u> wealth was partly caused by the baby boom. By the 1980s, most baby boomers had begun building careers. Many focused on acquiring goods and getting ahead in their jobs. Because there were so many baby boomers, their concerns helped to shape the culture. The strong economic growth in the 1980s mostly benefited middle- and upper-class Americans. By the mid-1990s, the top 5 percent of Americans earned more than 21 percent of the nation's income.

The 1970s and 1980s also featured a new approach to selling products to consumers. Discount retailing began in the 1960s and focused on selling large quantities of goods at very low prices. By 1985, this style of retailing generated annual sales of nearly $70 billion. While Wal-Mart was the most successful discount retailer, other franchises such as Home Depot and Best Buy successfully copied the same model.

Academic Vocabulary
accumulate: to gain over time (p. 903)

6. What was the main component of the new style of retailing that grew successful in the 1980s?

_____

_____

_____

_____

_____

_____

• Technology and the Media *(page 904)*

In the 1980s, the news and entertainment industry also transformed. "Superstations" like Ted Turner's WTBS sold low-cost sports and entertainment programs <u>via</u> satellite to cable companies throughout the nation. Similar networks, such as Robert Johnson's Black Entertainment Television (BET), appeared and helped spread cable television across the country. In 1980, Turner founded the Cable News Network (CNN)—the first 24-hour all-news station in the nation.

Academic Vocabulary
via: to have come by or through (p. 904)

Study Guide

Chapter 20, Section 3 *(continued)*

7. What characterized the new "superstations" of the 1980s?

_____

_____

_____

_____

• A Society Under Stress *(page 905)*

The United States continued to deal with many social problems in the 1980s. Drug abuse made many city neighborhoods violent and dangerous. Drug use spread from cities to small towns and rural areas. Alcohol abuse, particularly by teenagers, was a serious problem. Young people were involved in thousands of alcohol-related accidents. In 1980 Mothers Against Drunk Driving (MADD), a grassroots organization, was established to find solutions to underage drinking and drunk driving. In 1984 Congress cut highway funds to any state that did not raise the legal drinking age to 21. All states complied.

In 1981 researchers identified a disease that made young healthy men get sick and die. The disease was called AIDS, or "acquired immune deficiency syndrome." It weakens the immune system. HIV is the virus that causes AIDS. It is spread through body fluids. In the United States, AIDS was first seen among homosexual men, but it began to spread to heterosexual men and women. Some got it from blood transfusions. Some were drug users who shared needles with infected blood. Others were infected by sexual partners.

8. What was the purpose of MADD?

_____

_____

_____

_____

• Social Activism *(page 906)*

AIDS focused in on the gay and lesbian community in the United States. Some homosexuals had been involved in defending their civil rights since the 1960s. On June 1969, New York City police raided a Greenwich Village night-club called the Stonewall Inn. The police often raided the club and the clients because of their sexual <u>orientation</u>. The gay and lesbian onlookers in the club became frustrated with the police actions, and a public disturbance developed. The Stonewall riot was the beginning of the Gay Liberation Movement. The movement tried to increase public awareness of homosexuality.

Academic Vocabulary
orientation: position relative to a standard (p. 906)

Study Guide

Chapter 20, Section 3 (continued)

Social activism continued to be important in the United States in the 1980s. Many Americans became concerned about the environment. Some joined environmental groups such as the Sierra Club. The environmental movement that began in the 1970s continued to grow in the 1980s. Environmental groups campaigned against nuclear power plants. They also campaigned to protect fragile wetlands. Communities started recycling programs. Activists became concerned about the ozone layer and rain forests.

In the 1980s, many singers and other entertainers took up social causes. Bruce Springsteen gave concerts to benefit food banks and the homeless. In 1984 Irish musician Bob Geldof organized musicians in England to put on benefit concerts to help starving people in Ethiopia. The theme song "We Are the World" was a best-seller. Country singer Willie Nelson organized benefit concerts to help American farmers going through hard times.

Senior citizens became activists in the 1980s. With new medical technology, more Americans were living to an older age. Older Americans became more active in politics. They opposed cuts in Social Security or Medicare. Because they voted in large numbers, they were an influential group. Their major organization was the American Association of Retired Persons (AARP), which was founded in 1958.

9. Why were older Americans an influential group in the 1980s?

_____

_____

_____

_____

_____

• A New Era in Space (page 907)

New technology led to an increased interest in space exploration. After the moon landings in the 1970s, the National Aeronautics and Space Administration (NASA) concentrated on the **space shuttle.** This spacecraft looked like a huge airplane. It was reusable, going into space and then returning to Earth. The shuttle *Columbia* made its first flight in April 1981. In 1983 Sally Ride became the first American woman in space. Female astronauts became more common. In January 1986, Christa McAuliffe, a teacher, joined six others on the *Challenger.* As millions of Americans watched, the shuttle lifted into space and then exploded, killing everyone on board. Defective seals were blamed for the accident.

Despite the *Challenger* disaster, shuttle flights continued. Some of the shuttles carried satellites into orbit to gather scientific data. NASA also sent probes into space for further research. The probes sent back pictures of Jupiter,

Study Guide

Chapter 20, Section 3 *(continued)*

Saturn, and Neptune. The long-range goal of the shuttles was to set up **space stations.** These were orbiting platforms where continuous observation of the universe could take place. The goal was to set up a place where people could conduct research for a long period of time. The U.S. *Skylab* was launched in May 1973. In 1986 the Soviet Union launched the space station *Mir*. Since 1986, sixteen nations, including Russia, have participated in creating this space station.

10. What was the purpose of establishing space stations?

_____

_____

_____

_____

_____

Name _____ Date _____ Class _____

Study Guide

Chapter 20, Section 4

For use with textbook pages 914–919

THE END OF THE COLD WAR

CONTENT VOCABULARY

perestroika   a restructuring *(page 916)*

glasnost   openness *(page 916)*

downsizing   the practice by factories of laying off workers and managers in order to become more efficient *(page 918)*

capital gains tax   the tax paid by businesses and investors when they sell stocks or real estate for a profit *(page 919)*

grassroots movement   groups of people organizing at the local level *(page 919)*

DRAWING FROM EXPERIENCE

What issues were important in the most recent presidential election? What issues do you think will be important for candidates in the next election? Why do you think so?

The last section discussed the increased social activism in the United States in the 1980s. This section discusses the administration of President George Bush.

ORGANIZING YOUR THOUGHTS

Use the diagram below to help you take notes. During his presidency, Bush faced the task of improving the nation's economy. List the ways he attempted to do so.

Steps to Improve the Economy	1. _____
	2. _____

> **California History-Social Science Standards**
>
> **11.1** Students analyze the significant events in the founding of the nation and its attempts to realize the philosophy of government described in the Declaration of Independence.
>
> **11.8** Students analyze the economic boom and social transformation of post–World War II America.
>
> **11.9** Students analyze the U.S. foreign policy since World War II.
>
> **11.11** Students analyze the major social problems and domestic policy issues in contemporary American society.
>
> **Focuses on:** 11.1.3, 11.8.4, 11.9.5, 11.9.6, 11.11.7

READ TO LEARN

• **George Bush Takes Office** *(page 915)*

When President Reagan left office in 1988, most Americans wanted a continuation of Reagan's domestic policies. When George Bush accepted the Republican Party's nomination, he promised the Americans that he would not impose any new taxes. The Democrats wanted to regain the White House by promising to help working-class Americans, minorities, and the poor. Jesse

328

The American Vision: Modern Times

Study Guide

Chapter 20, Section 4 *(continued)*

Jackson ran for nomination. He finished second in the primaries and was the first African American to make a serious run for nomination. The Democrats' nominee was Massachusetts Governor Michael Dukakis. The Republicans pictured him as too liberal and not tough on crime. Bush won the election, but Democrats kept control of Congress.

3. Who did George Bush defeat in the 1988 presidential election?

_____

_____

• The Cold War Ends *(page 916)*

President Bush continued Reagan's policies with the Soviet leader Gorbachev. To save the Soviet economy, Gorbachev set up **perestroika,** or restructuring, of the economy. He allowed some private businesses and profit-making. Another part of Gorbachev's plan was **glasnost,** or openness. It allowed more freedom of speech and religion. It allowed people to discuss politics openly.

The idea of *glasnost* spread to Eastern Europe. Demonstrations took place in several Eastern European cities. Democratically elected governments began replacing Communist governments in Poland, Hungary, Czechoslovakia, Romania, and Bulgaria. The <u>revolution</u> reached East Germany in November 1989, when the gates at the Berlin Wall were opened. Many East Berliners began streaming through the gates. A few days later, the wall was leveled. A year later, East and West Germany had reunited.

Academic Vocabulary
revolution: an uprising to overthrow a government and replace it with a new one (p. 916)

Gorbachev faced criticism from opponents at home. In August 1991, some Communist officials started a coup, an overthrow of the government. Gorbachev was arrested and troops were sent into Moscow. There, Boris Yeltsin, the Russian president, defied the leaders of the coup. The coup eventually collapsed and Gorbachev returned to Moscow. After the coup, all 15 Soviet republics declared their independence from the Soviet Union. In December 1991, Gorbachev announced the end of the Soviet Union. Most of the former Soviet republics joined in a federation called the Commonwealth of Independent States.

4. What was the result of *glasnost*?

_____

_____

• The "New World Order" *(page 917)*

After the Cold War ended, President Bush had to redefine American foreign policy. His first crisis occurred in China, where Communist leaders were determined to stay in power. Although the Chinese government had <u>relaxed</u> some controls on the economy, it continued to forbid protests and political

Academic Vocabulary
relax: to be made less strict or severe (p. 917)

Study Guide

Chapter 20, Section 4 *(continued)*

speech. In May 1989, Chinese students and workers held protests for democracy. The government crushed their protests in Tiananmen Square in Beijing, China. Many demonstrators were killed and thousands were arrested. Some were sentenced to death. The United States and other countries reduced their contacts with China. The World Bank suspended loans.

A crisis also developed in Panama. In 1978, the United States had agreed to give Panama control of the canal by the year 2000, so it wanted to be sure that Panama's government was stable and pro-American. Panama's dictator, Manuel Noriega, had stopped cooperating with the United States. He aided drug traffickers and cracked down on opponents. In December 1989, Bush ordered American troops to invade Panama. Noriega was sent to the United States to stand trial on drug charges. U.S. troops then helped the Panamanians hold elections and set up a new government.

In addition to all these problems, President Bush also faced a crisis in the Middle East. In August 1990, Saddam Hussein, Iraq's dictator, ordered the invasion of Kuwait, an oil-rich country. American officials believed that this was Iraq's first step to capture Saudi Arabia and its oil reserves. President Bush persuaded other nations to join in a coalition to stop Hussein. The United Nations set a deadline for Iraq to withdraw or face the use of force. Iraq refused. On January 16, 1991, the coalition forces launched Operation Desert Storm. After about six weeks of bombing, the coalition began a ground attack. Just about 100 hours after the ground war began, President Bush declared victory. Iraq accepted the coalition's cease-fire terms, and Kuwait was liberated.

5. What action led to Operation Desert Storm?

_____

_____

_____

• **Domestic Challenges** *(page 918)*

In addition to handling crises in foreign affairs, President Bush had to address domestic issues. He faced a growing deficit and a recession. The recession was partly caused by an end to the Cold War. With the threat from the Soviet Union ending, the United States began reducing its armed forces and canceling orders for military equipment. This caused defense factories to lay off thousands of workers.

Other kinds of companies also began **downsizing,** or laying off workers and managers to become more efficient. In addition to the recession, the nation faced a huge debt. Americans had borrowed heavily during the 1980s. By the end of the 1980s, they had to stop spending and pay off their debts. The federal government faced a deficit, which meant that it had to borrow money to pay

Study Guide

Chapter 20, Section 4 *(continued)*

for some of its programs. The government had to pay interest on the debt, and that money could not be used to fund programs or to jumpstart the economy.

Bush tried to improve the economy. He suggested a cut in the **capital gains tax.** This was a tax paid by businesses and investors when they sell stocks or real estate for a profit. Bush thought that cutting this tax would help businesses to expand. Democrats believed it was a tax break for the rich and defeated the idea in Congress. Bush knew that the federal deficit was hurting the economy. He had to break his campaign promise of no new taxes. He made a deal with Congress, agreeing to a tax increase in exchange for cuts in spending. Many voters blamed him for increasing taxes and cutting programs.

President Bush and Congress did cooperate on other laws. One law was the Americans with Disabilities Act (ADA), which Bush signed in 1990. The law forbade discrimination in workplaces and public places against people who were physically or mentally challenged. The law resulted in access ramps being added in buildings and wheelchair lifts being installed on city buses.

6. Why did President Bush suggest a cut in the capital gains tax?

_____

_____

_____

• The 1992 Election *(page 919)*

Bush was the Republican nominee in the 1992 presidential election. He blamed the Democrats' control of Congress for the gridlock that seemed to take over the national government. The Democrats nominated Arkansas governor Bill Clinton. He promised to cut taxes and spending and to reform the nation's health care and welfare programs. Many Americans did not like either of the two candidates. This helped businessman H. Ross Perot to run as an independent candidate and to present a strong challenge to the other candidates. A **grassroots movement,** which are groups of people organizing at the local level, placed Perot on the ballot in all 50 states.

Bill Clinton won the election. The Democrats kept control of Congress. It was his <u>task</u> to revive the economy and guide the United States in a rapidly changing world.

Academic Vocabulary
task: an assigned job (p. 919)

7. What did Bill Clinton promise as the Democratic nominee for president in 1992?

_____

_____

Study Guide

Chapter 21, Section 1

For use with textbook pages 930–934

THE TECHNOLOGICAL REVOLUTION

CONTENT VOCABULARY

integrated circuit   a complete electronic circuit on a single chip of the element silicon *(page 931)*

microprocessor   a single chip that combined several integrated circuits containing both memory and computing functions *(page 931)*

software   the instructions used to program computers to perform desired tasks *(page 932)*

telecommute   to do a job via computer without having to go to the office *(page 932)*

biotechnology   the managing of biological systems to improve human life *(page 934)*

DRAWING FROM EXPERIENCE

Think of the ways that you use the computer. How important is it to your daily life? How important is the Internet to your daily life?

In this section, you will learn about the development of the computer and how it revolutionized science, medicine, and communications.

> **California History-Social Science Standards**
>
> **11.8** Students analyze the economic boom and social transformation of post–World War II America.
>
> **Focuses on:** 11.8.7

ORGANIZING YOUR THOUGHTS

Computers changed life in the U.S. List how they affected biotechnology.

How Computers Affected Biotechnology	1. _____
	2. _____
	3. _____
	4. _____
	5. _____

READ TO LEARN

- **The Rise of the Compact Computer** *(page 931)*

ENIAC (Electronic Numerical Integrator and Computer) was the world's first electronic digital computer. It went into operation in February 1946. This computer was large and weighed over 30 tons. In 1959 several young scientists and engineers designed the first **integrated circuit.** This was a complete electronic circuit on a single chip of the element silicon. It made computers easier to make. Other electronics companies started nearby in the area south

The American Vision: Modern Times

Study Guide

Chapter 21, Section 1 *(continued)*

of San Francisco, which was nicknamed Silicon Valley. In 1968 scientist Robert Noyce and colleague Gordon Moore started Intel, for "Integrated Electronics." This company revolutionized computers by combining several integrated circuits that contained both memory and computing functions on a single chip. These chips, called **microprocessors,** reduced the size of computers. They also increased their speed.

Stephen Wozniak and Steven Jobs used the microprocessor technology to build a small computer for personal use. In 1976 they founded Apple Computer and built their first machine, called Apple I. The next year they introduced the Apple II. This was the first practical and affordable computer for personal use. It sold well. In 1981 International Business Machines (IBM) introduced its own compact machine. It called it the "Personal Computer" (PC). Apple responded in 1984 with the Macintosh.

Bill Gates co-founded Microsoft to design PC **software,** or the instructions used to program computers to perform desired tasks. In 1980 IBM hired Microsoft to develop an operating system for its new PC. It became MS-DOS (Microsoft Disk Operating System). Microsoft also introduced the "Windows" operating system in 1985. It allowed PCs to use the on-screen graphic icons that Apple had made popular with the Macintosh, which users could <u>manipulate</u> with a mouse. Computers soon became essential in every kind of business—from large corporations to neighborhood shops. By the late 1990s, many workers used a home computer and electronic mail to **telecommute,** or do their jobs via computer without having to go to the office.

Academic Vocabulary
manipulate: to operate or arrange manually to achieve a desired effect (p. 931)

6. What was the significance of the development of Apple II?

_____

_____

_____

_____

• The Telecommunications Revolution *(page 932)*

In the 1970s, the government began to deregulate telecommunications. This led to competition in both the telephone and television industries. In 1996 Congress passed the Telecommunications Act. The law allowed telephone companies to compete with each other and to send television signals. This led to the development of new technologies, such as cellular phones.

Study Guide

Chapter 21, Section 1 *(continued)*

7. How did deregulation affect telecommunications?

_____

_____

_____

_____

_____

- ### The Rise of the Internet *(page 933)*

Digital electronics made a new world communications system possible. It
started with a computer networking system that the U.S. Defense Department's
Advanced Research Project Agency set up in 1969. This system linked government agencies, defense contractors, and scientists at various universities, and
they communicated through electronic mail. In 1985 the National Science
foundation funded several supercomputer centers across the country. This set
the stage for the Internet, a global information system that operated commer-
cially rather than through the government. With the development of the
hypertext transport protocol (http) and new software known as web browers,
the Internet rapidly expanded. Between 1997 and 2000, Internet use increased
almost 300 percent.

Academic Vocabulary
protocol: a standard for data that is transferred between two computers (p. 933)

The Internet also started a "dot.com" economy. This name comes from the
practice of using a business name as a World Wide Web address, followed by
".com." Many companies made millions of dollars for stock investors.
Internet-related stocks helped fuel the economy of the 1990s. However, the
stocks of these companies dropped drastically in 2000.

8. How did the Internet get its start?

_____

_____

_____

_____

_____

Study Guide

Chapter 21, Section 1 *(continued)*

- **Breakthroughs in Biotechnology** *(page 934)*

Computers helped scientists involved in **biotechnology,** the managing of biological systems to improve human life. Biotechnology helped researchers develop new medicines, genetically engineered plants, and industrial chemicals. The first steps toward biotechnology happened in 1953. American molecular biologist James Watson and his British colleague Francis Crick decoded the structure of deoxyribonucleic acid (DNA). DNA is the genetic material in cells that determines all forms of life. The work had a great impact. Being able to read the message of DNA improved medical research. It helped law enforcement by establishing that DNA was unquestionable in identifying a person. Research in biotechnology assisted in genetic engineering for plants, animals, and humans.

In 1990 scientists began using supercomputers to develop the Human Genome Project at the National Institutes of Health (NIH). The Human Genome Project recorded the DNA <u>sequence</u> of the human species. NIH put all of the data from the Human Genome Project on the Internet to make it available to scientists all over the world. The project published its first map of the human genome in February 2001. The information would help medical researchers determine which genes made people more susceptible to disease. This would help medical professionals improve their diagnoses and help them find cures.

Academic Vocabulary
sequence: an arrangement when objects follow one after the other (p. 934)

9. How would the map of the human genome help medical researchers?

_____

_____

_____

_____

_____

Study Guide

Chapter 21, Section 2

For use with textbook pages 935–941

THE CLINTON YEARS

CONTENT VOCABULARY

perjury   lying under oath *(page 940)*

ethnic cleansing   the brutal expulsion of an ethnic group from a geographic area *(page 940)*

DRAWING FROM EXPERIENCE

What foreign affairs is the United States involved in today? How is the president handling these affairs?

The last section discussed the impact of computers on different aspects of American life. This section discusses the administration of President Clinton.

ORGANIZING YOUR THOUGHTS

Use the diagram below to help you take notes. President Clinton faced several foreign policy issues during his administration. List the areas of foreign policy issues in the diagram.

> **California History-Social Science Standards**
>
> **11.11** Students analyze the major social problems and domestic policy issues in contemporary American society.
>
> **Focuses on:** 11.9.6, 11.11.2, 11.11.3, 11.11.6, 11.11.7

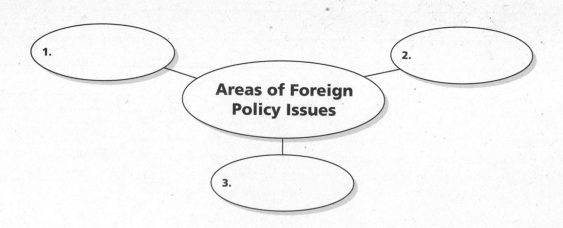

Study Guide

Chapter 21, Section 2 *(continued)*

• Clinton's Agenda *(page 936)*

When President Bill Clinton took office, he focused on domestic issues. He focused first on the economy. Clinton believed that the problem with the economy was the huge federal deficit, which forced the government to borrow huge amounts of money to pay for its programs. This helped drive up the interest rates. Clinton believed that it was important to lower interest rates. He believed that this would help businesses borrow more money to expand. It would also help consumers to borrow money for mortgages and other items. He hoped that this would help economic growth.

Clinton believed that one way to bring down interest rates was to reduce the federal deficit. He sent a deficit reduction plan to Congress. However, reducing spending would involve cutting entitlement programs, such as Social Security and Medicare. This would be difficult to do because many Americans depend on these programs. As a result, Clinton decided to raise taxes, even though he promised to cut them during the campaign. His plan called for tax increases on middle- and upper-income people. The tax increases were unpopular. A <u>modified</u> plan narrowly passed Congress.

> **Academic Vocabulary**
>
> **modify:** to make changes or alter (p. 936)

Another part of Clinton's domestic program was the health care system. Millions of Americans did not have health insurance. Clinton appointed a task force, headed by his wife, Hillary Rodham Clinton, to develop a plan that guaranteed health benefits for all Americans. The plan that was developed put too much of the burden of payment on employers. Small businesses, the insurance industry, and doctors opposed the plan. Many members of Congress opposed the plan. As a result, the plan never came to a vote.

Clinton was successful in having the Family Medical Leave Act passed. The law gave workers up to 12 weeks per year of unpaid family leave for the birth or adoption of a child or for the illness of a family member. Clinton was also successful in getting Congress to create the AmeriCorps program. It put students to work improving low-income housing, teaching children to read, and cleaning up the environment.

In his campaign, Clinton <u>stressed</u> the need to get tough on crime. He was successful in getting Congress to pass the Brady Bill, a gun-control law. Clinton also introduced an anticrime bill, which would provide states with extra funds to build new prisons and to put 100,000 more police officers on the streets.

> **Academic Vocabulary**
>
> **stress:** to place importance on something (p. 937)

4. How did Clinton fulfill his promise to get tough on crime?

_____

_____

_____

_____

Study Guide

Chapter 21, Section 2 (continued)

• The Republicans Gain Control of Congress (page 937)

Although he experienced some successes, by 1994 Clinton was very unpopular. He had raised taxes after promising to reduce them and he did not fix health care. Republicans in Congress, led by Newt Gingrich, created the Contract with America. The program called for several changes, including lowering taxes, welfare reform, and a balanced budget amendment. The Republicans won huge victories in the 1994 Congressional elections. They had a majority in both houses of Congress. The House of Representatives passed most of the Contract with America. However, the Senate defeated several parts of the Contract, and the President vetoed others.

In 1995 Republicans in Congress clashed with the president over the new federal budget. Clinton had vetoed several Republican budget proposals. He claimed that they cut into social programs too much. The Republicans believed that if they stood firm, the president would back down and approve the budget. If he did not, the entire federal government would shut down for lack of funds. Clinton refused to budge, and the government did shut down. Clinton's stand against the Republicans regained much of the support he had lost in 1994. The Republicans realized that they would have to work with the president. They eventually reached an agreement to pass the budget.

Before the 1996 presidential election, the president and Congress worked together to pass some new laws. In August, Congress passed the Health Insurance Portability Act. It improved coverage for people who changed jobs, and it lowered discrimination against people with preexisting illnesses. Congress also passed the Welfare Reform Act. It limited people to no more than two consecutive years on welfare and required them to work to get welfare benefits.

5. Why was President Clinton unpopular by the 1994 Congressional elections?

_____

_____

_____

_____

_____

• The 1996 Election (page 938)

In the 1996 presidential election, President Clinton was very popular. The nation was experiencing an economic boom, crime rates fell, and the number of people on unemployment declined. The Republicans nominated Senator Bob Dole as their presidential candidate to run against Clinton. H. Ross Perot also ran as a candidate for the Reform Party, which he had created. Clinton won the election, but the Republicans kept control of Congress.

Study Guide

Chapter 21, Section 2 *(continued)*

6. What were the results of the 1996 elections?

_____

_____

_____

_____

_____

• Clinton's Second Term *(page 939)*

The economy continued to expand during Clinton's second term. The president and Congress continued to work to shrink the deficit. In 1997, for the first time in 24 years, the president was able to <u>submit</u> a balanced budget to Congress. By 1998 the government began to run a surplus—it collected more money than it spent.

Clinton's domestic policy focused on the nation's children. He asked Congress to pass a $500 per child tax credit. He signed the Adoption and Safe Families Act and asked Congress to ban cigarette ads aimed at children. Clinton signed the Children's Health Insurance Program. This was a plan to provide health insurance for children whose parents could not afford it. To help students, the president asked for a tax credit, an increase in student grants, and an expansion of the Head Start program.

By 1998 Clinton became involved in a serious scandal. It began in his first term. He was accused of setting up illegal loans for an Arkansas real estate company, called Whitewater Development, while he was governor of Arkansas. Kenneth Starr, a former federal judge, was appointed by a three-judge panel to become an independent counsel to investigate the president. Then in early 1998, a new scandal became known. It involved a personal relationship between the president and a White House intern. Some evidence showed that the president had committed **perjury,** or had lied under oath, about the relationship. The three-judge panel directed Starr to investigate this scandal. Starr determined that Clinton had obstructed justice and committed perjury. He sent his report to the Judiciary Committee of the House of Representatives.

The House began impeachment hearings after the 1998 elections. On December 19, 1998, the House passed two articles of impeachment. The case went to the Senate for trial. On February 12, 1999, the Senate voted that Clinton was not guilty. However, Clinton's reputation had suffered.

7. Why was President Clinton investigated by independent counsel Kenneth Starr?

_____

_____

_____

Academic Vocabulary
submit: to put forward for consideration or judgment (p. 939)

Study Guide

Chapter 21, Section 2 (continued)

- **Clinton's Foreign Policy** (page 940)

Although the Cold War had ended, President Clinton had to deal with several regional conflicts. In Haiti, Jean-Bertrand Aristide, the democratically elected president, was overthrown by military leaders. Aristide sought refuge in the United States. The new rulers in Haiti used violence to keep down the opposition. Clinton urged the United Nations to set a trade embargo on Haiti. This caused severe economic hardships in the country. As a result, thousands of Haitian refugees fled Haiti to the United States. Clinton ordered an invasion of Haiti, but former president Jimmy Carter convinced Haiti's rulers to step down.

After communism collapsed in Eastern Europe, Yugoslavia, which was made up of many different ethnic groups, split apart. A civil war started in Bosnia, one of the former republics of Yugoslavia. The war involved Orthodox Christian Serbs, Catholic Croatians, and Bosnian Muslims. The Serbs began **ethnic cleansing.** This is the brutal expulsion of an ethnic group from a geographic area. In some cases, the Serbs killed the Muslims instead of moving them.

The United States convinced the NATO allies that military action was necessary. NATO warplanes attacked the Serbs and forced them to negotiate. Clinton arranged peace talks in Dayton, Ohio. The participants signed a peace plan known as the Dayton Accords. NATO troops were sent to Bosnia to enforce the plan.

Another war started in 1998 in the Serbian province of Kosovo. Two ethnic groups lived in Kosovo—Serbs and Albanians. Many Albanians wanted Kosovo to separate from Serbia. Serbian leader Slobodan Milosevic ordered a crackdown. The Albanians fought back. President Clinton again asked NATO to use force to stop the conflict. They began bombing Serbia. The bombing convinced Serbia to pull its troops out of Kosovo.

After the Persian Gulf War, President Saddam Hussein remained in power. He continued to make threats against his neighbors. In 1996 Iraq attacked the Kurds, an ethnic group whose homeland is in northern Iraq. The United States responded by firing missiles at Iraqi military targets.

Conflicts continued between Israel and Palestine. In 1993 Israeli Prime Minister Yitzhak Rabin and Yasir Arafat, the leader of the Palestine Liberation Organization, reached an agreement. The PLO recognized Israel's right to exist. Israel recognized the PLO as the representative of the Palestinians. President Clinton then invited the two leaders to the White House where they signed the Declaration of Principles. This was a plan for creating a Palestinian government. Opposition to the plan existed on both sides. In 1998 President Clinton met with Israeli and Palestinian leaders to work out details for the withdrawal of Israeli troops from the West Bank and the Gaza Strip. The agreement, however, could not solve the problem of Jerusalem, which both sides claimed. Talks between the two sides in 2000 also failed. Then in October of that year, violence broke out between Palestinians and Israeli soldiers.

Study Guide

Chapter 21, Section 2 (continued)

President Clinton left office with a mixed legacy. He had balanced the budget and had overseen the greatest period of economic growth in U.S. history. Clinton's impeachment, however, tarnished his successes. It also divided the nation and increased the gap between liberals and conservatives.

8. Why did President Clinton ask the United Nations to set up an embargo against Haiti?

_____

_____

_____

_____

_____

Name _____ Date _____ Class _____

Study Guide

Chapter 21, Section 3

For use with textbook pages 942–946

AN INTERDEPENDENT WORLD

CONTENT VOCABULARY

trade deficit   the situation in which Americans bought more from foreign nations than American industries sold abroad *(page 943)*

euro   a common currency for member nations of the European Union *(page 944)*

nuclear proliferation   the spread of nuclear weapons to new nations *(page 946)*

global warming   an increase in average world temperatures over time *(page 946)*

DRAWING FROM EXPERIENCE

What do you think is the most important issue facing the world today? Why do you think so?

The last section discussed the administration of President Clinton. This section discusses the interdependence of the world's nations regarding the economy, health, and the environment.

ORGANIZING YOUR THOUGHTS

Use the chart below to help you take notes. The world faced several environmental concerns in the late 1990s. List and describe those issues in the chart.

Environmental Concerns
1.
2.
3.

> **California History-Social Science Standards**
>
> **11.9** Students analyze the U.S. foreign policy since World War II.
>
> **11.11** Students analyze the major social problems and domestic policy issues in contemporary American society.
>
> **Focuses on:** 11.9.7, 11.11.5

The American Vision: Modern Times

Study Guide

Chapter 21, Section 3 (continued)

READ TO LEARN

• The New Global Economy (page 943)

By the end of the 1900s, the United States had become involved in many global issues. Computer technology and the Internet made a global economy possible. By the early 1970s, a serious **trade deficit** had resulted. Americans bought more from foreign nations than American industries sold abroad. Some people believed that the United States needed free trade because Americans benefited from buying imports. They believed that buying imports would keep consumer prices, inflation, and interest rates low. Those who wanted to limit trade believed it was necessary to prevent the United States from losing industrial jobs and manufacturing to lesser-developed nations.

One way to increase international trade was to set up regional trade pacts. In 1994 the North American Free Trade Agreement (NAFTA) joined Canada, the United States, and Mexico in a free-trade zone. Some Americans were concerned that industrial jobs would go to Mexico, where labor costs were lower. However, unemployment rates in the United States fell after the signing of NAFTA, and wages rose.

Other trade blocs developed in other parts of the world. The European Union (EU) was set up to promote economic and political cooperation among many European nations. The EU set up a common bank and the **euro,** a common <u>currency</u> for member nations.

The Asia Pacific Economic Cooperation (APEC) set up a Pacific trade community, which was the fastest-growing region in the world. Although APEC began as a way to promote cooperation and lower trade barriers, differences among its members prevented them from acting together.

The World Trade Organization (WTO) was important in promoting world trade. It administered international trade agreements. It also helped settle trade disputes.

China played an important part in world trade. It provided a huge market for American goods. However, many Americans were concerned, <u>citing</u> China's record on human rights. Despite the concerns, President Clinton believed that regularizing trade with China would help bring the nation into the world community. Clinton urged Congress to pass a bill to give China permanent normal trade relation status. Some groups opposed this. Labor unions were worried about inexpensive Chinese goods flooding U.S. markets. Conservatives opposed China's military ambitions. Environmentalists worried about pollution from Chinese factories. Despite the opposition, the bill passed in late 2000.

4. What was the purpose of the World Trade Organization?

_____

_____

Academic Vocabulary
currency: paper money used as a medium of exchange (p. 944)

Academic Vocabulary
cite: to point out as an example in an argument or debate (p. 944)

Study Guide

Chapter 21, Section 3 *(continued)*

- ## Issues of Global Concern *(page 945)*

    After the end of the Cold War, only a few nations had nuclear weapons. When Russia agreed to reduce its nuclear weapons, concerns arose about some of the weapons being lost, stolen, or sold in the black market. The United States provided funds for Russia to help it reduce its nuclear weapons. Congress also took measures to reduce the threat of **nuclear proliferation,** or the spread of nuclear weapons to new nations. Congress passed laws that cut aid and imposed sanctions on nations that wanted to get nuclear weapons.

    In the 1980s, scientists found out that chemicals called chlorofluorocarbons (CFCs) could use up the earth's atmosphere of ozone. This is a gas in the atmosphere that protects life on Earth from the cancer-causing ultraviolet rays of the sun. CFCs were used in air conditioners and refrigerators. Many people wanted the making of CFCs to be stopped. In 1987 the United States and other nations agreed to <u>phase</u> out the making of CFCs and other chemicals that might be weakening the ozone layer.

    In the early 1990s, scientists found evidence of **global warming,** or an increase in average world temperatures over time. This rise in temperature could lead to more droughts and other types of extreme weather. Many experts believe that carbon dioxide emissions from factories and power plants caused global warming. Others disagree. Some even question whether global warming even exists. The global warming issue is controversial because the cost of controlling emissions would fall on industries. These costs would eventually be passed on to consumers. Developing nations that are beginning to industrialize would be hurt the most.

    In 1997 thirty-eight nations and the EU signed the Kyoto Protocol. The nations promised to reduce emissions, although very few nations put it into effect. President Clinton did not present the Kyoto Protocol to the Senate because most senators opposed it. In 2001 President George W. Bush withdrew the United States from the treaty. He believed that it had flaws.

Academic Vocabulary
phase: a definite period of time over which a change is made (p. 946)

5. Why did President Bush withdraw the United States from the Kyoto Protocol?

_____

_____

_____

_____

_____

_____

The American Vision: Modern Times

Study Guide

Chapter 21, Section 4

For use with textbook pages 947–951

AMERICA ENTERS A NEW CENTURY

CONTENT VOCABULARY

chad   the piece of cardboard punched out of a ballot *(page 949)*

strategic defense   a military program to develop missiles and other devices that can shoot down nuclear missiles before they hit the United States *(page 951)*

DRAWING FROM EXPERIENCE

How important do you think it is for citizens to vote in elections? Are you looking forward to voting in local and national elections? Why or why not?

The last section discussed the common issues facing the nations of the world. This section discusses the controversies surrounding the 2000 presidential election and President Bush's first days in office.

> **California History-Social Science Standards**
>
> **11.11** Students analyze the major social problems and domestic policy issues in contemporary American society.

ORGANIZING YOUR THOUGHTS

Use the chart below to help you take notes. President Bush suggested programs for the nation's economy, education, and the military. List his proposals in the chart.

Categories	Bush's Proposals
Economy	1.
Education	2.
Military	3.

The American Vision: Modern Times

Study Guide

Chapter 21, Section 4 *(continued)*

- ## A New President for a New Century *(page 948)*

In the 2000 presidential election, the Democrats nominated Vice President Al Gore. The Republicans nominated Texas Governor George W. Bush. In the campaign, both candidates fought for independent voters. The campaign focused on what to do with the surplus tax revenues. Both candidates agreed that Social Security needed reform, but they disagreed on how the reform should come about. Both promised to cut taxes, but Bush promised a larger tax cut. Both men promised to improve education and to set up programs to help senior citizens pay for their prescription drugs.

The state of the economy helped Gore. However, some voters were concerned about what they believed was a decline in the moral values of the nation's leaders. Bush promised to restore moral leadership.

Consumer advocate Ralph Nader became a presidential candidate for the Green Party. Nader claimed that both Bush and Gore received campaign funds from large companies and that they would not support policies that favored American workers and the environment.

The election was one of the closest in American history. Gore won the popular vote. However, to win the presidency, candidates have to win a majority of the electoral votes. The election came down to the Florida vote. Both candidates needed the state's 25 electoral votes to win. The vote in Florida was so close that state law required a recount of the ballots using vote-counting machines. Thousands of ballots, however, had been thrown out because the counting machines could not detect a vote for president. As a result, Gore asked for a hand recount of ballots in the Florida counties that voted strongly Democratic. A battle began over the manual recounts. Most Florida ballots required voters to punch a hole. The piece of cardboard punched out is called a **chad.** Vote counters had a problem figuring how to count a ballot when the chad was still attached. On some ballots the chad was still in place and the voter had left only a dimple on the surface of the ballot. Vote counters had to look at the ballot and determine what the voter had intended. Different counties, however, used different standards to determine it.

Under Florida law, state officials had to certify the results of the election by a certain date. When it became clear that the count would not be finished on time, Gore went to court to postpone the deadline, and the Florida Supreme Court agreed to do so and set a new deadline. Bush then asked the United States Supreme Court to intervene to determine if the Florida Supreme Court acted unconstitutionally. While both sides prepared their case, the hand counts continued. Even with additional time, some counties were not able to meet the new deadline. On November 26, Florida officials certified Bush the winner, by 537 votes.

Gore's lawyers went back to court and argued that thousands of votes were still not counted. The Florida Supreme Court ordered all Florida counties to

Study Guide

Chapter 21, Section 4 *(continued)*

begin another hand recount of ballots that the counting machines rejected. The United States Supreme Court ruled that all recounts should stop until it made its ruling.

On December 12, 2000, in *Bush* v. *Gore,* the United States Supreme Court ruled 7–2 that the hand counts violated the equal protection clause of the Constitution. The Court argued that because vote counters used different standards, the recount was not treating all voters equally. The Court ruled that there was not enough time for a manual recount before the electoral votes had to be cast. The ruling left Bush the certified winner.

4. What argument did the Supreme Court use to stop the hand recounts?

_____

_____

_____

- **Bush Becomes President** *(page 950)*

Bush became the 43rd president of the United States. His first priority was to cut taxes. During the campaign, the economy began to slow. Some companies went out of business and many other businesses laid off workers. Congress passed a $1.35 trillion tax cut. The plan introduced tax cuts over a 10-year period. However, it also gave taxpayers an immediate rebate. By mid-2001, Americans began receiving tax rebate checks. Bush hoped the rebates would put about $40 billion into the economy to prevent a recession.

Bush's plan for improving public schools included giving annual standardized tests and allowing parents to use federal funds for private schools. Congress did not support the use of federal funds for private schools. It did support the idea of states being required to annually test reading and math.

Bush focused on a Medicare reform bill that added prescription drug benefits. The bill was <u>finally</u> passed in November 2003.

Academic Vocabulary
final: to be at the end of a process (p. 951)

Congress reacted to a number of corporate scandals. The government made regulations and penalties stronger.

Bush called for a review of the nation's military. He wanted to increase military spending. He also wanted to set up new programs. He favored a program known as **strategic defense.** Its purpose was to develop missiles and other devices that can shoot down nuclear missiles before they hit the United States.

5. Which of President Bush's education plans was supported by Congress?

_____

_____

_____

Study Guide

Chapter 21, Section 5
For use with textbook pages 954–961

THE WAR ON TERRORISM

CONTENT VOCABULARY

terrorism   the use of violence by nongovernmental groups against civilians to achieve a political goal *(page 955)*

state-sponsored terrorism   terrorism secretly supported by a government *(page 956)*

anthrax   type of bacteria used to create biological weapons *(page 959)*

DRAWING FROM EXPERIENCE

How did the terrorist attacks on the United States affect daily life in the nation? How did the attacks affect your community?

The last section discussed the 2000 presidential election and President Bush's programs to improve the economy, education, and the military. This section discusses the terrorist attacks on the United States and the nation's response to the attacks.

> **California History-Social Science Standards**
>
> **11.9** Students analyze the U.S. foreign policy since World War II.
>
> **Focuses on:** 11.9.6

ORGANIZING YOUR THOUGHTS

Use the diagram below to help you take notes. The United States government quickly responded to the terrorist attacks of September 11, 2001. List the ways it responded in the diagram.

Study Guide

Chapter 21, Section 5 (continued)

• September 11, 2001 (page 955)

On September 11, 2001, hijackers slammed two passenger jets into the World Trade Center in New York City. Hijackers crashed a third jet into the Pentagon in Washington, D.C. Hijackers also took over a fourth plane, but some of the passengers resisted them, causing the plane to crash in western Pennsylvania. Thousands of people were killed. These attacks were acts of **terrorism.** This is the use of violence by nongovernmental groups against civilians to achieve a political goal. Terrorist acts are done to fill people with fear and to get their governments to change their policies.

Most terrorist acts on Americans have been carried out by Middle Eastern groups. The reason for this traces back to the 1920s when oil became important to the American economy. The United States invested heavily in the oil industry in the Middle East. The industry brought great wealth to the ruling families in some Middle Eastern kingdoms. Most of the people, however, remained poor. Some of these people became angry with the United States for supporting the wealthy families. In addition, the growth of the oil industry led to increased contact with Western society and its values. Many devout Muslims feared that their traditional values and beliefs were being weakened by this contact.

New movements developed throughout the Middle East that called for a strict interpretation of the Quran, which is the Muslim holy book. These movements wanted to overthrow governments in the Middle East that were pro-Western. They wanted to set up a pure Islamic society. Muslims who supported these movements are known as fundamentalist militants. The vast majority of Muslims believe terrorism is <u>contrary</u> to their faith. Militants, however, began using terrorism to achieve their goals.

Academic Vocabulary
contrary: to be in disagreement with (p. 956)

Many people in the Middle East were also angry about American support of Israel. In 1947 the UN divided British-controlled Palestine into two territories. One part became Israel. The other part was to be a Palestinian state, but fighting between Israel and the Arab states left this territory under the control of Israel, Jordan, and Egypt. The Palestinians wanted their own nation. They began raids and guerrilla attacks against Israel. The United States gave Israel military and economic aid. As a result, Muslim militants began targeting the United States. In the 1970s, several Middle Eastern nations realized that instead of going to war with Israel and the United States, they could fight the two nations by providing terrorist groups with money and weapons. When a government secretly supports terrorism, this is called **state-sponsored terrorism.**

In 1979 the Soviet Union invaded Afghanistan. Muslims from across the Middle East came to assist Afghanistan in its fight. One of these people was Osama bin Laden. He was a member of one of the wealthiest families in Saudi Arabia. He used his money to help Afghan resistance. He also founded an organization called al-Qaeda, which recruited Muslims to fight in Afghanistan and channeled money and supplies to the nation.

Study Guide

Chapter 21, Section 5 *(continued)*

After fighting in Afghanistan, bin Laden believed that superpowers could be defeated. He also believed that Western society had contaminated Muslim society. He was angry when Saudi Arabia allowed American troops on its soil after Iraq invaded Kuwait. He changed al-Qaeda into a terrorist organization and started attacks against Americans. Bin Laden began operating from Afghanistan, which came under the control of Muslim fundamentalists known as the Taliban. He devoted himself and al-Qaeda to driving Americans and other non-Muslims out of the Middle East. He called on Muslims to kill Americans anywhere in the world. Truck bombs exploded soon after in the American embassies in Tanzania and Kenya in Africa.

President Clinton responded to the attacks by ordering cruise missiles to attack terrorist camps in Afghanistan and Sudan. The attacks destroyed the camps but missed bin Laden. He continued to target Americans. In October 2000, al-Qaeda terrorists crashed a boat loaded with explosives into the American warship USS *Cole*, which was docked in the Middle Eastern country of Yemen.

8. What did bin Laden and al-Qaeda dedicate themselves to do?

_____

_____

_____

_____

- **America Unites** *(page 957)*

The American people responded quickly to the terrorist attacks of September 11, 2001. Money, blood, and supplies were donated. Across the nation, flags were flown to show unity and resolve.

The government also responded quickly. The armed forces were put on high alert. Security at airports was increased, and the FBI began a massive investigation. President Bush declared a national emergency. Congress approved a $40 billion emergency aid package for rescue and repair work and for increased security. Intelligence sources and FBI investigations determined that the attack was the work of bin Laden and al-Qaeda terrorists. Secretary of State Colin Powell worked to form an international coalition to support the United States. Secretary of Defense Donald Rumsfeld began sending American troops, aircraft, and warships to the Middle East.

President Bush issued an ultimatum to the Taliban. He demanded that they turn over bin Laden and his followers and to close all terrorist camps in Afghanistan. He announced that the United States would not tolerate countries that helped or harbored terrorists. President Bush also warned Americans that the war would not end quickly.

Study Guide

Chapter 21, Section 5 *(continued)*

9. What ultimatum did President Bush issue to the Taliban?

_____

_____

_____

- **A New War Begins** *(page 958)*

Several challenges faced the United States as it began its war against terrorism. The president asked Congress to create the Department of Homeland Security. Its job would be to coordinate the dozens of federal agencies and departments working to prevent terrorism.

In late October 2001, Congress drafted a new antiterrorist law. The new law permitted secret searches and allowed authorities to obtain a single nationwide search warrant. The law also made it easier to wiretap suspects, and it allowed authorities to track Internet communications and seize voice mail.

On October 5, 2001, a Florida newspaper <u>editor</u> died from anthrax. **Anthrax** is a type of bacteria that can become lethal if left undetected. Several people died after becoming exposed to anthrax. Special teams in protective suits worked nonstop to check any reports of suspicious substances. The FBI has stated that it has no evidence linking al-Qaeda to the attack.

On October 7, 2001, the United States launched the first military operations of the war on terrorism. Warplanes began bombing targets in Afghanistan. The U.S. also began sending military aid to Afghan groups known as the Northern Alliance, who had fought the Taliban for several years. President Bush warned that other countries and groups might threaten the world by using nuclear, chemical, or biological weapons. These weapons of mass destruction could kill many thousands of people all at once.

In January 2002, President Bush warned that an "axis of evil," which he identified as Iraq, Iran, and North Korea, posed a grave threat to the world. Months later, North Korea announced that it had restarted its nuclear weapons program, arguing that they needed nuclear weapons to protect themselves from a U.S. attack.

Academic Vocabulary
editor: someone who arranges, alters, or corrects manuscript to be published in a book, newspaper, or magazine (p. 959)

10. What did the new antiterrorist law allow the federal government to do?

_____

_____

_____

_____

Study Guide

Chapter 21, Section 5 *(continued)*

- **Confronting Iraq** *(page 959)*

President Bush considered Iraq an immediate threat in developing and distributing weapons of mass destruction. Iraq's dictator, Saddam Hussein, had used chemical weapons in the 1980s. After the Gulf War, UN inspectors had found evidence that Iraq had biological weapons and was working on a nuclear bomb. In the summer of 2002, President Bush increased pressure on Iraq for a regime change, asking the United Nations to demand that Iraq give up its weapons of mass destruction.

While the UN was still debating the issue, in mid-October Congress authorized the use of force against Iraq. With the midterm elections coming up soon, many Democrats in Congress now wanted to turn to the poor economy. The president managed to keep the focus on national security issues. In 2002 the Republicans picked up seats in the House and kept control of the Senate. Soon after the elections, a new UN resolution threatened "serious consequences" if Iraq did not declare all of its weapons of mass destruction, stop supporting terrorism, and stop oppressing its people.

Weapons <u>inspectors</u> returned to Iraq. The Bush administration believed that the Iraqis were still hiding weapons, but other Americans thought the inspectors should be given more time. The Bush administration pushed for a war resolution in the UN Security Council. Although France and Russia refused to back it, the United States and Great Britain prepared for war. About 30 other countries supported the war, but many antiwar protests took place around the world.

On March 20, 2003, the U.S.-led coalition forces attacked Iraq and quickly seized control. On May 1 President Bush declared that the major combat was over. However, the fighting and controversy continued. During the first six months of the occupation of Iraq, Americans found no evidence of weapons of mass destruction, but bombings, sniper attacks, and battles plagued American troops. American deaths and expenses were mounting. President Bush began to seek support from the UN to help stabilize and rebuild Iraq. He was sure that democracy would succeed.

Academic Vocabulary
inspector: an official placed in charge of critically examining something for evidence (p. 960)

11. Why did President Bush consider Iraq to be an immediate threat?

_____

_____

_____

- **The 2004 Elections** *(page 960)*

The Democrats chose Senators John Kerry and John Edwards to run against Bush and Cheney. Kerry's service in Vietnam made him leery of war, but he voted to authorize President Bush to use military force in Iraq. When no

The American Vision: Modern Times

Study Guide

Chapter 21, Section 5 *(continued)*

WMDs were found, Kerry called the war a "diversion" from the hunt for al-Qaeda.

Bush and Kerry offered voters a sharp choice in a politically divided nation. There was a record turnout on election day. President Bush won reelection and the Republicans preserved their majorities in both houses of Congress.

12. Why did John Kerry call the war in Iraq a "diversion"?

_____

_____

_____